George Woodcock

British Columbia

A History of the Province

Douglas & McIntyre
Vancouver/Toronto

Douglas & McIntyre, 1615 Venables Street, Vancouver, British Columbia V5L 2H1

CANADIAN CATALOGUING IN PUBLICATION DATA
Woodcock, George, 1912–
        British Columbia, a history of the Province

        Includes bibliographical references.
        ISBN 0-88894-702-X
        1. British Columbia—History.   I. Title.
FC3811.W65   1990   971.1   C90-091395-9
F1088.W65   1990

Editing by Saeko Usukawa
Cover design by Robert MacDonald
Text design by Alexandra Hass
Maps by Lisa Ireton, base map by P. J. Jance,
Geography Department, University of British Columbia
Typeset by The Typeworks
Printed and bound in Canada by D. W. Friesen & Sons Ltd.
Printed on acid-free paper ∞

Contents

	PREFACE	vii
I	Before History	1
II	The Time of First Contact	15
III	The Alien Intrusions	23
IV	The Nootka Incident and Vancouver's Voyage	33
V	West from Canada	39
VI	The Doomed Equilibrium	50
VII	The Fur Empire: Flowering and Decline	61
VIII	The Colonial Era	83
IX	The Two Colonies	98
X	Prelude to Confederation	113
XI	The Decline and Fall of the Native Societies	125
XII	From Canada to the Pacific	142
XIII	Progress, Profits, Plunder	160
XIV	Party Politics	175
XV	War in a Land of Plenty	191
XVI	Doldrums and Depression	200
XVII	Once More unto the Breach	222
XVIII	The Tides of Change	230
XIX	Returning to the Equilibrium	253
	EPILOGUE	265
	FURTHER READING	270
	INDEX	274

*To Michael Mercer
and Jeani Read*

Preface

It is almost a third of a century since Margaret Ormsby's *British Columbia: A History* appeared in 1958, when the province was celebrating the centenary of its foundation. A solid, readable, conservative history, it took the record from the arrival of the first European explorers by sea in the late eighteenth century down to the early 1950s.

A decade and a half later, in the early 1970s, Martin Robin published *The Company Province*, a history of British Columbia in two parts—*The Rush for Spoils* (1972) and *Pillars of Profit* (1973)—which covered the period from 1871, the year of the province's entry into Confederation, to 1972, when Robin finished writing his books. Robin's volumes are revisionist and radical in approach, emphasizing the exploitative nature of the province's development and the part that greed has played in its politics; his is avowedly a political history, and a somewhat shrilly partisan one, though useful in filling many of the gaps in Ormsby's more cautious record. No other attempt at a comprehensive popular history of British Columbia has been made in recent years.

Valuable though they were in their time, both Ormsby's and Robin's books are now outdated, not merely because of events since they were written but even more because of shared limits of approach. Both are essentially histories from the point of view of the white population. You will look in vain in either of Robin's two volumes for an index entry relating to "Indians" or "Native Peoples," though racially exploited Chinese and Japanese appear as victims of rampant capitalism. A similar criticism applies to *British Columbia: A History*; it virtually begins in 1774 with a Spanish friar spotting the coast of the Queen Charlotte Islands through a fog from the deck of the ship in which the mariner Juan Josef Pérez Hernández was sailing up the coast from California. Afterwards the Indians appear only when they impinge on the white men's steady penetration and occupation of the province. No attempt is made to describe in detail the Indian culture, which the first white men encountered when they landed at Nootka Sound in the 1770s and which continued to flourish until the last quarter of the nineteenth century, or to tell what happened to the native peoples when the white men appropriated their lands and their all-important fisheries. In the index to *British Columbia: A History*, the Indians are indeed included, but references to the Chinese—a much smaller proportion of the population—are more numerous, for the simple reason that the presence of the Chinese, a rival group of immigrants, impinged more on the life of white men in British Columbia than that of the native peoples, most of whom lived outside the main theatres of white activity at that time.

Since Ormsby wrote in the 1950s, and even since Robin wrote in the early 1970s, there has been a change in our attitudes towards British Columbian and indeed towards Canadian history; it is increasingly difficult to defend an approach restricted to the white immigrant cultures that began to penetrate the country from the east in the sixteenth century and from the west in the late eighteenth century. Historians are increasingly inclined to take notice of the fact that, even if the native peoples of the Pacific coast kept no documentary records, and entered into actual history only at the point when the white keepers of records encountered them, theirs were the long millennia of human occupation and adaptation after their first arrival in the land that so late became Canada. And no true history of Canada or of any of its provinces can in fact be complete unless it takes into account the physical evidence offered by the archaeologists and the evidence in terms of myths and customs and traditions offered by the ethnologists.

It is not merely a matter of reconstructing as completely as we can the kind of life followed by people who lived before history or even of recognizing its distant continuity with our own; it is also a matter of recognizing how important an element the native peoples, with their traditions, have remained in British Columbian life. As late as 1871, the British Columbia that entered Canada had a population in which the Indians outnumbered the white people three to one; the native peoples had no voice in the matter of British Columbia joining Confederation, though this meant that white men were giving away to other white men the land of their ancestors.

It is true that the number of Indians declined both absolutely and also in relative terms by the end of the nineteenth century, and even ethnologists who should have known better saw them as a demoralized group of peoples whose extinction seemed imminent, the romantically celebrated but practically neglected "vanishing Red men." But since the 1930s the Indians of British Columbia have not only begun to increase numerically at a higher rate than any other group in the province. They have also recovered their pride in their native cultures. With varying degrees of success, they have asserted their claims to ancestral lands and have won back the rights to perform traditional ceremonies like potlatches and spirit dances, which were once prohibited at the instance of the missionaries. Adapted to modern conditions, their various ancient patterns of life are re-emerging, and have evoked external responses. During recent decades, for example, the artistic traditions of British Columbian native peoples, particularly the coastal groups, have been recognized worldwide as perhaps the greatest of all the so-called primitive traditions.

That such people should be left out of history is no longer tolerable, as it must have seemed thirty or even fifteen years ago, and perhaps the most important way in which my narrative will differ from that of my predecessors, Ormsby and Robin—whose example and insights I otherwise treasure—will be in the attention it pays not only to the past of the Indians before history but also to their changing role within the province's life after the wrenching impact between white and native cultures.

This book has gone through a long period of anticipation and preparation. I have been discussing it in a rather general way for at least five years with the publishers who are now offering it to the public. But my interest in British Columbian history is long-standing and has already in many ways affected the course of my writing.

I returned from England to Canada in 1949, and settled first on Vancouver Island. I soon became aware of the wealth of history and prehistory that the environment offered, and I would spend hours in the provincial museum, whose splendid collection of Coast Indian art was then housed in crowded cases in the basement of the parliament buildings; there I met the brilliant anthropologist Wilson Duff, who encouraged me to travel into the northern parts of the province and to visit the Indian villages beside the Skeena River. Also, in the provincial archives a floor up in the same building, I encountered Willard Ireland, a fine scholar of local history; he introduced me to some of the colourful public figures who, from Amor De Cosmos onward, have played such maverick roles in British Columbian public life and have made it, certainly as much as Québec, a province *pas comme les autres*.

It was with a good priming by Ireland and Duff, both now departed from the land they loved, that my wife and I set off in the fall of 1950 on a rambling journey up and down the province, out of which came my travel book *Ravens and Prophets*, published in 1953, a narrative of experiences and observations influenced by my historical interests. The "ravens" of the title already celebrated my dawning interest in the native cultures, while the "prophets" referred to the Doukhobors and other sectarians whose communities gave an exotic touch to the social and ethnic patterns of British Columbia.

Now, I regard *Ravens and Prophets* as an immature, apprentice work, jejune in its writing and superficial in its insights, so that I have a degree of sympathy with those British Columbians who reacted to it with hostility, seeing in it an assumption of superiority on the part of a person who, despite his Winnipeg birth, they regarded as a cocky Englishman. Still, I recognize in its pages the beginnings of an attachment to the setting and to the changing ways of life I observed, that would eventually lead me to spend the rest of my life in British Columbia.

For two decades after *Ravens and Prophets* I was engaged mainly on projects that took my time away from my chosen habitat. But my interest in British Columbia as a place and a past grew more intense as the years went on, and made me more closely committed to my regional loyalties, so that in the end I would proclaim myself to be "British Columbian first, and then Canadian."

And then, in the middle of the 1960s, Bill Toye of Oxford University Press invited me to write my second book related to British Columbia. Simma Holt had written her antagonistic account of the Doukhobors, *Terror in the Name of God*, which I had reviewed in the *Tamarack Review*, and Toye invited me to write a serious history of the sect that would counter Holt's negative treatment. I had already made contact with the Doukhobors and was deeply interested in them. I knew no Russian, but in the late 1940s I had collaborated with Ivan Avakumovic in a life of Peter Kropotkin, *The Anarchist Prince*, for which he had done the Russian research. Ivan had since moved to Vancouver, so that collaboration in the new book would be easy, and he immediately agreed to work with me. In 1968 our book appeared; *The Doukhobors* was the first definitive book on that sect in English and my own first book concerned mainly with British Columbian affairs since *Ravens and Prophets* a decade and a half before.

In the 1970s my interest in British Columbian subjects increased. In 1975 I published with Oxford University Press a biography of Amor De Cosmos, and in 1977 with Mel Hurtig a long introductory work on local native cultures, entitled *Peoples of the Coast*. Shortly afterwards Mel invited me to contribute to the series of illustrated histories of the provinces which he had launched. The resulting book, *A Picture History of British Columbia*, gave a concise account of British Columbian history, supported by much visual material, and first sketched out many of the insights I shall develop in this book.

Later, again for Hurtig, I began to compile an ambitious volume entitled *British Columbia: A Celebration*. Illustrated splendidly with landscape photographs by Janis Kraulis, it was a massive anthology of documentary and imaginative literature relating to British Columbia from the days of Captain Cook's arrival down to the present; some of the Indian tales that were included in translation may well have predated Cook's arrival. This book, which involved heavy forays into the sources of British Columbia's distinctive cultural life, appeared in 1983.

Finally came *Beyond the Blue Mountains*, the second volume of my autobiography. The first volume, *Letter to the Past*, which appeared in 1983, had taken my life up to the spring of 1949, when I finally left England and returned to pass the rest of my life in Canada. I went immediately to British Columbia, and *Beyond the Blue Mountains* picks up the narrative there. Since 1949 in fact, except for a year teaching in the United States (1954–55), a couple of fellowship years in Europe (1951–52 and 1957–58), and a few longish Asian journeys, I have spent all my time in British Columbia and have never been tempted to live elsewhere. Much of *Beyond the Blue Mountains* is concerned with how I became devoted to the region and how I centred there a world of friendships and interests that has always extended far, unhindered by my local loyalties. I have in fact found that the more deeply I experience and understand and love this region I have made my own, the more I understand other people who seek to sustain the autonomy of their own cultural and political lives. In this sense, I believe that a local patriot is a better internationalist than one whose loyalties are attached to the globally divisive concept of the national state.

Thus my interest in British Columbia's past became active more than a third of a century ago, in the months when I first settled in the province. It has continued ever since, has helped shape my political and cultural outlooks, and has formed the subject matter of a large proportion of my writing. This means that I have a long familiarity with much of the historical terrain I shall be covering in this book and that I write it not merely with a great deal of accumulated knowledge but also with a sense of creative involvement, which I believe is as necessary in history as in any other of the literary arts.

It means also that I have been able to see British Columbia as a land in its special right, a place and a culture whose changing patterns have their own life, for the province has belonged only relatively briefly and never completely to the larger political entities in which it has been involved. All through the long ages of prehistory, human society on the Pacific coast was locally oriented and its peoples had relations of trade and war that did not extend far beyond the mountain barriers. From the arrival of Pérez and Cook in the 1770s, the region had trading relations but virtually no political ones with the outside world of Europe, China and the eastern United States. From 1849, when the crown colony of Vancouver Island was established, with British Columbia to follow in 1858, it was one of the many remote and little regarded colonial fragments within the growing British Empire. In 1871 it uneasily entered the new Dominion of Canada and for many years threatened to secede over federal promises long unredeemed. But the one constant factor in the long narrative on which we are about to embark is the distinctiveness, from the days of the great coastal tribes onward, not only in terms of physical geography but also in cultural, ethnic and political ways, of the province on the Pacific. It is that distinctiveness I seek to capture.

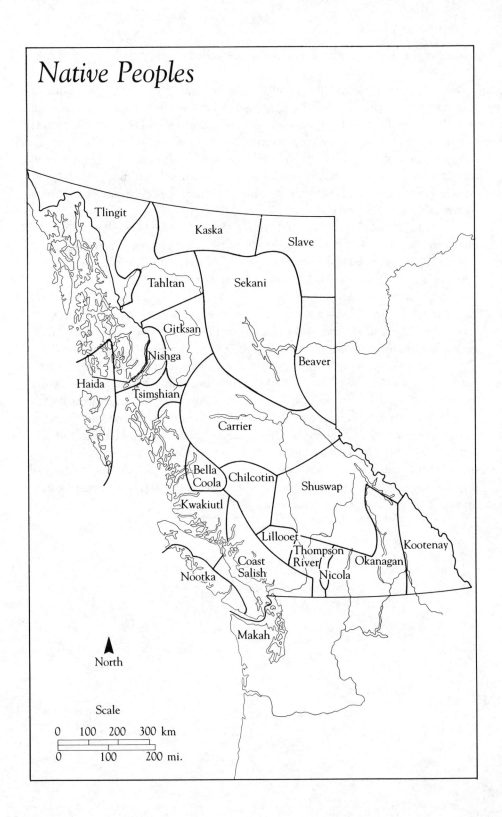

Native Peoples

Tlingit

Kaska

Slave

Tahltan

Sekani

Gitksan

Nishga

Beaver

Haida

Tsimshian

Carrier

Bella
Coola

Chilcotin

Shuswap

Kwakiutl

Lillooet

Kootenay

Thompson
River

Okanagan

Coast
Salish

Nicola

Nootka

Makah

North

Scale

0   100   200   300 km

0   100   200 mi.

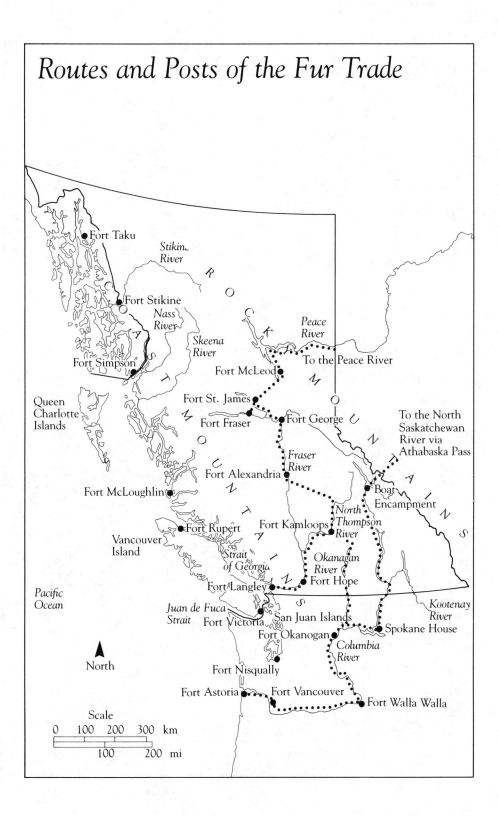

Routes and Posts of the Fur Trade

Fort Taku

Stikine River

Fort Stikine

Nass River

Fort Simpson

Skeena River

ROCKY

Peace River

To the Peace River

Fort McLeod

Queen
Charlotte
Islands

Fort St. James

Fort Fraser

Fort George

To the North
Saskatchewan
River via
Athabaska Pass

M O U N T A I N S

Fraser River

Fort Alexandria

Fort McLoughlin

Boat
Encampment

Fort Kamloops

North Thompson River

Fort Rupert

Vancouver
Island

Strait of Georgia

M
O
U
N
T
A
I
N
S

Okanagan River

Fort Hope

Pacific
Ocean

Fort Langley

Kootenay River

Juan de Fuca Strait

Fort Victoria

San Juan Islands

Spokane House

North

Fort Okanogan

Columbia River

Fort Nisqually

Fort Astoria

Fort Vancouver

Fort Walla Walla

Scale

0   100   200   300   km

100   200   mi

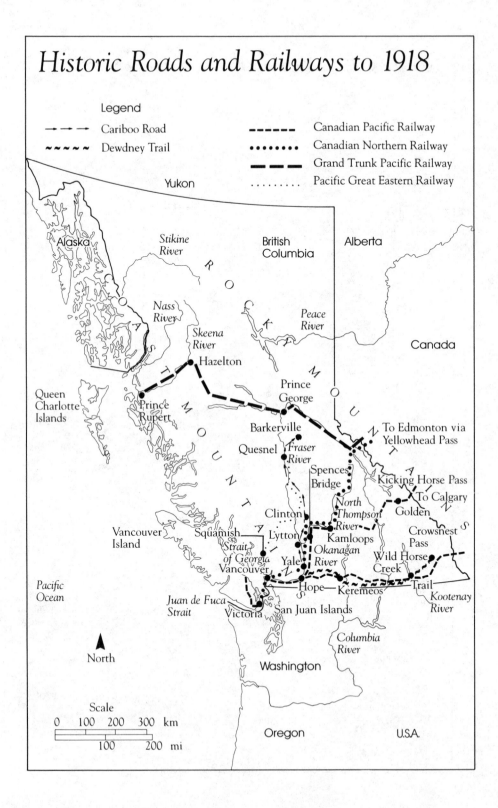

Historic Roads and Railways to 1918

Legend

→·—·→ Cariboo Road
~~~~~ Dewdney Trail

- - - - - - Canadian Pacific Railway
•••••••• Canadian Northern Railway
— — — — Grand Trunk Pacific Railway
········· Pacific Great Eastern Railway

Yukon

Alaska

Stikine River

British Columbia

Alberta

ROCKY

Nass River

Peace River

Canada

Skeena River

Hazelton

Queen Charlotte Islands

Prince Rupert

Prince George

MOUNTAINS

Barkerville

To Edmonton via Yellowhead Pass

Quesnel

Fraser River

Spences Bridge

Kicking Horse Pass

To Calgary

North Thompson River

Golden

Vancouver Island

Clinton

Squamish

Lytton

Kamloops

Crowsnest Pass

Strait of Georgia

Yale

Okanagan River

Wild Horse Creek

Pacific Ocean

Vancouver

Hope

Keremeos

Trail

Kootenay River

Juan de Fuca Strait

Victoria

San Juan Islands

Columbia River

North

Washington

Scale

0   100   200   300 km

100   200 mi

Oregon

U.S.A.

I

Before History

The Shape of the Land

British Columbia is separated from the rest of the world and the rest of Canada by great natural boundaries to the east and west, and by artificial political boundaries to the north and south. To the east is the mountain wall of the Cordillera, dominated by the Rocky Mountains, which the native peoples sometimes crossed in times before history, but which the first explorers—fur traders of the North West Company—penetrated only at the end of the eighteenth century, when Alexander Mackenzie made his famous trip overland to the Pacific in 1793. To the west lies the Pacific Ocean, whose northern parts also lay unexplored until the late eighteenth century, when Spanish mariners from Mexico and California and English naval ships began to enter these remote waters. By coincidence, one of Capt. George Vancouver's ships had just left the estuary of the Bella Coola River when Mackenzie arrived by land.

To the north, British Columbia was cut off arbitrarily in 1898 at the 60th parallel, which runs through desolate northern woodland; it was the time of the Klondike gold rush, when the federal government established Canadian sovereignty in the region by creating the Yukon Territory. The fear of American aggression which led to that act also dictated the southern boundary, which was established at the time of the Oregon Boundary Treaty in 1846. It ran straight east to west along the 49th parallel from the Great Divide of the Rockies to the Strait of Georgia, and dipped south to include all of Vancouver Island in British and, later, Canadian territory. Since that time British Columbians, from the first governor of the colony (Sir James Douglas) onward, have argued that in right of its discovery by Canadian fur traders, the northern bank of the Columbia River, which would have constituted a natural boundary, should have been the southern frontier, and in fact the northern parts of the state of Washington played such a role in the early nineteenth-century history of the British territories in the Pacific Northwest that they will inevitably take their place in this narrative.

This roughly rhomboidal territory that is now British Columbia, sloping southeast to northwest according to the line of the Cordillera, is more than 366,000 square miles (approximately 948 600 km^2) in area. Its northern and southern sides are mathematically straight, its eastern side follows the curving line of the Rocky Mountain crests, but its western side is so raggedly bitten by inlets and estuaries that though the province is a crow flight of 660 miles (1062 km) from north to south, its charted coastline totals more than 20,000 miles (32 186 km).

The Human Influx

Until approximately twelve thousand years ago, like the whole of the Americas, this area was an animal realm without either human or humanoid inhabitants. When people did arrive in the northwestern corners of the Americas and began the slow process of penetration that eventually would take them down the whole length of the two subcontinents to Tierra del Fuego, all the earlier human strains, like Neanderthal man, were extinct, and it was members of the species Homo sapiens and of the Mongoloid race that crossed the Bering land bridge from Siberia to Alaska somewhere about 10,000 B.C.

This was the end of the last great ice age, which terminated the Pleistocene Epoch. Alaska and parts of the present Yukon Territory had escaped being submerged by the great ice sheets that covered the rest of Canada. As the weather grew warmer there, large animals like mammoth and mastodon, horse and bison, caribou and muskox, began to move in and graze off the tundra vegetation that developed. Small groups of hunters bearing spears with characteristic fluted stone tips followed the animals out of Siberia; these were the first ancestors of the native peoples of the Americas.

During the tenth millennium B.C. the ice sheets began to melt quite rapidly, and soon a corridor of tundra was clear east of the Rockies, dividing the Cordilleran Ice Sheet in the west from the Laurentide Ice Sheet that covered the rest of Canada. Large glacial lakes formed in the corridor, and the grazing animals moved south from Alaska and north from the great plains, which had remained unglaciated; it is to this period, between ten and eleven thousand years ago, that the first finds of human artifacts in British Columbia can be assigned.

The contours of the terrain revealed as the ice sheet slowly melted away were those with which we are familiar today: the successive ranges running parallel from the Rockies to the coast to form the celebrated "sea of mountains," the narrow inland valleys and the deep fjords running down to the sea, the relatively small areas of flattish land that would eventually be suitable for farming and ranching, and a scattering of large and small islands offshore, dominated by Vancouver Island to the south and the Queen Charlotte group to the north. The area cleared of ice at first became tundra, and it is likely that the weather was dryer than in more recent millennia. A northern woodland of pine and spruce next appeared. Only when the climate changed about 5000 B.C. was the characteristic mixed rain forest of Douglas fir and alder, of cedar and hemlock, finally established on the coast; inland was a sparser boreal forest cover of birch and spruce and poplar, with a dry country of grass and sagebrush to the south.

There is debate, likely to continue, as to how the groups of early hunters first reached British Columbia and found their way to the coast, where in historic times the most sophisticated cultures eventually flourished. One theory is that their ancestors came down the corridor east of the Rockies while the coast was still under ice and pushed into the lightly wooded southern grasslands of what is now British Columbia and similar terrain in what is now Washington state. As the ice retreated northward, they found their way up through the Columbia and Kootenay river systems into the interior of British Columbia, and eventually down the Fraser, the Skeena and the Stikine rivers and other streams to the coast, where the abundance of marine food quickly converted them from hunting into fishing folk.

Support is given to this theory from a number of directions. First, there are peoples both in the interior of British Columbia and on the coast who share the Salishan group of languages. While it is unlikely that people already on the coast would willingly abandon its abundance for the hardships of an inland hunting life, hunters coming down the Fraser River and tasting its riches would probably choose to stay. One example of a group moving down to the sea is that of the Bella Coola, a small Salish-speaking group living along the valley and the river that bear their name. They are neighboured on the north and south by groups speaking Kwakiutl dialects, and inland to the east by the Athapaskan-speaking Chilcotin. They had no connection, by the time Mackenzie encountered them at the end of the eighteenth century, with any other Salishan group, and they had adopted cultures and ceremonial patterns similar to those of the great coastal tribes. They had retained their Salish dialect although they had no legends of how or when they had become separated from other Salish groups. The only conjecture which seems to fit their case is that they were part of a Salish group once inhabiting the Chilcotin plateau and thrust out of the territory by the present Chilcotin Indians.

The Bella Coola established themselves on salt water so long ago that the memories of their collective journey had vanished from their myths. But the likelihood of a downriver journey in their case is strengthened by the fact that when other peoples on the coast did have legends about arrival from elsewhere, they always spoke of downriver migrations. The Haida, Tlingit and Tsimshian groups of the northern part of the coast all claimed that their ancestors found their way to the sea by either the Skeena or the Stikine River. Moreover, the oldest archaeological finds in British Columbia, like the Milliken site near Yale in the Fraser Canyon, which was in use between nine and ten thousand years ago, tend to be on routes leading from the interior down to the coast.

However, the possibility that other groups found their way down the coast from Alaska and the Aleutians as the ice melted cannot be discounted, for there are very old sites in remote parts of the coast, like Skoglund's Landing in the Queen Charlottes, that could only have been reached by water, and the likelihood is that the first people to inhabit the north Pacific coast came by both land and sea.

A Babel of Languages

Whichever way they came, it must have been long enough ago for a number of sharply distinct languages in seven different families to form and survive. The southern interior was peopled when European travellers arrived by groups speaking a variety of Salishan dialects, related to other groups farther south in the coastal area. In the southeast corner of the province lived the Kootenay, who shared some of the customs of the prairie peoples, going over the Rockies each year to hunt the bison, but who spoke a language of their own that had no close relatives anywhere else in Canada. Much of the central and northern part of the province was inhabited by peoples who spoke various Athapaskan languages.

On the coast a number of languages had developed, many of them with no evident relatives anywhere else in the world. To the north, Tlingit was spoken mainly by the people of the Alaskan panhandle, though there were a few groups who used it in northwestern British Columbia. The Queen Charlotte Islands were inhabited entirely by speakers of Haida. On the mainland, opposite the Queen Charlottes and near the present site of Prince Rupert, the Tsimshian lived in a maze of channels and islands; related groups inhabited villages scattered along the main rivers of the region, the Nishga on the Nass and the Gitksan on the Skeena. South of them, inhabiting northern Vancouver Island and the opposite mainland, there were groups speaking a variety of Kwakiutl dialects. An enclave of Salish speakers, the Bella Coola, inhabited the inlet that bears their name. Along the Pacific shore of Vancouver Island lived the various groups who spoke dialects of Nootka. Some linguists have maintained that Nootka and Kwakiutl were related and have united them in a hypothetical Wakashan language group. South of Vancouver Island, on the Olympic Peninsula across Juan de Fuca Strait, lived the Makah, who were whale hunters like their congeners to the north and spoke a Nootka dialect. Salish speakers inhabited southern Vancouver Island and the lower Fraser Valley.

These distinctive coastal languages had remained unlike each other despite the exchange of customs and ceremonials that (by the time of Cook's arrival) had created a largely homogeneous culture from Tlingit to Kwakiutl territory, and this fact suggests that the ancestors of all these peoples must have lived together in the same localities for the millennia it would take for new languages to develop.

The End of Nomadism

Such a development was possible because of the natural abundance of wild foods that enabled people who settled the coast to modify the nomadic life their forebears had lived inland. They ceased in fact to be land peoples, for apart from the great trees of the rain forest for which they found a multitude of uses, the land provided them with little of what they needed. They feared the forest, populating it with hostile supernatural beings, though it offered them isolation and protection in the inlets where they mainly lived. Nomadism was reduced to the annual trips from their sheltered winter villages to the summer villages in more open settings which they inhabited during the seasons of fishing and gathering other marine foods, notably seaweed, shellfish and herring roe. The sea, essentially, was their territory and their highway, by means of which they traded and carried on the raids, mostly to collect slaves, that were their substitute for warfare. The abundance of fish and other products, which they learnt to preserve, not merely gave their life a stability usually found only in agrarian societies. It provided a superfluity of goods, so that the peoples of the coast were able to spend their winters developing and sustaining a rich ceremonial life and the arts that served it.

Historically and prehistorically the peoples of the coast were largely dependent on that marvellous all-purpose tree, the cedar. It provided the planks for their great houses, the poles they carved with heraldic motifs to celebrate rank and ancestry, the wood for great canoes, for masks, rattles, waterproof vessels, ceremonial seats, giant feast dishes; its bark they shredded and wove into garments and blankets.

This broad use of wood has deprived archaeologists of most of the material through which they might have traced the earlier development of the coastal cultures, which used little in the way of imperishable materials. They never developed pottery, and the stone figures and the petroglyphs that have been found on the coast and in the interior are comparatively rare, and seem to have been connected mainly with shamanic practices. Nevertheless even the oldest of them show certain formal and stylistic resemblances to later woodcarving, and suggest that the kind of perishable figures we associate with the Northwest Coast were being made millennia rather than centuries ago.

The First Villages

Round about the end of the fourth millennium B.C. the levels of the sea had stabilized with the final melting of the great ice sheets, and the vast annual migrations of salmon swarming up the coastal rivers increased, at about the same time as the cedar became an important component of the rain forests that hitherto had been dominated by Douglas fir. Nature was setting the stage for humans to flourish, and the migrant peoples began to establish themselves on sites they would often continuously occupy for many centuries.

We are helped to determine the age of such settlements by the fact that shellfish played so great a part in their diet, especially during the winter months when there were no great fish runs and the people were living mainly on dried or smoked foods. Most of the vast mounds of clam and oyster shells grew up on the edges of the villages, piling up year after year, century after century; some of them are still piling up today. Excavating them enables archaeologists to determine the age of the sites and provides a haul of stone and bone objects dropped by chance as people worked at opening the molluscs.

The sheltered waters around Prince Rupert are particularly rich in such sites; almost fifty prehistoric sites have been found in this area, half of which were still inhabited when the fur traders built Fort Simpson in 1831 and drained the inhabitants away to a set of new villages erected around the fort. Apart from the small objects found in the shell middens, excavations have revealed that large plank houses, similar to those traditionally associated with the Coast Indian cultures, were probably being built there about four thousand years ago. At roughly the same time some of the interior Salish people in the region of the upper Fraser and Thompson rivers were creating winter villages with round semiunderground houses like those used in historical times.

The region around the Fraser delta, rich in natural resources and obviously well inhabited at an early date, has been the source of other discoveries dating from well before the Christian era. One of the more prosperous Indian villages in British Columbia today is the community of Musqueam, on the north bank of the Fraser near the University of British Columbia campus in Vancouver. Recently a waterlogged shell midden was excavated at Musqueam. The damp had preserved otherwise perishable items for three thousand years; wooden dishes and pieces of basketry and matting were found whose techniques and designs showed a remarkable continuity with the artifacts that the Salish were producing on the eve of their contact with Europeans.

The Locarno Beach People: 1500 to 400 B.C.

The relics of Musqueam seem to have been associated with the rich finds at Locarno Beach on Burrard Inlet which gives its name to what the archaeologists call a "phase" rather than a separate culture, in this way recognizing a continuing evolution in the Fraser delta area and the lower Fraser Valley. In many ways the finds at Locarno Beach resemble the relics of European neolithic cultures. The abundance of easily caught food had obviously provided time for ingenuity and leisure to express themselves in perfecting tools and weapons from nonmetallic substances. The pebble tools had been replaced by elaborately chipped flint arrowheads and, later, by ground slate projectile points and knives adapted for a variety of functions. The uses of bone and antler were even more varied. There were weapons for hunting, and doubtless sometimes for warfare, like harpoon heads, fleshing knives and daggers. There were sewing needles for making skin garments, and netting needles suggest these people already made the nets of nettle fibres that native fishermen on the coast were making well into historical times. There were tools like awls and small adzes of both stone and bone, and sharpened beavers' teeth used to etch in the finer details of woodcarvings.

The Locarno Beach people had gone beyond the stage of merely utilitarian manufacture. Personal ornamentation had become important; women wore labrets—oval discs of stone or bone—in their lower lips and plugs in the lobes of their ears; the custom of using labrets survived into historic times, when they were a sign of rank. There were also necklaces of bone and slate beads and animal teeth, and bone finger rings.

Other purposes than personal decoration seem to have inspired many carvings found at Locarno Beach. All of them are small and all evoke the magical tradition within which these people enjoyed their mental and physical being. The end of a deer bone was meticulously carved into a tiny human skull an inch and a half (3.8 cm) high; in historic times such miniature skulls were part of a shaman's paraphernalia. A spear-thrower had been carved in the form of a human head, wearing what looks like one of the conical basketry hats still worn by Indians on the coast in the nineteenth century. A piece of antler shaped in the rough effigy of a killer whale suggests the existence already of clans who used the great dolphins for their crest—as their descendants have done in recent times.

The Marpole Phase: 400 B.C. to A.D. 500

Technology must have developed quite quickly in this vital region of the lower Fraser River, either through local evolution or the arrival of energetic invading groups. By about 400 B.C., the Locarno Beach phase had developed into the Marpole phase, named after a site on the Fraser River in south Vancouver. During the millennium of the Marpole phase, something very near to the Coast Indian culture as we have known it came into being.

The Marpole people possessed what the archaeologist Charles E. Borden called "the basic" triad of tools associated with the monumental woodworking tradition of the Coast Indian culture: large wedges of antler and wood to split the trunks of red cedar into broad planks; hand hammers of tough stone shaped in pestle form; and finishing adzes with finely polished blades of nephritic jade. With such tools, the Marpole people were able before the beginning of the Christian era to construct the great plank houses whose foundation holes and stone central hearths have been discovered. They lie on landlocked beaches that once faced on the waves but have long been isolated by the steady accumulation of silt in the Fraser delta. On the same beaches, in front of the great houses, the long canoes that the new tools had made must have been drawn up and protected by rush and cedar bark mats from the sun.

These large canoes and the great variety of fishing and hunting gear that the Marpole people created enabled them to diversify their sources of food and to accumulate the surpluses that subsidized their rich ceremonial life. Seals, sea lions and the Fraser River sturgeon, which then grew to a length of 20 feet (6 m), were caught. There was an abundance of salmon of different species in their appropriate seasons. Molluscs were collected on the beaches and sandbanks, and waterfowl taken in the great marshes whose remnants still survive along the shores of the Fraser delta.

Warfare and Trade

The Marpole people and their northern contemporaries around the mouth of the Skeena seem by this period to have been increasingly involved in warlike raids, and individual warriors—presumably men of rank—have been found buried with elaborately decorated weapons. Warfare was mostly hand to hand, a matter of quick surprise attacks in which clubs were widely used. One grave beside a shell midden in the Skeena area contained a stone club, another made from the jaw of a killer whale, and a third of carved whalebone, as well as a kind of corselet made of rods of native copper imported from Alaska.

Not all the relations between peoples in the coastal and inland areas were warlike. Patterns of trading were even older than patterns of settlement, and from the appearance of the early hunters, ten thousand years and more ago, the flint stones from which they made their spear and arrow points were moving over great distances from the rich quarries in the Mackenzie Valley and the southern prairies, following a complex pattern of exchanges over the Rockies into the central British Columbian plateau and down to the coast. Obsidian was particularly prized; at least five thousand years ago it was being excavated on Mount Anahim in the Chilcotin country and taken down the Bella Coola River to the sea verge. Native copper made into bracelets and other ornaments turns up quite often in early burials, evidently traded down the coast, as in historic times, from Copper River in Alaska. And round about the Locarno Beach period, people on the west coast of Vancouver Island and the Olympic Peninsula had begun to gather in deep water the tubular dentalium shells that were highly valued and carried through the southern interior and beyond the mountains to the prairies, where they were coveted by the Blackfoot.

As well as the trade in less perishable valuables, there must have been, as there was when the Europeans arrived, a considerable trade in preserved foods—meat to the coast and fish to the interior—as well as in hides and in the mountain sheep and mountain goat horns out of which the coastal people made the exquisitely carved spoons for their great feasts. One of the most important items of trade was the oil of the oolichan or candlefish, carried in leakproof wooden boxes over ancient paths known as "grease trails."

The use of labrets, that later sign of rank, the beginning of the practice of artificially flattening some heads but not others, and the presence of worked copper, shell and stone jewellery and other valuables in certain graves suggest that already a ranking system existed among the peoples of the coast. Another indication of degrees of prosperity and presumably of rank exists in the fact that, though no actual fabrics have survived, elaborately worked spindle whorls of stone and bone have been found in sites from the Marpole period. Evidently people were already using mountain goat wool and rearing the now extinct little dogs that the Salish up to early historical times bred for their fine curly hair, to be woven into blankets for people of high standing. Not everyone, even in those early times, was expected to be content with the simple cedar bark blankets ordinary people wore from day to day.

Not only weaving but everything else perishable has been lost from the sites of the Marpole period, so that we can envisage only in a fragmentary fashion the level of artistic achievement they attained. No wooden artifacts survive, and therefore we have little idea of the skill these people developed in making large carvings or their ability in painting. Yet it is likely that as early as the Marpole period, if not before, the houses and wooden utensils were decorated with carving, for the tools that were found included not only those appropriate for rough, house-building carpentry but also the jade adzes, sharpened beaver teeth, tiny nephrite chisels and sharp-edged fragments of quartz for working finer details of carving.

The Emergent Arts

With such a range of tools, the Marpole people could work not only perishable wood but also such durable substances as stone and horn. Fragments of antler were carved into charms in human and animal form, and some of these show features that foreshadow classic Northwest Coast art, such as heavily outlined and exaggerated eyes and bones shown in "X-ray" vision. Soft stones, like steatite and soapstone, were used for anthropomorphic images. Many of these were seated human figures, often with serpent attendants; they usually had bowls lodged between their knees and clearly had a ritual function connected with shamanism. Recent discoveries suggest that a stone-carving culture began in the Nass and Skeena region at about the same time and continued into the historic period.

There was a similar continuity in the petroglyphs pecked and scored into the surface of boulders, cliffs and rock outcrops down the whole length of the coast from Alaska to the Columbia estuary. Carbon 14 datings of early petroglyphs suggest that they were made at about the beginning of the Christian era. Some were related to shamanistic rituals; others were connected with the rituals practised to ensure the return of the salmon shoals. But sometimes they carried records of extraordinary events, which their carvers may have seen as supernatural; later petroglyphs made in early historical times portrayed ships and horses, and one, at Cloose on western Vancouver Island, recognizably represents the s.s. *Beaver*, a Hudson's Bay Company's boat that did not begin to ply the coastal waters until 1836.

The sense of a long prehistoric development one gains by studying the portable stone carvings and petroglyphs of the Alaskan and British Columbian coasts has a meaning beyond itself. In historical times, when stone continued to be carved, often for new and commercial reasons (like the little argillite sculptures of the Queen Charlottes), the carving in wood was always greater in quantity, and in quality more varied and—at its best—more satisfying. It is reasonable to assume that the easier craft of woodcarving was even more widespread in the past, and that stone carving was done mainly for magical uses. Coast Indian woodcarvings that survive are rarely even two hundred years old. But we can assume that the first such artifacts, brought to Europe by James Cook's companions, were the refined products of a tradition of craftsmanly work in both stone and wood lasting back at least two millennia and linking the ancient carvers of man-bowl figures with the men who created the great poles and house carvings of the Haida and Tsimshian and Kwakiutl during the final nineteenth-century blossoming of the Coast Indian cultures.

The archaeological record is a broken one in which long periods pass without a great deal of evidence showing up. In the Fraser Valley particularly there is a long hiatus between the Marpole culture and that represented by the old village of Tselax on the Musqueam reserve near Vancouver, which seems less than a thousand years old. In many ways the culture it represents resembled that of the Marpole phase, with little evident technological progress, though there was a change in burial practices, which suggests a new group with new customs may have moved into the area and influenced the older society. Instead of being buried on the verges of the shell middens, the dead were wrapped in blankets, with their most treasured possessions around them, and deposited in gravehouses outside the villages or in canoes placed in trees. These possessions were more modest than in earlier graves; there were fewer personal ornaments and stone carvings were entirely absent.

This was the immediate predecessor of the Fraser Valley Salish culture that Europeans encountered in the early years of the nineteenth century. Its technological stagnation, its poverty in artistic creation, suggests there had been a regression from the dynamic times of the Marpole culture a thousand years or more before. The impetus of development in fact seems to have moved during the first millennium of the Christian era away from the delta and the lower Fraser Valley and towards the northerly region where the Haida, Tsimshian and Kwakiutl faced each other across the waters of Hecate Strait and Queen Charlotte Sound. During this period when the northern cultures seem to have developed steadily in social and artistic complexity, the Salish or their predecessors had become less prosperous and less creative, and also less capable of defending themselves from the raids of their more aggressive northern neighbours. Warfare was rarely territorial, so that the Salish tended to retain their tribal lands and fisheries, but they paid a heavy toll in slave raids. Among all the northern tribes in historic times, the slaves were mainly Salish; so, ironically, were they among the Salish themselves, whose various villages raided each other but did not dare to raid the villages of the Haida or the Kwakiutl, their principal persecutors.

Ozette—The Pacific Pompeii

Fortunately, we have been given an extraordinary glimpse into the lives of the peoples of the Pacific coast near the time of their first contact with Europeans through a natural disaster that provided what has been described as "a North American Pompeii." It took place at Cape Alava, a little way south of Cape Flattery, inhabited in historic times by the Nootka-speaking, whale-hunting Makah. At a village the Makah now call Ozette, sometime in the sixteenth century a cliff collapsed in heavy rains and an avalanche of mud engulfed eight great plank houses. The slurry, kept damp over the centuries, preserved the dwellings and their contents. The slide must have happened at night, for the skeletons of at least twenty people, as well as dogs, were found in the first four houses to be excavated; it happened also in the spring, for the first excavators came across young evergreen leaves that withered once the air struck them.

The find at Ozette, made in 1971, revealed a community that had perhaps been in existence fifteen hundred years. It demonstrated that the material abundance and artistic fertility of native culture was not merely a late result, as has sometimes been suggested, of the influx of trade goods and of metal tools through the establishment of the fur trade.

In the first four houses, no less than 45,000 items of local manufacture or inter-tribal trading were discovered, including examples of every art with which we are familiar from later native production. There were cedar bark blankets, rugs of goats' and dogs' wool, the looms and spindle whorls used in making them, and even skeletons of the wool-bearing dogs. There were carved wooden bowls, sewn boxes of cedarwood elaborately painted with the owners' crests, and a multitude of woven blankets. There were wooden sculptures, ceremonial clubs carved out of stone, and the elaborate hats woven of spruce root, with whales and whalers represented on them, that appear in all the early white men's drawings of the Nootka peoples.

The excavations at Cape Alava also confirmed the repeated assertions by early mariners that the native peoples had a knowledge of metals. Not only copper but iron had reached these houses, which had been destroyed before the first Europeans even arrived in the area. And in fact the iron discovered at Ozette bore no resemblance to that made in preindustrial days by European ironmasters. It was nearer to the kind of metal then being used among the more primitive Asian peoples like the Siberian tribes and the Mongols.

Asian Hints

When they traded with the Haida in the 1770s and landed at Nootka Sound, the first Spanish and English explorers noted that the "rough knives with coarse wooden hafts"—as Cook's marine sergeant, John Ledyard, described them—were of unfamiliar manufacture. Some of the mariner diarists offered the suggestion that the blades might have been traded across Keewatin and over the mountains by successive Indian middlemen from the English posts on Hudson Bay. But the Cape Alava find dates from earlier than the beginning of trade on Hudson Bay, and the iron remains are unlike any known British iron. The blades must have been traded from some Asian source, carried across Bering Strait by the Inuit who now occupied both its shores, and found their way through the Aleut to the northern Tlingit. Once they reached Yakutat Bay, they would enter the North Pacific trading system and find their way down the coast in a chain of exchange.

These lingering contacts with Asia seem to have been of the same tenuous kind as those tribe-to-tribe chains that appeared in Asia itself in prehistoric times, carrying precious materials step by step from one tribal culture to the next in the days before Chinese and western merchants established a clearly marked Silk Road between China and Europe. Equally tenuous are the hints of influence one sometimes sees when comparing the stylization of human and animal shapes in the incised patterns of early Shang bronzes and those of Coast Indian artifacts. In fact there is not a scrap of hard evidence to suggest any direct contact in prehistoric times between the Coast Indian peoples and the leading civilization of contemporary eastern Asia, that of China.

There indeed have been theories of Chinese traders reaching the coast, of storm-driven Chinese junks fetching up on some Alaskan or British Columbian shore. But the only reference in the Chinese imperial records is one whose relevance is highly dubious.

This is the tale of the journey of Huei-Shin, a Chinese monk who travelled in the fifth century A.D. with a group of Buddhist priests across Siberia until he reached a land called Fusang; he returned in 499 to report his mission. Inhabited by a people of high culture, Fusang has been identified variously with Mexico and the Northwest Pacific Coast, but too many features of the account cannot be reconciled with either, such as domestic animals that resemble reindeer, a system of writing and the Buddhist religion.

The tale of Huei-Shin seems in fact to have been a synthetic account, prepared for promotional purposes by fifth-century Buddhist missionaries and including features of a number of lands, the only clearly identifiable one being the northern Siberian region. There is no reference that points specifically to the Pacific coast and, except in small details, the Kingdom of Fusang has no real resemblance to any territory in British Columbia or Alaska.

Thus there are no authentic records, either in historic or in prehistoric times, and no archaeological evidence of travellers having found their way directly from China or other Asian realms to the coast of British Columbia. The last migration from Asia appears to have been that of the ancestors of the modern Inuit, who found their way along the shores of the Arctic Sea five thousand years or so ago to create the characteristic native culture of the Canadian north and of Greenland. These early Inuit did not find their way down the coast to British Columbia or have any influence over its cultures. They only played their part in the trading chain that was in existence long before the white men superimposed their own commercial network.

The Shamanic Connection

But there is another direction in which one can find clear and copious evidence of a common origin between the Coast Indian cultures and those of prehistoric Eurasia, and a continuing affinity. That is the complex of beliefs, rituals and magical practices known as shamanism, which one still finds tenaciously surviving as a kind of parareligion in a great arc that begins with the Bon who preserve the ancient pre-Buddhist beliefs of Tibet, sweeps through the native tribes of Siberia and Mongolia to the Bering Sea, and flourishes in many forms among the Inuit and most of the Indian peoples of the Americas.

In its classic form, shamanism exists in Siberia; the very word *shaman* is a Russian adaptation of a word originally used among the Tungus. The origins of shamanism lie far in the human past. It is possible that the painters of the Lascaux caves were recording shamanistic concepts of the linked destinies of men and animals as well as carrying out mere hunting magic, for which much less naturalistically elaborated figures of animals would have been sufficient. It is even possible that a primitive form of shamanism was emerging in the quasireligious rituals we now believe Neanderthal men practised in their caves fifty thousand years ago.

Forms of shamanic practice occur in most parts of the world. But the particular current of shamanism that flourished among the Coast Indians of British Columbia originated in Siberia and was brought over the land bridge by the first waves of migrants. Significantly, the last migrants, the Inuit, retain a type of shamanism almost identical with the cults surviving in present-day Siberia, whereas practice and doctrine have undergone modifications in Pacific North America.

In both traditions the novice shaman receives a qualifying spiritual experience, either sought or unsought, often at the end of an illness. Meeting a supernatural being, he falls into a deep trance in which he encounters the spirit who will be his guardian and lead him into the underworld. There, at the hands of spirits who are really dead shamans, he undergoes the dismemberment of his body, the reassembly of his bones, and the renewal of his organs. He believes himself to be an entirely transformed being, and from this basic original transformation he gains the power of further transformation at will.

From this point he acquires knowledge in two ways: by repeated entrancement, and through the esoteric oral teachings of the older shamans who have accepted his initiation. He can change himself into animal form, for he has regained the power of interchangeability that all beings possessed in a happier past. He can detach his soul from his body for journeys into the underworld or the heavens. The universe, through which he moves with such facility, is centred on a great World Tree or Tree of Life, up which he can climb to the heavens its branches touch, and down which he can descend to the underworld.

The influence that a shaman can wield as a wise man in a community varies greatly in accordance with the social structure; in some situations he acquires a considerable degree of temporal power; Sitting Bull, after all, was a shaman. But among the Coast Indians, at least in historic times, many of the socially necessary contacts with the spirit world had passed into the hands of ritualists of other kinds, like the chiefs who performed the welcoming ceremonials for running salmon. The particular role that the shaman always played in the community was a healer, but even here his functions were related to his ecstatic role, to the insights he had acquired on entering the freemasonry of the world of spirits. Other kinds of healers, like wise women who knew the properties of herbs and primitive chiropractors, were also present with their spirit helpers, but the shaman specialized in illnesses attributed to souls wandering away from bodies and in illnesses attributed to the intrusion of negative forces or foreign substances into the body, either through sorcery or supernatural beings angered by the breaking of taboos.

Yet shamanism, and concepts related to it, had a permeative and shaping influence on the Coast Indian culture that reached its height in the centuries before the Europeans arrived. Transformation, which was at the heart of the shamanic experience, played a great part in Coast Indian beliefs and rituals. Raven, the local Prometheus who in his role as trickster benefited mankind at the expense of less generous supernatural beings, was regarded as the great Transformer. In the winter ceremonials of the dancing societies among the Kwakiutl and other tribes who imitated them, special masks and other illusionist devices enacted transformations before the eyes of the audience. Symbolic death and dismemberment, theatrically rendered, were as much a part of these winter ceremonials as they were of shamanic initiations, especially in the performance of the ghost dancers, where burial alive and decapitation were regularly mimed. Even in art the concept of dismemberment and re-creation became dominant. The literal forms of nature were cavalierly butchered, just as the spirits symbolically dismembered and reassembled the shamanic initiate, to fill the area being decorated, for Pacific coast artists had a horror of empty spaces. An animal might be shown kippered down the backbone to fit into a rectangular form; its bones and organs might be clearly delineated, X-ray wise, within its body; its joints and genitalia might be moved into quite unnatural compositions to satisfy the needs of design and the symbolic expression of clan or secret society myth, or both might be represented by eyes or faces.

Spirit Quests

The evolution that sharply distinguishes American from Siberian shamanistic beliefs led to a widespread recognition on the coast that the spiritual world was open even to those who were not initiated warlocks. The guardian spirit quest existed among all Coast Indian peoples and penetrated far beyond the professional ranks of the shamans. Every man with a special skill, whether a carver, a canoe maker, a hunter, or a warrior, felt that he had gained his ability from a spirit helper. Every nobleman traced the crests that appeared on his poles and other property to encounters with the supernatural he or his ancestors had experienced. Membership in the prestigious secret societies of the Kwakiutl and the northern tribes depended on real or simulated spirit encounters. Among the Salish, where the social order was least stratified and society more naturally democratic, probably a majority of individuals of both sexes underwent guardian spirit quests, which might bring them special skills or even turn them into shamans, but usually merely provided them with a personal song and a dance that established both their positions in mundane society and their links with the supernatural.

Just when this generalization of spiritual searching among the Coast Indians began and how much can be attributed to such factors as the greater leisure enjoyed during the winter months, or the spectacular and awe-inspiring features of the setting of coast and rain forest and mountain, it is virtually impossible now to determine. But the ultimate fact is that, though we cannot doubt the common origin of Siberian and Coast Indian cultures, and especially of shamanism in the two regions, by the end of the eighteenth century A.D. there was a striking difference between the hard and frugal existence of the Siberians, and the materially wealthy and ceremonially complex life of the Coast Indians with their surplus economy, their conspicuous spending, their love of overtly displayed honours, their remarkable artistic and inventive talents, and their diffused spirituality. It was the latter society, at the height of its prehistoric flowering, that the first European voyagers encountered in the 1770s.

cautious, is definitely circumscribed, being partisan and anti-capitalist. What both have in common is that neither considers the reality of the Native presence.

In *British Columbia: A History of the Province*, Woodcock is the first popular historian to tell exactly who these people were who met the first intruders. In describing the rich ceremonial life of the tribes of the coast and comparing it with the habits of the European sailors, there is no necessity for the author to spell out which had the more sophisticated culture. Woodcock later describes what happened to the Natives once their land, their fisheries, and even their ceremonies were taken from them.

He emphasizes that other than some small-scale treaty-making by Sir James Douglas in 1850, among Natives of Vancouver Island, and the few Peace River bands affected by the Government treaty of 1898, "no Indian in British Columbia has ever been included in a treaty since successive Provincial administrations have refused or neglected to recognize aboriginal title."

his own undercutting bid and awarded his firm the contract. When challenged, the premier told a house committee it was no more wrong for a company owned by the premier to do business with the government than", "a member who is a lawyer, or is Attorney General and his partner takes charge of looking after a Private Bill for anybody and lobbying it through the house."

One would not be surprised to hear it put just that way today. Back then, however, the Lieutenant-Governor threw those rascals out of office, which indicates the progress British Columbia has made in 88 years.

The history of B.C. is not merely a chronicle of contrasting forces and perspectives, but of contrasts within those forces and perspectives. When it is approached by a writer with a sense of drama combined with a crystalline clarity of style, the result is a rare thing indeed — an immensely satisfying historical panorama. Woodcock calls to mind some trail-blazer that Mackenzie or Thompson might have sent into the rugged terrain, completely confi-

not fail to mention, for instance, that Indian men from northern Vancouver Island needed no encouragement to bring boatloads of their women to Victoria to sell to sailors; or that whatever ill may be spoken of the early many missionaries, it is also true that they won over many Natives by not viewing them as inferior. As well, the author reveals the role of labour unions in the province's scandalous history of racism, and points out that in its early days under W.A.C. Bennett, the Socreds and not the CCF were the true populist party, opposing the vested interests.

Through all of Woodcock's work — biography, literature, travel, or history — there is a unifying theme, the opposition to any authority that would limit the freedom and imagination of men and women. Thus in this work Woodcock exposes the Philistines, the racist and the rapacious, white or Indian, boss or union. This theme is like a river, Heraclitus's river, timeless and "ever renewed" even if "the water is never the same."

Jan/Feb
1991

BLAZING THE TRAIL

By Jim Christy

BRITISH COLUMBIA: A HISTORY OF THE PROVINCE

by George Woodcock
Douglas & McIntyre, 276 pages, $34.95 cloth
(ISBN 0 88894 702 X)

In SKETCHING THE SCENES of first contact between the indigenous inhabitants of British Columbia and European explorers, George Woodcock underlines the "tragic separation" between them. Other writers have, of course, attempted to do the same but none has invested it with such poignancy and drama.

There have been two previous full-dress histories of British Columbia: Margaret Ormsby's *British Columbia*, published in the 1950s, and Martin Robin's two-volume treatment in the '70s (*The Rush for Spoils*

Thus, the problems of 200 years ago resonate across the long decades. As for other aspects of white people's politics in B.C., it seems that little has changed but the names. The current administration is merely part of an infamous tradition. In fact, the history of B.C. provincial politics sounds like a cacophonous litany of scandal. For the shenanigans of the Van der Zalm government there are, if you'll excuse the pun, Prior examples. In 1903, the premier was one Edward G. Prior, who also owned an engineering firm. His government accepted bids

Unemployed men board an On-to-Ottawa train at Kamloops in June 1935

dent he'd negotiate the peaks and pitfalls to bring back real goods.

One can think of a couple of prominent Canadian writers of popular history who manipulate their material as if it were the ingredients for a TV mini-series, or who trot out one colourful character after another. There are enough interesting figures in B.C. history — such as Maquinna, Matthew Baille Begbie, Amor de Cosmos, John Robson, Billy Barker, and Genevieve Mussel — that Woodcock doesn't need to push them onto stage in brackets that des-

II

The Time of First Contact

Native Societies and Cultures at the Time of First Contact

With the help of archaeological and linguistic studies, it is possible to envisage the continuities between the British Columbian aboriginal population when Europeans first encountered them, and their prehistoric ancestors. But there is still a special drama about the moment of first contact, the day when a Haida or a Nootka chief danced before a Spanish or English captain, scattering the eagle down of welcome over the water and taking his place—the first of his kind—in the actual historical record. Much as we may sift the physical debris of the past, it is the living race as it enters history, with its myths and customs and languages, with its physical appearance recorded visually and verbally, that we come to know in ways we can never envisage the people who went before, no matter how rich their relics or how close their links with the people of history.

Perhaps the most striking collective fact about the native peoples of British Columbia at the point of first contact is their linguistic diversity and complex social organization. There were perhaps between two and three hundred Indian bands—nomadic groups or settled villages—scattered between the Rockies and the Pacific at the end of the eighteenth century. They belonged to ten different linguistic and cultural areas. Seven of them were situated on the coast: going from north to south, they began with a group of Tlingit bands from the Alaska panhandle who had settled in the northern interior of British Columbia, followed by the Haida, the Tsimshian, the Kwakiutl, the Nootka, the Bella Coola and the Coast Salish. In the mountainous southeast corner lived the Kootenay. The rest of the interior was inhabited by bands of Interior Salish in the south, and of Athapaskans or Dené in the centre and north, each band speaking its own dialect.

These people of greatly differing languages and cultural traditions in no way constituted a nation, nor could that title be applied even to the linguistic groups, which had developed nothing resembling the political organization created by the Blackfoot on the prairies or by the Iroquois confederacy of the Six Nations in the eastern woodlands. Each band or village was a loose entity of its own. The large coastal villages consisted of a number of clans or lineages, each of which owned certain fishing, hunting, berry-picking and similar rights and lived in a common house over which a hereditary chief ruled. Each of the clans owned a number of titles, with accompanying masks and dances, that were distributed among its "noble" members, to whom the commoners were more or less distantly related; every clan member, noble or commoner, shared in its resources, and each had to contribute towards its collective celebrations, notably the great giving feasts or potlatches at which the chiefs would validate their titles and proclaim their importance. The slaves, people taken in war or their children, were the third element in the clan, and these were chattels, with no right even to life if the chief chose to kill them.

Within each village, the chief of one house was usually regarded as *primus inter pares*, wielding influence rather than power over his neighbours and acting as their spokesman in relations with outsiders. Alliances between two villages speaking the same language were much less frequent than conflicts, and unless ceremony marked and demanded it, any contact was usually a matter of mutual suspicion.

A similar lack of political organization marked the interior groups, especially the Athapaskan speakers, whose basic group was often the nomadic extended family wandering over large areas in regions where the game was not abundant. At the same time, some groups of Interior Salish, especially the Thompson River Indians, had moved nearer to community organization by the establishment of winter villages of semipermanent underground dwellings covered by conical roofs.

In spite of the lack of political or linguistic unity and in spite of the differences between their myths of origination, most of the coastal peoples—Tlingit, Haida, Tsimshian, Bella Coola, Kwakiutl, Nootka and Coast Salish—had entered into a remarkable common culture, distinguished by its emphasis on rank and ceremonial and on a high craftsmanship often reaching the level of true art.

The culture centred on two kinds of ceremonial, both of which were carried on mostly during the winter months when the bands would literally shift house, taking the planks from the frames of their summer houses, which were near the fishing grounds, and attaching them to other frames in their winter village sites up the protected inlets. The move from summer to winter home was an elaborate operation involving the transportation of large quantities of dried fish and shellfish and of personal possessions and household goods packed in the painted and carved rectangular chests that the craftsmen so carefully carpentered out of cedar wood.

The potlatch was the more personal of the two ceremonies, a feast that affirmed a chief's rank, enhanced his personal status, and cast reflected glory on the members of his clan. There were a number of occasions when a potlatch must be held; it must accompany the raising of a memorial pole to a dead chief, or the raising of a crested pole telling a living chief's mythic origins and supernatural encounters. A new chief gave a potlatch to validate his acceptance of a hereditary title, and an established chief gave one to celebrate his daughter's puberty or to initiate a son into one of the clan's lesser titled roles.

When the potlatch was planned, heralds were sent inviting the other clans of the village, and often the chiefs of neighbouring villages, who would come standing on platforms built across their canoes and dancing in accordance with the mask and costume they wore. They arrived in all their noble splendour, and when they had danced on arrival, they would doff their masks and wear the ceremonial Chilkat blankets of goat's wool woven by Tlingit women according to sacred designs drawn by the men; sometimes they also wore dancing skirts or leggings of Chilkat weave. Diadems would proclaim their rank; often they were of intricately carved alder wood inlaid with abalone, with a kind of coronet of sea lion whiskers and ermine skins hanging on each side of the face and over the shoulders. In their hands they would carry finely carved rattles in the shape of birds, most often Raven, the great Trickster and Transformer. The ladder of precedence was observed as punctiliously as in a European court of the Victorian age. The visiting chiefs were seated according to rank, and a mistake in the ordering would be construed as an insult and might even lead to a bloody feud.

The host chief would be the star of the evening, wearing in turn the masks to which he was entitled as he danced his various dances and sang his various songs, with his clansmen acting as chorus and orchestra, beating out the time on boards. Leaning on his carved talking stick, he would invite his guests to partake of the abundant dishes (all well garnished with oolichan oil) that were served in great wooden bowls carved in the shape of animals; the guests would eat with their own spoons finely carved from the horns of mountain goat. As the feast went on, the chief, assisted by his heralds, would present the gifts that were the main purpose of the occasion. They were graded according to rank, and their value was almost always calculated so that the host gave something more valuable than he had received at his guest's last potlatch; in fact, it was demeaning to attempt anything less. The giving was accompanied by boastful speeches, verging on insult; they proclaimed the chief's generosity in giving away the wealth he had accumulated and by implication challenged the visiting chiefs to better his gift at their own potlatches. Often—and especially in the mid-nineteenth century—the chiefs would go beyond mere giving and compete in the actual destruction of property. Slaves would be killed; sometimes they were even crushed to death by the butt of a totem pole as it was raised into place. Canoes might be dragged into the feast house and burnt in the central fire, which was often fed by enormous libations of oolichan grease; as the flames burnt high, the guests seated in the places of honour close to the fire were expected to show their indifference by sitting there impassively even though their eyebrows might be singed off and their hair set on fire. A special role in the potlatch complex was played by coppers, which were engraved, shield-shaped sheets of metal highly prized by the chiefs. Frequently sold, like celebrated paintings today, they would gain ever-increasing prices, some of them being worth many thousands of blankets; then they would have their own names and be famous up and down the coast. At last, as a high gesture combining both gift and destruction, a chief would decide to destroy one, breaking it up and distributing the fragments among his guests. Fortunate the chief who, by various purchases, could gather together all the scattered pieces and then have the copper rewelded into a shield that had acquired the accumulated value of all the exchanges! After such a potlatch the visitors departed, imbued with the will to meet the challenge the host chief had offered them and to do even better in giving and destruction.

The potlatch might seem extravagant and bizarre to nineteenth-century Caucasians, the devotees of frugality and the accumulation rather than the dispersion of wealth, yet it was a key factor in the economic and social lives of the coast peoples. By constantly confirming rank, it provided a well understood social order in a society that had no genuine political structure. It ensured the circulation of wealth, for even the slaves benefited from the largesse of such occasions, provided they survived them. And the potlatch also served as a kind of primitive insurance system. A chief and his clan stripped themselves of all they had accumulated over a period of years, but they were left with their honour and spirit intact, and the next summer of hard work the accumulation of goods could begin all over again. Moreover, the erstwhile givers were now in the receiving line. Potlatches were not frequent events in a chief's life. On the top of a heraldic pole there would often be a little seated human figure with a chief's conical hat on his head. On top of the hat little circlets were added, each representing a potlatch given; one rarely sees a figure with more than four of these circlets, which means that most of the time chiefs were receiving rather than giving. It was a way of casting bread on the waters and receiving it back.

All the coast peoples were actively potlatching by the time of their first encounter with white men, and the custom spread so that within historical times at least two Athapaskan-speaking groups—the Tahltan who were neighbours to the Tlingit and the Carriers who were neighbours to the Gitksan (Inland Tsimshian) on the Skeena—adopted ranking systems, heraldic poles and the potlatch.

It is uncertain among which language group the potlatch, ranking and totem pole complex developed, but there is good reason to believe that the other type of winter festival, which consumed even more energy and ingenuity, the quasi-religious winter dances, originated among the Kwakiutl and reached the other peoples by imitation, gift and purchase. Certainly the Kwakiutl staged winter festivals—and still do—more lavishly than the other coastal peoples, though it seems likely that they themselves were elaborating on a simpler model—that of the spirit dance as practised by the Salish to the south of them.

The Salish spirit dances celebrated the links between humans and the forces of nature. Young men would go out as novices into the wilderness, enduring hunger and cold, until in a trance induced by their privations, they would encounter their spirit guides. These guides often determined their occupations; a young man who encountered a supernatural woodpecker was regarded as having a vocation for woodcarving. After their experiences in the wilderness, the young men would return as initiates to dance the dances and sing the songs the spirits had given them, which remained inalienably their personal property.

The Kwakiutl winter dances also depended on the initiation experience—in this case initiation into powerful secret societies, which explored that mysterious borderland where humans confront the natural and supernatural forces that control the world.

Winter was a highly organized season in the Kwakiutl villages. It began after men and women had come back from their summer activities, bearing the abundance of preserved food they had accumulated over the season. First they gathered together in their clans to sing the personal songs of those who had died since the last winter; on these occasions the relatives wore special mourning masks. There followed a period of saturnalia called Klasila, when the people relaxed after the summer's labours, displayed their family masks and dances, and feasted joyfully. Very soon the spirit whistles would begin to sound in the woods, and the people would disperse for the ritual ablutions that prepared them for Tsetseka, the winter ceremonial season.

During this season, the summer order of life was abandoned. People ceased to be known by their usual names and titles and accepted those they possessed in the dancing societies, whose ceremonial officers now replaced the house chiefs in ordering village life. People saw themselves as members of a confraternity rather than as members of a lineage. Forgetting their clan divisions into Eagles and Wolves, into Ravens and Hawks and Killer Whales, they now found themselves divided into Seals and Sparrows.

The Seals were members of the eight dancing societies, at their head the Hamatsa or Cannibal Society, under the patronage of Baksbakualanu Xsiwae, the Cannibal from the North End of the World. This formidable being presided over the winter festivals invisibly, the breathing of the thousand mouths that studded his body simulated by wooden whistles blown by mortals. These societies were highly exclusive; the Hamatsa Society would admit only those who held validated ranks within their clans.

The dance societies were the intermediaries through which, during winter, the supernatural world was brought directly into the affairs of humans, as the dancers spinning around the fires in the great houses manipulated their ingenious masks in the flickering half-light to mime the presence of spirits with whom they were held to be in close communion.

Everything was done with superb stagecraft. The dances of the Hamatsa Society, whose novices celebrated their initiation by simulating the eating of human flesh, had a kind of grim and macabre austerity. Its ecstasies were simulated with the minimum of theatrical apparatus and were the more effective for this reason, as the novice clad in simple boughs whirled in his frenzy, as his naked woman assistant danced before him with a desiccated corpse in her arms, as the dancers bearing the great masks of mythical birds clacked the six-foot-long (1.8-m-long) beaks in chorus, dancing on their haunches, and the snarling grizzly bear dancers kept silence with their menacing presence.

But there were other dances with a range of conjuror's devices. This was especially the case with the Tokwit dance, when a girl was dismembered, stabbed with spears, burnt in a box, and went through many other cleverly simulated torments, which at the same time delighted and mystified the noninitiated audience. In other dances, people were entirely dismembered and then at the end returned whole to the firelight, rather as the shaman's spiritual body was dismembered in his initiatory trances. Many of the masks were ingenious transformation devices, worked by strings, in which the face of one creature would slowly open, as the tempo of the drumming changed, to reveal a quite different being, an eagle turning into a man or the rays of a sun mask reforming themselves into the tail of a whale. Tsetseka was indeed a time when, as the word suggests, "everything is not real." It was also a time when the particular mechanical talents that distinguished the Kwakiutl from the other coastal peoples had full scope to develop outside the limited area of shamanistic gimmickry. Many of the products of the artisans' ingenuity have in their fantasy a beauty that far excels any mere conjuror's adeptness that they may also reveal.

The winter dances showed a completely different aspect of Kwakiutl society from the potlatch. A temporary transformation of the social order took place during Tsetseka, so that the Kwakiutl were able to relate to each other anew in an order that horizontally embraced people from every lineage. The conduct of village affairs temporarily lapsed out of the hands of the house chiefs, and was assumed by a group of ceremonial officials, mostly senior members of the dancing societies who had retired from active roles. They made sure protocol was observed and appointed proctors and other officials to maintain order while the dances went on. It was the season when the village was most clearly a unity; it was characteristic of Coast Indian society that such a unity should be achieved in a ceremonial rather than a political context.

The art so characteristic of the Coast Indian peoples, assuming local styles among the various groups from the Tlingit south to the Nootka, was the product partly of the beliefs expressed in the potlatch and the winter dances, and partly of the great abundance of natural resources that provided the leisure to follow artistic pursuits and the goods to pay the artists, who depended on the patronage of chiefs and dancing societies. The ranking order, with its emphasis on ostentation, provided a market for carved poles of various kinds, for carved and painted decorations on house fronts and canoes, for chiefly seats and massive food vessels to be used at the potlatch feasts, for the masks and diadems, rattles and talking sticks, used by the chiefs during their celebrations. The dancing societies demanded their own kinds of masks and paraphernalia, which were carved by a special group of craftsmen who worked in secrecy until their products were revealed in the appropriate ceremonial setting.

Among the inland peoples both social and ceremonial patterns were far less complex. Still, once one overcomes the cliché of lumping together as nomadic hunters these sixteen tribal groups, belonging to three separate language groups (Interior Salish, Kootenay and Athapaskan), their considerable cultural differences emerge as much more than linguistic variety.

They were of course united by the physical fact that the abundance of resources to be found on the coast, though it extended to a degree up the lower courses of the four great rivers, the Fraser, the Skeena, the Nass and the Stikine, did not exist in the plateaus and mountains of interior British Columbia. Indeed, it diminished in proportion to distance from the coast. All people in the area west of the Rockies depended not only on hunting for their survival but also on the great salmon runs that found their way to spawning grounds in remote rivers and creeks almost as far as the Great Divide. Even deep in the interior there were great fishing sites at places like the falls at Lillooet on the upper Fraser or the Bulkley River canyon in Carrier country, where even today the Indians fish by handnet and spear. Elaborate wicker fishtraps were to be found on streams distant from the ocean, and in years of large runs people everywhere in the region prospered. But groups like the Athapaskan-speaking Carrier, Beaver, Sekani and Slave peoples in the north and in the northeast over the Rockies often suffered because they were at the end of the fishing chain and could depend only on runs much depleted by groups downstream. When the fish supplies were low, and big game like moose and deer elusive, they had to depend on small kine like hare, but the hares were liable to periodic declines in population; in years when the fish runs were scanty and the hares were scarce, there were often local famines in the remote interior, which show in the records of the North West Company's New Caledonian posts and which even at times affected the traders and their employees, who in the winter also lived largely on dried salmon and sometimes came near starvation.

The material life of the native peoples in the interior, varying according to locality, markedly affected their social patterns. The Athapaskan peoples of the northeast tended to be actual nomadic hunting groups, wandering much of the year in extended families but coming together periodically on occasions like the salmon runs; they had the most rudimentary political organization and no real ranking patterns. Other groups, farther to the south and nearer to the coast, like the Salishan-speaking Thompson River Indians, were moving towards a more settled pattern of life. They would spend the warmer seasons on hunting and fishing expeditions, but they had also established villages of semiunderground dwellings—pits with conical roofs entered by notched logs serving as ladders—where they would store their dried and smoked food and live in relative comfort over the winter.

Situation also tended to modify cultural ways, particularly where Athapaskan, Salish or Kootenay speakers came into contact with groups that in some ways were more developed in their technologies or social patterns. Even before the fur traders came by sea and land, the Kootenay were using horses that had passed by trade or theft northward through the American West from Spanish colonial territories; they became marginal prairie Indians, riding over the Rocky Mountain passes to hunt the bison in season and enduring retaliatory raids of Peigan horsemen into their own territory.

Interior peoples often had quite elaborate animistic beliefs, and recent books like Hugh Brody's *Maps and Dreams* and Robin Ridington's *Trail to Heaven* have revealed sophisticated patterns in which dreams, as among the Australian aborigines, chronicled not only the mythical histories of their groups but also dominated basic techniques of survival like those related to hunting. The Salish groups, both on the coast and along the Fraser and Thompson, cultivated the spirit quest, with its supernatural experiences in the wilderness, its revelatory trances, its personal songs and dances. And in marginal areas, particularly when coastal groups had extended themselves up the great rivers, Athapaskan or Salish tribes would adopt and adapt elements of the more elaborate cultures, so that the potlatch and the winter dances, and even at times ranking and clan systems, spread from the Gitksan on the Skeena to their Carrier neighbours, from the Tlingit on the Stikine to the Athapaskan, Tahltan and Tsetsaut (the latter of whom they eventually absorbed), and from the Kwakiutl to Salishan groups on Vancouver Island.

Constant intercourse assured these patterns of influence. A kind of raiding warfare was endemic among these peoples, inspired by concepts of manhood and honour that Homeric warriors might have understood and sometimes by more material motives such as the capture of slaves or the theft of horses. But they met much more often for the peaceful procedure of trade, and it was in such unbelligerent encounters, exchanging oolichan grease for mountain goat horn, or dried salmon for dried moose, or dentalia for argillite, that they most influenced each other, sometimes by example but sometimes by the highly commercial procedure of trading dances or ceremonials. Indeed we get the religious ambiance of this area in a true—if ironic—perspective when we remember that nothing among the peoples from the Rockies to the coast was too sacred to be marketable. Even ancestors' revelations and family legends were possessions and hence had their price.

III

The Alien Intrusions

Drake's Landfall

Literal mists, not merely those of prehistoric conjecture, enwreath the first arrival of white travellers on the Northwest Pacific Coast. In June 1579, Capt. Francis Drake was sailing up the coast north of California in the *Golden Hind*; one of his companion ships, the *Marigold*, had sunk, and the *Elizabeth* had become separated and would eventually find its own way home to England. Drake himself, with the many tons of silver, gold and jewels he had looted from the great treasure galleon *Nuestra Senora de la Concepcion* off the coast of Nicaragua, was seeking the western end of the Northwest Passage in the hope of finding a safe escape route by way of the Strait of Anian, a flight of cartographer's imagination that had appeared only a few years before on a 1574 map by Abraham Ortelius, which showed it probing to a wide open channel leading towards the Atlantic.

The *Golden Hind* reached what according to Drake and his companions was the 48th parallel, which would mean they were off the Olympic Peninsula, the home of the southernmost Coast Indian people, the Makah. According to the account prepared by the preacher Francis Fletcher and some of the other voyagers, *The World Encompassed by Sir Francis Drake*, they landed on this shore in bitter cold:

> The 5th day of June, wee were forced by contrary windes to runne in with the shoarr, which we then first descried, and to cast anchor in a bad bay, the best roade we could for the present meete with, where wee were not without some danger by reason of the many extreme gusts and flawes that beate upon us, which if they ceased and were still at any time, immediately upon their intermission there followed most vile, thicke and stinking fogges, against which the sea prevailed nothing.

It was no place to stay, and too cold to sail northward against the contrary winds, so Drake turned and went southward again without encountering any of the inhabitants, to head west to the East Indies and circumnavigate the globe.

There was controversy even in Drake's day over whether or not he actually had reached the 48th parallel, and today some historians argue that he may have reached only the 43rd parallel (which his description of cold in June makes unlikely), and others suggest that through errors in dead reckoning he may have placed his turning point too far south and have actually made his anchorage on the coast of Vancouver Island at about the 50th parallel.

An Old Greek's Tale

The next account, of the discovery of Juan de Fuca Strait, by the Greek mariner Apostolos Valerianos (whom the Spaniards called Juan de Fuca), is as controversial as that of Drake's landfall, with which it is curiously linked. Sailing off Valparaiso, Drake captured a Spanish ship of which de Fuca was the pilot. The Greek was captured again a few years later by another English gentleman pirate, Capt. George Cavendish, and put ashore in 1587 in lower California, whence he proceeded to New Spain (Mexico) and was employed by the viceroy on exploratory voyages.

In 1596 de Fuca was on his way home to Cephalonia (the next island to Odyssean Ithaca) where he meant to live out his old age, and in Venice he encountered an English merchant, Michael Lok, who shared the intense interest in the Northwest Passage that obsessed the English of his time. He was a ready audience for the old Greek's recollections, which told how in 1592 the Viceroy of Mexico

> sent him out . . . with a small *Caravela* and a Pinnace, armed with Mariners only to follow the said voyage, for discovery of the said Straits of Anian, and the passage thereto, into the Sea which they call the North Sea, which is our North-west Sea. And that he followed his course in that Voyage West and North-west in the South Sea, all alongst the coast of Nova Spania, and California, and the Indies, now called North America . . . until he came to the Latitude of forty-seven degrees, and that there, finding that the Land trended North and North-east and North, and also East and South-eastward, and very much broader sea than was at the said Entrance, and that he passed by diverse Ilands in that sayling. And that at the entrance to this said Strait, there is on the North-east coast thereof, a great Hedland or Iland, with an exceeding high pinnacle, or spired Rocke, with a pillar thereupon.
>
> Also he said, that he went on Land in divers places, and that he saw some people on land, clad in Beasts skins: and that the land is very fruitfull, and rich of Gold, Silver, Pearle and other things, like Nova Spania.

The reference to gold and other precious substances, so inaccurate for this particular region, suggests that the old pilot was working hard to arouse Lok's interest. But though some historians have dismissed his story entirely, mariners long familiar with the coast noted that not only was the description Lok transmitted of Juan de Fuca Strait and the Strait of Georgia beyond it substantially correct but also that the "spired Rocke" stands exactly where Juan de Fuca had placed it.

Brobdingnag and Other Fantasies

For a century and a half after the voyages of Drake and de Fuca, the Pacific coastline was treated with a surprising lack of interest. During the seventeenth century the European powers interested in the Americas were occupied in consolidating the bridgeheads they already had—the French in Québec and Acadia, the British in the Thirteen Colonies and the Caribbean, the Portuguese in Brazil, and the Spaniards in Central and South America. They were in no hurry to explore further what early travellers described as an inhospitable coastline, and for a century and a half after the voyages of Drake and de Fuca, the region was left to be filled by the invention of fiction writers and the fantasy of mapmakers. Into this great *terra incognita* Jonathan Swift inserted a whole imaginary country—Brobdingnag— when he wrote *Gulliver's Travels* in 1726. Gulliver, we are told, was stranded there in 1703 and found a race of giants inhabiting a great peninsula jutting out from the coast roughly where the Queen Charlotte Islands actually lie.

The old concept of the Strait of Anian as the westernmost stage of the Northwest Passage was still regarded as geographical fact, and as late as 1750 two French cartographers, Philippe Buache and Joseph-Nicolas Delisle, prepared a map of "New Discoveries North of the Southern Sea," which delineated the Mexican and Californian coasts fairly accurately but farther north lapsed into conjecture, showing a great inland sea reached by the mythical strait that covered the whole of later British Columbia. The myth of this Mer de l'Ouest was current among the French in Québec during the eighteenth century, and with the ostensible aim of discovering it, the Sieur de la Vérendrye and his son set out in 1731 on their expeditions in the Canadian West.

Russians and Spaniards

From an unexpected direction, and by an unexpected and secretive rival to the western European powers, the first real exploration of the Pacific Northwest began when the Danish mariner Vitus Bering, in the employment of Russia, voyaged to Alaska in 1741. He did not reach the future British Columbia, for he died of scurvy late in the same year on Bering Island off Kamchatka, but his successors would reach the Alaskan panhandle, trade with the Tlingit for sea otter skins, and eventually after Tsar Paul founded the Russian American Company, establish a capital at Sitka, about 200 miles (322 km) north of the eventual boundary between British Columbia and Alaska.

Though they had done nothing to secure them, the Spaniards regarded the virtually unexplored regions of the Northwest Pacific as theirs by virtue of the 1493 Bull of Pope Alexander VI, which had divided the New World between Spain and Portugal. And when King Carlos II of Spain heard through his ambassador in St. Petersburg of covert Russian activities on the American continent, he recognized that the time had come for claims to be made and reinforced by action. His wish to propel Spanish power northward was complemented by the desire of the mission clergy in Mexico to begin the conversion of the Californian Indians. In 1760 land and sea expeditions were sent north from San Blas in northwestern Mexico and the first mission was founded at San Diego by the Franciscan priest Junipero Serra. An overland supply route across the deserts of Sonora and Arizona was established in 1773, and in June 1774 the frigate *Santiago* was dispatched from the new harbour at Monterey to find out what the Russians really were doing.

The *Santiago* was commanded by ensign Juan Josef Pérez Hernández, who sailed with instructions to proceed north to the 60th parallel, and on his return voyage to make acts of possession at suitable places, to spy out activities by Europeans other than Spaniards, and to establish contact with the native peoples. Only the last of these instructions was met, for Pérez turned back just north of the 55th parallel, somewhere near Ketchikan; he was alarmed by the complex shoals and islands in the Alexander Archipelago, his men were getting sick, and he met Drake's enemies, contrary winds and bitter cold. He did not even make a landing and sailed home with the unplanted cross his carpenters had made, which bore a message claiming the land in the name of Spain. The two missionaries who accompanied him, Fray Juan Crespi and Fray Tomas de la Pena, had no opportunity to practise their skills of conversion, but perhaps they left a better heritage in their journals describing the first encounters between Europeans and the Indians of the Pacific Northwest.

For Pérez not only made an authentic sighting of the British Columbian coast when, on the morning of 18 July, through screens of rain and mist, his men saw the rocky shores of the Queen Charlotte Islands; he too was sighted. As the *Santiago* sailed slowly parallel to the coast, he could see the smoke of the fires with which the inhabitants were signalling to each other the presence of strangers. Two days later, on the afternoon of 20 July, the first encounter took place when Haida canoes came out from the shore, some of them almost as long as the tiny *Santiago*. The attitude of the Indians seems to have been friendly but cautious, for though they refused to come on board to trade, they made all the customary gestures of welcome:

> While they were still some distance from the bark we heard them singing. . . . They drew near the frigate and we saw there eight men and a boy in the canoe, seven of them rowing, with the eighth, who was painted, standing up in the attitude of dancing, and throwing feathers on the water.

Other canoes approached, and the Spaniards did a little trading with one of them, letting down trinkets on a rope's end and receiving dried fish in return; they noted that one of the Indians had a harpoon with an iron head.

The next day the *Santiago* lay becalmed off Langara Island, waiting for a wind to cross Dixon Entrance, and now the Haida gathered in numbers, twenty-one canoes containing more than two hundred "well formed Indians, with good faces, rather fair," as Crespi remarked, Pena adding that the women were "as fair and rosy as any Spanish woman" but that they had disfigured themselves horribly by the use of labrets in their lower lips.

The occasion became a regular market; the Indians sang and drummed and danced in their canoes, and in return for the Spaniards' knives and cloth and beads, offered beaver and other skins (doubtless sea otter), often made into cloaks "sewn together so skilfully that no tailor could have done it better." They also offered the first examples of Coast Indian artifacts to pass into European hands: conical painted hats, horn spoons, carved wooden platters, a couple of carved and painted wooden boxes ornamented with seashell, and Chilkat blankets (which the Tlingit were already trading down the coast) "of fine wool, woven and worked with thread made of the same hair in several colours, principally black, white and yellow. It is so closely woven that it seems to have been made on a loom," as, indeed, it was.

On his return voyage, Pérez had a first encounter with another native people on 8 August, when he put in to what was probably the entrance to Nootka Sound on Vancouver Island. This time the local Indians were not immediately welcoming. A few men came out from the shore in small canoes and sang wailing songs with dismissive gestures; later three larger canoes arrived and remained until after dark, their crews howling in what seemed to be lamentation. Native accounts of the event suggest that the Nootka feared the ship might contain avenging spirits. When nothing fearful happened overnight, they gathered courage, and next morning fifteen canoes with about a hundred people came and traded for the brilliant abalone shells the Spaniards had brought from Monterey; right from the start they established the Nootka reputation for light-fingeredness, one of them stealing from the second officer, Esteban José Martínez, some silver spoons that four years later would be offered in trade to members of Captain Cook's expedition.

Disappointed by the results of this expedition, the viceroy sent the *Santiago* back north in the spring of 1775. This time it was captained by Bruno de Hezeta, with Pérez demoted to first officer, and was accompanied by a smaller ship, the *Sonora*, commanded by Juan Francisco de la Bodega y Quadra, whom we now—forgetting Spanish usage—celebrate as the distinguished navigator Quadra.

Hezeta was told to sail north as far as the 65th parallel and there make the required act of possession. In fact, he achieved even less than his predecessor, turning back when he was off the southern tip of Vancouver Island, and it was left to Quadra in the 36-foot (11-m) *Sonora* to probe high into the Alexander Archipelago and make an act of possession a few knots north of the 57th parallel. Neither Hezeta nor Quadra appears to have landed on what later became British Columbian soil.

Content for the time being with Quadra's symbolic gesture, the viceroy decided to suspend further northerly sailings and to establish a strong Californian base; not until the end of the following decade would Spanish ships again sail northward.

Cook at Nootka

Spain was not the only European power interested in the news of Russian activities in the North Pacific area. The Admiralty in Britain had already heard of them and of the equally secretive activities of the Spaniards (for no account had been published of the Pérez expedition), and the news revived the old British obsession with the Northwest Passage.

In 1776 the Admiralty decided to send off an expedition to find out what was happening. James Cook, whose two great voyages earlier in the decade had led to a general opening of the knowledge regarding the South Pacific, was becoming restive in his virtual sinecure as Fourth Captain at Greenwich Hospital. The distant waters called him, and he quickly requested and secured command of the expedition, which his very presence raised to the level of a major enterprise. He sailed once again on the *Resolution* and was accompanied by the smaller *Discovery*, commanded by Capt. Charles Clerke. Leaving in June 1776 and revisiting Tasmania, New Zealand and Tahiti on the way, he sailed north across the Pacific and discovered Hawaii, which he named the Sandwich Islands after the sailorly Earl of Sandwich. The winter of the northern hemisphere was passing away, and he pushed on, reaching the Oregon coast on 7 March 1778. But storms kept him offshore, and though he saw and named Cape Flattery on 22 March, he was pushed too far out to see the entrance to Juan de Fuca Strait and sighted land again on 29 March, when he rediscovered Nootka Sound on Vancouver Island.

More than thirty welcoming canoes put out as Cook's ships sailed into the sound. A chief danced and sang in his canoe, waving his bird-shaped rattle and scattering eagle down on the water. Looking at the people crowded in the canoes, the English officers found it hard to penetrate imaginatively below the layer of what seemed to them dirt, though in fact it was largely paint arranged in patterns that expressed identities and protective grease used against insects and sunburn. Several of these officers, who had encountered a wide variety of peoples on their way through the Pacific, remarked that the Nootkans were the "dirtiest set of people" they had ever seen. Lieutenant King's description was typical:

> It will require the assistance of one's imagination to have an adequate view of the Wild, savage appearance & Actions of these first Visitors, as it is difficult to describe the effect of gestures & motions. Their dark coppery colour'd bodies were so cover'd over with filth as to make it a doubt what was really the proper Colour; their faces were bedaub'd with red & black Paint & Grease, in no regular manner, but as their fancies led them; their hair was clott'd also with dirt, & to make themselves either fine, or frightful, many put on their hair the down of young birds, or platted in it sea weed or thin strips of bark dyed red; the Dress of some was a loose skin thrown round their Shoulders, & which was not seemingly intended to hide their private parts, which in many were expos'd.

Even Cook found it impossible to make the leap of comprehension between one culture and another, and his own comment on his first sight of the Nootka was that of a reasonable man faced by the appearance of gross unreason:

> If travellers or voyagers in an ignorant or credulous age, when many unnatural and marvellous things were supposed to exist, had seen a number of people decorated in

this manner, they would readily have believed, and in their relations would have attempted to make others believe, that there existed a race of beings partaking of the nature of men and beasts.

In an ironic way he had unwittingly grasped at a corner of truth, for the Indians themselves saw a common identity between human and beast, the sense of which Europeans had long lost. But what Cook really meant was that the customs of the Indians, which he did not understand, seemed to place them on the verge of humanity as he knew it. In adopting this attitude, he was anticipating the tragic historic separation that developed in British Columbia, as in so many other places, between the indigenous culture and that of the European intruders.

It is true of course that during the four weeks he spent on Nootka Sound, Cook and his crews were much concerned with their own tasks. The masts of the two ships had to be repaired or replaced, spars had to be cut from local trees and rigging refitted. Spruce beer had to be brewed as a preventive for scurvy and the water casks filled. And there was plenty of work for the astronomers, the only scientists the expedition carried on board.

Though a rudimentary attempt was made to compile a Nootka vocabulary, relations were conducted mainly by signs and gestures. Cook appears to have got along well with the leading chief of the summer village of Yuquot, but significantly he never mentions his name; he would certainly have been one of the bearers of the hereditary title of Maquinna, used since before memory by the head of the most important clan on the sound. Yet, even if he gained no idea of the rich ceremonial life of these people and seems to have had no appreciation of the extraordinary sense of form their artifacts displayed, Cook did admire the efficiency of their carpentry and the great houses partitioned by mats and planks for the numerous families inhabiting them. Some of his crewmen wrote interestingly on practical matters, as in the descriptions by the marine sergeant, John Ledyard, of the clothes the Nootka made and wore and the ingenious variety of their fishing tackle.

But we probably get our best idea of the Coast Indian villages and villagers at this time of first encounter from the work of John Webber, the expedition's artist. To him we owe our visual sense of the great houses, with their sleeping benches and central hearths, fish hanging in lines to dry below the roof and the tall pillars, carved with grotesque faces, that supported the beams. He showed the people resting and working—cooking their meals and weaving their garments of cedar bark on large looms. Through his eyes, a way of existence becomes alive and believable. Unfortunately, in the beginning there were not many sympathetic mediators like John Webber between the two worlds.

On 28 April, Cook sailed out of Nootka Sound, and the first extended visit of Europeans to a Coast Indian community came to an end. It had been a remarkably pacific one, with no major clash and little bloodshed, the most serious occasion being one on which, exasperated by Nootka thievery, Cook peppered a few behinds with smallshot from his musket. The chief and the people gave the English a ceremonial farewell, as the men in the longboats bent to their oars and towed the two ships into the open ocean.

Cook did not revisit Nootka Sound, though it would be more than three years before his ships returned to England. He himself went on to his death on Hawaii in February 1779. Charles Clerke, commander of the *Discovery*, took over the expedition and, in the last stages of tuberculosis, insisted on sailing north in the effort to find a way through the Bering Sea. Having almost reached Kamchatka, he died in August 1779, and Lieut. John Gore took command of the expedition on its voyage southward to Macao and Canton and back to England, arriving home in August 1780.

There, the news of Cook's achievements took on an unexpected kind of significance. Knowing they would be sailing north into harsh climates, the sailors had traded with the Nootka for robes made of sea otter skins and other furs. On reaching the China coast, they discovered that the greasy garments they had used as blankets in Alaskan waters were bought eagerly at high prices, and when they returned to England in 1780, the news of the possible fortunes to be made out of Pacific coast furs seemed almost as important as the details of Cook's last discoveries.

All at once the secrecy maintained by both the Russians and the Spaniards was broken. The Admiralty tried to prevent publication of any account of the voyage before the official one, largely because it was hoped to use the proceeds of sales to help Cook's widow, but as early as 1781 a publisher named Newbery hired a ghost to make a sensational *Journal of Captain Cook's Last Voyage* out of the journals of Lieut. John Rickman.

William Ellis, surgeon's mate and the expedition's second artist, published in the following year his *Authentic Narrative of a Voyage Performed by Captain Cook and Captain Clerke*. And in 1783 Sgt. John Ledyard, having deserted from the Royal Navy, introduced the whole story to New Englanders by publishing in Hartford, Connecticut, his *Journal of Captain Cook's Last Voyage to the Pacific*, in which he did not hesitate to point out the advantages of trading to Nootka, since "skins which did not cost the purchaser sixpence stirling sold in China for 100 dollars." And when *A Voyage to the Pacific Ocean . . .* , the official account of Cook's voyages, finally did appear in 1784, the last volume, written by Captain (formerly Lieutenant) King on events after Cook's death, contained a positive incentive to anyone who wished to profit from the situation:

> When . . . it is remembered, that the furs were, at first, collected without our having any idea of their real value; that the greatest part had been worn by the Indians, from whom we purchas'd them; that they were afterwards preserved with little care and frequently used for bed-clothes, and other purposes, during our Cruize to the North; and that, probably, we had never got the full value for them in China; the advantages that might be derived from a voyage to that part of the American coast, undertaken with commercial wisdom, appear to me of a degree of importance sufficient to call for the attention of the public.

King George Men and Boston Men

From the beginning, political and commercial interests, the will to power and the desire to trade were mingled in the attitudes of the European intruders towards the land and the people of what eventually became British Columbia, with the commercial motive quickly becoming dominant and long remaining so.

The Russian interest was almost entirely commercial; the imperial government in the late eighteenth and most of the nineteenth century was too involved in absorbing its recently acquired lands in Siberia and the central Asian emirates to seek further territorial expansion, and contented itself with profit rather than power.

The Spaniards and the British were more intent on establishing spheres, perhaps not of sovereignty, but certainly of influence, though the Spanish found in proselytization an extra excuse for intrusion, just as the English did in scientific enquiry. And when the news of Cook's expedition began to become public in 1780, the reaction on the part of the Spaniards was a political one. The other reaction was a commercial one on the part of English and American trading interests, and it was this that first manifested itself and quickly changed the earlier relationship of guarded friendliness between the natives and the newcomers on the coast.

On 15 April 1785, Capt. James Hanna, a seaman of shadowy antecedents, set sail from Macao in the brig *Harmon*, with the financial backing of John Henry Cox, an English merchant in the China trade. It was on Hanna's visit to Nootka in August the same year that the first serious clash between native people and Europeans took place, and several natives were killed. There were varying accounts of the incident. Hanna blamed it on the Nootka trying to steal iron tools from him. But Maquinna told the Spaniards when they returned to Nootka in 1789 of a brutal and insensitive trick of which he had been the victim and which had enraged his followers. Invited on board the *Harmon*, he had been placed on a chair; there was a small pile of gunpowder beneath it, from which one of the sailors drew a thin powder trail that he ignited. The chair, with Maquinna on it, was thrown into the air; four years later he could still show Esteban José Martinez the scars on his behind.

Somehow, probably by making gifts in compensation for the deaths and for Maquinna's literally wounded dignity, relations were mended between Maquinna and Hanna, who was able to depart with a good cargo of sea otter skins. He returned the following year to find that rival captains were now arriving from both England and Bombay, under arrangements with the East India Company and the South Sea Company, which theoretically shared the monopoly of trading under the English flag in the Pacific Ocean. The King George's Sound Company in London sent two captains, Nathaniel Portlock on the *King George* and George Dixon on the *Queen Charlotte*, both of whom would play a considerable role in the exploration of coastal waters between Cook's voyage and Vancouver's in the 1790s. From the name of Portlock's ship, English traders would henceforward be called King George Men, while Americans, when they came, would be called Boston Men.

James Strange, the trader accompanying the *Experiment* from Bombay, persuaded the young surgeon on the ship, John Mackay, to go and live among the Nootka people until the *Experiment* returned the following year. Maquinna took Mackay into his house and assured Strange "that my Doctor should eat the Choicest Fish the Sound produced; and that on my return I should find him as fat as a Whale."

The *Experiment* did not return to Nootka, but in 1787 Capt. Charles Barkley arrived in command of the *Imperial Eagle*, flying Austrian colours to circumvent the South Sea Company's monopoly. It was Barkley's honeymoon, and his seventeen-year-old bride, Frances, was on board the *Imperial Eagle*; she was the first European woman to visit British Columbia. At Nootka, Barkley encountered Mackay, who had been forced to go more native than he had originally bargained for: "the natives had stripped him of his clothes, and obliged him to adopt their mode of dress and filthiness." It is not recorded whether he had also become "as fat as a Whale." Mackay eagerly accepted Barkley's invitation to join him on the *Imperial Eagle* and proved very useful as an interpreter and general go-between in trading with the Indians up and down the coast.

The most ambitious of all these early traders to the Northwest Pacific was John Meares, who first appeared in the autumn of 1786, having sailed from Calcutta on the *Nootka*, commissioned by the Bengal Fur Company, in which he seems to have had a controlling interest. He stayed too long on the Alaskan coast, where he got caught in the ice and many of his men died of scurvy. He was rescued in 1787 by Portlock and Dixon, whose ships were sailing under licence of the South Sea Company. They regarded him as a poacher, yet released him when he signed a bond to desist from further trading on the coast. But he gathered quite a few pelts before he headed for Hawaii, and this was typical of the man. He was bold and even rash in his enterprises, yet he was also devious and dishonest, and such a liar that nothing he said about his exploits in his prolix *Voyages Made in the Years 1788 and 1789 from China to the North West Coast of America* can be accepted without confirmation.

As first comers, these English captains established such harmonious trading relations with the people of Nootka Sound that when the first American trading ships arrived from Boston in the early autumn of 1788, they found that the sound was commercially closed to them while the English vessels were trading there; as one of the Yankees recorded, "they monopolized all the skins nor could we get intercourse with one of the Natives even for the purchase of fish or deer." It was not until the English departed to spend a warm winter in Hawaii that the Americans could enter the depleted market.

IV

The Nootka Incident and
Vancouver's Voyage

John Meares and the Nootka Incident

In the spring of 1788 John Meares was back again on the Northwest Coast with
the *Felice*, joined in August by the *Iphigenia*, flying the Portuguese flag and financed by the same John Henry Cox as had ventured with Captain Hanna.
Meares sent Captain Douglas in the *Iphigenia* to gather furs in the Alaskan islands
and sailed the *Felice* into Nootka Sound. He intended to establish a base, and obtained a piece of land from Maquinna. The nature of the arrangement is obscure,
for the Coast Indians had no concept of the transfer of property in the European
manner, since rights over land belonged to lineages and could not be alienated;
Maquinna had probably merely agreed to use of the land in return for the eight
sheets of copper that Meares gave him.

On the *Felice* Meares had brought European artisans, as well as seventy Chinese, who now began the long history of their people in Canada. They first
erected a building very much like the forts that the English traders had put up
around Hudson Bay: rooms for the officers, a mess hall, a dormitory for the men,
workshops, stores and a smithy, all surrounded by a palisade. It was the first
European-style structure built on the Pacific coast north of San Francisco, and
Meares followed it up with yet another innovation, "the first bottom ever built
and launched in this part of the globe." The "bottom" was a neat 40-ton (36-t)
sloop, designed for working in the coastal inlets, which Meares launched with
great festivities on 20 September and named the *North West America*.

It seemed a time of triumph for Meares. His second ship, the *Iphigenia*, had just
arrived heavily loaded with furs from Alaska, he himself had established good relations with another powerful chief on Vancouver Island, Wickanninish of Clayoquot Sound, and Maquinna had just returned triumphant from a raid on his local
enemies, well pleased with the English captain for providing him with arms.

But the good times did not last long. Three days before the launching of the
North West America, the first American had appeared in Nootka Sound, while
that summer, unknown to either King George Men or Boston Men, a couple of
Spanish ships had sailed quietly up the coast into Alaskan waters. They had not
only learnt of British activity there but had also listened to the big talk of some of

the Russians about occupying Nootka Sound and driving out the English and the Yankees.

Antonio Florez, the new viceroy of Mexico, decided that action must be taken to assert his king's rights. He evidently regarded the situation as potentially explosive, for he instructed Esteban José Martínez, the commander of the new expedition, to "behave with appropriate firmness, but without being led into harsh expressions that may give serious offence and cause a rupture."

Florez had reckoned without the arrogant stupidity of his own commandant and the equally arrogant effrontery of Captain Meares. In the frigate *Princesa*, with the *San Carlos* (commanded by Gonzalo López de Haro) as its consort, Martínez reached Nootka Sound in May 1789. He formally claimed it as part of the Spanish king's domain by right of prior discovery, without considering the aboriginal rights of the local people. He declared Meares's title void, which it probably was, and built his own fort with a cluster of houses around it, the first actual settlement in British Columbia. And he seized the *North West America* and turned it to his own uses.

While all this was going on, Meares was still on the China coast. There he met with the other English interested in the fur trade, and without knowing of the Spanish initiative, they decided to pool their resources to combat the American intruders. They formed a new enterprise, the Associated Merchants of London and India, which in 1789 sent out two vessels, the *Argonaut* under Captain Colnett and the *Princess Royal* under Captain Hudson. Meares remained on the China coast, and it was not until November that he heard of the disaster that had overcome his enterprises. Martínez had seized both his vessels and made their crews prisoner, while he had conscripted the Chinese labourers to work on his own fortifications. However, his triumph was at best a Pyrrhic one, for when the supply ship came from Mexico that summer, it carried instructions to dismantle the fort and return to San Blas.

With the British eliminated, the Americans temporarily scared away, and the Spaniards in strange retreat, Nootka was left for a short time to its native people. Meanwhile, the incident at Nootka had been blown into an international crisis by the efforts of Meares, who hurried to London and presented a Memorial setting forth in lurid terms the injustices he had experienced from the Spanish authorities. Given the history of British-Spanish relations, nothing could have been better contrived to stir the anger of trueborn Englishmen, and the government knew it had popular support when it induced Parliament to vote funds to prepare for hostilities with Spain. The Spaniards were equipped neither militarily nor morally to undertake a war at this time, and they agreed to immediate negotiations, out of which emerged the Nootka Convention of October 1790, which paid Meares more compensation than he deserved, provided—without consulting Maquinna—for the restitution of the land Meares had occupied, and declared that British subjects were free to trade anywhere in the Pacific Ocean, on the condition they avoid areas already occupied by the Spanish.

Even before the Nootka Convention, the Spaniards were back, for a new viceroy, the Conde de Revillagigedo, ordered the reoccupation of the sound, and in
February 1790 sent Francisco Eliza north with three ships and a contingent of
troops. Work began on a miniature colonial capital, with a church, a governor's
residence, and a hospital, and Pedro Alberni, who commanded the troops, set
about establishing the first garden ever cultivated in the area; he also introduced
cows, so that 1790 in Nootka can fairly be regarded as the beginning point of British Columbian agriculture.

The Spaniards dramatically increased their surveying activity and supplemented
it with the work of scientific enquirers of many kinds who arrived in August 1791
on the *Descubierta* and the *Atrevida*, the ships of Alejandro Malaspina's world voyage, intended as the Spanish equivalent to Cook's voyages. In 1790 and 1791 Eliza
and Manuel Quimper surveyed much of the Vancouver Island coastline.

Vancouver and Quadra

For their part the British decided to carry through with a plan already sketched
out: a new expedition to the Pacific Northwest to chart the numerous inlets the
trading captains had reported along the coast, once again in the hope of tracking
down that ancient quarry, the Northwest Passage. The command of the *Discovery*
went to Lieut. George Vancouver, who was given a double mission: to survey and
chart the coast from 30 degrees to 60 degrees north, and to accept the restitution
of territory at Nootka Sound.

Vancouver set out from Falmouth on 1 April 1791, sailing to the North American coast by way of the Cape of Good Hope. He took a good year to get there, arriving in the middle of April 1792 off Cape Mendocino, and surveying his way
methodically northward, reached Juan de Fuca Strait in May.

While Vancouver had been outfitting his ships and making his slow way across
the Pacific, Nootka Sound had once again become the centre of activity.

In 1792 Juan Francisco de la Bodega y Quadra, who had been commander of the
Sonora in 1775 and was now admiral of Spanish naval forces in western North
America, came from San Blas to Nootka, commissioned to negotiate restitution
with the English representative. Upon his arrival, the pace of activity sharply increased, with the obvious intent of establishing a highly visible Spanish presence
in the region by the time Vancouver arrived. Jacintho Caamano was sent north to
explore the Queen Charlotte Islands, while Dionisio Alcalá Galiano and
Cayetano Valdés, with the *Sutil* and the *Mexicana*, continued the exploration of
Vancouver Island, Juan de Fuca Strait and the Strait of Georgia. Quadra remained
at Nootka, gathering evidence to put a good case for ceding to the British as little
territory as possible.

Unaware of happenings at Nootka, Vancouver started his own survey of the
coast in the late spring of 1792, proceeding along Juan de Fuca Strait and the
Strait of Georgia, claiming all the lands he set eyes on in the name of King George
III, without knowing that everywhere—except Puget Sound, which he actually

discovered and explored—the Spaniards had been there before him. He realized this fact on 22 June 1792, when he entered Burrard Inlet, and, off the shore that he named Spanish Banks in memory of the meeting, encountered the *Sutil* and the *Mexicana*. The Spanish commanders welcomed him and his officers to "a very hearty breakfast" on one of their ramshackle little boats, which he described as "the most ill-calculated and unfit vessels that could possibly be imagined for such an expedition." Not to be outdone in urbanity, Vancouver suggested that they continue their surveys together; the Spaniards agreed, and the four ships sailed off in company, though Vancouver's vessels were the larger and swifter, and by the time he sailed into Nootka Sound on 28 August and Quadra's pilot guided him to anchorage, he had left the Spanish barks three days behind.

The good will that had been established continued. Vancouver sent Lieutenant Broughton ashore to intimate to Quadra that if he were prepared to salute the English flag, he would do likewise to the Spanish. Quadra complied, and a thirteen-gun salute was fired on each side. The exchange of courtesies developed into a round of splendid hospitality. Vancouver and his officers—as well as the commanders of the trading vessels that happened to call in during this generous summer—were repeatedly guests at Quadra's table, where five-course meals were served on solid silver plates; even the English crews benefited, because Quadra sent them fresh vegetables from the garden Alberni had planted and bread from the bakery at the fort. Quadra went so far as to make peace between the English and Maquinna over an unintended insult when the chief had not been recognized by a duty officer and had been refused permission to board the *Discovery*.

Vancouver and Quadra developed an increasingly close personal friendship that neither forgot in the few years of life that remained to them, for Quadra died in 1794 and Vancouver in 1798, regretting, as "a painful consideration," that he never met his Spanish friend again after they both left Nootka. When he came to naming on his maps the features of the coast, Vancouver acknowledged the Spaniards' contribution to the exploration of the region by using the names they had given to natural features. And at the end he paid tribute to his Spanish friend by naming the land on which they met "Vancouver and Quadra Island." Friendship was evidently not a virtue greatly valued by the naval cartographers, who quickly dropped Quadra's name.

And, in fact, friendship was not allowed by Quadra and Vancouver to influence their decisions in the political situation that brought them together, and one cannot fail to be impressed by the courteous obstinacy with which Quadra sustained the interests of his Spanish masters. Vancouver had come expecting substantial concessions: perhaps the abandonment of all Spanish interests in the Nootka region, perhaps the recognition of the right of English mariners to trade anywhere they chose on the Pacific coast north of the area the Spaniards had begun to settle around San Francisco. Quadra, however, interpreted his role as that of negotiating the Nootka Convention so that the Spaniards would surrender as little as possible.

In adopting this attitude, Quadra relied largely on the reports of Martínez, but also on the opinions expressed by the Boston Men, impelled not merely by trading rivalry but also by anti-English fervour developed during the American War of Independence, which had ended less than a decade before. The English may have been right, for Quadra was much taken with a young American captain, Joseph Ingraham, who commanded the *Hope* of Boston and who led Quadra to the conclusion that the British had no right, even under the convention, to more than the restoration of the patch of land seized from Meares.

This was the ground Quadra stood on. The cove where the *North West America* had been built and launched would return to Britain, but Spain would retain title to the rest of Nootka Sound, though the British would be allowed to use it. Quadra also argued that because the Spanish had built a small post at Neah Bay on the Pacific shore of the Olympic Peninsula, Juan de Fuca Strait must be regarded as the northern boundary of Spanish territory, and the British would have rights to settle or trade on the coast only north of there.

Vancouver argued that the post at Neah Bay had been erected after the Nootka Convention was signed; at that time the northernmost Spanish settlement had been San Francisco, and he would only accept an agreement that acknowledged the right of both powers to trade or settle on the Pacific coast north of a spot ten leagues north of that settlement. Moreover, he had not been sent all the way to North America to accept nothing more than the tiny patch of land Meares claimed to have bought.

The talks ended in deadlock, but there was a provision in the Nootka Convention that allowed the commissioners to refer disputed matters back to their governments. Vancouver arranged for Lieutenant Broughton to sail on a trading vessel bound for Canton, so that he could carry news of the breakdown back to Britain. Then he sailed down the coast, following Quadra who had left to report to his superiors in Mexico. On the way Lieutenant Broughton entered the estuary of the Columbia and explored the lower 80 miles (129 km) of the river, claiming its shores in the name of King George III. Unfortunately, the American fur trader Gray had named it after his ship, the *Columbia*, and this scant act of exploration the Americans were to use effectively when in later years they laid claim to the Columbia River valley.

Vancouver returned to the Pacific coast in the summers of 1793 and 1794, and surveyed the Alaskan coast northward to the 56th parallel, the edge of Russian territory. Meanwhile, political events in Europe, notably the French Revolution and the execution of Louis XVI and Marie Antoinette, had drawn Spain and England together, and they had concluded a military and commercial treaty in May 1793. This led to a desire to clear up outstanding differences, among which the unresolved Nootka issue ranked high. At last, on 23 March 1795, Brigadier General Alava and Lieut. Thomas Pearce of the Royal Marines arrived at Nootka to exchange the agreements signed by their respective governments. The final agreement provided that neither Britain nor Spain should have a permanent establishment at Nootka and that they should co-operate in preventing any other country from establishing sovereignty there; meanwhile the coast north of San Francisco was open to trade.

No Spanish naval vessel did in fact return to British Columbian waters. By the end of the eighteenth century the rule of Spain everywhere in the Americas was becoming unstable; in 1810, only fifteen years after the surrender of Nootka, revolution would begin in Mexico, and in 1821 Spain would acknowledge the independence of a country that would be much too involved in its internal disagreements and in its differences with the Americans to be concerned with anything as remote as the rugged coasts and islands of British Columbia.

V

West from Canada

Mackenzie's Journey to Bella Coola

The eventual abandonment by both Spain and England of the right to maintain establishments at Nootka might indeed seem like an act of political renunciation. In fact, while virtually eliminating Spanish interests from the region, it transformed the area south of the Russian domain into a British sphere of influence, even if it was to be maintained for the time being with nothing more formal than the occasional visit of a naval vessel.

In the summer of 1793, as Vancouver was surveying northward up the coast, the first fur trader to cross the Rocky Mountains found his way across the interior plateau of British Columbia to the coast. There, on the shore of Dean Channel, not far from Bella Bella, he recorded his arrival by painting his message with a mixture of vermilion and melted grease on a rock just above tide line.

> Alexander Mackenzie, from Canada, by land, the twenty-second of July, one thousand seven hundred and ninety-three.

Immediately, in response to hostile gestures from the Indians he encountered there, he turned and made his way back through the mountains to his base at Fort Chipewyan in what is now the Northwest Territories.

This was the first occasion on which the name of Canada was associated with the lands west of the Rocky Mountains; the reference, of course, was not to the nation that would take another three-quarters of a century to come together, but to the province of Lower Canada, created under the Constitutional Act of 1791. Mackenzie had originally come into the country east of the Rockies from Montreal, where he had started his career as a trader.

The fur trade in British North America was at this time undergoing rapid transformation. Ever since the 1670s, the London-based Hudson's Bay Company had been operating from the great inland sea whose name it adopted, trading mainly with Indians in the tundra and arctic forest regions inland from the shores of the bay. Since its beginning the company had experienced competition from French traders operating from Montreal into the regions north of the Great Lakes. After the conquest of Québec by the British, French traders were quickly shouldered out by mainly Scottish merchants who came in the wake of the British troops that occupied Québec. These were reinforced at the end of the American War of Independence by exiled Loyalists—often former officers. Mackenzie himself was the son of an officer who had died while serving the British cause; he had been sent to school in Montreal, where he remained after the end of the war. He showed great aptitude for the fur trade, and in 1784 he was made a partner in his firm, Gregory MacLeod and Company. In 1787 Gregory MacLeod joined other competing firms in the North West Company, which would become the Hudson's Bay Company's formidable competitor.

Theoretically the North West Company had no political status, unlike the Hudson's Bay Company, which operated under royal charter and acted as a kind of surrogate for political government in Rupert's Land, the drainage basin of Hudson Bay, which Charles II had deeded to it in 1670. In fact the HBC exercised only a shadowy semblance of power, maintaining its fortified trading posts and sustaining the routes between them, without attempting to impose authority on the Indian population, whose adherence it hoped to ensure by making them dependent on British goods. Only if the native people showed violence towards its officers or servants did the Company reply in kind, but that was self-defence rather than policing a territory.

The North West Company was clearly trespassing when it moved west of Lake of the Woods and into the prairie that formed the southern part of Rupert's Land. And though its partners were not afraid to challenge the rule of the Hudson's Bay Company or the charter on which it was based, they were also anxious to move into territories where they would be able to offer the justification of first discovery. Peter Pond gave them this justification in 1778 when he followed an old Indian trail across Methye Portage into the Athabaska country, rich in furs, whose streams all ran into the Mackenzie River basin and eventually into the Arctic Ocean. In Athabaska, with their forts and brigade routes reaching back to Montreal, the North West Company became as much a shadowy state within a state as the Hudson's Bay Company in Rupert's Land and defended its interests with great vigour.

Peter Pond was the first of a series of notable trader-explorers of the Canadian West whose activities were encouraged by the North West Company's need for ever new sources of fur. Through his own observations and Indian reports, Pond had become convinced that even if the existence of the Rockies—known since Anthony Henday had sighted them in 1754—had disposed of the idea of a great Mer de l'Ouest, there must still be a natural means of communication with the Pacific. He had observed the great stream that flowed out of Great Slave Lake and had decided that Cook Inlet in Alaska must be its estuary. This would provide a way to the western ocean and eliminate the need for the North West Company to maintain the costly route by which furs and trade goods travelled between Montreal and the far west. Mackenzie spent a great deal of time with Pond when they jointly founded Fort Chipewyan on Lake Athabaska, listening to his theories, studying the crude maps he drew, and being infected with his enthusiasm. After Pond had departed, Mackenzie decided to set out and follow the directions shown on the maps. His first effort, in 1789, took him down the river posterity has named after him but which he called the River of Disappointment, for at the end of it he found the great salt marshes of the Mackenzie delta and the shores of the Arctic Ocean, which he reached on the day the Bastille fell in Paris.

Still, Mackenzie was convinced that there was a way to be found to the Pacific, even if it might not take the form of a broad and easy river. To establish "the practicability of penetrating across the continent" became, as he later admitted, "the favourite project of my ambition," and he thought of it continually and obsessively until, in October 1792, he set off once again. He wintered at Fort Forks, at the junction of the Peace and Smoky rivers, and in May 1793 started off again with a large birchbark canoe 25 feet (7.6 m) long and 4 feet 9 inches (1.5 m) in beam, into which he stuffed 3,000 pounds (1360 kg) of cargo ("provisions, goods for presents, arms, ammunition and baggage") as well as ten people. Alexander Mackay, a young clerk with the North West Company, went as his lieutenant, and there were six *canadien* voyageurs and two Indians taken as hunters and interpreters. The extraordinary hardships that Mackenzie and his men underwent finding a way across the Rockies have been told too often to need repeating. The important fact is that he found the Rockies were penetrable by land; others who followed, notably Simon Fraser twelve years later, would locate a more practicable route.

Ascending the Peace, Mackenzie soon entered what would eventually become British Columbian territory and faced such difficulties negotiating the Peace River canyon that his men were on the verge of deserting. However, they battled their way over rocks and against waters until they reached the point where the Finlay and Parsnip rivers came together to form the Peace; accepting the advice of local Indians, Mackenzie turned south up the Parsnip, and at its headwaters crossed the mountains and descended the McGregor River to the Fraser, which he thought must be the upper reaches of the Columbia. He proceeded downriver until other Indians (probably the Shuswap) told him it was not a good way to the sea; on their advice he turned north and started along what he called the West Road River, where Indian trails took him over the Coast Range into the Bella Coola Valley, down which he travelled to the ocean. On his way he passed as the first white visitor through the territory of a number of Indian peoples, the seminomadic interior tribes like the Sekani and the Carrier, the Shuswap and the Chilcotin, and the settled Bella Coola with their villages of large coast-style houses; Mackenzie admired the skill of their carpentry and remarked on the quality of their woodcarving. From Fort Forks to Bella Coola he encountered slight and passing hostility, usually the results of fear, and the Bella Coola welcomed him with great hospitality. Throughout his journey he depended on the advice of Indians, which he shrewdly took, and benefited from Indian guides, as did most of the explorers of Canada whose "discoveries" we praise.

It was only at the end of his journey, on 21 July at Dean Channel, that he encountered Indians who had already met white men face to face and who resented the experience. These were the Heiltsuk (or Bella Bella), a northern Kwakiutl tribe who received him with such open hostility that his Bella Coola guide advised him to turn back if he wanted to stay alive. Now he knew the way, Mackenzie returned very quickly, leaving Dean Channel on 22 July and reaching Fort Forks on 24 August.

Simon Fraser and the Beginnings of White Settlement

It would be more than a decade before the North West Company seriously followed Mackenzie's lead by moving into the area between the Rockies and the sea; the delay was due to further dissensions in the Montreal fur trade, during which Mackenzie himself left the North Westers to join in a new XY Company. Not until 1804 did the XY traders join or rejoin the North West Company. A tentative overland attempt at trading was indeed undertaken in 1800 by a couple of *canadiens* employed by the North Westers, La Gassi and Le Blanc, who attached themselves to a band of Kootenay Indians hunting bison on the prairie and accompanied them back across the Rockies. But this was an isolated foray, and not until 1805, the year after the absorption of the XY Company, did Simon Fraser cross the mountains with the intention of establishing a continuing fur trade. In doing so he created the first permanent settlements, other than those of the Coast Indians, in British Columbia.

Fraser—an American-born Loyalist who had come to Montreal as a child after his father died in prison—set off in the autumn of 1805 with a party of twenty men. They followed the Peace and, like Mackenzie, ascended the Parsnip; but instead of proceeding to its headwaters, they turned off westward along the Pack River and reached Trout Lake, as Fraser called it, where he established his first log-built post. The lake was eventually renamed McLeod Lake, and the post became Fort McLeod; it survives as a small settlement, the oldest white community in British Columbia. Fraser was delighted with the quality of the furs he acquired there and regarded the tiny post as the beginning of a large enterprise in New Caledonia, as he named the country, because its forested hills reminded him of his mother's description of her native Scotland.

In the following years Fraser moved deeper into this northern country, the land of the Carrier Indians. In 1806 he established Fort Fraser on Fraser Lake and Fort St. James on Stuart Lake, which eventually became the centre of trading operations for this northern region. In 1807 he built Fort George at the confluence of the Fraser (which he still believed to be the Columbia) and the Nechako.

From Fort St. James on a bright May day in 1808, Fraser set out on the canoe voyage that would make him famous; he had a small flotilla of four craft and was accompanied by John Stuart and Jules Quesnel, nineteen voyageurs and two Indians. It was not the best season to have chosen, for as they travelled south, the spring freshets steadily raised the volume and level of the river. By the beginning of June the situation had become alarming; on the second of that month Fraser noted a rise of 8 feet (2.4 m) in a single day. More and more they had to land their canoes and carry them over rough portages. An old Shuswap chief had joined them as a guide, and on 6 June he and other Indians warned Fraser—as Mackenzie had been warned fifteen years before—that he would never get his craft through the canyons and rapids which faced him. Fraser ignored them, for his intention to follow the great river to its mouth was fixed, but a few days later, in the territory of the Lillooets, he realized that he could not proceed by water. He stored his canoes and set out on foot through Lillooet territory and into that of the Thompson River Indians, whom he found friendly and helpful.

He certainly needed help at this point, for he faced the intimidating task of finding a way down the Fraser Canyon, where at points, such as Hell's Gate, there was no ordinary trail but the mere ghost of a path they could not have followed without the guidance of the Indians, and then did so at great peril.

> We had to pass [said Fraser] where no human being should venture. Yet in these places there is a regular footpath impressed, or rather indented, by frequent travelling over the very rocks. And beside this, steps had been formed like a ladder, or the shrouds of a ship, by poles hanging to one another and crossed at certain distances with twigs and withes, suspended from the top to the foot of the precipices, and fastened at both ends to stones and trees, furnished a safe and convenient passage to the Natives—but we, who had not the advantages of their experience, were often in imminent danger, when obliged to follow their example.

Below the canyon, the river again became navigable, but the people less friendly. Somewhat grudgingly, the Indians below the canyon agreed to rent canoes to Fraser, but they warned him against the Cowichan people, who were reputed to be a ferocious group, at the mouth of the river.

By now Fraser had experienced the same kind of disappointment as Mackenzie on his first voyage. He had realized that the river entered the sea nearly three degrees north of the mouth of the Columbia; he had found neither the objective he sought nor a practicable trading route. But he persisted in continuing to the sea, and when he reached the village of Musqueam at the mouth of the Fraser, he found the warnings justified, as he saw the warriors making "their appearance from every direction, howling like so many wolves, and brandishing their war clubs." He retreated immediately, harried by the peoples of the lower Fraser Valley until he reached the canyon and, once again, a friendly reception from the Thompson River Indians. When he got back to Lillooet he recorded in his diary that he would have turned back from there if he had known the ardours of travelling down the canyon and in the end not gaining his objective. Nevertheless he had added notably to knowledge of the interior of British Columbia, and his memory was left for posterity when David Thompson gave the name of Fraser to his particular river of disappointment.

David Thompson, the Mapmaker

David Thompson's name was already attached to the terrain by the time he named the Fraser, for at a place where the town of Lytton now stands, Fraser had seen a river of clear blue-green glacial water flowing into the Fraser and mingling with its murky waters. He had named it after Thompson, the third of the great fur trader–explorers of British Columbia.

Thompson stood rather apart among the Scots—highland and lowland—who were in the majority among the traders of the North West Company. Despite his name, he was of Welsh ancestry, born in London, and he had started out in 1784 as an apprentice in the employ of the Hudson's Bay Company, where he learnt his skills as a surveyor and mapmaker and acquired a flair for prose that made his travel journals by far the most interesting among those of early travellers in British Columbia. Unlike most of the fur traders, he was religious in the early nineteenth-century evangelical manner and combined his piety with abstemious habits. Yet he had a scientific bent, and the exactness of his descriptions of the animals he saw suggests that in another situation he might have been a great field naturalist in the Victorian manner. In 1797, discontented with the lack of support for his surveys, he terminated his service with the Hudson's Bay Company and joined the North Westers, who received him with open arms and immediately employed him mapping their trade routes and carrying out explorations east of the Rockies. In 1806 he was commissioned to supplement Fraser's travels from the Peace River by seeking a way through the Rockies farther to the south; ultimately, he was expected to locate the headwaters of the Columbia and follow the river down to the sea.

In the spring of 1807 he set off from Rocky Mountain House and followed the North Saskatchewan to its headwaters, where he located and crossed Howse Pass. On the other side of the mountains he followed the Blueberry River and reached the Columbia, establishing close to Lake Windermere a fort he called Kootenae House. There he spent the winter trading and observing the skies and the countryside, and in 1808 he occupied himself mainly with following the Kootenay River down to Kootenay Lake. He showed a surprising disinclination to follow up his principal commission, and 1809 found him still in the mountain country of Idaho and Montana, where he established Kalispell House and Salish House. Then in 1810 he set off back to Montreal, to be intercepted when he reached Rainy Lake House by categorical instructions to proceed immediately to the mouth of the Columbia and establish a post there before John Jacob Astor's Pacific Fur Company, which—the North Westers had heard—had dispatched an expedition by sea.

He was delayed on his way by threats from the Peigan Indians and the need to make a diversion to avoid them, which led him to Boat Encampment at the Big

Bend of the Columbia. Again he procrastinated unjustifiably, for the river was clear, yet he built a winter camp and spent valuable months gathering a crew to replace men who had deserted. Not until 15 July 1811 did he reach the mouth of the Columbia, precious weeks after the American traders who had already built a post and named it Fort Astoria. Thanks to the multiple delays of this brilliant but unreliable man, the Americans had been given yet another reason for their eventual claim to the Oregon territory. Yet Thompson remains one of the most remarkable explorers of Canada, a man whose skill as a surveyor enabled him to create the first even remotely accurate maps of the interior of British Columbia and write the journals that bring the country two centuries ago alive to us as none of the other travel narratives of the time can do.

The Pacific Fur Company at Fort Astoria

At first, with the Pacific Fur Company established on the Columbia, it looked as though a full-scale fur war would develop between the new trading enterprise and the North West Company, which was still only precariously established in the territory west of the Rockies. David Stuart, in charge of Astoria, started up the Columbia in 1811, founding Fort Okanogan at the junction of the Okanogan River and the Columbia, then pushing on into the dry country of British Columbia and building Fort Kamloops on the Thompson River. Shortly afterwards, a party of North Westers arrived and set up a rival post at Kamloops.

However, the Pacific Fur Company had already suffered a setback when its ship, the *Tonquin,* was destroyed in an Indian raid in Clayoquot Sound. And now, early in 1813, the American traders heard of the war in Canada between Britain and the United States that inevitably imperilled their situation. At least a British blockade of the one American settlement on the Pacific coast seemed likely, and the traders decided to abandon Astoria and make an overland journey to St. Louis in the spring.

Meanwhile the North West Company had sent out a ship of its own, the *Isaac Todd,* which had letters of marque as a privateer. At the same time, John Stuart, Simon Fraser's associate, had led a party of seventy fur traders and voyageurs across country from the Fraser by a new route to the Thompson and the Okanagan. He continued down the Columbia and camped close to Fort Astoria, awaiting the arrival of the *Isaac Todd* with its cannon before he attempted an assault. It was a situation curiously devoid of enmity, for most of Astor's men were former North Westers. A good deal of casual socializing went on, and out of it emerged a realization on the part of the Pacific Fur Company men that they did not have to abandon Fort Astoria; they could sell it. And this eventually happened, for the North Westers handed over bills of exchange amounting to $80,000, and on 16 October the fort, with all its trade goods and the furs gathered since it had come into existence, was handed over to the North Westers, while most of its traders rejoined the Canadian company.

Legally, it was an excellent solution as far as the Canadian fur trade was concerned; the only existing American title to land in the Pacific Northwest had been liquidated by mutual agreement and purchase. But all the benefit gained in this way for British interests was to be negated by a blunder as harmful as Thompson's procrastinations. At the end of November, Captain Black of the Royal Navy sailed the HMS *Raccoon* into the mouth of the Columbia River. He was annoyed to see the fort already in the possession of the North Westers, but he decided to carry out at least a ceremonial seizure, and went ashore with a party of marines and sailors. A flagstaff had already been erected. There—a witness recorded—the captain took a British flag that he had brought for the purpose and raised it to the top of the staff; taking a bottle of Madeira, he smashed it against the pole, proclaiming in a loud voice that he took possession of the establishment and the country in the name of his Britannic majesty and named it Fort George. In this way a peaceful transfer of property was turned into an act of war, with all the consequences that were to emerge in a few years' time.

The transformation of Fort Astoria into Fort George placed the North West Company in a favourable position on the Pacific coast. This dominance was reflected in the growing transportation network that developed to link the original North West posts, those taken over from the Pacific Fur Company and those more recently established, like Fort Walla Walla and Fort Alexandria. While New Caledonia remained a separate department administered from Fort St. James, a new department of Columbia was created and supplied by sea. The traders there enjoyed a luxury of living rather like that which prevailed in the company's headquarters in Fort William, but in New Caledonia the shortage of any food more palatable than dried fish forced Daniel Williams Harmon to begin at Fort St. James the first farming on the mainland of British Columbia, growing cold climate crops of barley and potatoes, turnips and carrots, to vary the diet and cut the risk of scurvy.

However, the attempt to dominate coastal and ocean trading as well as inland commerce remained unsuccessful. The North Westers never competed successfully against the Boston Men who still traded into the inlets of the heavily indented coast, and their attempt to enter the China trade was unsuccessful because the East India Company would not allow the *Isaac Todd* to buy the tea whose profits would have enabled the ship to bring back British trade goods to Fort George on the last lap of its voyage. Furthermore, the North Westers were reaching the critical stage of their great battle with the Hudson's Bay Company for domination of the entire fur trade in British North America west of Montreal, while the consequences of Captain Black's folly at Fort Astoria were working themselves out in the negotiations that brought the War of 1812 to an end.

The Treaty of Ghent was a *status quo ante bellum* agreement in which each power returned to the other the territory taken during the war. Astoria had been both purchased and taken, and the Americans stressed the taking rather than the buying. In the first of a series of unnecessary concessions to Yankee bluster, the British gave in. On 18 October 1818, HMS *Blossom* of the Royal Navy moored off

Fort George, and British and American commissioners went ashore to exchange documents. The American flag was raised over Fort George, and the *Blossom's* guns saluted it.

There was no immediate or dramatic change in life on the Pacific coast. John Jacob Astor was not interested in resuming trading there, and the North West Company continued as before in the fort it had purchased. But from 1818 onward the British no longer held the unchallenged sway they had enjoyed since the termination of the Nootka Incident. On 20 October the same year, Britain and the United States signed a convention, of which Article II provided for their equal political status in the territory west of the Rockies.

The situation created by this convention continued almost to the middle of the nineteenth century, when it was brought to an end by the Oregon Boundary Treaty of 1846. It had been defined when in 1819 the Spaniards agreed with the Americans to surrender their rights west of the Arkansas River and north of the 42nd parallel. In 1821 the Russians had further delineated spheres of influence of the coast when they issued an ukase claiming exclusive rights north of Queen Charlotte Sound, and abandoned their claims to other territories in treaties signed with the United States in 1824 and with Britain in 1825. This meant that the whole territory between 54°40′ and 42° was open to the competition of British and American interests, with no danger of interference from Spain or Russia.

A political arrangement had been made regarding the temporary disposition of the land west of the Rockies, without its original and most numerous inhabitants being consulted. There were treaties between intruders, but none between the intruders and the native peoples; there was no recognition of aboriginal right, a situation that may have been due in part at least to the assumption of a divinely approved right of ownership on which both the Spanish and the Russians, the first intruders on the coast, had operated.

Yet at the same time there was no implementation of the sovereignty that both the British and the Americans tentatively claimed. Neither a colonial administration nor a protectorate—not even a condominium like that many years later between the British and the French in the New Hebrides—was established. There was no seat of government, and there were no permanent military forces; the only token manifestations of power were the rare occasions when American or British warships sailed the coast.

The Hudson's Bay Company: Discipline and Dependence

But if there was as yet no political infrastructure, a commercial one quickly developed, and it did so especially after the next significant date in the history of the Pacific coast. After years of bitter conflict, verging on warfare, in the Athabaska country, the two great fur-trading enterprises decided to bury their quarrels and unite in a great monopoly that would cover most of British North America. Agreement was signed in London on 26 March 1821, and the new organization took on the name and also the charter of the Hudson's Bay Company. It also assumed its hierarchical structure, with its rigid distinctions between gentlemen and others. The gentleman would start as an apprenticed clerk and could rise to the rank of chief trader (in charge of one of the larger forts) or chief factor (in charge of a district or a department). In the days of the North West Company there had been flexibility in ranking, so that employees—voyageurs, artisans, interpreters—might on occasion become gentlemen officers. There had also been comparatively little stress on racial origins; a number of important traders before 1821 had been the Métis sons of wintering partners, given a good British education in Montreal or even Scotland. Within the new dispensation, under Governor George Simpson, the caste lines were quickly frozen. A man who started out as a boatman or a carpenter could never hope to become an officer. The highest position he could attain was that of postmaster, in charge of some small and remote establishment. The same applied to men of mixed blood, no matter how capable and whether their male ancestry was English or French.

All this was part of a reorganization of the Company to make it more tightly controlled and better adapted for the vast role it now assumed. To strengthen the new Company and to give more unity to the British possessions in North America, the British government had vastly and officially extended its sphere of privilege. The Company received an exclusive licence to trade in parts of western Canada—e.g., the Athabaska country—that were outside Rupert's Land. Another licence gave it a monopoly on trading in the area between the Rockies and the Pacific coast. These were virtually expansions of the charter, and they made the Company the only power, *de jure* and for long *de facto*, in the vast area extending westward from the Great Lakes to the western ocean and northward as far as they cared to venture.

In the manner of the classic chartered trading companies, the Hudson's Bay concentrated its energies on its commercial activities. Except for trading with them, it sought to interfere as little as possible with the native peoples, respecting their customs and ignoring their wars. This policy went so far as discouraging missionaries, who might change the nomadic habits of the native people which were advantageous to the fur traders, and until relatively late almost no attention was given to education except among the children of Company officers. At an earlier stage on Hudson Bay itself, Company employees had even been forbidden to enter into sexual relations with native women, but the North Westers introduced easier manners they had inherited from the French *coureurs de bois*, and—until British women began to arrive in the mid-nineteenth century and introduced Victorian morals—informal marriage *à la façon du pays* became customary and led to the considerable Métis or mixed-blood population that was one of the main heritages of the fur trade.

This essentially commercial power of the Hudson's Bay Company was sustained by a scattering of forts and a thin network of brigade routes. Overland stretches—extended portages—served by teams of pack animals would alternate with long waterways served by brigades of *canots de nord,* or York boats in the more navigable stretches. One of the main routes ran south from Fort St. James through Fort Kamloops, Fort Okanogan and Fort Walla Walla to the Columbia estuary at Fort George, or later Fort Vancouver. Another major route, often called "The Communication," went northward following the Columbia to Boat Encampment and then struck overland to Jasper House in the Rockies and eventually, by the Saskatchewan River system, to York Factory on Hudson Bay, which after 1821 became the Company's Canadian headquarters and the transshipment point for furs destined for England. Montreal was superseded as a fur-trading centre, and the voyageur from Québec became an anachronism, replaced in the canoes by Iroquois and western Métis paddlers, and in the oar-propelled boats by Orkneymen. Later on, the inland forts would be supplemented by a chain of forts dotted up the coast to intercept trade that might go to the freelance sea traders; and trading schooners and—later on—steamers would furnish a marine equivalent of the inland trading routes.

Though the Columbia department was more amply staffed, that of New Caledonia, extending over the whole of northern British Columbia as far south as Fort Alexandria on the Fraser, was administered by a chief factor, a chief trader and nine or ten clerks, supported by fifty or sixty employees. They were many times outnumbered by the native people around them, and one of their principal means of protection—like that of the sahibs in India—was the awe they could establish among the native peoples, which was just as important as their superior weaponry and their usually rather flimsy fortifications.

But even more important was the sense of dependence the fur trader developed among the Indians. It is not accidental that the tribes in Canada who longest maintained a proud show of independence were those, like the Blackfoot, who were most resistant to the attraction of white men's goods (except for guns and horses). Most of them found that once they had become used to steel hatchets and iron pots, there could be no retreat to stone axes and basketwork cooking pots. Alcohol also created a dependence, and though this was much exaggerated in evangelical accounts of the fur trade, it did contribute to a sense of alarm that arose among the Indians at the thought of the traders ceasing to supply the new needs that were changing their lives and turning them from independent hunters into servile trappers. The fact that there were no longer rival companies trying to win them over with competing prices made the Indians only more dependent on the monopoly that remained.

So the Company started its last decades of dominance in British Columbia with a power that was shadowy in substance if one considers political structure and military resources, but strong in spirit, maintained on the one hand by the courage and capacity of its highly selected personnel and on the other hand by the needs and desires that had almost insensibly been implanted in the minds of the native peoples.

VI

The Doomed Equilibrium

Changing Indian Populations

The trade routes of the fur traders would later help to define the transport lines of modern Canada and the forts they founded would provide the nuclei for some of British Columbia's major communities, including Victoria and Prince George, Kamloops and Nanaimo. Yet the railway builders and the miners contributed just as much in this respect, and perhaps more. The importance of the Hudson's Bay Company in terms of an evolving western Canadian history has tended to cast a forward shadow from the events of that time, giving the actions of white men on the coast and on the inland plateaus and valleys of British Columbia a romanticized importance that was not evident in the thin but tenacious network which the Hudson's Bay Company then cast over the region. A recent popular historian of the Hudson's Bay Company, Peter C. Newman, took a phrase from one of the fur traders and called his book *Caesars of the Wilderness*. But these were no Caesars; they conquered nothing, and the people over whom their charter gave them a kind of suzerainty never became their subjects. The first half of the nineteenth century was a period of suspended decision, a time when two societies existed in precarious equilibrium. For many years they occupied the same territory without either establishing dominion over the other: the tightly organized fur trader society of a few hundred white gentlemen officers and Métis, Iroquois and Orkney servants, and the mass of the Indian population who inhabited the vast areas. Throughout the nineteenth century, population figures are uncertain, but anthropologists have established a plausible curve which suggests that the native population at the time of Cook's arrival was probably round about 100,000. Even at that time, before they had seen a Caucasian, the Indians were being reduced by white men's diseases, especially smallpox, which is mentioned by some of the earliest sea traders such as Captain Portlock, who in 1787 told of an epidemic that had struck the Tlingit some years before. The same epidemic may have affected the Haida, for in 1829 the American missionary Jonathan Green picked up recollections that must have referred to it.

> Some thirty or forty years since, the smallpox made great ravages among them. This disease they call Tom Dyer, as some supposed from a sailor of the name who in-

troduced it, though it is probable it came across the continent. Many of their old
men recollect it, and they say, that it almost decimated their country. I can not
learn that any general sickness has been prevalent since that time, but their vices are
fast hastening them to ruin.

Green was almost certainly correct in his assumptions, for the trading routes
over the Rockies, which had existed for millennia, would have transported infec-
tions as effectively as they transported coastal valuables like dentalium and
abalone shells in the days before the white men came.

When Green talked of the "vices" that were hastening the "ruin" of the Coast
Indians, he was probably referring both to their predilection for alcohol, which
they learnt to enjoy after first rejecting it with distaste, and to venereal diseases,
which were spread through the custom of the chiefs profiting from the prostitution
of their female slaves to visiting seamen. But other white men's diseases against
which the Indians had developed no immunities were equally ravaging; they included measles, tuberculosis and influenza.

During the following years, there were further catastrophic smallpox epidemics.
An epidemic in 1836 badly reduced the northern tribes, particularly the Tsimshian gathered around Fort Simpson, of whom James Douglas estimated that a
third died. Yet, though the survival of many groups appeared precarious early in
the present century, only two small Athapaskan-speaking bands and one Salish
band became extinct in historical times. They were the Tsetsaut, whose survivors
were absorbed by the Nishga of the Nass River; the Nicola, whose survivors joined
the Thompson River Indians; and the Pentlatch in the Fraser Valley, whose survivors melded with neighbouring groups. Territorial claims in the sense of use rather
than ownership on the part of the various lineages were so traditionally defined
that annexation hardly entered into the pattern of Indian warfare even after the
reduction of populations by sickness, and the only dramatic instance of the dis-
placement of one people by another was that of the Salish who occupied Cape
Mudge at the south end of Quadra Island. They were pushed out by the Kwakiutl-
speaking Euclataw, an aggressive group who used Cape Mudge's situation on Seymour Narrows to carry on a profitable piracy.

Rivals in Trade

A census made by a Hudson's Bay Company clerk in 1845 seems to confirm the
opinion of many modern ethnologists that the native population of British Columbia was about 70,000. The HBC estimate covered the whole of the districts of
New Caledonia and Columbia; it established a total of just under 87,000 persons,
counted tribe by tribe. Given, owing to the density of the coastal population
north of Juan de Fuca Strait, that a majority of the 87,000 would have lived in
what is now British Columbia, a total of between 60,000 and 70,000 seems a reasonable guess for the native population north of the 49th parallel in 1845. The
employees of the Company in both New Caledonia and Columbia at this time to-
talled 635; this figure included Iroquois, Métis and Kanakas as well as white men,

talled 635; this figure included Iroquois, Métis and Kanakas as well as white men, so that whatever distant political ambitions the governments of Whitehall and Washington may already have harboured, the proportion of Caucasians to the native people was much less than 1 to 100. These strangers made no immediate claims over the actual land except for the sites of their posts, and until the arrival of the gold seekers at the end of the 1850s, the various Indian peoples held their traditional fishing and hunting grounds without challenge.

It was a situation that suited the fur traders, who enjoyed commercial advantages without having to assume political responsibilities, and in many ways their presence must have seemed like the introduction of a new tribe into the population complex of the region, for the relations between the Hudson's Bay Company men on one hand and the native peoples on the other closely resembled those between the various aboriginal groups. They were, after all, based on trade and on occasional bursts of what passed on the coast as warfare, and trade and warfare were traditional occupations of all the peoples of British Columbia at the time of their first encounter with white men.

Trading relations on the coast by the late eighteenth century were based on the fact that the main cultural and linguistic regions had already been established on the coast and in the interior many centuries before the white men came, so that even an isolated enclave like the Bella Bella had no traditions about how and when they became isolated from their congeners. The situation had achieved such a stability that even today there has been no basic change to the situation Pérez and Cook encountered more than two centuries ago. The same peoples live mostly in the same places, and their languages have not substantially changed, nor has any new language except English appeared.

With the arrival of the Europeans, the simple trading patterns of precontact times became diversified and extended. A coastal trade brought items like abalone shells from as far south as California, while at the mouth of the Columbia the Chinook people were so deeply involved in trade that a kind of pidgin based on their language had become the commercial *lingua franca* of the whole Pacific Northwest even before the white traders arrived.

Farther north, trade went on around the islands and up the inlets, and trade routes crossed the interior mountains of Vancouver Island from east to west. Since the Fraser River was not navigable, the main communication routes between coastal and inland peoples were the larger northern rivers, the Skeena, Nass and Stikine, with the Bella Coola River as a lesser artery.

The area occupied by the coastal Tsimshian around the present site of Prince Rupert was a particularly important focus of commercial activity, since not only was there trade up the Skeena and the Nass into the territory of the inland Tsimshian-speakers (the Nishga and the Gitksan), who carried the trade on to the Athapaskan tribes farther east, but a considerable traffic went on up the coast of Alaska into Tlingit territory and across the strait to the Haida villages of the Queen Charlottes. Even before the white men came, the trade was extremely var-

and a variety of manufactured objects. From Alaska, for example, there came native copper, iron that had found its way through the Aleutians from Siberia, and the fine blankets and other weavings of the Chilkat people. From the Queen Charlottes came great cedar canoes, sea otter furs, and dried halibut and black cod. From the inland peoples came obsidian and amber, sheep and goat horns for carving into spoons, and goat wool for weaving into blankets, as well as furs, deer and moose hides, dried berries and stone tools.

From the Prince Rupert area, perhaps the most important export in all directions was the oolichan grease prepared in enormous quantities when the fish ran each year up the Nass. Other exports from this focal region included killer whale jawbones, which could be transformed into clubs, and sea lion whiskers, which were used to decorate chiefs' headdresses. Local manufactures for export also formed a considerable part of the trade, including armour, clubs made from whalebone, wooden items such as carved and painted boxes and vessels, while as middlemen the Tsimshian traded Haida canoes and Kwakiutl secret society paraphernalia to the Tlingit.

The native trade had its organization and its experts. It was carried on by the various lineages represented by chiefs like Maquinna and the famous Shakes on the northern coast, who gained a name as a tough bargainer among the white traders. The general assumption of the white traders was that the chiefs were acting for their own profit, but the situation was more complicated, since the goods that were traded represented the communal surplus production of the lineage, and it was sold on their behalf, even if some of the goods gained in exchange would end up gracing a chief's potlatch.

The chiefs and their clans often controlled major waterways leading into the interior where their representatives acted as middlemen in the exchange of coastal for interior products. The Kitselas Canyon on the Skeena was one of the key situations; middlemen in the villages of Gitsaex and Gitlaxdawk on either side of the canyon entrance controlled the whole traffic up the river.

It is possible to see the trade carried on by the independent sea traders (whose numbers reached their peak when twenty-three British and Boston ships arrived on the coast in one season) as an extension of this pattern, since the native people continued accumulating surpluses to sell for their potlatches, and the arrival of the whites meant more than anything else an increase in the number of available commodities and of trading partners. Indeed, there were many instances when white men actually followed the old patterns of the trade, as when Vancouver's men took north with them the fine abalone shells they had found at Monterey in California and sold them at high prices on Vancouver Island. Very quickly the trading chiefs realized that they could increase their profits by monopolizing local commerce with the white traders, and as early as 1778 Cook's men witnessed a barely averted battle when the people of Nootka Sound, led by Maquinna, prepared to fight off another group who had come to trade directly with the English seamen.

Already expert traders, the Indians quickly learnt how far they could press their demands for goods in exchange for furs, and the trade changed as certain desires were saturated. The heavy initial demand for iron was replaced, for example, by a demand for other metals, notably brass and copper, though there were some commodities, like firearms and ammunition, blankets and tobacco, for which it never diminished, while the call for alcohol increased. Women, particularly among the Tsimshian where they had a high status, seem to have become deeply involved in the bargaining process and even to have dictated the trading at times, for some of the ships' captains were astonished to see the wives beating their menfolk when they did not make good enough deals. Perhaps it was the close involvement of the women that made the Indians carry on their trading with an eye to the quality of trade goods as well as to the price being paid. Just as some of the fur traders became expert at judging the pelts that were offered them, so there were experts among the Indians, for the British free trader Captain Bishop described how, when he went to trade with Shakes and his people in 1801, there was first a ceremonial encounter with Shakes himself, eating biscuits and butter and drinking wine, and then, after the chief's withdrawal to his own canoe,

> the Trade commenced an old good Humered Blind (but cunning Man) conducting the whole of it, for all the Cannoes, who whould sell nothing, till the Goods had been put into his hands and his Assent given. It was a matter of astonishment to us, to see how readily he would find a Flaw in the Iron &c and by feeling the Furs, the price they ought to fetch.

The effect of the first century of trading between the Indians of British Columbia and the various traders they encountered was especially complex among the culturally advanced coastal peoples, already wealthy in terms of their own world.

In the simpler world of the interior hunting peoples, the effects were more dramatic and direct and resulted usually in a dependence from which they have never really recovered. Once they had taken to firearms and metal tools and traps and utensils, once they had discovered that in many ways cloth was more practical than skins, they seemed never to have the will—whatever the necessity—to return to their old ways; when ammunition became difficult or impossible to obtain, hunters would starve rather than return to bows and arrows, whose use they forgot remarkably quickly. Their dependence on the muskets and cooking pots, the axes and chisels, the knives and blankets that they could obtain only by trade forced them into a new pattern of living in which trapping for sale largely replaced hunting for subsistence, and in which they found it increasingly difficult to escape from their roles as clients to the traders. Their fragile cultures were diminished rather than enriched by the trading relationship.

On the coast, the effect of the fur trade was to stimulate an already dynamic culture, for, as Wilson Duff said in his *Impact of the White Men* (1964), it brought "prosperity, an increase in wealth in a society already organized around wealth." To begin, it increased the existing native trading network, as the middlemen chiefs of the coast traded inland the goods they had obtained from the trading ships. In a society based on conspicuous consumption, chiefs became richer than ever, and this brought a rapid stimulus to ceremonial life and even more to its artistic activity. Rapidly increasing stocks of wealth, often in the form of novel and therefore temporarily valuable items bought from the ships, encouraged the multiplication and magnification of potlatches and of ceremonies of all kinds. And this in turn meant a sudden efflorescence of the various arts that had already been developed before the white men came.

Some ethnologists, notably Marius Barbeau, have argued that Coast Indian artistic traditions in fact developed almost entirely as a result of the introduction of metal tools after the arrival of the white man. Barbeau has even suggested that the freestanding heraldic pole was itself a product of this period. However, there is strong evidence, in the accounts of early trading captains and in the discovery of prehistoric artifacts at Ozette and elsewhere, that the distinctive coastal art style and the main types of crafted objects with which we are now familiar were already flourishing by the time Pérez and Cook made their first contacts in the 1770s.

As new wealth permeated the Coast Indian society by the middle of the nineteenth century, there was a great upsurge of ceremonial and artistic activity. The patrons, rich clan chiefs, demanded more poles and elaborately decorated house fronts, more masks and headdresses, rattles and talking sticks, feast dishes and spoons, and illusionary devices for the winter dances.

The artists in their turn became more capable of responding to the demand as they worked with metal tools, which allowed quicker and more accurately detailed production than the jade blades and beaver teeth of the past. The tricks performed in the winter ceremonials became more elaborate and mechanically ingenious, and in the "public" art of poles and house fronts a veritable golden age developed when the great groves of highly symbolic heraldic poles were erected along the beaches of the northern villages during the mid-nineteenth century. The splendid products of Coast Indian art that are scattered in museums across the world almost all date from this relatively late but richly productive era. The works of the native artists even entered the mainstream of commerce when the Haida, in particular, invented new craft genres—and incidentally earned more wealth to potlatch—by making small carvings of argillite stone and silver jewellery with native motifs that appealed to the outside market.

Much less beneficial in its effects was the introduction of firearms. The appearance of guns and horses had already transformed the native cultures of the prairies, and horses and guns came to the interior groups of British Columbia by exchange with other Indians or by theft from them even before the first white man made an appearance. Horses never assumed any importance on the coast, but guns, traded abundantly by both King George Men and Boston Men, rapidly spread, often with disastrous intervals when one village had bought its muskets and a neighbouring settlement had not. As early as 1794 Vancouver was noting that in order to sell more weapons, the Boston Men were not above a little local warmongering.

Trade and Warfare

By the end of the eighteenth century, the welcoming friendliness that Cook and the earlier Spanish voyagers encountered had come to an end. Relations between white men and Indians did not cease, for trading continued, but it went on in an atmosphere of mutual distrust punctuated by occasional and often sensational outbursts of violence.

While among the prairie Indians something resembling a chivalric code may have developed, which saw honour in taking risks and in single combat among warring chiefs, the warfare of the coast peoples was one of ruse and surprise, aimed at obtaining slaves, booty and the heads of victims, with as little damage to the attackers as possible. Since the idea of alliance between villages hardly existed, nobody was immune from a surprise attack, though in fact the culture was too stable for major raids to have been frequent before the introduction of firearms. The situation seems to have been mitigated by the existence of phratric bonds, which loosely united people who shared the same clan crest, no matter what their villages or languages. This phratric bond imposed certain limitations, including that of exogamy; an Eagle from one village could not marry an Eagle from another. But it also provided certain protections; an Eagle would not enslave another Eagle and would try to avoid killing him in battle, while he would give him hospitality and protection if he came as a stranger to his village.

When the white men came, the Indians were unsure of their visitors' identities. The marvellous things they possessed, guns and telescopes, clocks and watches, gilded buttons and large quantities of iron, suggested that they might be supernatural beings, perhaps manifestations of the Transformer himself. But once the novelty wore off, the Indians realized that the whites were merely men after all, members of strange and distant races. Since they were not in any sense relatives, it was permissible to deal with them as one might with any other strangers on the coast—to steal from them, even to kill them if necessary to satisfy the great desire that the coastal peoples so quickly developed for the white man's goods. Before the end of Cook's month at Nootka, the thieving had begun, and the killing had begun even earlier on a small scale, for in July 1775 a boat's crew of seven men from Quadra's ship, the *Sonora*, was attacked and killed on Destruction Island in Juan de Fuca Strait; and afterwards the Indians tried to board the *Sonora* itself from their canoes but were beaten off. However, these were isolated rather than typical incidents, and it was not for another decade that extensive violence between white and Indians became a habitual feature of coastal life. It started with the arrival of Captain Hanna in 1785 and the incident of Maquinna's humiliation already described; the desire of the Indians to trade saved the day on this occasion, and Hanna got away without harm, but the incident rankled, and particularly among the members of Maquinna's clan, with tragic later consequences.

The pattern of dishonest trading and violent methods that marred early commerce on the coast was really initiated by two Boston sea traders, Captain Kendrick and Captain Gray, the reputed discoverer of the mouth of the Columbia. Kendrick and Gray were among that first batch of American traders who arrived in Nootka Sound in the autumn of 1788 to find that Meares had cleared out all the available supplies of otter pelts. They remained over the winter and in 1789 moved north to the Queen Charlottes, where Kendrick performed his first outrage and almost died for it.

The Haida had stolen some linen from his washing lines, and he complained that when he demanded it back, it was not all returned. So he removed a small cannon from its carriage, seized Koya and another chief, tied them to the carriage, cut off their hair, painted their faces ludicrously, and, not content with humiliating them, threatened to kill them unless the Indians sold him all their furs at his low price, which they did. However, his deeds were not forgotten, and two years later, when Kendrick entered the same inlet, the people recognized him, and, getting onto the ship, they seized the arms chests and forced the crew below decks. There the officers distributed their personal weapons, and after a short and hard skirmish defeated the Indians, who were urged on by a woman chief Kendrick described as "a proper Amazon" and who was killed in the fray. Not content with having escaped alive, Kendrick proceeded to teach the Indians a lesson. As one of his later officers remembered Kendrick's account of the incident, "a constant fire was kept up as long as they could reach the natives with cannon or small arms after which they chased them in their armed boats making the most dreadful havoc by killing all they came across."

Gray's depredations in 1792 were even worse. He wintered over from 1791 in Clayoquot Sound, where he built a sloop, the *Adventure,* and eventually—according to his account—heard of a plot by the Indians, who were all now well armed and who resented his ill treatment of one of their chiefs, to attack his ship, the *Columbia,* and take revenge. He moved the ship quickly into a safer place and, maintaining careful defences, completed his sloop; as his last act in Clayoquot Sound, he dramatically punished the Indians for merely plotting an attack. On 27 March he sent his fifth mate, the young John Boit, with three boats loaded with well-armed men to destroy the village of Opitsaht. Boit noted in his journal:

> It was a command I was no means tenacious of, and am griev'd to think Capt Gray shou'd let his passions go so far. *This* Village was about half a mile in Diameter, and Contained upwards of 200 houses, generally well built for *Indians.* Ev'ry door that you enter'd was in resemblance to an human and Beasts head, the passage being through the mouth, besides which there was much more rude carved work about the dwellings some of which was by no means *inelegant.* This fine Village, the Work of Ages, was in a short time totally destroy'd.

Gray went north to the Queen Charlottes, and on his way back down the coast of Vancouver Island at the end of May became involved in yet another violent incident. According to him, the Indians of one village were preparing to attack, and when a war canoe came near the ship, he opened fire with his cannon, killing or wounding all the warriors. The Indians complained to Quadra at Nootka with quite a different story; according to them, a Boston ship with a one-eyed captain (Gray was one-eyed) had attacked an Indian settlement, killing seven men and wounding others, and stealing sea otter skins. They brought one of their wounded for the surgeon at the fort to treat, and Maquinna asked Quadra to punish the aggressors.

But the Spaniards did nothing, and this was characteristic of a period when the European powers were content to establish their claims to territory in the Pacific Northwest without in any way attempting to police it, so that it was left for the white captains, a few of whom followed the examples of Kendrick and Gray, to establish their ascendancy by terror, including massacres, the kidnapping of chiefs, and the extortion of furs at cannon point.

Among peoples as warlike and as concerned with matters of honour and prestige as the Coast Indians, an extreme reaction to such treatment was inevitable. There were further attacks on small boats belonging to Captain Barkley and Captain Meares in 1787 and 1788 respectively, both in Juan de Fuca Strait; and in 1790 Captain Colnett lost a boat's crew from the *Argonaut* who had been shipwrecked on a reef and were massacred by the Indians. The attacks assumed tragic proportions in 1794 when the Haida chief Cumshewa led a raid on the American ship *Resolution* and massacred its crew, leaving one survivor.

A number of sensational incidents followed in the early years of the nineteenth century. Up to then, Nootka Sound had been relatively peaceful, with the various high chiefs who bore the title of Maquinna maintaining on the whole good relations with their visitors, whether Spanish, British or American. At the same time, memories of Captain Hanna rankled, while more recently a certain Captain Tawnington had raided one of the villages when the men were away and stolen all the furs from the terrified women. And in 1803, when Captain Salter of the *Boston* spoke insultingly in English of Maquinna, the chief (whose knowledge of English the captain had underestimated) resolved to take revenge.

The *Boston* was invaded after Maquinna had performed what turned out to be a masked war dance on its deck. All the officers and seamen were slaughtered, except the armourer, John Jewitt, and an older seaman named Thompson, while the ship was plundered. Jewitt was taken as Maquinna's personal slave, and the result of his two years' sojourn at Nootka was *A Narrative of the Adventures and Sufferings of John R. Jewitt*, the first account to be published of life in a Coast Indian village seen from the inside. Jewitt was finally rescued by the captain of the *Lydia*, another American trading ship, who in 1805 lured Maquinna on board his ship and held him hostage until Jewitt was released.

Parts of the coast were no longer safe sailing—or rather safe landing—for the trading ships. During the summer of Jewitt's rescue from Nootka, the Bella Bella Indians of Milbanke Sound went on board the schooner *Atahualpa* with evidently friendly intent. The leading chief then attacked and killed the captain, and this was the signal for a general boarding of the ship in which half the crew were immediately killed, including the first and second mates as well as the captain. The survivors managed to get to their arms and drive off the Indians, and they successfully sailed their ship out of the sound and eventually to Hawaii.

The most sensational attack of the period, at least in its consequences, was that on the *Tonquin*, the Pacific Fur Company's vessel that in 1811 had brought to the mouth of the Columbia the traders who established Fort Astoria. While the latter began to build up their trade on the Columbia, Captain Thorn took the *Tonquin* north up the coast of the Olympic Peninsula and Vancouver Island. There he entered Clayoquot Sound, the domain of Chief Wickanninish, and began trading.

What Thorn did not know was that a sealing captain, another American named G. W. Ayres, had recruited a dozen Indians there for one of his expeditions and had failed to bring them home as promised. Instead, he had marooned them off the California coast, and when they tried to go north to their home, they were either killed or enslaved by other Indians. Under the vendetta rules that prevailed on the coast, any member of the group to which a person responsible for a death belonged could be killed in revenge, and to the people of Clayoquot Sound all Boston Men were fair prey in avenging themselves on Ayres.

They came on board the *Tonquin* with bundles of furs, but the Indian interpreter whom Thorn had picked up along the coast suspected their intent from some of the remarks he overheard; he warned Thorn, who gave orders to put to sea, and the crew began hoisting the sails and raising the anchor. At this time the Indians produced weapons hidden in their furs and attacked the crew, most of whom they massacred immediately. Four or five men retreated to the stern cabin, from which they climbed into a small boat and escaped in the general confusion. They did not get far before they too were hunted down and killed. But they had left a slow fuse burning towards the powder magazine, and when the Indians swarmed on to the *Tonquin* to plunder it, the ship blew up and two hundred natives died. The only survivor from the *Tonquin* was the Indian interpreter, who made his way back to Fort Astoria with his news.

John Jewitt had plenty of opportunity to hear the Indian point of view, and in his *Narrative* he had some reflections about "the manner in which our people behave towards the natives" that his fellow countrymen might profitably have considered:

> For though they are a thievish race, yet I have no doubt that many of the melancholy disasters have principally arisen from the imprudent conduct of some of the captains and crews of the ships employed in this trade, in exasperating them by insulting, plundering and even killing them on small grounds.

However, instead of heeding Jewitt's reproach, the Boston Men—and some of the British traders as well—continued in their own ways, and relied on greater precautions against attack. When they went to trade with a tribe suspected of violent intent, they would post sharpshooters at the mastheads, load and man their cannon, and cover the deck with great boarding nets that prevented any aggressor from leaping on board. They would carry on their trading through the portholes. Such practices were continued even after the Boston Men no longer came, by the Hudson's Bay Company vessels as they traded up and down the coast.

But it was not the fear of Indian attacks that drove the free traders from the coast. It was economic warfare, the concerted action of the Hudson's Bay Company and the Russian American Company in systematically overbidding the interlopers, as they called them, until for individual entrepreneurs the profit went out of the trade.

In the beginning the Indians had been so eager for the white men's goods, and especially for metal and for firearms, that they would pay high prices in furs, and Captain Meares gave an amusing (though perhaps exaggerated) account of how he exchanged two copper teapots for a large pile of sea otter pelts. But very quickly the Indians realized that there was competition among the white traders themselves, and they soon fitted their demands to the situation. By 1835 the Hudson's Bay Company, with its own trading vessels as well as its coastal forts, was competing directly with the remaining American traders. In that year Chief Trader John Work accompanied Captain McNeill of the HBC ship *Llama* on a trading trip to the mouth of the Nass, where they found Captain Allan of the Boston boat *Europa* already trading. Work noted in his journal:

> *Sunday, May 17.* Still fine weather. The Indians assembled again in the morning as usual, and kept going between us and our opponents as usual. During the day we traded 94 Beaver, 5 Otters, 28 Bears, 21 Martens. We had more customers than our opponents owing to the superior quality of our Rum and Tobacco. Capt. Allan who must have been perfectly aware of our scale of trade, came aboard and enquired what we were giving, and on being told, got in a violent passion and declared that he would do his utmost to rise the price and make us pay as high as possible for all the furs we would trade on the coast this season, that he had plenty of goods to do so (& as our deck was full of Natives busy trading) without waiting to be spoke to went over the side and proclaimed to the Indians that he would give 4 gall. Rum & 8 heads of tobacco with one of his large blankets for a beaver. The Indians . . . immediately ceased trading and began to clear off to his vessel. It remained with us either to lose the beaver or rise our price, the latter was preferred and we accordingly offered 5 gall. Mixed rum & 10 heads tobacco with a blanket per beaver, the result of which was that we secured, as we think, the best share of the day's trade.

VII

The Fur Empire: Flowering and Decline

The Great United Company

To the Indians they all seemed interlopers, whether they were the Boston captains or the American mountain men who were appearing in the Rockies or the Hudson's Bay traders who competed with a show of legitimacy under their antique charter and its recent extensions. And in so far as they remained traders instead of settlers, drawing exportable wealth from the land instead of committing their lives to it, they did remain strangers who often died in a land they had not made their own.

All this was to change, with negative consequences for the native societies, during the half century following the union of the fur companies in 1821. It was the period when the original commercial infrastructure of white presence on the Pacific Northwest was transformed, by the arrival of white men other than fur traders, into a political structure, substituting for the suzerainty of a chartered company the sovereign power of political states.

The first part of this period was dominated by the reorganization and rationalization of the fur trade west of the Rockies into a single commercially efficient organization.

The takeover of New Caledonia and Columbia by the recreated Hudson's Bay Company in 1821 was itself something in the nature of an invasion. The two districts had always been the terrain of the North West Company, into which the Hudson's Bay Company had made only two minor fur-collecting forays, each without any followup. This meant that there was no memory of internecine conflict between fur traders to be eliminated. It also meant that almost all the officers in these areas who accepted the Deed Poll of 1821, and as chief factors and chief traders became shareholders as well as officers in the reconstituted Company, were former North Westers, accustomed to a different style of operation than that which had been directed from Hudson Bay.

They first became aware of the change through the actions of George Simpson (later "Sir George") who presided over the Company's affairs in Canada, first as governor of the Northern Department and then as governor-in-chief from 1821 to 1860; a diminutive authoritarian of enormous energy, he earned the title of "the

Little Emperor." From the day the companies united, Simpson was concerned with rationalizing the unwieldy structure, which had acquired a single head but still in effect had two bodies consisting of the companies' transport systems and their networks of forts. He was intent on abandoning the long, uneconomical northwest route from Montreal through Fort William into the West, and on making York Factory on Hudson Bay the sole transshipment point for outgoing furs and incoming trade goods. Simpson also proposed to reduce drastically the number of forts and posts, needlessly numerous because of the practice of duplicating each others' establishments, which the companies had followed during their struggle for ascendancy; he also planned to trim the employment rolls and create a leaner and more efficient system. He was particularly concerned with the logistical problems of carrying on an operation west of the Rockies, and early on he set about discovering how to make New Caledonia and Columbia more self-sufficient and how to deal with the American threat, which became evident during the 1820s with the penetration of traders and trappers through the Rockies as an advance guard of the ever-moving frontier.

The second dominant figure in the new order was John McLoughlin, a Canadian-born Scot of gigantic build with a mane of prematurely silvery hair, whom the Indians are said to have called "the white-headed eagle." He has his place in the hagiography of the American West as "the father of Oregon" and was described by his fellow fur trader John Tod, with equal accuracy, as an "ambiguous mammoth." McLoughlin had taken medical training and always used his title of doctor; since 1803 he had worked for the North West Company, first as a surgeon, then as a fur trader, becoming a wintering partner in 1814. He was a man of broad reading and considerable intellectual powers, with a touch of radicalism that made him sympathetic to republican ideas and popular movements. When the union of the two companies was mooted, McLoughlin was delegated by the wintering partners to represent them at the discussions between the two concerns, and when the amalgamation did take place, he was absorbed into it with the rank of chief factor. In 1825 Simpson picked him out as the man most likely to carry out a reorganization of the departments beyond the Rockies, and he went there as superintendent, the only one with that rank in the service, second only to Simpson. For the next twenty years he would direct the Company's affairs on the Pacific coast and the hinterland stretching back to the Great Divide of the Rockies; he did so in increasing conflict with Simpson.

Under McLoughlin's shadow would develop the dour and capable figure of James Douglas, who bridged the transition of British Columbia from a fur-trading territory to a pair of crown colonies, and himself would symbolize the transition by being the only HBC officer to serve at the same time as governor of a colony. Born in Demerara, the son of a Scottish merchant and a creole woman, and educated in Scotland, Douglas entered the North West Company's service as a youth of sixteen in 1819. When the companies united, he was still a clerk, sent in 1825 to Fort St. James in New Caledonia, where he completed a hard apprenticeship. A man of impatient arrogance, Douglas was often in conflict with the Indians, who once captured him and threatened him with death, and in 1830 he was transferred to Fort Vancouver on the Columbia, as much for his own safety as for the smooth running of the trading operation in New Caledonia. There his administrative abilities became evident, and he caught the attention of George Simpson, who in 1832 wrote down an assessment of his character, as he was wont to do in the case of men he was considering for promotion.

> A stout, powerful active man of good conduct and respectable abilities; tolerably well Educated, expresses himself clearly on paper, understands our Counting House business and is an excellent trader. Well qualified for any Service requiring bodily exertion and the exercize of sound judgment, but furiously violent when roused. Has every reason to look forward to early promotion and is a likely man to fill a place on our Council board in course of time.

Promotion in fact came quickly. Douglas became a chief trader in 1835, a chief factor in 1839. When McLoughlin resigned in 1846, Douglas was the man most fitted to take his place, and, after the Oregon Boundary Treaty of that year, to supervise the withdrawal of the Company's western headquarters from Fort Vancouver on the Columbia to Fort Victoria on Vancouver Island, whose site he had chosen. Unlike McLoughlin, Douglas had no love for the Americans or for their democratic pretensions.

Simpson's Grand Tour

By 1824 George Simpson had set on foot the reforms he considered were needed everywhere in the Hudson's Bay Company's domain except the districts beyond the Rockies. He was impatient to see the situation in these areas, of which he had heard mainly through rumour or by reports he suspected of being self-serving.

In New Caledonia and Columbia, the "commissioned gentlemen" had been awaiting his inevitable visit with a mixture of optimism and apprehension. He was reputed to be acute in judging the characters and abilities of men, and surely he would recognize the special knowledge they had gathered of a territory different in so many ways from the rest of the great Company's domain. On the other hand, they were almost all former North Westers, and in the great struggles of the later 1810s in the Athabaska country, Simpson had been one of their bitterest enemies. Bygones—in the reconstructed Company—were supposed to be bygones, yet there were instances of North Westers too militant in their hostility to the old Hudson's Bay Company having been punished by temporary ostracism; it had happened to Samuel Black and to Cuthbert Grant, each allowed to cool his heels for a couple of years before a position was found for him.

When McLoughlin was appointed in charge of the Columbia department in the summer of 1824, Simpson decided to accompany him, so that the reforms McLoughlin would have to direct might be fitted in with the general plan Simpson had in mind for the reorganization of the Company. McLoughlin set out in the latter part of July, while Simpson waited at York Factory for the ship that would bring his annual instructions from the Committee in the City of London, the Company's highest authority. By the middle of August he realized that unless he left, the weather would make his journey impossible until the following spring; on the fifteenth of the month he ceased waiting for the mail ship and set out. Accompanying him in his *canot du nord* with its picked crew of eight voyageurs was Chief Trader James McMillan, who had been with David Thompson on his exploratory journeys beyond the Rockies.

Simpson incorporated into his cult of efficiency the belief that "time is money," and just as he never wasted an hour in his office, so he never wasted a day on the road. He insisted on taking a difficult new shortcut and triumphantly overtook McLoughlin, who had started twenty days before him, on the Athabaska River. McLoughlin, who had been travelling in the leisurely manner customary to potentates of the North West Company, was vexed and embarrassed, particularly as he now had to adapt to Simpson's pace—with its early risings and long days. By the time they reached Fort George on the Columbia, they had achieved a record time for the journey, completing it in 84 days as against the previous record of 104 days. It was a foretaste of the kind of efficiency Simpson would demand when he set about reforming the western departments.

Simpson was preoccupied with two major problems as he crossed the mountains: the first was reaching Jasper's House ahead of the winter weather on the tenth of October and Boat Encampment on the Big Bend of the Columbia by the nineteenth.

The inevitability of trouble with the Americans in at least the southern part of the district of Columbia was much in the minds of the Hudson's Bay Company's London directors and of the imperial officials in Westminster. The Convention of 1818 still held, and in fact it would be renewed for another decade in 1827, but Foreign Office representatives had already expressed pessimism about retaining any long-term rights in the country east of the Columbia and south of the 49th parallel. For its part the Company had already responded to the situation by abandoning its traditional conservationist policies and organizing its annual Snake River expedition of trappers and traders, led first by Alexander Ross and later by the more aggressive Peter Skene Ogden, aimed at harvesting to elimination point all fur-bearing animals in the country between the Rockies and the Columbia and so offering the equivalent of scorched earth to the American trappers pushing in from the Missouri Valley.

The second and more urgent problem was the condition of the Columbia department. Simpson's route did not take him to the bleak posts of New Caledonia, where life was meagre and austere. But what he saw of the Columbia posts south of the 49th parallel, as he made an exploratory diversion to Fort Spokane and then went down through Fort Walla Walla to Fort George, aroused his concern, and a week before he reached the coast he noted angrily in his journal that it seemed as though "from the Day of its Origin to the present hour" the Columbia department had been "neglected, shamefully mismanaged and a scene of the most wasteful extravagance and the most unfortunate dissension." He noted that everything here *"except the Trade"* was on too high a scale, and that the officers had shown such "an extraordinary predilection for European Provisions that they may be said to have been eating Gold." He concluded ominously: "It is high time the system should be changed and I think there is an ample Field for reform and amendment."

When he reached Fort George, Simpson's criticisms were broad. He observed that the traders at Fort George had made no effective effort to compete with the interloping traders who swarmed unopposed up the coast, and they had made little effort to push their trading into the area closest to the fort, between the Columbia and Puget Sound. But he was equally concerned that—unlike Harmon in New Caledonia—nobody had attempted to grow food in the rich lands of the region and reduce the great cost of supplying the various posts with food imported from England. When a clerk objected that their business was to gather furs and not to farm, Simpson replied: "Every pursuit tending to lighten the expense of the trade is a branch thereof," and in saying so he opened a line of policy that would turn the Hudson's Bay Company into an activating force in the early settlement economy, establishing the directions that major British Columbian industries would later follow.

Simpson's presence over winter at Fort George invoked an immediate upsurge of activity. The matter of urgent concern—even more urgent than starting agriculture or expanding the coastal trade—was the protection of the Company's operations from an eventual American takeover of most if not all of the area south of the 49th parallel. Clearly, Fort George, which lay south of the Columbia and over which the Americans had re-established their claims, was in imminent peril of takeover, while the brigade route southward down the Columbia ran through what might well eventually become American territory.

Evidently, Simpson was not fully aware of the difficulties Simon Fraser had encountered on his journey to the coast, for he considered the Fraser River a possible route between New Caledonia and the sea. One of his first acts after reaching Fort George was to send James McMillan northward with a strong expedition to find a suitable spot for a fort on the lower Fraser. McMillan set off on 18 November, accompanied by three clerks and thirty-six paddlers, including Kanakas (Hawaiians) as well as French-Canadian voyageurs. They went up the coast to the Chehalis River and portaged to Puget Sound, afterwards tracing a way through its islands until they reached Semiahmoo Bay on the Strait of Georgia, where White Rock now stands. At Mud Bay, just beyond, they found the mouth of the Nikomekl, and followed this tiny river to the marshy plain later called Langley Prairie. A short portage took them to the meandering Salmon River and down to the Fraser; they saw plenty of evidence of beaver on the way. The local Indians—people "of low stature" with "flattened heads"—turned out to be friendly and eager to trade.

McMillan identified a likely place for a post and returned to Fort George by the end of the year.

Simpson was pleased with McMillan's report, particularly since he had come to realize that the Columbia had a major natural disadvantage to add to its political ones; the bar at its entrance was dangerous and already several ships had been wrecked there. Still, for the time being, he felt that the most urgent task was to transfer the headquarters of the department of Columbia to politically safer territory north of the river. He sent McLoughlin and Chief Factor Alexander Kennedy in search of a suitable site; they had to go 80 miles (36 km) upriver to find it, at the spot which Lieutenant Broughton thirty years before had named Belle Vue Point. It was a splendid situation, near the confluence of the Columbia and Willamette rivers, in the midst of fertile grassland admirably suited for the farming operations Simpson anticipated. Work on constructing the buildings started over winter, and when Simpson arrived in the spring on his return journey to Hudson Bay, the fort was almost complete. On 19 March 1825 he "Baptised it by breaking a Bottle of Rum on the Flag Staff" and "Gave a couple of Drams to the people and the Indians." He named it Fort Vancouver, "to identify our claim to the Soil and Trade with his discovery of the River and Coast on behalf of Gt Britain." It would remain the centre of the Company's operations on the Pacific coast for the next twenty-four years. In 1826 the brigade route from New Caledonia was rerouted so that it ran south from Fort Alexandria on the Fraser and then via Okanagan and Walla Walla to Fort Vancouver, so that all operations on the West Coast would be consolidated, with the traffic to London going via Fort Vancouver instead of York Factory.

Simpson continued on his way, leaving bags of seed potatoes as he went as an incentive to start food-growing and making decisions on the spot regarding the inland establishments. He had been tempted to decree the abolition of Fort Kamloops, which brought in very little fur, but decided to maintain it as a necessary link in whatever pattern of brigade routes might eventually evolve. But he decided to abandon Spokane House and instead to build a new post near the junction of the Kettle River and the Columbia, since at Kettle Falls near this point the Indians gathered in great numbers for the fishing. He himself lined up the site for a building 150 feet square (45.7 m^2) overlooking the Columbia, which he named Fort Colvile, in honour of Eden Colvile, associate governor of Rupert's Land.

Running the Canyon

Like many vigorous entrepreneurs, George Simpson combined ferocious efficiency with a romantic response to the grandeur of natural phenomena, and he seemed to enjoy travel for its own sake as much as for the information he gathered. On his original western journey, approaching the Rockies in 1824, he had been impressed by the mountains that rose "perpendicular to a prodigious height." He was also charmed by the beauty and variety of the country as opposed to the monotonies of the northern woodlands and the prairies with which he was familiar. In a rare moment of introspection, he confessed in his journal the "extraordinary interest" he found himself taking in the affairs of the Columbia department. In 1828 he decided to return, partly to see how the plans he had made in 1824–25 were being carried out, and partly to decide how to direct the Company's operations northward in view of the growing danger of American penetration.

In 1828 Simpson travelled no less rapidly than in 1824, but somewhat more spectacularly, and he decided to start with a first visit to the forts of New Caledonia. It was a larger party this time; Simpson rode in his own canoe with a bagpiper and nine voyageurs wielding vermilion paddles, and a second canoe carried Chief Trader Archibald McDonald and Dr. Richard Julian Hamlyn, both bound for posts in the Columbia district. The expedition left York Factory to a seven-gun salute at one o'clock on the morning of 12 July and sped across the parkland waterways at between 90 and 100 miles (145 and 161 km) a day. This meant that they would start at two every morning, and the paddlers carried on until eight each evening, with only a brief halt at mid-day; they were also expected to carry exceptionally heavy burdens of 100 pounds (45.4 kg) each at the portages instead of the customary 90 pounds (41 kg).

By 11 September, travelling Mackenzie's old route along the Peace and the Parsnip, they reached Fort McLeod and found John Tod and his men starving because the fishing that summer had been so poor; Tod was "so pale and emaciated" that Simpson had difficulty recognizing him. After this first glimpse of the meagreness of existence in New Caledonia compared with the relative luxury in which men lived in the forts farther south, Simpson and his party set off overland for Fort St. James. Tod had provided horses for Simpson and the other officers, but the expedition moved at the speed of the burdened men travelling on foot, and took five days to cover the 100 miles (161 km) between the forts. Archibald McDonald's often cited description of their arrival at Stuart Lake is worth reproducing once again because it shows the air of pageant Simpson sought to create to impress the Carrier Indians; he had already acquired a name for magical power by contriving to make them believe that the sounds from his musical snuffbox were in fact produced by his dog. On the morning of the day they expected to reach Fort St. James, the men changed into clean blue uniforms.

The day, as yet, being fine, the flag was put up; the piper in full Highland costume; and every arrangement was made to arrive at FORT ST. JAMES in the most imposing manner we could, for the sake of the Indians. Accordingly, when within about a thousand yards of the establishment, descending a gentle hill, a gun was fired, the bugle sounded, and soon after, the piper commenced the celebrated march of the clans—'Si come leun cogadh shea,' (Peace: or War, if you will it otherwise.) The guide, with the British standard, led the band; then the Governor on horseback, supported by Doctor Hamlyn and myself on our chargers, two deep; twenty men, with their burdens, next formed the line; then one loaded horse, and lastly Mr. McGillivray . . . closed the rear.

A "brisk fire of small arms and wall-pieces" saluted them from the fort. They were met by "Mr. Douglas," a young clerk who, as Sir James Douglas, would eventually govern this great domain beyond the Rockies in the name of Queen Victoria.

A few days later, at Fort Alexandria on the Fraser, the party divided. The clerk James Murray Yale took the canoes with fourteen men down the Fraser to its junction with the Thompson, to await the rest of the party, who set off on an eight-day horseback journey to the North Thompson. There Simpson met the assembled Shuswap nation and made presents to their chiefs before he set off, again by canoe, down the Thompson to the rendezvous with Yale. Though he narrowly escaped drowning when his canoe was caught in a whirlpool, Simpson insisted on doing what no man—in history at least—had done before: going through the Fraser Canyon by water.

He survived, and the painters later on would imaginatively represent him sitting imperturbably in his beaver hat among the straining paddlers as the canoe crested the formidable white water, but he did not minimize the perils of the situation:

> (a)ltho we ran all the Rapids in safety, being perfectly light, and having three of the most skilful Bowsmen in the country, whose skill however was of little avail at times, I should consider the passage down, to be certain Death, in nine attempts out of Ten.

Simpson came out alive, indeed, only because he made his journey in the autumn, when the spring freshets had long ended and the waters were at their lowest level. He realized that ideas of a Fraser Valley route for the fur brigades, which he had cherished so long, had little relation to the realities of British Columbian geography.

Eventually, years afterwards, on the eve of the Hudson's Bay Company's removal north of the 49th parallel, a difficult but practical route over the mountains by way of the Coquihalla River to Hope was discovered. It was opened in 1849 and at last, after many years of frustrated exploration on the part of the fur traders, the Fraser took its place among the arteries of commerce.

But when Simpson sailed on down the river and saw the fresh new timbers of Fort Langley, completed in anticipation of the fur brigades during 1827, he must have felt that the impressive new establishment, 136 feet by 100 feet (41.5 by 30.5 m) within its palisades, with two bastions well defended by cannon, was far too elaborate for what it would now become, one of the several new posts marking out HBC territory in British Columbia. A few years before, in 1822, Fort Kilmaurs (better known as Fort Babine) had been opened on Babine Lake, and in 1826 James Douglas had built Fort Connolly high up the map of New Caledonia on Bear Lake north of the 56th parallel. It was meant to establish a territorial claim, for the Anglo-Russian Convention establishing the *lisière* (later called the panhandle of Alaska) had been signed in 1825, and founding Fort Connolly validated a claim to land east of the *lisière*.

Fort Langley now seemed relegated to the same role of a flag-showing establishment. But Chief Trader Archibald McDonald, who came to the fort in the middle of 1828, was soon finding a new use for it, and creating an early white man's industry in British Columbia: the catching and preservation of fish on a commercial scale. He began the salting of salmon, not only for the use of the Hudson's Bay Company post but for export as well, and, though the product did not keep well enough to stand transport around Cape Horn to Europe, it found a ready market in Hawaii, and thus diversified the Company's income as well as helping render the trade itself more self-subsistent.

From Fort Langley, Simpson went by boat to Fort Vancouver, where some of the officers under McLoughlin had been rather rough in their reprisals for Indian attacks, and the prevalent resentment in the Puget Sound area was bad for trade. In addition, there were ominous signs of American infiltration over the Rockies, for when Simpson reached Fort Vancouver, he found among the guests there the noted mountain man Jedediah Smith, who had escaped slaughter when a party of Missouri trappers was massacred by the Umpqua Indians and who had accepted McLoughlin's hospitality. Despite the kindness with which he was treated by McLoughlin and—less willingly—by Simpson, Smith resumed his hostility to the British as soon as he returned to the mountains and became one of the most active promoters of the American penetration into Oregon.

On the other hand McLoughlin had taken very seriously Simpson's concern for the self-sufficiency of the establishments west of the Rockies. The staff of the fort had been reduced to little more than half that of Fort George four years before, yet it was surrounded by fields of already partly harvested wheat and barley, corn and oats, peas and potatoes. More than 150 cattle were grazing in the fields of the Willamette Valley, while a sawmill and a flour mill were already in operation. A pattern of new white men's industries was emerging in the lower Columbia Valley— logging and farming as well as commercial fishing—that would later be replicated in British Columbia when the trade moved northward.

Simpson saw immediately the possibilities beyond the mere supplying of the forts and the fur brigades. Though he could not foresee the great crisis that would overtake the North American fur industry when the Florentine hatters invented the silk topper and the beaver hat went out of fashion in the 1840s, he knew already that his Asian markets for fur had disappeared through his failure to persuade the East India Company to allow the Hudson's Bay Company to trade in Canton. And he therefore began to see the districts beyond the Rockies as ripe for a diversification in trading as well as in production patterns. Sawn timber, as well as salted salmon, would find markets both in Hawaii and in California where settlement was beginning to spread. The Russian forts along the Alaskan *lisière* seemed to offer a market for farm produce.

But for this kind of traffic, as well as for a serious campaign to seize the coastal trade from the interloping Boston Men, an effective network of coastal posts linked by trading ships was needed, and by 1828 it hardly existed.

In that year the Company had no fort on salt water, and only a tiny fleet of ships that were of little use for trading. In 1825, to reconnoitre the situation, the Company's supply ship, the *William and Ann*, had been sent north during the interval between its arrival from England at Fort George in the late spring and the coming of the brigades in the fall with the furs it would take back to England. Captain Hanwell of the *William and Ann* seemed uninterested in trading, and while he was in the Queen Charlottes he kept his ship so far away from the dangerous-looking shores and the equally dangerous-looking inhabitants that he collected no more than four hundred pelts on his whole voyage, though he garnered some useful scraps of information. One was that the Nass River was an excellent place for trading because of the Indian markets already existing there, and another was that Nootka had become almost wholly depleted of fur-bearing animals. A third—perhaps the most important—was that after a long history of attacks on trading craft by resentful or rapacious Indians, modifications of the ships for both trading and defence had taken place, and a mere transport vessel like the *William and Ann* was quite unfitted for the trade.

The same applied to the two small vessels acquired by the department of Columbia in 1827. The small schooner *Cadboro* was no longer than a large Indian war canoe and even lower in the water, so that it was highly vulnerable to boarding. The other boat, the *Vancouver*, had been constructed at Fort Vancouver from local timber by carpenters unused to shipbuilding, and was almost unseaworthy.

Over Simpson's second winter on the Pacific coast, he and McLoughlin worked out a strategy for conquering the coastal trade. They were fighting against foes who had established themselves, despite the resentment their methods had aroused among the Indians, by dealing in liquor and firearms, a traffic the Company's policy rejected. They boldly trespassed in the waters nominally dominated by the Russian American Company as well as on those over which the Hudson's Bay Company claimed rights. They contrived ways of trading into the Asian market and so were able to establish a pattern by which they could obtain high prices in China, enabling them to buy their trade goods advantageously and so undercut the Company. Also, they were evading the Russians, encroaching on the Alaskan panhandle, and feeding the extensive Tlingit middleman trade.

The policies that Simpson and McLoughlin worked out over the winter of 1828–29 gradually opened out in their application over the next decade. Despite initial losses, the Company's traders matched the prices offered by the interlopers, and McLoughlin quickly overcame his scruples when it came to evading the Company's rules against selling alcohol and ammunition.

A series of coastal establishments was built. In 1831 Lieut. Aemilius Simpson of the Royal Navy, who was a kinsman of George Simpson and who later entered the Company's service, founded Fort Simpson at the mouth of the Nass River; three years later it was removed to the Skeena and became present-day Port Simpson. In 1833 Fort McLoughlin was built on Milbanke Sound near Bella Bella, and in the same year, at the southern end of Puget Sound, Fort Nisqually was established, not as a trading post but as a centre for provisioning. Finally, in 1834, Peter Skene

Ogden made his frustrated attempt to establish Fort Taku on the Stikine River.

But the network of forts was of little use without a fleet to support it and compete with the interlopers in trading up the inlets. The turning point here came in 1832, when McLoughlin sent Chief Factor Duncan Finlayson to Hawaii to buy an adequate craft with the proceeds of the salmon and timber trade to the Sandwich Islands. Finlayson achieved a double bargain, not only acquiring the American brig *Llama*, which had been adapted and armed for the coastal trade, but also engaging her captain, a Boston Man named W. H. McNeill, who became a good and resourceful officer of the Company.

But the *Llama* itself was not sufficient to turn the scales against the interlopers. As long ago as 1826 McLoughlin had been advocating the introduction of a steamboat, which would have far more flexibility of movement than the sailing ships. As Simpson would later remark, when he wrote to London asking for such a craft:

> A steam Vessel would afford us incalculable advantages over the Americans, as we could look into every Creek and cove while they were confined to a harbour by head winds and calms, we could ascend every stream of any consequence upon the coast, we could visit our establishments at stated periods, in short a Steam Vessel would, in our opinion, bring the contest to a close very soon, by making us masters of the trade.

In May 1835 the *Beaver*, a sturdy rather than a comely little boat of 109 tons (111 t) and 101 feet (31 m) in length, was launched from a London yard; by August it was fitted out and ready to sail around Cape Horn. It made the voyage by sail, rigged as a brig with its paddles unshipped, and voyaging in the company of the bark *Columbia*, the latest addition to the Company's fleet of large sailing ships, of which there were six by 1836. With some difficulty, the *Beaver* crossed the bar of the Columbia on 19 March 1836 and proceeded to Fort Vancouver, where her paddle wheels were fitted and her boilers and engines connected; they gave her a speed of almost ten knots. Dr. J. S. Helmcken, who sailed in her during her most active days, round about 1850, described her as being "flush fore and aft and schooner rigged."

On 17 July the *Beaver* finally set out on its first cruise, and though it remained in the Company's service for almost forty years, it never again entered the Columbia for fear of the river's bar. The cost of operating the *Beaver* at first appalled McLoughlin and made him doubt the wisdom of his original idea; to provide adequate defence and fuelling, it required a crew of thirty-one, including thirteen woodcutters engaged in chopping the six or seven cords of wood it consumed every day. Not until the late 1840s would a reliable source of coal become available on Vancouver Island.

Yet the *Beaver* quickly proved its value, saving time and magnifying the Company's image. Unlike the sailing vessels, it was not dependent on the winds, and in almost all weathers could make its way up the narrow, tortuous inlets, and never wait becalmed. But its importance as a symbol of the Company's power far outweighed any practical use it may have had, for the Indians, though they were themselves great masters of illusion, regarded it for a long time as the product of a consummate magic in which the white men must have been assisted by powerful spirit forces.

The event that sealed the ascendancy of the HBC over the interlopers was the recognition by the Russian American Company that it had enough common interest with its British counterpart to conclude an agreement. The convention of 1825, by creating the *lisière*, had introduced a source of conflict that, long after the Russians departed, would bedevil British-American relations, since the lower courses of the rivers here were in Russian hands, but the British, who owned the upper courses, had rights of navigation to the sea.

By 1838 an agreement seemed possible, and McLoughlin was called to London for consultation. He left Fort Vancouver in the charge of Chief Trader James Douglas, who from this time onward played a steadily greater role in developments west of the Rockies. Simpson, freshly knighted for supporting the British authorities in the Canadian rebellions of 1837–38, was already in England, and eventually, after talks in St. Petersburg, the HBC's governor-in-chief and Baron Wrangell of the Russian American Company met in Hamburg and worked out an agreement that was highly advantageous to both of them and equally detrimental to the American interlopers. The Russians leased the coastal strip to the Hudson's Bay Company as far north as Mount Fairweather and handed over their own post of Fort Stikine; the agreement did not cover the offshore islands. For its part the Hudson's Bay Company agreed to provision the Russian American Company's posts farther north in Alaska and to ship to them at a fair price from Britain all the trade goods they needed. Russian trade with the Americans came to an end, and after fifty years the Boston Men were finally and quickly frozen out of the coastal trade.

The provisioning clauses of the agreement were to have a profound effect on the Company's Pacific coast operations. Already at Fort Langley, Fort Vancouver and Fort Nisqually, a surplus of food was being grown, though not enough to fulfil the contract with the Russians.

A dilemma appeared at this point, illustrating the rapidly changing character of the economy over which the Hudson's Bay Company presided in western Canada. There was abundant and fertile farming land for the taking, since at this point nobody in the fur trade thought of concluding treaties with the native peoples for the use of their terrain. The difficulty was one that affected the Hudson's Bay Company's right to operate west of the Rockies. Its licence there—and its charter in Rupert's Land—recognized its existence as a fur-trading firm, and the use of its capital on an agricultural enterprise might—its lawyers suggested—render it vulnerable to criticism and lawsuits. What the lawyers did not say, but many of the experienced fur traders recognized, was that when the farmer appears the day of the trader is visibly ending, since the cultivation of the land means the subjection of the wilderness habitat of fur-bearing species.

Stimulated by the possibilities of a virtual monopoly along the whole Pacific coast between California and northern Alaska, the Company went ahead in spite of its officers' misgivings. It established a nominally independent organization, the Puget's Sound Agricultural Company, largely financed by shares bought under pressure by the chief factors and chief traders. The land already being used for pasture and tillage at Fort Nisqually and in the Cowlitz Valley was handed over to the new enterprise. Cattle were brought from California and sheep from England. In a few years, by 1846, the activities of the Puget's Sound Agricultural Company had expanded so far that the 167,000 acres (67 585 ha) of pasturage around Fort Nisqually provided grazing for almost two thousand cattle, almost six thousand sheep and two hundred horses. In the Cowlitz Valley ten thousand bushels of grain were being harvested every year and another fifteen hundred livestock found grazing. In addition nineteen French-Canadian families brought from the Red River were farming land and had established their own village near the Cowlitz farm.

Americans by Sea and Land

Years later, in the 1850s, when George Simpson was almost perjuring himself trying to demonstrate that the prairies were useless for agriculture, he was influenced by recollections of the way in which settlement, largely inspired by the Company's successful farming experiments at Fort Vancouver and Nisqually, brought an unexpectedly rapid end both to British influence and to the Hudson's Bay Company's hegemony south of the 49th parallel.

Simpson made his third and final visit to the department of Columbia in 1841, as part of the round-the-world trip by way of Siberia and Russia which took him well into 1842 and was recorded in the two-volume *Narrative of a Journey Round the World, During the Years 1841 and 1842* (1847), ghostwritten by Adam Thom from Simpson's diaries. Always bold in his travelling, Simpson this time followed an unorthodox route, ascending the Bow River and crossing with an Indian guide the unfamiliar Simpson Pass, which was named after him. He reached the headwaters of the Columbia and then worked his way overland to Fort Colvile, from which he descended the Columbia to Fort Vancouver.

Simpson's thought as he reached the Pacific coast region centred on three main problems: he wanted to find out how the Company's arrangement with the Russians was progressing; he wanted to see how the Puget's Sound Agricultural Company was working out in practice; and he wanted to resolve some of the differences that over the last decade had emerged between him and McLoughlin, a man who in his own territory was liable to be as autocratic as Simpson in the Company's wider domain. In particular they differed about the way to carry on the coastal trade, McLoughlin being in favour of the system of forts he had built up, united by periodic visits of ships like the *Beaver*, and Simpson preferring the idea of a trade carried out entirely by well-protected steamboats, with one or two central depots. To complicate matters, without waiting for Simpson's arrival or approval, McLoughlin had authorized James Douglas to set up a new fort at Taku in Alaska in 1840, and early in 1841 to establish a mercantile depot at Yerba Buena in San Francisco harbour to start up a trade in hides and tallow.

After a mere week at Fort Vancouver, Simpson set off north to inspect the farms on Puget Sound and to meet the Russian representatives in Alaska, looking at the Company's coastal forts on the way. Before he went, he was made rather dramatically aware of an even more ominously looming problem, for he was present at the lavish banquet McLoughlin gave to the officers of the American expedition led by Commodore Charles Wilkes of the USS *Vincennes*. Wilkes had a mandate to explore Puget Sound and also the Columbia River as far as Fort Colvile, though these of course had been thoroughly explored already by Vancouver and the British fur traders. Simpson's suspicion that the expedition had a much more political intent was increased when one of the American officers told him that Wilkes intended "to recommend strongly to his Government to claim the whole of the territory on the shores of the Northern Pacific, from the Mexican northern boundary at Latitude 42° to the Russian southern boundary at Latitude 54°40'." (This, in fact, was what Wilkes did eventually recommend.)

Carrying this further problem on his mind, Simpson set out on his journey. He travelled along the Cowlitz River to Puget Sound, observing as he went the terrible effects of the "intermittent fever" (probably malaria) on the native people since he had last been there in 1828. At Fort Nisqually, McLoughlin was awaiting him but decided not to accompany him on the long trip north on the *Beaver*. James Douglas instead was Simpson's companion, and this was the real beginning of Douglas's climb to power on the Pacific coast.

Steaming out of Puget Sound, they crossed Juan de Fuca Strait to the southeastern corner of Vancouver Island. There, Captain McNeill of the *Beaver* had found in 1837 what he described as "an excellent Harbour and a fine open country along the sea shore, apparently well adapted to both tillage and pasturage." McLoughlin, who was attached to his own creation, Fort Vancouver, was not greatly taken with the site, partly because he had his own reasons for not being as alarmed as his associates about the danger of American penetration into the Columbia Valley. But Simpson was impressed, describing the site as "well adapted for colonization," remarking on its "excellent harbour and abundance of timber." He thought: "It will doubtless become, in time, the most valuable section of the whole coast above California." McLoughlin's inertia had to be brought to an end, and by the summer of 1842 Douglas would be back again selecting a site for a new depot.

They sailed north, putting in at Port McNeill, Fort McLoughlin near Bella Coola, Fort Simpson and Fort Stikine, and finally Fort Durham, the northernmost HBC post, at Taku, opened just a year before. Afterwards they sailed south again to Sitka, where Simpson stayed four days as the guest of the Russian Governor Adolph Etolin, enjoying an interlude of French cooking and flattery as the Russians displayed the St. Petersburg culture they had imported to this far and frosty wilderness. The two fur potentates decided that the Boston Men had been effectively eliminated from the coast, and agreed to cease trading liquor.

Simpson decided that Captain McNeill's way of trading from the ship's deck was more effective and economical than trading from a series of remote posts. Accordingly, he decided to close all the forts north of Juan de Fuca Strait, except for a single depot, Fort Simpson. Taking a trip southward, to California and then across to Honolulu, he also decided to close the post at Yerba Buena, which was being operated inefficiently by McLoughlin's son-in-law. Most important, he decisively turned against Fort Vancouver as the centre of the Company's Pacific coast operations after being held at the bar of the Columbia for three weeks by inclement weather before he could make his southward trip. On mere grounds of commercial efficiency, Fort Vancouver must be replaced by a post with an open harbour, and preferably within territory that was likely to remain British.

All these decisions, reflecting on his own judgment, rankled with the proud McLoughlin, and the difficulties between the two men were aggravated by an incident in the spring of 1842, before Simpson left on his trans-Russian journey. On his way to Sitka, he learnt that John McLoughlin, the chief factor's son, left in charge of Fort Stikine, had been murdered. The men were unanimous in their story that McLoughlin had been violently drunk and that the man who killed him had acted in self-defence. Knowing that young McLoughlin had been something of a scapegrace before entering the Company's service, Simpson concluded their account was correct. The killer was handed over to the Russian authorities, who took no action against him, and Simpson sent McLoughlin a coldly tactless letter that earned him the White-headed Eagle's lasting enmity: "The occurrence having taken place within Russian territories, no legal steps against the parties can be taken by me; but my belief is, that any Tribunal by which the case could be tried, would find a verdict of 'Justifiable homicide.'" The incident aggravated a disagreement that had already gone deep, partly because of differences over how to run the coastal trade and partly because of McLoughlin's equivocal attitude towards the Americans.

Years before Commodore Wilkes arrived with his flotilla in 1841, Americans had begun to appear overland in the district of Columbia. First there were the fur traders and trappers from the Missouri Valley region, against whom the Snake River scorched-earth expeditions were organized. The mountain men retaliated by trying to inflame American opinion against the Hudson's Bay Company. In 1830 Jedediah Smith and his trading partners appealed to the American secretary of war, claiming that the HBC was cleaning "American" territory of fur, and demanding that the Convention of 1818 be abrogated and the Company driven from the Pacific coast.

More serious was the actual arrival of settlers in the early 1830s. The first came almost fortuitously in 1832, when a group of American overland travellers, led by Nathaniel Wyeth of Boston, arrived at Fort Vancouver. They were expecting to meet a supply ship so as to set up a small trade in furs and smoked salmon, but the boat had been lost in the South Pacific and they were stranded. McLoughlin not only fulfilled the normal calls of hospitality, he even assisted two of them to settle in the Willamette Valley, and helped the rest on their way back to the Missouri.

Two years later Wyeth was back again, with a company of prospective settlers, accompanied by the American Methodist missionary Jason Lee. McLoughlin did nothing to discourage them; on the contrary, as Jason Lee noted in his diary:

> Dr. McLoughlin, the governor of the fort, seems pleased that the missions have come to the country and freely offers us any assistance that is in his power to render. It is his decided opinion that we should commence somewhere in this vicinity.

Jason Lee and his settlers remained, and when they needed cattle, McLoughlin put some of his own money into an Oregon Cattle Company to buy livestock in California and drive them to the Willamette Valley. Wandering missionaries arrived and took the good news back with them to the eastern states, and most of the HBC men—including Douglas—suspected Lee and the other clergymen of being political stalking horses. Simpson was certainly well enough aware of the problem, and sent out French-Canadian settlers from the Red River not only to Nisqually but also to the Willamette Valley around Fort Vancouver. In 1842 there were almost a hundred of them, outnumbering the fifty Americans. The situation was reversed when the first overland party of American immigrants came in the fall of 1842, 140 persons under the leadership of Dr. White, who carried a commission—the first sign of overt American political influence—appointing him subagent of Indian affairs. Others followed, and by the spring of 1843 there were three hundred Americans in the Willamette Valley.

McLoughlin disobeyed the Company's orders by letting them have seed and equipment on credit. His consistent help for the American settlers from their first arrival until his departure from the Company in 1846 led to his being portrayed as a kind of villain by Canadian nationalist historians and supporters of the Hudson's Bay Company, and as a kind of hero—"the father of Oregon"—by the Americans. In fact he was a man of radical political opinions that did not accord very well with the loyalties he had assumed in turn to the two great fur companies.

Most of the fur traders were of Loyalist descent, by the 1840s the sons or grandsons of men who had fought on the British side in the American War of Independence. They tended to retain the loyalties of their forebears, and even those who were not Loyalists by descent were so by sentiment, like George Simpson and James Douglas.

McLoughlin was not among them. In 1852, after the whole Oregon boundary question was settled and he was now an American citizen and proprietor of a general store in Oregon City, he made an open statement of his long-held convictions.

> I was born in Canada and reared to manhood in the immediate vicinity of the United States. . . . The sympathies of my heart and the dictates of my understand-

ing, more than thirty years ago, led me to look forward to a day when both my relations to others and the circumstances surrounding me would permit me to live under and enjoy the political blessings of a flag which, wherever it floats, whether over the land or the sea, is honoured for the principles of justice lying at the foundation of the government it represents, and which shields from injury and dishonour all who claim its protection.

We may perhaps find a clue to the origins of McLoughlin's republican attitudes in the fact that he studied medicine in Québec, where he would be followed only a few years later by those medical revolutionaries, the brothers Robert and Wolfred Nelson, who played such an important role in the Lower Canadian uprisings of 1837–38, led by Louis-Joseph Papineau. Certainly in 1837, McLoughlin, unlike Simpson, expressed his sympathy for Papineau, and in 1841, just as the American immigration into Oregon was beginning, he let down his guard sufficiently to remark to one of his fellow traders that "the constitution of Canada . . . is a Despotism in Disguise." Later, in his 1852 statement, he equated "the march of civilization" with "the progress of peopling the American territories," and he remarked that "this could neither be successfully resisted, nor did I see it politic or desirable to attempt it. In this spirit I prepared myself to encourage, hasten and further what I thought would be not only attended by good, but inevitable."

There is no evidence that McLoughlin was suborned by the United States government or that he gained any personal profit as a result of his encouragement of American immigrants. He seems to have been an example of the True Believer, the moral man true to an idealized cause and seeing no difficulties in breaking his word or his faith to serve it. Undoubtedly McLoughlin thought humanity would benefit from his actions, whose results are clear and unequivocal in terms of demographic and political change.

It was in 1843 that politics in a more direct way than the suzerainties rather vaguely wielded by Spanish and British authorities first began to enter the Pacific Northwest in the guise of American democracy. By the beginning of that year there were more than three hundred American settlers in the Willamette Valley, and they considerably outnumbered the French Canadians. In March, sixty-five of the settlers drew up a petition to the United States Senate asking it to annex the territory. In May the American settlers gathered at Champoeg and created a provisional government that adopted the laws of Iowa, supplementing them in a July meeting with a series of land laws that already assumed the land was American territory. What the provisional government lacked in legality it quickly made up for in numbers, for in the fall of 1843 the first of the Great Migrations described by Francis Parkman in *The Oregon Trail* came over the mountains and deposited almost nine hundred new settlers. It was to be exceeded in 1844, when fourteen hundred settlers came; by June of that year the provisional government was talking of raising its own militia.

By now the British government was becoming as concerned as the Hudson's Bay Company over the future of New Caledonia and Columbia. The boundary east of the Continental Divide was already agreed on as the 49th parallel; west of that point the Convention of 1818 still held, but obviously with the increasing American population along the Willamette River, this situation could not be long maintained. The Americans were already preparing for war with Mexico in order to seize territory, and, apart from the visit of Commodore Wilkes, American officers had been examining the passes of the Rockies and a secret agent named William A. Slacum had taken back a report of the Oregon territory. The British in their turn sent a warship, HMS *Modeste*, while two army officers, Lieutenants Vavasour and Warre, went in from Red River. The reports of these agents were not encouraging; it was obvious that the whole area south and east of the Columbia would have to be abandoned to the Americans. North and west of the Columbia, however, there were no Americans; the settlement of the land had been carried out entirely under British auspices, and it was along the line of the river that the Hudson's Bay officials felt a stand should be taken as negotiations between the British and American governments began, with a flotilla of the Royal Navy for the first time assembling near the entrance to Juan de Fuca Strait in case of war.

As Yankee politicians whipped up public feeling with calls for annexation of the whole region between California and Russian Alaska, using the slogan "Fifty-four Forty or Fight," representatives of the British and American governments met to make a final apportionment of territory. Neither side had any desire to fight, the British because the War of 1812 had given a lesson in the difficulty of fighting long wars far away, and the Americans because they were about to take on Mexico. But the Americans had just enough extra gall to insist on gaining both banks of the Columbia, so that the boundary agreed on 15 June 1846 was the 49th parallel from the Rockies to the coast, with Britain retaining the whole of Vancouver Island, though its lower end dropped below the line. Thus, the future political boundaries of British Columbia were defined in a treaty that ignored the native peoples, still the most numerous population in the region.

The Company Moves North

Once Columbia ceased to be an Anglo-American no man's land, and British and American interests were marked off by the fragile line of the 49th parallel, the Hudson's Bay Company had to adjust itself quickly to the new situation. As a British company under an imperial charter, it was resented by the American immigrants, and both Governor Simpson and the London Committee were fully aware of the kind of harassment that might be practised, through customs regulations and disputes over land titles, by a hostile administration.

It was during this period of major adjustment that John McLoughlin fell from grace and power. After the reports of Lieutenants Warre and Vavasour, which stressed how much the influx of American settlers had been due to his mistaken policies, he was increasingly blamed for the Company's troubles. The Committee of the Northern Department, the body of high officials that with Simpson controlled the Company's affairs in Canada, clearly linked his errors in this respect to what Simpson had perceived as a failing capacity to handle the increasingly complex activities on the Pacific coast. They decided in 1845 to replace the office of superintendent of the Columbia department by a board of management, of which McLoughlin would serve as a member, but only for a year. In the spring of 1846 he was instructed to hand over the conduct of affairs to a triumvirate consisting of James Douglas, John Work and Peter Skene Ogden. He chose the occasion as a reason to resign three months before the land south of the 49th parallel became the Oregon Territory of the United States. He remained, and died an American citizen in 1857, harried to the end by the very people he had helped, who attempted to dispossess him of his lands and otherwise treated him as if he were still a representative of the hated British company. Only posthumously would the Americans recognize his service to them.

Douglas and McLoughlin were like men on a swing; as one fell the other rose, for the real beginning of Douglas's career can be traced to the period of 1841–42 during which McLoughlin's star was in decline. Douglas had been appointed a chief factor in 1839, and on him fell the responsibility for adjusting the Company to its new circumstances and its restricted area of operation. He returned in 1842 to the area on the southern end of Vancouver Island which Captain McNeill had shown him and Simpson in 1841. Though his stubbornness and rectitude earned Douglas the nickname of "Old Squaretoes," he was at times inclined to lyrical outbursts in the manner of the new reign of Victoria. After walking over the oak-studded parkland of southern Vancouver Island, with its meadows blue with flowering camas, he wrote that:

> The place itself appears a perfect 'Eden' in the midst of the dreary wilderness of the Northwest Coast, and so different is its general aspect, from the wooded, rugged regions around, that one might be dropped from the clouds into its present position.

He chose a place he called Clover Point, and in March returned on board the *Beaver*, arriving on the thirteenth and picking a spot which, as he noted, "will allow of vessels lying with their sides grazing the rocks, which form a natural wharf, whereof cargo can be conveniently landed from the ship's yard." Provisionally he called the post he was about to build Fort Camosun, from his own understanding of a local Indian name. Later it was proposed to call it Fort Albert after the prince consort, but eventually it was named Fort Victoria after the young queen.

Douglas immediately set twelve of the men who had accompanied him to work, digging a well and preparing squared timbers for the buildings; he also drove a sharp bargain with the Indians of the Songhees band. He supplied them with good axes and agreed to pay one 2½ point Hudson's Bay blanket for each batch of forty cedar pickets 22 feet (6.7 m) long and a yard (91 cm) in circumference. Ignoring a cautious order from McLoughlin that the area of the fort should be 210 feet square (64 m^2) , he laid out a rectangle within the palisades 330 feet by 300 feet (100.5 by 91.4 m) and made provision therein for six buildings each 60 feet (18.3 m) long.

Then he set off north in the *Beaver*, with the *Cadboro* accompanying, to close Fort Durham in Alaska and Fort McLoughlin at Bella Bella. At the beginning of June he was back with fifty men and three officers from the abandoned forts, and the construction work at Fort Victoria went ahead under the clear skies of a rainless summer. Three hundred Songhees Indians provided the unskilled labour, and by the end of September the palisades were up, dominated by an octagonal bastion three storeys high, armed with swivel guns and blunderbusses, and three of the buildings—a large storehouse and two dwellings—were complete. Douglas returned to Fort Vancouver, leaving Chief Trader Charles Ross in command; Ross died early in 1844 and his place was taken by Roderick Finlayson.

Perhaps the most striking feature of Fort Victoria from the beginning was the extent to which its functions diverged from those of the ordinary trading fort. Southern Vancouver Island was poor in fur resources, and in the first year the fort bought only four hundred pelts. But other aspects of the Company's rapidly diversifying activities were admirably served by the new establishment and the fine open lands in its vicinity. During the first summer, horses and cattle were brought up from Fort Nisqually, and late in the year 5 acres (2 ha) were sown with winter wheat. It was in the minds of Simpson and Douglas that not only the trading operations of Fort Vancouver but also the farming operations of the Puget's Sound Agricultural Company would sooner rather than later have to be transferred northward, and season after season the land under tillage at Fort Victoria and the livestock there were both increased, while Indians were trained as farm workers to supplement the labour force. A similar expansion was going on at Fort Langley up the Fraser Valley, where 240 acres (97 ha) were now under cultivation. There was a ready market for surplus grain and meat, not only with the Russians and among the Boston whaling ships that had replaced Boston trading ships on the coast but also with the ships of the Royal Navy that, from the time of the Oregon boundary crises, made regular visits to the Pacific coast.

Very quickly the remaining basic industries of white men in British Columbia began to appear as part of the new HBC pattern. The salmon fishery at Fort Langley continued to flourish under the enterprising James Murray Yale, while in 1848 the first sawmill in British Columbia was opened near Fort Victoria and was soon exporting sawn timber to San Francisco, now an American city and in a spurt of growth that would reach boom proportions with the California gold rush of 1849, which also increased the demand for the agricultural products of Fort Victoria, Fort Langley and Puget Sound. Another industry linked to building would be started shortly afterwards when in 1851 the Hudson's Bay Company imported the brickmaker George Mason.

Finally, mining began in British Columbia under HBC auspices with the discovery of coal, first at Beaver Harbour and then at Fort Rupert, both on the east coast of Vancouver Island. A potential demand already existed, to replace wood fuel on the *Beaver* and to supply the Company's smiths, and also to coal the naval ships that were increasingly in evidence on northern Pacific waters. In 1849 the Com-

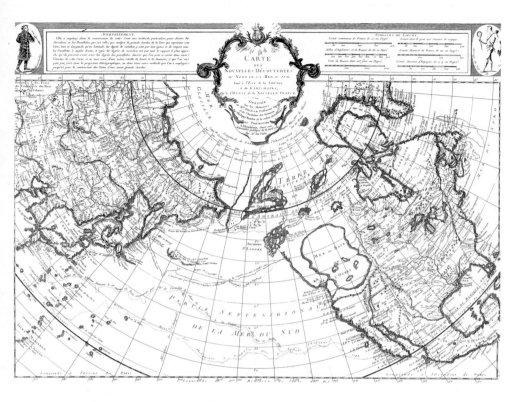

Top:

An early chart of the Pacific Northwest, titled "New Discoveries North of the Southern Sea, East of Siberia and Kamchatka, and West of New France," compiled in 1750 by Philippe Buache and Joseph-Nicolas Delisle. The chart shows the great inland Mer de l'Ouest (covering what is the interior of British Columbia), which is connected to the Mer du Sud (the Pacific Ocean) by the mythical Strait of Anian.

NATIONAL ARCHIVES OF CANADA, CARTOGRAPHIC AND ARCHITECTURAL ARCHIVES DIVISION/NMC 21056

Bottom:

Capt. James Cook. NATIONAL ARCHIVES OF CANADA/C 17726

Top:
Maquinna's potlatch, c. 1789, to celebrate his daughter's puberty. B.C. ARCHIVES AND RECORDS SERVICE/PDP229

Bottom:
Capt. George Vancouver. B.C. ARCHIVES AND RECORDS SERVICE/PDP2252

This early photograph of Hell's Gate in the Fraser Canyon, with the Indian drying racks for salmon on the rocks, shows the fearsome terrain through which Simon Fraser descended to the sea.

Simon Fraser. B.C. ARCHIVES AND RECORDS SERVICE/PDP2258

Governor James Douglas. B.C. ARCHIVES AND RECORDS SERVICE/HP2656

Top:
The *Beaver,* which arrived in 1835 and revolutionized coastal trade. B.C. ARCHIVES AND RECORDS SERVICE/HP127

Bottom:
Matthew Baillie Begbie. B.C. ARCHIVES AND RECORDS SERVICE/HP24288

Amor De Cosmos. B.C. ARCHIVES AND RECORDS SERVICE/HP2624

Dean Cridge of Christ Church Cathedral, Victoria, led a schism in the Anglican Church and became Bishop Cridge of the Reformed Episcopal Church. B.C. ARCHIVES AND RECORDS SERVICE/ HP43512

Salish grave monuments beside the Fraser River. B.C. ARCHIVES AND RECORDS SERVICE/HP83245.

Nanaimo in 1859, showing the fort and coaling installations. NATIONAL ARCHIVES OF CANADA/
C 9561

Boats of the *Devastation* and *Sutil* bombard the Indian villages of Clayoquot Sound with rockets, 1864. B.C. ARCHIVES AND RECORDS SERVICE/PDP84

Great Bluff on the Cariboo Road north of Yale, where the Royal Engineers had to blast a way through the rock walls. B.C. ARCHIVES AND RECORDS SERVICE/HP763

The Overlander Catherine Schubert gave birth on 14 October 1862, at Fort Kamloops, to Rose, the first white child born in the interior of British Columbia. B.C. ARCHIVES AND RECORDS SERVICE/HP7106

The pattern of flumes at Camerontown, c. 1865. B.C. ARCHIVES AND RECORDS SERVICE/HP10501.

Surveyors of the 1870s, portaging a dugout canoe between waterways. NATIONAL ARCHIVES OF CANADA/PA 22618

Having their own lavish regalia, Coast Indians like these Haida chiefs took happily to European official and formal garb. B.C. ARCHIVES AND RECORDS SERVICE/HP66699

The Haida village at Skidegate in 1887. B.C. ARCHIVES AND RECORDS SERVICE/HP33784

Francis Rattenbury's parliament buildings, just completed, proclaim British Columbia's late nineteenth-century ambitions, particularly in this unique photograph where the old Birdcages are still standing in the foreground. B.C. ARCHIVES AND RECORDS SERVICE/HP8090

The Chinese were eager to show loyalty in the hope of diverting prejudice and built welcoming arches, like this one in Nanaimo, to honour visiting dignitaries. B.C. ARCHIVES AND RECORDS SERVICE/HP11323

Stanley Park was founded in 1888, and the Hollow Tree immediately became a place of rendez-vous. VANCOUVER PUBLIC LIBRARY/13253

Vancouver, four weeks after the great fire of June 1886. The line of forest is at Burrard Street. The smoke is from land-clearing fires on the site of the present-day Richards, Granville and Hornby streets in the heart of the city. VANCOUVER CITY ARCHIVES/WAT.P.3.N.10

pany imported John Muir and a number of other miners from Scotland to work the Fort Rupert seams. Fort Rupert was built largely to protect the mine and its workers.

Like the other infant industries of British Columbia, mining was stimulated by the California gold rush, for the HBC gained a contract to supply coal to the newly founded Pacific Mail Steamship Company, which was carrying mail and miners from Panama to California and the Oregon coast. But the Fort Rupert mines were never very productive, and the HBC soon had its eye on other prospects. Sometime in 1849 a Salish chief named Che-wich-i-kan arrived at Fort Victoria, and saw coal burning in the smithy. He remarked that he knew where plenty of black rocks like that were to be found. The blacksmith did not take him very seriously but suggested he might bring a few of the rocks next time to came to Victoria. In a few months Che-wich-i-kan arrived with a canoe load of coal, for which he gratefully accepted a bottle of rum and repairs to his musket. Shortly afterwards the Hudson's Bay Company laid claim to the shore at Nanaimo where Che-wich-i-kan (known afterwards as "the Coal Tyee") had loaded his canoe, and sent another Scottish miner, Robert Dunsmuir, to supervise its operation.

The year 1849 was in many ways a crucial date in the transformation of the Company's role on the Pacific coast and the development of the still unnamed and politically still unformed British Columbia. It was in this year that a brigade route from Fort Kamloops north of the 49th parallel was first used. It ran up the Similkameen River, across Hope Pass and down Peers Creek and the Coquihalla River to the Fraser. At the point where it reached the Fraser, Fort Hope was built, and in 1849 the first brigades made their way over this all-British trail. Fort Langley at last began to fulfil the role for which it had been planned, that of a major focal point in the trade network linking the interior and the coast, since here boats could be loaded to transport goods to and from Victoria.

The establishment of a satisfactory route from New Caledonia was the development for which both Simpson and the London Committee had been waiting before transferring the Company's headquarters on the Pacific coast. The Oregon Boundary Treaty had robbed them of the Columbia Valley, but Fort Victoria was assured by the same treaty. The Company's assets in American territory, it was decided, would be sold, and compensation sought for the common law rights it might have acquired over lands in the Oregon Territory.

The Company's most urgent task now was to establish a new centre and direct from there what salvage operations it could; early in 1849 Douglas received orders to vacate Fort Vancouver and take charge of the Company's affairs on the Pacific coast from Fort Victoria. By the autumn he had evacuated all his men and all the Company's movable possessions from Fort Vancouver, together with what he described as "the richest freight that ever left these shores"—round about 100,000 pounds sterling in gold, bills and furs, which he took over the portage to Fort Nisqually and shipped thence to Victoria.

When he got there, he found that Roderick Finlayson had completed the buildings, erecting a second bastion and equipping both the wooden towers with nine-pounder guns. Already the fort was beginning to take on the look of a village as well as a trading establishment, for some of the Company's officers, active and retired, were building themselves log cottages. In other ways, the nature of the establishment began to change, particularly as naval vessels patrolled increasingly in these waters; when they anchored off Victoria or in Esquimalt harbour, they added a social dimension to the fort's quiet life. Yet for almost a decade after the transformation of Fort Victoria into the headquarters as well as the provisioning and shipping centre for the coast, the old ceremonials of the fur trade were continued with solemnity and strict protocol. The officers dined in their mess hall with Douglas at the head of the table (his wife Amelia dined separately with their children), and the senior officers chatted and smoked the evening away after the toast to the queen had been the juniors' signal to depart.

In 1859 young Dr. John Sebastian Helmcken arrived to act as the Company's surgeon at Fort Victoria, and many years later he wrote a recollection of his first evening there which stands as a monument to the already obsolescent dignities treasured by the Company that had been chartered by King Charles II and whose royal first governor had been Prince Rupert of the Rhine. In a remote outpost its traditions were drawing to an end.

> After making ourselves decent, for I was told that Mr. Douglas was rather particular about this, the "bell and the gongs" told us it was time for dinner, and to it nothing loath we went. The mess room was more than thirty feet long, by say twenty feet wide, a large open fire place at one end and large pieces of cordwood burning therein. A clock on the wall, a long table in the middle, covered with spotless linen, the knives and forks clean, decanters bright, containing wine and so forth. The chairs of wood (Windsor) but everything European. There must have been twenty people in the room, when Mr. Douglas made his appearance—a handsome specimen of nature's noblemen, with a grave bronzed face, but kindly withal. After the usual greetings, he took the head of the table, Mr. Finlayson the foot. . . . Grace having been said by Mr. Douglas (the chaplain did not dine in the mess, but all the other married officers did) on comes the soup, then the salmon, then the meats—venison on this occasion and ducks—then the pies and so forth, and down they go into their proper receptacle, each one ready and willing to receive them. Having done justice to the dinner and taken a glass "to the Queen", many of the junior officers left, either to work or to smoke their pipes in their own quarters. We remained; the steward, a Kanaka (the cook was also a Kanaka) brought in tobacco and long clay pipes of the type called "alderman." Mr. Douglas took *his* pipe, which I noticed was beautifully coloured, showing slow and careful smoking, (the clerks used to like to get hold of his coloured pipes) and others took pipes either from the heap or from their pockets. Everybody seemed to smoke calmly and deliberately.

VIII

The Colonial Era

The Seven Shillings a Year Colony

By the time James Douglas established the Hudson's Bay Company's western administration at Fort Victoria, the little commercial centre had also become a miniature capital. Following on the Oregon Boundary Treaty, the British government found itself in a political dilemma. In the 1840s, before the great flowering of imperial feeling that followed the Indian Mutiny in the following decade, Britons in general tended to look on their empire with impatience as a burdensome cluster of possessions that needed constant and expensive defence. On the other hand Earl Grey, the incumbent colonial secretary, realized that any further retreat before American manifest destiny was politically impossible. Vancouver Island had to be anchored into the empire as it had never been in a formal way before, and this must be done in a manner that protected the Company's interests without making unconditional concessions to the HBC, which, like its fellow the East India Company, was becoming increasingly unpopular in an age of economic liberalism when companies chartered by the whims of kings seemed obsolete.

Accordingly, Vancouver Island, but not the mainland where the Company still operated under its trading licence, was created a crown colony, the first part of British North America west of Upper Canada to become formally a part of the empire. At the same time, on 13 January 1849, it was granted to the Hudson's Bay Company for a rent of seven shillings on condition that the Company establish "a settlement or settlements of resident colonists, emigrants from our United Kingdom of Great Britain and Ireland, or from other our Dominions."

Sceptical observers concluded that, in accordance with the fur trader's traditional dislike for the settler, the Company would carry on no more colonization than was needed to maintain its rights on the island and increase its profits, and by and large this happened.

But first there were certain formal requirements to be met for Vancouver Island to become a crown colony in fact as well as in name; a governor must be appointed who must in turn appoint his council. The original plan had been to appoint James Douglas, the most important authority figure in the region. However, both the HBC committee and the Colonial Office had second thoughts; as the Company's chief factor and agent of the Puget's Sound Agricultural Company, Douglas already engrossed all the economic power on the island, and to add political authority would allow the Company's critics to declare the arrangement a sham that protected HBC interests. Accordingly, it was decided to appoint a governor who had no links with the Company whatsoever.

What other qualifications the appointee Richard Blanshard had to offer as a colonial governor it is hard to imagine. He was a barrister in his early thirties, who doubtless had political pull, but certainly no previous experience of colonial administration. He was so eager to get a foothold in the service that he expressed his willingness to accept the office with no initial salary, expecting to be paid later from the colonial revenue. Nor could he rely on any of the infrastructure of a colonial administration being in place by the time he arrived. As Margaret Ormsby aptly remarked, "without salary, without headquarters, without law officers, without an army, without police, Queen Victoria's representative was expected to introduce the pattern of government existing in all British colonies."

Blanshard arrived on 9 March 1850 to find that there was as yet only a single independent settler on the island, the flighty half-pay officer of the Scots Greys, Capt. Walter Colquhoun Grant, who had taken land at Sooke, 30 miles (48 km) west of Fort Victoria, with a team of eight farmhands. Otherwise, Blanshard had no company but the tightly knit group of Hudson's Bay officials, conscious that their interests and his authority were inevitably at odds.

A more cynical man might have traded concessions and adapted himself to the situation, and a tougher man might have forced Douglas into compromises, but photographs of Blanshard portray him as a sensitive, weak, well bred and probably well intentioned young man with the look of never being far from tears. He seems as ignorable as he seems estimable, and it was precisely in this way that he was seen and treated by tough immovable James Douglas, who made sure that Blanshard knew from the beginning that the chief factor had all the authority. The house the Company had promised Blanshard was not even complete when he arrived, and at first he had to live like a clerk in a room in the fort, charged at the highest rate (cost plus 300 per cent) for anything he bought in the HBC store.

Hemmed by both the Company and the Colonial Office into his figurehead role, he took an initiative as governor on one occasion, when there was complex trouble up the island at Fort Rupert. The miners there had downed tools—the first strike in British Columbia's turbulent labour history—and the clerk temporarily in charge had imprisoned two of them. There had also been desertions from the Company's supply ship *Norman Morison*—sailors intending to head for California—and three of them had been murdered by local Kwakiutl Indians. Blanshard sent Dr. Helmcken to Fort Rupert with a temporary magistrate's commission, and followed him in HMS *Daedalus*, which happened to be in local waters. The strike had ended and the imprisoned miners had been set free, but the murderers of the three sailors had not been caught, and Blanshard's little expedition departed after the *Daedalus* had shelled a village where they were thought to be hiding.

By November 1850 Blanshard wrote to offer his resignation, pleading that his health was destroyed and he could not sustain himself on his private means. Blanshard received scant gratitude from the Colonial Office, which insisted that he pay his own passage back to England and declined to offer the further colonial appointment he had been expecting. Before his departure, he performed his one constitutional task of any significance by giving the colony the beginnings of a political structure. A tiny group of settlers had petitioned him to appoint a legislative council, and he did so on 27 August.

Douglas himself was the senior member, and the others were Chief Trader John Tod, who had formerly run Fort Kamloops and had now retired to farm near Victoria, and Capt. James Cooper, who had entered the Company's service as a ship's master in 1844 and now had resigned to run his own farm, which he operated with an English bailiff and Kanaka labourers, and to operate a small iron schooner, which he had brought over in sections and assembled at Fort Victoria to trade to San Francisco and Hawaii. Tod remained a loyal Company man to the end, but Cooper was alienated because the Company squeezed him out of his coastal trading business, and eventually, when the population became large enough for a genuine opposition to the Company and to Douglas personally to emerge, he would be one of the leaders among the malcontents.

Old Squaretoes' Realm

When Blanshard resigned, nobody could be found quickly to take on the thankless figurehead task he had abandoned, and in October, Douglas received his commission as governor of the colony. Since he was already chief factor, agent for the Puget's Sound Agricultural Company and the Company's agent in land sales, this meant that he was the unchallenged controller of political and commercial affairs in the colony. But the power he wielded was slighter than his titles might indicate or than most historians have suggested, since his direct authority was secure only in Fort Victoria and even there apprehension was created by the unpredictability of the local Songhees Indians and by the fact that bellicose northern Indians, particularly the Haida and the Kwakiutl, were gathering in increasing numbers (eventually reaching thousands) on the beaches outside the fort.

Elsewhere on the island, the Indians continued to live according to their own customary patterns, carrying on their internecine wars and vendettas without interference as long as white men were not harmed. British power was represented only by the armed vessels of the Royal Navy and the Company which sailed along the coasts and occasionally put into an inlet, the *Beaver* being supplemented by the screw steamer *Otter*, which arrived in 1853. There was no police; punitive parties of bluejackets and armed servants of the Company acted, usually with little investigation, in their place. There was not even a judge until 1853, and then he was a man with only negative qualifications. David Cameron, an unsuccessful businessman in Scotland and plantation manager in Demerara, who happened to be Douglas's brother-in-law and had been brought in to work as a clerk in the coalfield at Nanaimo, was appointed judge of the supreme court, though he had no previous experience either as a lawyer or as a magistrate.

It was a society in modest transition over which Douglas ruled. Victoria was now almost entirely devoted to functions ancillary to the fur trade. The actual trade flourished up the coast and in New Caledonia, and both Fort Victoria and Fort Langley had become transshipment ports rather than gathering posts. The fertile land began to draw in immigrants, and in the beginning this happened more through the Company's own effort by way of the Puget's Sound Agricultural Company than through independent settlers. The Agricultural Company was organized to make it an instrument of colonization as well as a provisioning agency. It established four farms, at Viewfield, Constant Cove, Craigflower and Colwood, all in the Victoria parkland, and on each of them placed well constructed barns and farmhouses. The handsome Craigflower house, built in 1853, still survives beside the road westward out of Victoria, and gives a fair idea of the high style in which the "gentlemen bailiffs" who ran the farms actually lived. Chosen, it would appear, for their social connections more than for their experience in farming, the bailiffs were paid small salaries and a share of the profits of their farms. The labourers brought out to work on the farms were paid £17 a year plus their keep and were promised 20 acres (8 ha) of free land after five years of service.

The great mistake the Company made was to give the bailiffs not only free houses but also free food. Some of them chose the opportunity to act like modern executives with access to lavish expense accounts. The most extreme case was that of Capt. Edward Edwards Langford, late of the 73rd Regiment, who arrived in May 1851 with his wife and five sprightly and personable daughters to take over the operations of Colwood Farm; they were the first actual English family to emigrate to Vancouver Island. Langford's principal fault was not a neglect of his duties as bailiff, for Colwood Farm was relatively productive in his time; it was, rather, the conspicuous manifestation of his gentlemanliness. During his incumbency, he turned Colwood Farm into the virtual social centre of the colony, with his handsome daughters attracting the naval officers from any vessel that might be moored in the vicinity as well as the young sparks of the fur trade. There were dinners and socials, picnics and riding parties, over the Victoria parkland, and all were charged against the Puget's Sound Agricultural Company as part of Langford's food allowance. During 1853—as the Committee in London noted with anger—he had spent on such matters eight times his actual salary; included in his account were such items as 1,606 pounds (728.5 kg) of sugar, 257 pounds (116.5 kg) of tea, 70 gallons (318 L) of liquor and wines. He was reprimanded, and somewhat mended his ways, but the reproaches rankled, and very soon he would join the growing opposition to the Company's rule.

In addition to the land it appropriated for the Puget's Sound Agricultural Company, the HBC was selling plots to prospective settlers, but in a way that discouraged any large-scale immigration of the poor. Both Earl Grey and the London representatives of the Company were much taken with the colonialist theories of Edward Gibbon Wakefield, by which land would be sold to relatively prosperous settlers who would guarantee to bring a minimum number of landworkers with them. This, it was thought, would recreate in the colonies an English-style rural society of squires, yeoman farmers and labourers living in harmony away from the corrupting cities. The idea was already being tried out in New Zealand. In the version worked out for Vancouver Island, the price of land was set at £1 an acre, which it was felt—rightly as it turned out—would keep out the kind of Americans who had settled in Oregon. Twenty acres (8 ha) was the minimum area that could be purchased, and every new landowner was expected to bring out five single men or three married couples for each 100 acres (40.5 ha) he might purchase. This, the London Committee believed, would introduce "a just proportion of labour and capital," and also prevent "the ingress of squatters, paupers and land speculators."

Though this policy led to no mass immigration, it meant that a steady trickle of newcomers arrived at Fort Victoria on the Company's vessel, the *Norman Morison*, and on other ships that put into the harbour. By January 1853 the *Norman Morison* had made three voyages carrying immigrants—80 of them in March 1850, 35 in October 1851, and roughly 80 in January 1853. Captain Grant's 8 men were among the 18 new arrivals on the *Harpooner* in the summer of 1849, and two years later, in May 1851, the *Tory* brought 140. In other words, within four years of the foundation of the crown colony, about 350 people were added to the original 50 men and officers of the Company who had inhabited the fort since 1843 and the small additional group who had been brought from Fort Vancouver in 1849. If one takes into account the drift to the California goldfields over this period, the total non-Indian population of Vancouver Island was not much more than 400, mostly from England and Scotland, though a few Kanakas from Hawaii were employed on farms and at the fort. There were outlying pockets of population around the coal mines at Fort Rupert and later Nanaimo, and also at Sooke, where in 1853 the miner John Muir took over the sawmill Captain Grant had started and began to exploit the forests of western Vancouver Island.

Slowly the colony on the island was beginning to diversify. Apart from the individual farms, a few private enterprises began to emerge—though the Company still clung to its trading monopoly. As well as the sawmill at Sooke, there was another privately owned mill at Victoria, in which James Douglas himself had shares. However, the people of the island still bought most of their goods at the HBC store and paid its high prices.

Yet it was obvious that such a situation could not go on indefinitely. A change was already taking place in the look of the place. In 1851 Joseph Despard Pemberton arrived as the Company's surveyor for its land sales, and in 1852 he started to lay out a townsite on the area outside the fort. Little white log cottages began to appear outside the palisades (including one—which still stands—built by Dr. J. S. Helmcken, who in 1852 married Douglas's daughter Cecilia), and some of the outlying farmhouses could be seen from the bastions. With its increasingly busy harbour, it began to take on the look of an early Victorian small English town set down on an unusually exotic coast.

Gradually the characteristic institutions of Victorian England established themselves, particularly the church and the school. Established religion appeared with the Reverend Mr. Staines, who carried on his services in the fort, but there was no actual Anglican church until Christ Church opened in 1856, with the incumbent chaplain Edward Cridge becoming its vicar and afterwards, when it reached cathedral status, its dean. In this area, the Roman Catholics were ahead of all the Protestant sects, for one of their priests, Father Jean Baptiste Bolduc, had accompanied Douglas to the site of Fort Victoria in 1843 and had started missionary work among the Songhees Indians. On the mainland, Fathers François Blanchet and Modeste Demers had begun their missions in New Caledonia as early as 1838. Demers, a talented linguist, established a formidable conversion record, so that when the Catholics decided to establish a diocese on the Pacific coast, he was consecrated first Bishop of Victoria in St. Christopher's at Esquimalt, which had been established in the same year.

Education was carried on roughly rather than readily during the early days of Fort Victoria. The fur traders had set no greater store on education than on conversion, both of which seemed likely to change native societies in unpredictable ways and interfere with the traditional relationship between trader and trapper. But the creation by the fur traders themselves of a progeny not entirely Indian necessitated some kind of educational facility, a need that would grow when, as in the 1850s at Fort Victoria, British wives would arrive and bring or produce British offspring. Not only must the children of the Company's officers and of the gentlemen farmers and bailiffs be provided for, but also the families of the workers of many kinds which the colony now employed. The Reverend Mr. Staines and his shrewish, snobbish wife Emma Frances ran a school in one of the buildings of the fort at which some of the students were boarders, children of upcountry fur traders, who long remembered its spartan disciplines. Douglas quickly became conscious of the need for elementary schooling, and in 1852 he was able to import teachers and set up a day school for boys in Victoria. In the following year he put up another school on Craigflower, whose modestly classical clapboard building still stands beside the Gorge outside Victoria. At the same time, Captain Langford's sister started at Colwood Farm an Academy for Young Ladies brought daily from Victoria to learn the social graces. Even the Victorian concern for popular culture swept lightly over this distant outpost. Amateur plays were staged in the mess hall of the fort as the number of young people in the community grew, and in 1854 the settlers at Craigflower organized a "scientific" institute on the lines of the mechanics' institutes in England.

Sailors on Sea and Land

At this transition period between Fort Victoria and the city of Victoria (which would be formally incorporated in 1862), the little community no longer enjoyed the self-contained isolation characteristic of traditional fur-trading posts. Links with the American territories to the south continued, though they were less with the Oregon and newly created Washington territories than with California, whose entrepreneurs sought supplies on Vancouver Island for the gold-mining camps. The Company still traded to Hawaii, and the Polynesians from those islands played a notable minor role in early British Columbia history. They served the Company and later on were among the early gold miners; several Kanaka Creeks and Kanaka Bars were named after them.

But the most constant link with the outside world was that provided by the ships of the Royal Navy, which after the foundation of Fort Victoria were to be found increasingly in the waters off Vancouver Island. The concentration of naval attention that had begun in 1844 when the sloop HMS *Modeste* sailed up the Columbia to Fort Vancouver to show the flag as the Oregon boundary dispute was moving towards its climax. It was joined off the coast by other ships like the *Cormorant*, the *Fisgard* and the *Pandora*, which maintained vigilance against American intrusions and continued Vancouver's work of surveying the coastline. The men-of-war made use of Esquimalt harbour, which the *Fisgard* and the *Pandora* surveyed in 1847, and the interest of the Admiralty was increased by the discovery, at this period when the navy was rapidly changing from sail to steam, of ample coal deposits at Nanaimo in the early 1850s. The first step towards making a permanent establishment came during the Crimean War. An unwritten armistice had been reached between the Hudson's Bay Company and the Russian American Company that ruled out hostilities in the Pacific Northwest, but the Admiralty felt the need for some kind of establishment to service its ships patrolling the Pacific.

In 1855 the first naval buildings were erected at Esquimalt to serve as a hospital. Land was reserved for a naval depot in 1859, and in 1860 the Fisgard Lighthouse was erected at the entrance to Esquimalt harbour. In 1862 the decision was made, in view of the advantages of having an establishment on British soil, to transfer the Royal Navy's Pacific station from Valparaiso in Chile to Esquimalt; a fully functioning naval yard was opened by 1864, and afterwards for many years Vancouver Island was anchored to Britain by considerations of imperial defence as well as by sentiment.

Some of the ships had stayed for long periods in Vancouver Island waters even before the Pacific command moved to Esquimalt; the *Plumper*, for example, carried on its survey work up and down the coast from 1857 to 1861, and its commander, Lieut. Charles Mayne, became so familiar with the affairs of the region at the dramatic point of the early gold rushes that he wrote an excellent book about it, *Four Years in British Columbia and Vancouver Island*.

Other vessels remained for shorter periods, but their officers gave a great stimulus to the social life of the tiny capital, attending the balls and parties to which people found their way through often muddy streets, joining in picnics, and taking part in the annual horse races over the camas-blue grassland of Beacon Hill, named after the beacon the Hudson's Bay Company had erected there to warn incoming craft of a dangerous rock.

Sometimes the naval vessels would organize parties or dances on their own decks, and Victoria society would drive or ride out to the small boats awaiting them on the shore at Esquimalt and return long after midnight. Occasionally the officers would organize a ball on land, and in 1859, after the population had been somewhat increased by the merchants arriving in the trail of the gold rush, two ships combined to put on such an occasion, which Lieut. Charles Wilson described in what amounts to an ironic comment on the social pretensions of the island.

> Every body was quite delighted & it goes by the name of 'the Party par excellence'; nobody says ball in this part of the world, it is always party. The ladies were very nicely dressed, & some of them danced very well, though they would look much better if they would only learn to wear their crinolines properly. It is most lamentable to see the objects they made of themselves, some of the hoops being quite oval, while others had only one hoop rather high up, the remainder of the dress hanging down perpendicularly.

No Taxation without Representation

From 1853 to 1858, the comfortably autocratic rule of Vancouver Island by Governor Douglas and his appointed council came under attack. Unrest began to appear despite all efforts to ensure that its inhabitants were of the right class and character. Douglas was to find that the discipline and the grimly exacted loyalties of the fur-trading era were unattainable in a colonial setting; he did so immediately he tried to raise money by taxation, imposing licensing on the saloons that were beginning to appear and levying a duty on timber. The tavern-keepers—and the drinkers, who were many—resented the first, and their case was argued with vehemence by James Yates, a former employee of the Company who himself operated a saloon. Landowners like the Reverend Mr. Staines—and Captain Cooper, who already resented Douglas's interference with his own private trading—objected to the duty on lumber and went about uttering the old colonial complaints about "taxation without representation." Captain Langford, who had his own grievances against Douglas in the latter's role of agent for the Puget's Sound Agricultural Company, joined in their agitation.

Douglas saw no reason to change his ways; he described Staines in his reports to the London Committee as a "preacher of sedition," and secured the termination of his contract as schoolteacher. Staines decided to return to England and lay before the colonial secretary a protest on behalf of the settlers. But the lumber ship in which he sailed from Sooke on the way to San Francisco sank off Cape Flattery, and he was drowned.

After the death of Staines, the agitation was carried on by Cooper, Langford, Yates and Thomas James Skinner, another of the gentlemen farm bailiffs. They had copies of the various petitions made and sent off to the Colonial Office, and eventually the agitation had its effect, largely through pressure from William Ewart Gladstone, who was a dedicated opponent of the Hudson's Bay Company.

The law officers of the crown were consulted and gave the opinion that the governor and council had power to administer but not to legislate. The colonial secretary decided that an assembly must be convened, and in February 1856 he so informed a disconcerted Douglas, who realized that the Company's half-hearted efforts at settlement had produced a scanty base of voters. The franchise was limited to owners of 20 acres (8 ha) or more of land, which effectively disenfranchised the more numerous dwellers in the embryo towns of Victoria and Nanaimo. The council established four electoral districts to make up an assembly of seven representatives, and set a £300 property qualification for candidates. In the event, just over forty people could be found qualified to vote, and everywhere but in Victoria it was a matter of nomination and acclamation. The seven members of this first parliamentary body in the future Canada West were Dr. John F. Kennedy for Nanaimo, the former miner John Muir for Sooke, Dr. J. S. Helmcken and the bailiff Thomas Skinner for Esquimalt, and for Victoria, Captain Langford, the surveyor J. D. Pemberton and the saloon-keeper James Yates. Captain Langford's qualifications were challenged, and his election was found null and void; J. W. McKay, a Company officer, was chosen in his place.

All the elected representatives had at some time been in the employment of the Hudson's Bay Company or the Puget's Sound Agricultural Company, but this did not mean that the assembly became a ready tool for Douglas. Two of its members, Yates and Skinner, were already declared enemies of the Company and James Douglas. Dr. Helmcken, who was chosen as speaker, was anxious to demonstrate that his relationship with Douglas did not affect his judgement, and he did this by becoming a stickler for the privileges of the tiny parliament, and in the end was as much a thorn in Douglas's side as his declared enemies.

In fact there was little that the assembly—which had no building of its own and had to meet in a smoky room in the fort—could do in the way of independent action, since the grant of the island to the Company made this a colony unlike any other. The only source of revenue over which the assembly had control was the proceeds of liquor licences, and it did not have the power to borrow. On the other hand the Company, its rival in authority, commanded large revenues not only from trade but also from selling land; even the royalties the company paid for the coal extracted at Fort Rupert and Nanaimo were administered directly by the governor.

But the assembly served a purpose in those early days by acting as a forum for public criticism of an administration in which the affairs of the Company and those of the colony were mingled inextricably. Administration was carried on by Douglas and his council, which remained an establishment enclave; its only dissident, Captain Cooper, went back to England in 1856, though he returned to Victoria as harbour master in 1859. The council was completed by the addition of John Tod, later replaced by Donald Fraser, and Judge Cameron, all of whom could be relied on to support Douglas's viewpoint and the Company's interests.

The assembly remained devoted to the pursuit of fuller parliamentary democracy, and enjoyed a great deal of support, particularly outside the palisades of the fort. Having been established on the basis of a suffrage limited to the well-to-do, it did not seek to turn that situation to the advantage of its own members, some of whom may have had personal grievances but were still moved by a great deal of genuine public spirit. The assembly refused to levy new taxes and customs tariffs to pay for a road to Sooke on the grounds that it was not fully representative and therefore did not possess the powers of taxation. Helmcken, as speaker, was as firm on this point as his fellow assemblymen. They proposed the extension of the franchise to small property owners and to tenants in the town of Victoria, but the council refused to endorse the assembly's bill until 1859, and by that time great changes had taken place in the population of Vancouver Island.

The Gold Rush and the Second Colony

To Lieutenant Wilson and his fellow naval officers, the young ladies of Victoria may have seemed a set of jolly colonial dowds, but by the time of his ball Victoria had in fact been transformed almost unrecognizably. It happened dramatically between breakfast and dinner on a single day, and historians are rightly fond of telling the story. Under the influence of Governor Douglas, the inhabitants of the fort and its environs were a pious lot, on Sundays at least, and as usual on the morning of 25 April 1858, they had packed into their new little Christ Church with no idea of what Providence had in store for them. They were emerging, many of them somnolent after one of Edward Cridge's long and moralistic sermons, when they saw in the harbour downhill an American ship, the side-wheeler *Commodore*, unloading its passengers. There were 450 of them, more than the population of the little settlement and its surrounding farms at this time, and most of them were the kind of men who had not been seen in Victoria before. Sunburnt and bearded, clad in red shirts and knee boots and wide-brimmed hats, they were gold miners leaving the dwindling fields of California—impatient men who replenished their supplies at the Company's store and the few independent shops that by now had appeared, then hurried across the Strait of Georgia in whatever craft they could and went up the Fraser to the newly discovered goldfields on the mainland.

This was not the first British Columbian excitement over gold. In 1852 it had been found in small quantities on the Queen Charlottes, to which a few miners from California made their way. They were hindered and harassed by the Haida, who naturally resented their presence, and they actually found little gold. But their presence was enough to arouse in Douglas the not unjustified fear that this might be the beginning of an American invasion like that which had engulfed the Oregon Territory. He immediately alerted the authorities in Westminster; a warship was sent to ensure British sovereignty over the archipelago, and Douglas was appointed lieutenant-governor. Under this commission, he issued a proclamation vesting all gold mines in the crown, and devised a system of mining licences similar to those being used in the Australian goldfields. The flurry in the Queen

Charlottes never developed, but Douglas had created a precedent for the serious rush that did develop later.

On the mainland a few prospectors from California seem to have reached the upper Columbia as early as 1855, and in 1857 the HBC officers at Fort Kamloops informed Douglas of the discovery of scale gold on the Thompson River by local Indians, whom the Company provided with iron spoons to dig it out of the crevices on the bed rock.

In spite of Douglas's efforts to keep it secret, news of the Thompson River finds gradually spread, and a few miners from the United States found their way there by the end of 1857. In the early spring of 1858 rumours of gold discoveries not only on the Thompson but also on the Fraser began to spread in the little ports of Puget Sound; pioneer prospectors began to make their way up the coast and overland to Fort Langley. But it was not until 3 April, when a ship reached San Francisco carrying the first consignment of gold to the assay office, that the real rush began. Douglas feared his nightmare of an American invasion had in fact come true. All that summer boats loaded with miners followed each other into Victoria harbour; estimates of the number of men who arrived during that season vary between 25,000 and 30,000, and well over 80 per cent of them pushed on into the trackless wilderness of the interior where, apart from a few dozen fur traders, the only inhabitants were the Indians who considered the land their own.

Even though he had no political authority over the mainland, Douglas with a great deal of prescience had prepared to receive the miners in a way that would boldly assert a British sovereignty he had no military means to sustain. On 28 December 1857, illegally but effectively, he issued a proclamation that all gold mines in the Fraser and Thompson areas belonged to the crown, and shortly afterwards he announced a system of mining licences, to be obtained in Victoria at the cost of a guinea a month. The Colonial Office recognized the pragmatic wisdom of Douglas's action but also realized that they must have a firmer political base, which would inevitably change the status of the mainland territory. But at this time the Colonial Office itself was going through a phase of ministerial musical chairs, and it was hardly in a position to offer immediate suggestions to Parliament. Henry Labouchère had been followed by Lord Stanley, who quickly resigned, leaving the office of colonial secretary open to the popular Victorian novelist Sir Edward Bulwer Lytton, and it was not until 2 August that the bill making the mainland a crown colony received royal assent. The Company's trading monopoly west of the Rockies would expire at the same time. To avoid confusion with the French colony in the South Pacific which Captain Cook had named New Caledonia, the new colony would be called British Columbia, a name selected personally for it by Queen Victoria.

Meanwhile Douglas, who did not hear of the Act until September, had been forced to improvise regulations in the face of a mounting flow of American commercial interests following in the wake of the miners. His solution was the controversial proclamation he issued on 8 May, which shows Douglas as governor listening to the prompting voice of Douglas as chief factor. It forbade American vessels to carry firearms, ammunition or liquor up the Fraser. For any other goods, they had to obtain both a licence from the Hudson's Bay Company and clearance from the customs officer in Victoria, both of which requirements were later replaced by an *ad valorem* tariff of 10 per cent on all goods; a party from the crew of HMS *Satellite* was stationed at Fort Langley to enforce the new rules, and confiscations were made at both Victoria and Fort Langley. When Lytton reprimanded him, pointing out that the Company had exclusive rights only to trade with the Indians, Douglas defended himself sturdily, maintaining that as the influx of miners and the traders who followed them had created an urgent need for revenue, it was only fair that they should help to meet it. Something of his sense of standing alone in the face of a threatening flood of American democracy comes out in his reference to the "stern necessity . . . either to take the initiative and to give a direction to the masses, or to submit to their dictation."

And in their own way the imperial bureaucrats seem to have recognized the value of Douglas in the current situation on the Pacific coast; a man obstinate enough to stand firm and treat an invasion of Americans as something different from an American invasion. Douglas's policy was one of controlling the miners from the beginning, so that the American authorities would never have the excuse of intervening to establish order in a disorderly place. Lytton had no desire to go through a repetition of the Blanshard fiasco; the solution he found was to use Douglas—the man who had already acted so firmly on the spot—but to detach him from the unpopular Hudson's Bay Company. On that condition, Douglas was offered the governorship of the new colony, which he would administer at the same time as Vancouver Island, though they would remain separate entities. For the two offices he was to receive a salary of £1,800, with promises of an increase as soon as the colonial revenues allowed it.

The legislation establishing the colony provided that there should be a governor in council with an assembly, but to what extent the assembly was to be elected was not specified; until the council could be nominated and the assembly created, Douglas should rule with virtually autocratic powers, as in fact he was already doing. Lytton also appointed the principal colonial officers, carefully choosing men with no HBC connections. The most important, legendary figures in their own time, would be the judge of the new colony, Matthew Baillie Begbie, Inspector of Police and Chief Gold Commissioner Chartres Brew, and Chief Commissioner of Lands and Works Col. Richard Clement Moody, who was also the lieutenant-governor.

Begbie was a Scottish giant, six-foot four inches tall and possessed of a cavalier kind of handsomeness he emphasized with his long black cloak, his broad-brimmed hat and his Van Dyck beard. He came from the same kind of background as Blanshard; his father had been a member of the gentry-officer class, serving as a colonel in the Royal Engineers, and he himself, like Blanshard, had been educated at Cambridge and called to the bar at Lincoln's Inn. He was a cultured man who spoke French and Italian, had done his own version of the Grand Tour in Europe, and knew much about music; and, again like Blanshard, he had been a young briefless lawyer who was glad of an opportunity to prove himself abroad, though he was too shrewd to do it unpaid.

At this point the resemblances ended, for Begbie presented a remarkable mixture of qualities. He was an engaging man whose kindness and hospitality became almost proverbial in the world beyond the mountains that he accepted so readily as his home. Yet he was impartial and firm in his decisions, and the whiff of corruption never hung in the red judge's robes he wore with as much formal dignity when he was making judgement on horseback in a fly-by-night Cariboo mining camp as when he was performing the same function in a New Westminster courtroom with the royal coat of arms hanging over his head. He had the taste for adventure needed in a judge who set out to administer the law fairly among thousands of men, intolerant of discipline, wandering over a vast territory. He refused to be browbeaten by Douglas, who realized that he needed him and treated him accordingly. He was even, though those who faced him in the dock may rarely have thought so, a man of great inner humility; when he died, this strange, flamboyant figure had a simple phrase carved on his gravestone: "God be merciful to me, a sinner."

Chartres Brew, his friend and companion for years in the task of creating some kind of order in the goldfields, was eventually buried in the old miners' cemetery at Camerontown on the edge of Barkerville. The epitaph, which can still be read, is said to have been written by Begbie: "A man imperturbable in courage and temper, endowed with a great and varied administrative capacity, a most ready wit, and most pure integrity and a human heart." Brew, the son of a stipendiary magistrate in Ireland, had fought as a young man in the British Legion during the Carlist Wars of the 1830s in Spain, and later had risen to the rank of assistant commissary-general during the Crimean War; when Lytton sought him out for service in British Columbia, he was inspector of the Royal Irish Constabulary in Cork. A year after his arrival in British Columbia, Brew was also appointed chief gold commissioner for the colony, which meant that he was virtually in control of all relations between the government and the miners except those related to Begbie's court. A genial and physically cumbersome man as he appears in photographs, Brew died in 1870 relatively young, worn out by hard work and the Cariboo winters, at the age of fifty-five, but by that time he had left an indelible mark on the administration of the colony.

Like Douglas, Begbie and Brew lived out their lives in the British Columbia they created, but Colonel Moody was a bird of passage. He arrived as commander of the detachment of 172 Royal Engineers that Lytton had decided to send out with a double purpose. They might act as a deterrent to any kind of violent uprising on the part of the miners, who were mostly armed and who in July 1858 had rioted in Victoria so that the soldiers guarding the Boundary Commission then working in the Fraser Valley had been brought over in HMS *Plumper* to restore order, and yet as engineers they might be expected to cause less offence to the American government than a combat unit. At the same time, the Royal Engineers would play a vital role in developing the new colony, surveying townsites and planning and partially building a road system. Moody, who with Douglas and Begbie formed a kind of *ad hoc* executive council, had his own experience of imperial administration as governor of the Falkland Islands in the 1840s, and his paraded knowledge in the field of colony building often led him into conflict with Douglas during the five years they worked together. Moody's charm was expansive, as was his chivalry (he named Lulu Island for a visiting actress whose performances took his fancy), but so were his plans, and he moved several decades ahead of his time in his ambition not only to design towns in defensible sites but also to create grandiose examples of public and private architecture in the wilderness, as if British Columbia were the long and much inhabited Mediterranean. Yet it was impossible for Douglas entirely to ignore this extravagant and land-avaricious gentleman, who acquired more than 3,000 acres (1200 ha) of real estate before he left in 1863, since Moody had been appointed not only chief commissioner of lands and works, but also lieutenant-governor—Douglas's successor in the event of his death. Like many heirs apparent, Moody tended to exploit his position and often to get his way in situations where disagreements arose.

An example was that of the capital for the new colony. Lytton and Douglas had agreed that a town should be built near the mouth of the Fraser as a commercial and administrative centre; such a town would doubtless become the capital of the new colony. Though Fort Hope and Fort Yale on the lower Fraser Canyon were developing as business centres for the miners operating the nearby gravel bars, they were too far from the sea. Fort Langley, established for thirty years on navigable waters and already a considerable trading centre, seemed the obvious choice.

Before Colonel Moody's arrival, plans were made to establish a townsite there and call it Derby in honour of the Earl of Derby, who was then prime minister of England. On 19 November 1858, Douglas sailed to Fort Langley with Begbie and other dignitaries on the *Otter*, accompanied by an advance party of the Royal Engineers under Captains Parsons and Grant. It was a rainy British Columbian autumn day as the party trudged through the mud to the fort, but the *Beaver*, which had joined the flotilla at the mouth of the Fraser, gave an eighteen-gun salute as the Union Jack was unfurled over the fort in place of the Hudson's Bay Company's flag. Douglas swore Begbie in as judge of the colony, and Begbie swore Douglas in as governor; proclamations were read ending the Hudson's Bay Company licence of exclusive trade in New Caledonia, establishing the government of British Columbia, indemnifying Douglas and his officers from all acts committed prior to the creation of a formal government, and extending British law—both civil and criminal—to the new colony. Subsequently a townsite was laid out, and many of the merchants who had recently settled in Victoria speculatively bought lots by public auction.

When Moody arrived, however, he immediately decided that strategically the site of Derby was extremely vulnerable to a possible American attack. It had virtually no natural defences, and a force following the old Hudson's Bay Company route up the Nikomekl River and across Langley Prairie could attack it with ease. The capital must be on the north side of the Fraser, and he picked a hilly site, about 20 miles (32 km) upriver from the estuary, that would be easily defensible with sufficient artillery and would have great facilities for communication by water and, as he put it presciently, "by future great trunk railways into the interior." Douglas and Moody were still at the early, easy stage of their relationship, and the governor accepted the recommendation. On 14 February 1859, to the intense chagrin of the land speculators who had invested in Derby, he proclaimed that the capital of British Columbia would be built on the site Moody had chosen and that it would be called Queensborough. The name shocked Lytton's literary sensibilities. Once again, the inventiveness of the Great White Queen was called upon, and she named it New Westminster.

IX

The Two Colonies

Governor Douglas's Double Realms

The events of 1858 meant the transformation of Victoria within a few months from a trading post into a bustling town, and added to the mainland population of Indians and fur traders a fluid element consisting of the miners who scattered over the interior of the colony, establishing temporary communities as they went but creating little in the way of permanent settlement. In the process they led the way for the agrarian settlers and the woodsmen, whose transformation of the land would be extensive and permanent.

All through the summer of 1858, the California shipping companies carried on a price war, reducing their fares from $75 to $30, that attracted thousands of passengers to the overloaded ships which lurched up from San Francisco to Vancouver Island. When the Reverend Matthew Macfie reached Victoria in 1859, memories of the previous years were still green, and he could describe vividly the effects of the gold rush on both California and Vancouver Island:

> Individuals of every trade and profession in San Francisco and several parts of Oregon, urged by the insatiable *auri sacra fames,* threw up their employments, in many cases sold their property at an immense sacrifice, and repaired to the new Dorado. This motley throng included, too, gamblers, 'loafers', thieves, ruffians, with not a few of higher moral standard. The rich came to speculate, and the poor in the hope of quickly becoming rich. Every sort of property in California fell to a degree that threatened the ruin of the State. The limited supply of provisions in Victoria was speedily exhausted. . . . Twice the bakers were short of bread, which had to be replaced with ship's biscuit and soda crackers. Innumerable tents covered the ground in and around Victoria as far as the eye could see. The sound of hammer and axe was heard in every direction.

In every gold rush there are those who understand that the surest way of making money out of such an occasion is not the hard and chancy work of finding, digging and panning gold dust but rather the provision of goods and services the miners need. So, out of the 450 men who landed from the *Commodore* on that April morning in 1858, 50 or so stayed behind as the real miners hurried on to the Fraser River bars. Many of the English residents were contemptuous of these new settlers in Victoria, and racial prejudice rang high in their denunciations. Alfred Waddington, for example, described the immigrants who chose to stay in Victoria as "an indescribable array of Polish Jews, Italian fishermen, auctioneers, hangers-on at auctions, bummers, bankrupts and brokers of every description."

In fact, the new Victorians included many men of substance, among them merchants who transferred their businesses and their stock from a faltering California economy to prospering Victoria, which had been named a free port; during July no less than $800,000 worth of merchandise was moved northward from San Francisco to the new gold-mining centre, thirty times as much as in the whole of 1857. By the middle of June already 225 new buildings had gone up, most of them of frame construction with impressive false fronts, though the first brick building, the Hotel Victoria, had already started construction. Two hundred new buildings were stores, and sixty of them were occupied by importers, whose competition effectively brought down the prices the Hudson's Bay Company had been charging in its own store.

A land boom continued all summer, lots being taken up so quickly that more than once sales had to be halted while the surveyor measured out the land. Prices, which had begun round about $50 a lot, rose to well over $2,000 before the summer had ended, and the Hudson's Bay Company, which held most of the land close to the harbour, profited immensely.

One result of this rapid development was that building went ahead of the efforts of the small chain gang who were Victoria's first public workers, and when the winter rains came on, the unpaved streets became almost impassable. "In the town of Victoria," wrote one visitor who was there in December 1858, "the mud is so deep that it comes up to the horses' girths & foot-passengers can only cross on planks laid across; indeed it is so bad that a story is told of a merchant who wished to carry on a conversation with a person on the other side of the street, hiring an Indian to shoot letters over with his bow and arrows."

The community that developed among these raw buildings and muddy streets was perhaps less American in its make-up and its attitudes than Douglas and his fur trade associates had feared. By the late 1850s the original American migrations to California had been overlaid by waves of people from other countries and continents, and the flavour the new town acquired was less American than San Franciscan in a specific and rather international way. The San Franciscan influence was particularly evident in the architecture of the new mercantile houses, and to this day on Wharf, Johnson and Yates streets, one can see surviving the kind of early San Franciscan buildings that were wiped out in their original home during the great earthquake and fire of 1906.

It was the cosmopolitan nature of early Victoria that struck visitors from eastern Canada. When George Monro Grant came to the city on his trans-Canadian journey a few years after its foundation, he was astonished:

A walk through the streets of Victoria showed the little capital to be a small polyglot copy of the world. Its population is less than 5,000; but almost every nationality is represented. Greek fishermen, Jewish and Scottish merchants, Chinese washermen, French, German and Yankee officeholders and butchers, negro waiters and sweeps, Australian farmers and other varieties of the race, rub against each other, apparently in the most friendly way. The sign boards tell their own tale. 'Won Shing, washing and ironing'; Sam Hang, ditto; 'Kwong Tai & Co., cigar store'; 'Magazin Français'; 'Teutonic Hall, lager beer'; 'Scotch House'; 'Adelphic' and 'San Francisco' saloons; 'Oriental' and 'New England' restaurants; 'What Cheer Market' and 'Play me off at ten-pins,' are found written within gunshot, interspersed with more commonplace signs.

Among the most distinctive groups in this heterogeneous colonial population were those who were also the most visible minorities, the blacks and the Chinese. The vanguard of the blacks actually arrived on the *Commodore*; they were freemen, persecuted in California, who sought a refuge under the British flag, which they associated with the abolition of slavery, and it was in this spirit that Governor Douglas welcomed them. Some were men of substance and education, and indeed one of the leading new mercantile houses established in 1858 was operated by two California blacks, Peter Lester and Mifflin Gibbs. Others opened restaurants, barbers' shops and cartage businesses, while there was at least one black lawyer.

Not all of them lingered in Victoria; soon they were opening stores in Esquimalt, and they were among the first pioneer settlers on Saltspring Island. On the whole they were regarded as one of the most orderly, sober and thrifty sections of the population, while their loyalty to their newfound flag was passionate; to show their gratitude for its guarantee of a free life, they organized the first volunteer armed force for the defence of Vancouver Island, the Victoria Pioneer Rifle Corps, outfitted largely at their own expense.

The blacks who came to Vancouver Island had already assimilated the dominant culture of North America; they were English-speaking, church-going Christians, and they fervently accepted the commercial ethics and the middle-class social norms of the Victorian age. The Chinese, on the other hand, must have seemed foreign in every way to the people of the colony. They lived apart, fed on their own strange and frugal diet, dressed differently, saved but also gambled fervently, and worshipped their own Taoist deities or country spirits in their own josshouses. Their years of participation in the California gold rush had established roles for them which they continued to follow from the time the first of them arrived on the ships from San Francisco in 1858. They worked in the mines; they provided services to the miners as laundrymen; they started truck gardening where they could find fertile land in the vicinity of the mines; they panned the less profitable bars and tailings other miners had abandoned.

Victoria became the commercial and social centre of the Chinese immigration, and merchants from the Canton area established themselves in the quarter around Fisgard Street, where the city's Chinatown has remained ever since. The merchants throve by import and export as well as by tending to the needs of their fellow countrymen, and Chinatown developed into a little ghetto that came to be regarded as self-policing. Separation provided a setting where the Chinese could live without disturbance almost as they did in their own country, but it also encouraged an apartness from the general community that had its negative results. For example, the Chinese—living economically in communal houses consisting of bachelors belonging to the same clan or village—could afford to work more cheaply than the whites when the placer mining ran out and the miners had to turn to labouring for the mining syndicates that operated the deeper diggings. Out of this practice arose a class resentment among the white workers that was fanned by racial prejudice, and well into the twentieth century British Columbia labour unions would be opposed to Chinese immigration, and the Chinese would remain the most isolated group of the non-native community in British Columbia.

Small as it was, Victoria soon developed into a city of varied entertainments, characterized by a great deal of the permissiveness that had been evident in the California gold rush communities. By the early 1860s, it boasted no less than eighty-five *licensed* drinking houses, many of which were said to be brothels and gambling houses as well. But it also had restaurants where the food was reputed to be of Parisian excellence and where the champagne flowed freely; notable among them was the Colonial on Government Street, run by a chef of legendary prowess, Sosthenes Driard, who later established the elegant Driard Hotel. Nor were the arts neglected. Judge Begbie established himself as their special patron and was active in founding the Victoria Philharmonic Society, of which he was first president, in 1859. He was also the moving spirit in the creation of the Victoria Theatre by converting a group of fur warehouses the HBC had ceased to use. Touring players, some of them celebrated, soon came to perform in this 500-seat theatre. They included Lulu Sweet, who in 1861 played Lucrezia Borgia with the John D. Potter Dramatic Troupe and after whom Colonel Moody named Lulu Island in the Fraser delta, and in 1864 the famous Shakespearean couple, Charles and Ellen Keen.

Victoria was not officially chartered as a city until 1862, but by then it had already acquired the characteristics of a settled community, and though its population would fluctuate with the varying fortunes of the gold-mining areas during the 1860s, it remained until the appearance of Vancouver in the late 1880s the unchallenged commercial and cultural centre of British North America west of the Rockies.

In Douglas's other realm of British Columbia, there was little—until the second great rush of 1862 into the Cariboo country and the emergence of Barkerville—that could compare with it. New Westminster, named a city on its foundation in 1859, three years before Victoria, never equalled it in population, and struggled unsuccessfully to establish a commercial ascendancy over it. Even as a government centre, New Westminster showed little of the modest social glitter of Victoria, since most of its principal officials followed the example of the governor and maintained their actual residences in the island capital, while the active ones, like Begbie and the ten gold commissioners who also acted as stipendiary magistrates, spent much of their time following the itinerant miners from one makeshift settlement to the next as the goldfields flourished and declined.

Most of the settlements in the interior were small, primitive and usually temporary. A *Harper's Weekly* drawing of Fort Yale in 1858 shows a camp of tents with a few small frame buildings clustering around the palisaded HBC fort. A slightly later photograph shows a single front street with a line of stores, small hotels and eating houses, facing the Fraser River where a sternwheeler is moored, and a few other houses, with a church the Royal Engineers built. Essentially the single commercial street, with the huts of the miners scattered often over a wide area, became the basic form of the mining settlement even when Barkerville developed into a considerable centre of population in the 1860s.

By 1859 the bars of the lower Fraser had already been worked out, and the gold miners left them to the Chinese who were willing to labour for small takings. Those who did not return to San Francisco began to move northward, following dangerous foot trails along the Fraser Canyon to Boston Bar, Lytton and Lillooet. There was an alternative route up the Harrison River to the now extinct little settlement of Douglas at the head of Harrison Lake, and thence by a trail Douglas persuaded the miners to make during the high water season when they could not work the bars. It went by way of Seton and Anderson lakes to Lillooet, which became a halting and staking place for miners proceeding farther up the Fraser; eventually it would become Mile 0 of the Cariboo Road.

In 1860 the surveyor Edgar Dewdney established the Dewdney Trail from Hope to the Similkameen River, much the same route followed by the present Hope-Princeton Highway, and later the Royal Engineers widened both the Douglas and the Dewdney trails into good wagon roads, beside which primitive inns were built to shelter travellers and refresh their animals. There was a certain political intent in building these roads, and particularly the Dewdney Trail, which it was hoped would prevent the economy of the border districts from being dominated by American merchants in Washington Territory.

By 1860 the northward flow of miners was stimulated by rich finds of gold at Horsefly east of Lac la Hache and on the Quesnel River. The prospectors had reached the verge of the Cariboo country. Later that summer the American "Doc" Keithley discovered the creek that bears his name, and the miners stampeded there and to nearby Antler Creek. Next winter "Dutch William" Dietz crossed Bald Mountain from Keithley Creek and gave his name to Williams Creek, where the deep gravels offered the richest yields of all. By 1861 almost equally productive veins had been found in the neighbouring Lightning and Lowhee creeks, and by 1862, as the news reached the outer world, an even bigger stampede than the original Fraser River rush was on. Tens of thousands of men—and not a few women—

were on the move, making their way to the Cariboo from Canada, from the United States, and this time in large numbers from Britain and Europe. In the spring of that year alone, five thousand miners went north by whatever foot and packhorse trails existed to join the great human agglomeration forming beside Williams Creek at the place that would be called Barkerville. All these movements of people and transport confirmed Douglas in his view that a Great North Road was needed which would take the most direct way through the Fraser Canyon.

It was an unsettled society that emerged in the gold-mining country. The miners were nomads, staying for a while where prospects seemed promising and moving on when chance seemed to offer something better. This meant a highly mobile population and towns that were sojourning places rather than settlements; real settlement did not begin until the emergence of agriculture tied men to the soil. Such societies are usually as unorganized and undisciplined as they are fluent, and the lawlessness of the mining frontier in the United States was notorious.

That this did not happen in British Columbia was due partly to the fact that Douglas and his officers established a framework of law and administration from the beginning, and partly to the fact that the miners, contrary to many expectations, seemed to accept the British system quite willingly and never resorted to the vigilante law that at times had created a reign of terror in the California goldfields.

Douglas's resolve to establish a law-abiding mining community was linked with his fear of American invasion; he wanted to establish a system that would maintain order while acting fairly towards British and foreigners alike, so that the Americans would have no excuse to interfere in the territory. And in fact, with a relatively small group of active and plucky men (most of them Anglo-Irish), he succeeded surprisingly well. The ten stipendiary magistrates, with their few constables, could be relied upon to appear where trouble threatened, and often to quell it by sheer effrontery. This, according to legend, Peter O'Reilly did when he arrived at the height of a riotous situation in one of the Kootenay gold camps, riding into the midst of the crowd and roaring out: "Now, boys, there must be no shooting, for if there is shooting there will surely be hanging!" And behind the magistrates loomed the tall figure of Begbie, enduring increasingly arduous rides as the prospectors went farther afield and administering what he saw as justice, which sometimes meant hanging on one of the rare occasions when a jury could be rallied into bringing a verdict of guilty, but more often brought a reversal on appeal of one of the magistrates' sentences. Begbie's interest in the drama was not accidental; he was a superb actor on the bench, simulating both ferocity and high rectitude as they were needed, and all this, with his imposing stature and physical toughness, aroused the admiration of the miners and made him a legend in his lifetime.

Though there were some early incidents between Indians and miners, there was only one occasion when authority appeared to be seriously challenged among the miners, and that had a genial ending. News reached Victoria in January 1859 of trouble at Hill's Bar near Yale, and Douglas decided to act immediately. Colonel Moody had arrived a few weeks before, so he sent him, with Lieutenant Mayne of HMS *Plumper*, and with Judge Begbie following quickly after, to investigate the troubles. They took a group of Royal Engineers under Captain Grant and some sailors and marines from the *Satellite*. At the centre of the dispute, they had heard, was an American miner, Edward McGowan, who had already made California too hot for him.

Moody and Begbie found the dispute had begun between two self-important lay magistrates, at Hill's Bar and Yale respectively, each of whom claimed jurisdiction over a certain prisoner and his alleged crime. The Yale magistrate had the man arrested; the Hill's Bar magistrate sent his constables to Yale and seized the man from the local gaol. One of the constables was Ned McGowan, who behaved in a characteristically flamboyant manner, and this, with his past reputation, had created alarm.

Everything had simmered down by the time the official expedition arrived, and Ned McGowan visited Moody to make a formal apology and explanation. He was fined by Begbie on one count of assault, and then invited the colonel, the judge and the junior officers to what Lieutenant Mayne described as

> a collation in his hut, where we drank champagne with some twelve or fifteen of his Californian mining friends. And, whatever opinion the Vigilance Committee of San Francisco might entertain of these gentlemen, I, speaking as I found them, can only say that, all things considered, I have rarely lunched with a better-spoken, pleasanter party.

So ended Ned McGowan's War, as it immediately became known, and Douglas never again had to call out the troops on undisputed Canadian territory. Disputed territory was another matter, and very shortly afterwards he would be assembling his forces in the squabble that would be known by the derisive name of the Pig War.

Canadian Democrats and American Expansionists

For James Douglas and his conservative associates, the main enemy of monarchical and autocratic order seemed to be American republicanism. But when the real challenge built up between 1858 and the governor's retirement in 1864, it came not from Yankee intruders but from British North Americans following the reformist tendencies of the eastern colonies of Nova Scotia and Canada. And when the trumpets sounded for the struggle, they were blown from the offices of the newspapers that now appeared for the first time in British territory beyond the Rockies and gave a uniting voice to a growing opposition, drawn from the new arrivals who wished to see a system nearer to those that already flourished in the colonies from which they had come or in Britain itself.

At this point the government of Vancouver Island retained the shape it had developed before the gold rush—a governor with an appointed council and an elected assembly. No approach had been made towards responsible government; public offices were all held by appointees of the governor or the Colonial Office, and in practice the elected assembly had very little legislative power beyond the approval or disapproval of money bills. In British Columbia there was not even the semblance of democracy; no appointed council of local worthies and no elected assembly. Douglas ruled in Cromwellian style through his ten gold commissioners with their constables, and the only elective body was the municipal council of New Westminster.

The transformation of West Coast political life through the power of the press began with the arrival of one of the most remarkable men to drift in on the crest of the rush from California. He was a Nova Scotian, born William Smith, who had gone to the California goldfields and done rather well speculating on real estate. Finding that the number of Smiths in Mud Springs, where he settled, made it difficult for him to get his mail, he decided to change his name, perhaps inspired by the fact that Mud Springs had transformed itself into El Dorado. The name he chose, Amor De Cosmos, would be his for the rest of his life; when asked to interpret it, he said, "its meaning tells what I love most, viz: love of order, beauty, the world, the universe."

Amor De Cosmos never lifted a shovel in California to find gold, and he had clearly resolved to extend the same wise abstention to British Columbia. He arrived by the *Brother Jonathan* in May 1858, in a small party of Canadians and Englishmen, liked what he saw, returned to El Dorado to clear up his affairs, and at the end of June was back. Of what De Cosmos did in his first Victoria months little is known, but he seems to have resumed his speculation in real estate. He was one of those who bought land at Derby late in 1858 and, after expressing his indignation when the site of the capital of British Columbia was changed, accepted lots in New Westminster in compensation. He moved freely among the people in Victoria, particularly the English and Canadian newcomers, and he probably communicated the ideas on democracy he had absorbed in Nova Scotia from Joseph Howe, whom he greatly admired. By the time he decided to start a newspaper to provide a forum for the critical discussion of government policies and action, he had gathered a group of sympathizers ready to support him. In one of his more frivolous moments, he claimed, "I started the *Colonist* for amusement during the winter months," but his intent was obviously to promote reform.

His *British Colonist* was not the first newspaper to appear on the Pacific coast of British America, though it was certainly the first politically independent journal. Earlier in 1858 two issues of a French-language paper, *Le Courrier de la Nouvelle Calédonie*, had appeared under the editorship of a French political refugee who called himself Count Paul de Gallo; it was sponsored by the Catholic bishop of Victoria, Modeste Demers. Shortly afterwards two Americans, Williston and Bartlett, started a paper they proposed to call *The Anglo-American*. They were sensitive enough to the reactions such a title might arouse in Fort Victoria (where they started publication) to change it before the appearance of their first issue to *Victoria Gazette*. Within a few weeks the original owners sold out to Abel Whitton. The word "gazette" gave a quasi-official flavour to the paper, and from the beginning of his ownership Whitton trimmed close to the Douglas line.

The *British Colonist* began as a weekly four-page sheet, printed by Count Paul de Gallo on the flat-bed press he had used for *Le Courrier de la Nouvelle Calédonie*, and sold for that now extinct coin, the "bit" of 12½ cents. De Cosmos was critical from the beginning, and often fiercely so, as he reached into the rhetoric of Nova Scotian and Canadian political struggle to portray Douglas's rule as a kind of company-family compact (the "Fort Clique"), dominated by the HBC's authoritarian traditions and serving its interests. On the positive side, he called for responsible government of the kind he had seen initiated in Nova Scotia under Joseph Howe, and by 1860 he had added a plea for the amalgamation of all the British North American colonies into a single nation. He began, as a stage on this course, by advocating the union of the two West Coast colonies.

In 1859, exasperated by the paper's relentless criticism, Douglas tried to suppress the *British Colonist* by invoking an old English law that required massive sureties for a newspaper to appear. It was a self-defeating act, for De Cosmos's popularity leapt immediately, and the citizens of Victoria, at a public meeting in which Douglas's old enemy Captain Cooper played a leading role, subscribed the funds necessary for the bonds; soon the *Colonist* became a daily instead of a weekly thorn in the side of Douglas and his government.

The time, De Cosmos felt, had now come to move from journalism to political action, and in 1860 he tried to gain election to the legislative assembly. Twice that year he was defeated by election frauds that were allowed to go unremedied; not until 1863 did he eventually enter the enlarged assembly of fifteen members and immediately become the leader of the opposition. His methods were flamboyant but arresting. He was often drunk when he spoke, and frequently he became involved in fights with opponents on whose heads he would freely use the heavy walking stick he carried. Once he and another legislator wearied their more numerous opponents into submission by speaking in turn for twenty-six hours on end; such methods gained and held admiration in a young and somewhat repressed community.

Meanwhile an equally active and vocal advocate of democracy had emerged in New Westminster, a man who would be the enemy as often as he was the ally of De Cosmos, yet who worked consistently for the same general goals. John Robson was a Canadian, from Perth in the Ottawa Valley, who arrived just after the first impetus of the Fraser gold rush had diminished in 1859, and competed for manual work in a situation where the supply of labour quickly exceeded the demand.

By 1861 Robson had accumulated enough money to start the first newspaper in the mainland colony, the *British Columbian*, which followed the line De Cosmos had pioneered in the *British Colonist*—hard-hitting criticism of the existing regime accompanied by strong demands for constitutional government, an aim that was even more urgently felt in New Westminster because of the lack of even the semblance of a democratic colonial government. Robson made his complaints and criticisms without fear of person, and published one item relating to Matthew Baillie Begbie which the judge regarded as contempt of court; he briefly imprisoned Robson, who continued to write angry editorials from his cell. Highly popular among the discontented inhabitants of British Columbia, "Honest John," as he quickly came to be known, was elected to the New Westminster municipal council and became its chairman.

The agitations that in the end would change the political shape of the western colonies were thus led by men who were born British subjects; their aims lay within the British parliamentary rather than the American republican tradition. On the whole the Americans expressed little interest in local politics. Where they did loom politically at this time was in a small no man's land in which the adjustment of frontiers laid down in the Oregon Boundary Treaty had not been completed, and here there was talk of war. The dispute was over the San Juan Islands, which lay at the southern entrance to the Strait of Georgia, between southern Vancouver Island and the American mainland. The wording of the 1846 treaty was vague enough for both parties to claim the islands, and on the largest, San Juan, the Hudson's Bay Company had set up a sheep station. The Americans countered by officially including the islands in a newly founded Washington Territory, and in 1859 the shooting of a Hudson's Bay Company pig by an American settler pushed the confrontation to the edge of war.

As charges and countercharges of violated sovereignty were exchanged, the Americans established a military force on San Juan Island, and Governor Douglas proposed to retaliate in kind. It was only the restraint of Rear-Admiral Baynes, then in charge of the Royal Navy's Pacific station, that kept the peace until a temporary compromise was worked out. Gen. Winfield Scott was sent out from Washington, D.C., to ensure that the islands were jointly occupied by equal forces from the two countries until the dispute over ownership was settled.

Governor Douglas had seen the incident as a heaven-sent opportunity to recover as British territory the land that the Hudson's Bay Company had lost owing to the treaty of 1846. As late as 1861 he was urging the British government to take advantage of American attention being distracted by the Civil War and send an expedition to occupy Puget Sound and establish a permanent frontier on the Columbia. To his chagrin, Douglas was ordered to maintain a strict neutrality towards both sides in the American conflict.

Even without Douglas's impetuosity, the 1860s were a period of tension in western North America, and a large British naval force, sometimes with as many as sixteen warships and never with less than twelve, was centred on the new base at Esquimalt. The Civil War ended in 1865 with a revival of American expansionist blustering. The confederation of Canada angered many American leaders who talked once again of annexing British Columbia. The purchase of Alaska by the United States in the same year made the situation even more precarious, and the continuing disagreement over the San Juan Islands remained a local irritant.

Finally, in the Treaty of Washington 1871, where outstanding American and British differences were worked out, it was decided to subject the fate of the San Juan Islands to arbitration by Kaiser William I of Germany. In 1872—doubtless to annoy his relative, Queen Victoria—the kaiser decided in favour of the Americans. From this time onward there was no physical threat of the Americans to British Columbia, now a part of the Dominion of Canada.

The Road to Cariboo

There were many directions from which men approached the Cariboo in the enthusiastic years of the early 1860s. Some followed Alexander Mackenzie's return journey, climbed up from the sea at Bella Coola and crossed the Chilcotin plateau. A more famous group—the Overlanders—set out in the summer of 1862 from Canada to traverse the prairies and cross the Rockies. There were 160 of them to begin with, of whom 125 finally set off on 29 July from Fort Edmonton through the mountains. Among them, sketching the incidents of the journey and the country through which they travelled, was the painter William G. R. Hind. Just after the party reached Kamloops, Catherine Schubert, the only woman among the Overlanders, gave birth to a daughter, Rose, who was the first white child born in British Columbia. The Overlanders were not very lucky in finding gold, but many of them remained to become important citizens of the colony-province they made their home.

Few of the travellers to Cariboo went by such perilous routes as the Overlanders. Most of them proceeded northward by the trails that already existed, and many of them were arriving at Williams Creek before the construction of the Cariboo Road actually began. Douglas decided to build the road by a combination of military and civilian labour. In May 1862 the Royal Engineers under Captain Grant began to work on the difficult section from Yale to Boston Bar, and also on a section along the Thompson River near Spence's Bridge, in both of which the blasting of rock faces and the construction of cribbing to support the road would be needed. The rest of the road was to be built by civilian contractors, one of whom was Joseph W. Trutch, who later played an equivocal role in British Columbia's entry into the Canadian confederation.

By 1863 the stagecoaches were running and the ox-drawn wagon trains were crawling between Yale and Soda Creek, well north of the Fraser Canyon, whence passengers and cargo proceeded by river steamer to Quesnel; from there Captain Grant had cut a trail to Williams Creek by way of Cottonwood River. By the autumn of 1865, the highway link had been made between Soda Creek and Quesnel, and the trail between Quesnel and Williams Creek had been turned into a wagon road along which the stagecoaches could ride to Barkerville and Richfield, the twin centres of the Cariboo goldfields. Gone, now, were the expensive pack trains of the early days, which once had included camels brought from the Australian goldfields; they were abandoned because horses and mules were deeply offended by the stench of the camels and sometimes fell over precipices beside the road in trying to avoid the offensive intruders.

The Cariboo Road ended at what was sometimes said to be the largest North American community west of Chicago. It was the one gold-mining settlement to acquire a certain permanence and consisted of a trio of towns that sprang up beside Williams Creek—Richfield, and then Barkerville, and finally Camerontown. Richfield—where a permanent courthouse was built for Begbie's cases to be heard and a jail to hold his prisoners—became the centre of government. Camerontown was named after the famous John Cameron—"Cariboo Cameron"—who made and lost one of the great fortunes of the Cariboo. When his wife died, he took her out for burial to Scotland, preserved in a lead coffin filled with whisky.

But it was Barkerville that became the real centre of life on Williams Creek. Billy Barker, after whom it was named, was a Cornishman, sometime potter and clay miner, who had gone to sea, and at Victoria in 1858 deserted the whaler on which he was sailing to join the rush to the Fraser Canyon. He later joined in the rush to Williams Creek, where he obstinately sank his shaft deeper and deeper until, at 42 feet (13 m), he hit pay dirt; he and his partners brought up $600,000 in gold. He lost it all to a calculating woman, and though he wandered the goldfields for years, he never made another fortune and died a pauper in 1894. Billy Barker would enter a saloon half-seas over, and dance a little hornpipe of his own while he sang his personal song:

> I'm English Bill,
> Never worked, never will.
> Get away, girls
> Or I'll tousle your curls.

There seems to be no accurate record of how many people lived at its height in the community where Barker and Cameron shone as men of fortune. Guesses run up to thirty thousand, but the highest are certainly exaggerated, though the three towns of Williams Creek at their height had at least ten thousand inhabitants when Victoria had six thousand and New Westminster only a few hundred.

In appearance Barkerville was more like a rough, huge mountain village than a town, though it had a surprising selection of urban amenities for those who could afford them. It had no real centre, but coalesced along a narrow street, usually deep in mud, that straggled along the valley bottom. Behind high sidewalks stood buildings of whipsawn lumber that housed hotels and restaurants, banks and barber shops, laundries and bakeries, groceries and blacksmiths' shops. There was a Theatre Royal used by miners' amateur groups and by touring dramatic and variety companies from San Francisco. There was a weekly newspaper, the *Cariboo Sentinel*. The terpsichorean art was served by the Hurdy Gurdies, German girls dressed in vaguely Tyrolean garb who were sent up from California in the company of a kind of duenna by a San Francisco entrepreneur. The miners would lift them high in energetic whirling dances to the tune of fiddles.

For those who wanted something more serious, there were several churches of competing sects and a good library. There was even a resident poet, James Anderson, who wrote plays for the amateurs at the Theatre Royal and in 1868 brought out a slim collection of verse, *Sawney's Letters: Or Cariboo Rhymes*, which was the first literary work to be published in British Columbia.

The population of Barkerville during the 1860s was overwhelmingly male. It is true that Baroness Burdett-Coutts, one of the great philanthropic ladies of the Victorian era, had sent out, in 1862 and 1863, two shiploads of respectable working-class girls to provide wives for the miners, but most of them were snapped up on the wharves at Victoria and very few reached the Cariboo. As in most essentially bachelor societies, there was a vigorous evening and nightlife in the saloons, which usually had dance halls and card rooms attached. There the liquor flowed freely, and so did the gold dust, for the cheapest grade of champagne cost $10 a bottle, and only successful miners could in fact afford to patronize the saloons. The settlement attracted its card sharpers, confidence men and bullies, like all other gold rush towns, but the shadow of Begbie and the presence of Chartres Brew and his men were so palpable that there were no classic western gunfights in the streets of Barkerville or in its drinking places. Banditry was so rare that the miners actually preferred to send their gold out by the stagecoaches of Barnard's Express rather than pay the extra cost of entrusting it to the Cariboo Gold Escort, which the government organized to take gold from Barkerville down to New Westminster, where an assay office and mint were established and which actually produced a tiny issue of handsome $10 and $20 gold pieces—British Columbia's only local currency.

The Cariboo settlements had their visible minorities—a few Kanakas and blacks and a larger group of Chinese, who had their own quarter of small log huts, stores, eating houses and a Masonic Hall. Racial prejudice was scanty in comparison with later decades in British Columbia. The attempts at discrimination that blacks had experienced in Victoria seem not to have been repeated in Barkerville, and the well-known barber W. D. Moses, who invented a much advertised "Hair Invigorator," was a respected citizen.

The presence of Barkerville and its sister communities gave a start to the agricultural settlement that eventually would transform large areas of interior British Columbia. By the middle of the 1860s cattle ranchers had already appeared in the natural grassland country to the south and west of Fort Kamloops and in the southern Cariboo around Ashcroft, from which large herds would be driven up to Barkerville, and the fresh meat they provided, together with the vegetables the Chinese began to grow, provided a welcome change to the bacon, beans and bannock that formed the gold miners' traditionally unhealthy diet.

Like most such instant communities, Barkerville could be a good place for the rich and a hard place for the poor, who were in the great majority, for the cost of transport kept prices high even when placer mining by individuals or small groups, with its unpredictable but often almost instant fortunes, began to be replaced by syndicates operating the deeper and more difficult shafts with wage labour.

Neither the prosperity nor the population of Barkerville would outlast the 1860s. In 1868 a miner tried to embrace a young laundress, and in their struggle a lit oil lamp was knocked over. Within an hour and twenty minutes, the whole commercial area of the town was destroyed; the damage, enormous for the period, reached $690,000 in buildings and $700,000 in goods. Nevertheless the gold-mining colony was so resilient that the town was rebuilt and resumed its air of prosperous gaiety by the summer of the next year. Still, the decline had already begun, and people were drifting away as the actual supply of gold dwindled and newer methods requiring less labour were introduced, including hydraulic sluicing with powerful water jets and dredges scraping the valley bottom.

How much gold was dug in Barkerville and its environs has never been accu-rately established. Almost $20,000,000 was reported during the 1860s, but it is known that large quantities were taken out clandestinely, particularly by miners returning overland to the United States. The total was probably not far off $30,000,000, a very large sum of money for the nineteenth century.

The End of the Bastions

The year 1864 marked the end of an era in the two colonies on the West Coast; the last bastion of Fort Victoria was demolished, and the core of what was already the city of Victoria was completely transferred to commercial use. It was also the year when the human bastion of the older order, James Douglas, departed and cleared the way for an era of rapid political change.

The demolition of the fort and its buildings had been going on since 1860 and had run parallel to the transfer of effective power out of the hands of the Com-pany. In 1860 also the legislative council had moved out of its smoky room in the fort to new government buildings on the south shore of Victoria harbour. They were designed by an itinerant artist-architect, Hermann Otto Tiedemann, who also did some interesting drawings of early Victoria, and they reflected the preoc-cupation with Oriental styles that was spreading in Europe at the time, for they had pagoda roofs and the woodwork was coloured lacquer red. They aroused great criticism and were called many names, of which the most affectionate was "The Birdcages," but at least they asserted the assembly's emergence from the Com-pany's shadow. Increasingly concerned with realizing profits from land sales and withdrawing from active agriculture, the Company also abandoned in Victoria its original mercantile activities, and from now onward it was the city's retail trade that it sought, with considerable success, to dominate.

The departure in 1863 of the Royal Engineers, including Colonel Moody, signi-fied the beginning of the end of Governor Douglas's long domination of the Pa-cific coast. In fact, there were very few sappers left to return to England, for all but fifteen of them had accepted their discharges and the pieces of land offered to them near the village of Sapperton, which they had established upriver from New Westminster.

By the time Moody and the remnant of the Royal Engineers had left, the British politicians and their Colonial Office advisors had come to the conclusion that it was time Douglas stepped from office. His road works had been costly—even if necessary—and he had been somewhat grasping on his own account, raising his salary from £1,800 to £3,800. Moreover, through the years since he first assumed governorship of Vancouver Island, he had not failed to make enemies, and some of them were persistent, like Captain Langford who surfaced in the early 1860s to accuse Douglas of despotism, while new enemies, like John Robson in New Westminster, sent in their petitions demanding at least a taste of democratic government in British Columbia.

To placate the New Westminster radicals, an act was passed in the British Parliament in July 1863 that provided for the inclusion in British Columbia of the Stikine territory as far north as the 60th parallel, but which also allowed for the establishment of the first legislative council in the colony. It did not meet the full demands of Robson and his associates, for it was not an assembly, and would consist of eight appointed officials and magistrates and five elected representatives. The Duke of Newcastle suggested that Douglas's retirement might be timely, and the governor agreed. Newcastle had decided to appoint separate governors for the two colonies, and Douglas would leave office when they arrived in the spring of 1864. Though he directed the formation of the new legislative council of British Columbia, and presided on 22 January 1864 over the opening of its first session in the old Royal Engineers' barracks at Sapperton, it was his successor who would effectively govern through this body. Meanwhile, Old Squaretoes departed in modest glory. He was knighted, while inhabitants of both Victoria and New Westminster gave splendid banquets in his honour, and even old enemies, like the *British Colonist* and De Cosmos, put aside past rancours to remark on the appropriateness of the honour done to him when he received his KCB.

X

Prelude to Confederation

Douglas's Successors

The men who separately succeeded Douglas in Victoria and New Westminster were both, unlike him, veterans of the colonial service. After a military career, Arthur Edward Kennedy had been governor of Gambia, and then of Sierra Leone, and finally for eight years of Western Australia before he went to Victoria. Frederick Seymour had been lieutenant-governor of the tiny colony of British Honduras. Both at heart were authoritarians, but their differences in style made Kennedy a total failure and Seymour a comparative success in the special political circumstances of the West Coast colonies.

Kennedy was a proud, aloof man, and his autocratic attitude and manner had been little challenged in the colonies where he had hitherto ruled, which had no elected legislatures. The more snobbish Victorians were taken by his looks and his manner, but even the genial Gilbert Sproat, variously lumber magnate, amateur anthropologist and in the 1860s a government official, who was capable of liking such diverse types of men as De Cosmos and Kennedy, remarked of the governor that "it was not easy for me, his inoffensive personal friend, waiting the announcement of dinner, to rid myself of the suspicion that I was in the guardroom, and that I deserved it." Kennedy once said that Victoria was inhabited by two kinds of people, "the convicts and those who ought to be convicts," and if even Sproat sensed the vibrations of this disapproval, one can imagine the hostility Kennedy harboured towards those he would soon describe as the "very unscrupulous men" in the assembly, by whom he meant not only De Cosmos but even Helmcken, whom Kennedy's governorship turned into something near a reformer.

Before Kennedy came, the assembly had passed resolutions calling for responsible government and for a single administration of the two colonies that would lead to eventual political union. When he arrived, the legislators not only learnt to their annoyance that their recommendations had been ignored but also that they were now expected to provide out of colonial funds a new residence for the governor and a salary for his private secretary. De Cosmos, the fiery democrat, and Helmcken, the stickler for parliamentary rights, united to lead the assembly in protest and in voting against providing a residence at the expense of the revenue.

De Cosmos and Helmcken considered that in this matter they were honourably defending the interests of their fellow islanders, and they were therefore mortified to find themselves momentary villains. The citizens of Victoria regarded the action of the assembly as a great discourtesy to the new governor, who on first appearance seemed such a courteous gentleman. Thomas Harris, the butcher mayor of the city, though a friend of De Cosmos, called on the governor to offer apologies in the name of Victoria. A meeting was held in the Victoria Theatre at which Helmcken and De Cosmos were shouted down when they tried to justify their actions to an ungrateful populace.

Eventually, the assembly did vote the funds for a governor's residence, and the Colonial Office agreed to pay the secretary's salary. But even these gestures of reconciliation went astray, for instead of spending the colony's grant on builders' wages, Kennedy paid $40,000 on buying Cary Castle (more often known as Cary Folly), the pretentious mansion built by the widely detested George Hunter Cary, who since 1859 had been attorney general of Vancouver Island and also (very much *in absentia*) of British Columbia until his resignation in 1864. De Cosmos had a new reason to rise in the assembly and point the finger of accusation. And the rest of Kennedy's administration, until his departure in 1866, was marked by an interminable series of wrangles over money.

Small and bald-headed, Seymour had none of Kennedy's immediate impressiveness, but his easygoing nature fitted him admirably for a role in New Westminster, where his inclination to gambling and high living found a quick response in the expansive gold rush cast of mind. He immediately showed a practical concern for the welfare of his people, upgrading the school in the little capital, and making personal gifts of books and magazines to the library and hospital. He spent public money on extending Government House, building a ballroom for two hundred people, guest accommodation and supper rooms, but he won the approval of the citizens of New Westminster when he provided lavish entertainments at his own expense, so that even the reformist *British Columbian* wrote ecstatically about the "viands of the most *recherché* character" which "were provided in prodigal abundance, and displayed in the most elegant manner." English games like cricket and tennis flourished under his benign eye (Begbie was a rival tennis fan), and so did amateur theatricals. He got drunk often but, as with Sir John A. Macdonald, such a tendency did not diminish the prestige of nineteenth-century political figures. Above all, under his rule the British Columbians appreciated the end of absenteeism. Now they had a governor actually living among them and so congenially that they felt they could think of him as one of their own.

Nor did he ignore the Indians. In fact, Seymour was exceptional among the British officials who found their way to the West Coast colonies in his concern for their welfare, though he developed no Indian policy. He showed a particular interest in the activities of missionaries like William Duncan of Metlakatla, who were trying not merely to convert the Indians but also to prepare them for entry into the new world that the white men were creating among them. And he relished his role as representative of the Great White Queen when on 24 May he invited the Indians of the Fraser River to join him in a jamboree for the queen's birthday. They responded with the alacrity of a people accustomed to grand festivities, and 3,500 of them paddled their canoes in a great flotilla that grew as it passed each village on the way to New Westminster, where they remained encamped for a week. When they departed, Seymour ceremonially presented the chiefs with gilt-headed canes and Union Jacks and invited them to return next summer. The Indians sang and drummed to show their friendship as they paddled past Government House on their way home.

There was policy as well as friendliness in this gesture on Seymour's part, for it was made in the midst of the first crisis to face him in his colony, the so-called Chilcotin War—a misleading name for a police operation that barely resembled the exterminatory Indian wars then being waged by American cavalry south of the border.

The Chilcotin War arose out of an effort to discover a route to the Cariboo goldfields that would bypass the Fraser Canyon and, at the same time, benefit Victoria. Between 1858 and 1863 no less than four officially sponsored efforts were made to find possible routes by way of the coastal inlets on the mainland, but none was successful. Even the route Alexander Mackenzie had followed down to Bella Coola did not seem suitable for a wagon road.

In spite of all these unfavourable reports, Alfred Waddington, an Englishman of parts who began as a Victoria merchant and later became inspector of schools for Vancouver Island, decided that it was possible to build a road 175 miles (282 km) shorter than the Cariboo Road that Douglas was building. It would start at the head of Bute Inlet, where a port would be built for the ships sailing from Victoria, and would proceed by way of the Homathko Valley and the Chilcotin plateau to the mouth of the Quesnel River, where it would link up with the existing road to Williams Creek.

Waddington communicated his enthusiasm to a group of Victoria businessmen who agreed to support him financially, and Douglas gave him a charter to construct the road. Waddington's enthusiasm sustained him and his supporters to such an extent that speculators put their names down for lots in a townsite he had laid out near the mouth of the Homathko River. But carrying the road over the precipitous sides of Mount Waddington offered such immense problems—it would involve making almost eighty zigzag curves—that the scheme would probably have been abandoned as too expensive if, before that, it had not provoked the anger of the Chilcotin Indians. In fact, the work crews that Waddington introduced in 1863 never even reached the really difficult construction area. Early in the second season, 1864, a band of hostile Chilcotins appeared, killed a ferryman on the Homathko, and then attacked work crews and a pack train. In all, thirteen of Waddington's men were killed.

In the next chapter I will discuss what may have motivated the Indians in making these attacks. For the white men then, there seemed little time to speculate on

such matters. The fur traders' rule had been to react against violence with violence and to afflict such punishment as would discourage further attacks. Now,
added to this primitive *lex talionis*, was the need to maintain the authority of the
state, which in practice meant the authority and welfare of the imperial race.

News of the killings was slow to reach New Westminster. Governor Kennedy
heard in Victoria on 11 May, but the incident had happened outside his territory,
and he showed no urgent concern, sending a message by the regular mail steamer
instead of dispatching one of the several naval vessels lying at Esquimalt. It took
two days to reach Seymour, and the delay earned Kennedy his lasting enmity. Seymour acted immediately, sending an urgent message to William George Cox, now
gold commissioner in charge at Rock Creek, and ordering Chartres Brew to organize a small expeditionary force. On 15 May, HMS *Forward*, commanded by Lord
Gilford, sailed for Bute Inlet with Brew's small volunteer force, which consisted
largely of Royal Engineer veterans.

Within a couple of weeks, news came through that Brew had been unable to
mount an effective pursuit and was returning for reinforcements. Kennedy now offered the help of volunteers from Vancouver Island, but Seymour pointedly refused and chose to rely on mainland resources. He ordered Cox to organize a volunteer force of miners in Barkerville and take them up the Fraser to Alexandria
and then across country into the Chilcotin. He also mobilized a second party,
consisting of the New Westminster Rifle Corps and the Hyack Fire Brigade, under
Chartres Brew, and with a characteristically egalitarian gesture enrolled himself in
the Rifle Corps so as to accompany the expedition as it sailed northward in HMS
Sutlej to Bentinck Inlet.

From Bella Coola the Brew expedition went 250 miles (402 km) by Mackenzie's
route as far as Puntze Lake, to rendezvous with Cox and his volunteers. Eventually
Chief Alexis, one of the most important local Indian leaders, arrived at Puntze
Lake, and Seymour persuaded him to co-operate in searching out the murderers.
After this Cox had no difficulty obtaining the surrender of a number of suspects,
and they were taken to Quesnel, where Begbie presided over their trial and the
condemnation to death of five of them, who were duly hanged in the presence of a
subdued audience of Indians.

Having prevented what might have developed into an Indian war, with its perils to the mining population, Seymour established his popularity right at the beginning of his term of office; and on his way back from Chilcotin, he broadened
his links with the population under his governorship by choosing a route that
would lead him to the goldfields and Barkerville. Douglas had never done this during the whole of his six years in office as governor of British Columbia, and the
people of the Cariboo—then at the height of prosperous optimism—felt that at
last they were being recognized by the queen's representative. They responded
with enthusiasm and generosity, firing royal salutes, raising leafy triumphal arches
and presenting addresses.

This direct introduction to the country he ruled over filled Seymour with constructive zeal, and he used his instant popularity to work well with his only partly elected legislative council. He proposed road improvements, including an extension of the Dewdney Trail into the Kootenays, where a find at Wild Horse Creek had provoked a new rush north over the border. He built bridges and improved the navigation of the Fraser. He encouraged street improvements in New Westminster and the general tidying up of his miniature capital. And to do all the work, which helped to counter the recession that set in at the end of 1864, he earned the ready consent of the legislative council to an export duty on gold and an increase in customs duties.

The recession, which affected Vancouver Island even more severely than the mainland, gave a new urgency to the matter of the union of the colonies, which was being approached from three different directions without all the parties being aware of it. The Duke of Newcastle and his officials in the Colonial Office had seen the wisdom from an imperial viewpoint of a single administration and had given both Kennedy and Seymour confidential instructions to work towards it.

As the depression deepened in 1864, members of the assembly on Vancouver Island became reconciled to the idea that colonial union would offer at least a partial solution to their economic problems. They wanted it to be a federal union, with a representative political system and the capital established in Victoria, which would remain a free port. Then the procrastinations of the Colonial Office and the continuing difficulties of working with Governor Kennedy encouraged more desperate proposals; in January 1865 Amor De Cosmos decided to leave the issue of responsible government in abeyance and introduced a resolution calling for unconditional union of the two colonies. It was passed, but aroused great indignation among the mercantile community in Victoria, which looked with consternation on the prospect of the city no longer being a free port. De Cosmos immediately resigned and sought re-election. He won handsomely, and from this point there was no doubt that union would follow quickly.

The question now was the terms the imperial government would impose, and here Seymour was the key figure, for it was already decided in London that when a union came he should govern what would be essentially an enlarged British Columbia. Seymour had closely observed events in Victoria and, despite his democratic manners, he had no love for democratic practices as demonstrated by the elected assembly on Vancouver Island. But he gave an appearance of not having made up his mind about union until he went to England in 1865 to consult with the imperial authorities (who had already decided on union to cut costs) about the political structure of the united colony. It was only after the act of union was passed in the British Parliament and had been duly proclaimed in November 1866 that the Vancouver Islanders realized how much they had lost through their own rashness in demanding union at any cost and through Seymour's duplicity. Their elected assembly was abolished; the new British Columbia would be ruled by an enlarged legislative council, in which the nine elected members—four from the island and five from the mainland—would be more than balanced by the six gov-

ernment officers and the seven stipendiary magistrates who sat as appointed representatives. Victoria would be deprived of its privileges as a free port and be
replaced as the colonial capital by the more rustic centre of New Westminster.
Vancouver Island was clearly being subordinated to the mainland, and De Cosmos
and his followers were not the only people to be alarmed. As he listened to the naval vessels at Esquimalt firing their salutes for the occasion, Sir James Douglas
noted: "A funeral procession, with minute guns, would have been more appropriate to the occasion."

Nevertheless, both De Cosmos and Douglas remained silent in public. De Cosmos clearly believed that a united colony, even if it were for the time being auto-
cratically ruled, would have more chance than two divided colonies of weathering
the economic crisis and of facing the pressures that would undoubtedly be asserted
from the south now the American Civil War had come to an end.

Accordingly, he developed his policy in the legislative council, when it first
met early in 1867, in two directions. First he revived the joint issues of an elected
assembly and responsible government, and in this he allied himself, at least temporarily, with the democratically inclined mainland representatives, John Robson
and George Anthony Walkem, surveyor, lawyer and gifted Sunday painter, who
represented Cariboo. All three were destined eventually to become premiers of
British Columbia.

Yet the alliance, particularly between De Cosmos and Robson, was strained
over the question of the capital of the enlarged province. Conscious that the roots
of his own influence lay on the island, De Cosmos advocated a return to Victoria;
Robson felt that the relatively greater economic strength of the mainland justified
a mainland capital. Here De Cosmos sought other allies, and he found them
among the appointed members of the council, the government officials with their
preference for the comforts of living in Victoria. Those preferences carried the issue when a free vote was held, and in March 1868, by a majority of fourteen to
five, the five being the elected mainland representatives, the council chose to depart to Victoria. There it prepared to debate the step that might follow on colonial
union—confederation with the Dominion of Canada.

The Cautions and Calculations of Confederation

With the rapid progression towards Confederation among the eastern colonies of
British North America during this period, the question of whether British Columbia should join the other colonies inevitably dominated attention. Generally
speaking, the former Hudson's Bay men and the British-born officials were opposed to Confederation, which they regarded as contrary to their interests, and it
quickly became evident that Seymour was sympathetic to them. De Cosmos, on
the other hand, had been advocating some kind of confederation since 1860,
when he celebrated the Prince of Wales's visit to North America with a call in the
British Colonist for the initiation of a "British North American policy to put an end
to disjointed provinces." After 1863, when he entered the Vancouver Island legis-

lative assembly, he had advocated the consecutive process of a union of the far western provinces and then a general Canadian confederation.

In 1866, as it became evident that the negotiations between the Canadas and the Atlantic colonies were moving towards some kind of conclusion, De Cosmos gained the rather unexpected support of the conservatively inclined Helmcken, who had a considerable influence on the older population of Victoria. Together with two other members of the council, they approached Seymour in March 1867, suggesting he cable the Colonial Office asking that provision for the admission of British Columbia be made in whatever law might be passed to confederate the eastern colonies. In spite of his personal opposition to Confederation, Seymour duly dispatched a telegram. A few days later, swayed by the persuasions of De Cosmos, the council unanimously called on the governor to take "whatever steps he deemed advisable to bring British Columbia into Confederation, this Council being confident that in advising this step they are expressing the view of the Colonists generally."

This time Seymour procrastinated; he did not send a second telegram to the Duke of Buckingham, the new colonial secretary, until September, three months after the Dominion of Canada had been proclaimed. By this time news had already reached the West Coast that Clause 146 of the British North America Act provided for territories other than the original three colonies to enter the dominion from time to time until it was complete, in the words of its motto, "from ocean even unto ocean." Seymour finally heard from the Duke of Buckingham in November, expressing the view that British Columbia could hardly be incorporated into Canada until the status of the intervening territory of Rupert's Land, still a chartered realm of the Hudson's Bay Company, had been determined. Seymour regarded this as settling the matter for the time being, but De Cosmos did not agree.

He decided to appeal to the people, and on 29 January 1868 he and James Trimble, the mayor of Victoria, called a public meeting at which De Cosmos made the principal speech proposing a resolution that the colony should seek immediate admission into Canada, with an overland wagon road to be completed from the head of Lake Superior within two years as the essential condition. An ad hoc committee was elected, which decided to bypass Seymour and to send the resolution directly to Governor General Lord Monck. In doing so, the committee pointed out how Seymour had neglected the matter, and asked for the intervention of the Canadian cabinet, "since without the help and support of the Government of the Dominion, the time will be remote when this Colony will be admitted into the Dominion."

The Victoria meeting had mixed results, and it showed how uncertain the feelings of British Columbians about Confederation still were. A counter-petition against Confederation was organized in Victoria, and though it was signed by only 164 people (4 per cent of the city's population), one of them was Dr. Helmcken. "I came out against Confederation distinctly," he explained later, "chiefly because

I thought it premature—partly from prejudice—and partly because no suitable terms could be proposed." On the other hand, the defection of Helmcken was compensated for by the final commitment of John Robson to the Confederation cause, and his support for a resolution in the legislative council calling directly for British Columbia's entry into Canada under Clause 146.

By now the official members of the council had been encouraged by the evidence of opposition to Confederation to veer back to their original position, and they defeated the resolution, to Seymour's delight. De Cosmos and his allies refused to accept defeat, and in May 1868 they formed the Confederation League, the first body resembling a political party ever created in British Columbia. The league's orators toured the colony, and in September 1868 called together in Yale a "Convention of Delegates, for the purpose of accelerating the admission into the Dominion of Canada, upon equitable and beneficial terms, and also to devise means to secure Representative Institutions with Responsible Government." Twenty-six delegates arrived at Yale from all parts of the colony, and their resolutions in favour of Confederation and responsible government won wide support. Yet the official minority in the legislative council still opposed Confederation until changing circumstances convinced its members that the development was inevitable and might even be turned to their own personal advantages.

Among these circumstances was the unexpected death in June 1869 of Governor Seymour. Seymour had gone north the previous month to deal with a series of disputes that had broken out among the Indians on the coast. He set off on HMS *Sparrowhawk* and successfully mediated a dispute among the chiefs of the Nass River. He went on to Skidegate to make peace among the Haida, and there he was taken ill with dysentery. But, minimizing the seriousness of his condition, he insisted on putting in on the return journey at Bella Coola, for yet another powwow. There he died on 10 June, and on 14 June the *Sparrowhawk* docked in Victoria with his body on board. All seemed to be forgiven in the splendour of Victoria's mourning, with full military honours given in the naval cemetery at Esquimalt after an elaborate service in Christ Church Cathedral with Sir James Douglas among the mourners. Yet there were many who regarded Seymour's death as providential, since it removed the principal barrier to the interests working towards Confederation.

Apart from the popular movement led by De Cosmos and Robson, two other interests had become involved. The Colonial Office, having successfully rid Britain of its responsibility towards the eastern colonies through creating the Dominion of Canada, was anxious to achieve the same with regard to areas west of Lake Superior, and in mid-1869—with Louis Riel yet barely on the horizon—negotiations regarding the ultimate fate of Rupert's Land seemed to be proceeding well. Accordingly the Duke of Buckingham picked, as Seymour's successor, Anthony Musgrave, who had been governor of Newfoundland and was known to favour British Columbia's entry into Confederation, which he had instructions to expedite. Finally, there were the Canadians, who were anxious to acquire British Columbia as the anchor for their dream of a British North American nation stretching from coast to coast. Macdonald had evidently not seen De Cosmos as a sufficiently malleable tool when they met in eastern Canada in the autumn of 1867, for he chose instead to work through his friend Dr. R. W. W. Carrall, a Canadian, who represented the Cariboo in the legislative council.

The entry of British Columbia into Confederation has often been represented as a triumph for the democratic forces on the West Coast, but this was not in fact what happened. Only De Cosmos, Robson and their associates were committed to the democratic proposals of responsible government and a representative assembly. When Confederation was in fact achieved, it was through a series of cynical political deals, in which Musgrave, with Macdonald's assistance, won over officials by assuring them that their interests would be protected. The attitude of the officials themselves, once they realized the Colonial Office was promoting Confederation, is shown in a revealing letter Peter O'Reilly, stipendiary magistrate for Yale and Lytton, wrote to the attorney general of the colony, Henry Crease. "I suppose there is little doubt we shall have Confederation sooner or later, but it appears to me that our only chance is to work together, & battle against it until a satisfactory provision is made for us." By "a satisfactory provision" he meant of course adequate pensions or posts for facilitating British Columbia's entry into Canada. This was promised by Musgrave with Macdonald's tacit approval.

Once they had been assured of their future, the officials turned the tables on their democratic critics by themselves introducing, on 9 March 1870, the motion for union with Canada. During the long debate that lasted almost a month, they defeated all attempts by the reformers to get the demand for responsible government incorporated in the resolution. When it was finally decided to send a delegation to Ottawa to discuss the terms of entry into Confederation, the officials gained a further triumph, for here Governor Musgrave exercised his prerogative, and in making his choices he ignored the men who had worked most devotedly, first for colonial union and then for union with Canada. De Cosmos was not chosen, nor was Robson. Dr. Carrall, Macdonald's man in the Cariboo, was picked, and so was Joseph W. Trutch, the incumbent chief commissioner of lands and works, himself an official. As third member, a highly reluctant Helmcken was persuaded to go, for his role in colonial politics since he became first speaker of the Vancouver Island legislative assembly gave a certain legitimacy to the delegation. In all this the Indian majority of the population had gone entirely unconsulted, and there had been no attempt to test the feelings of the population through a plebiscite. It was, essentially, an undemocratic arrangement between the governor, the British Columbian officials and the Tory political leaders in Ottawa.

The delegates were welcomed in Ottawa with even better terms than they had asked, for Sir George Etienne Cartier, who led the negotiations in Macdonald's absence through alcoholically induced sickness, offered not a wagon road but a railway across the prairies to British Columbia, to be started in two years and completed in ten. The terms of the agreement were proclaimed in Victoria on 30 August and a new legislative council—now representing the province and no longer the colony of British Columbia—ratified them in January 1871. The colony on the Pacific had become the western rim of a dominion that not only had shores on two oceans but was also the second largest nation in the world.

The Colony That Became a Province

The British Columbia that entered Confederation in 1871 was an area almost as large as the original Dominion of Canada, and larger than any land in Europe except Russia. No accurate census had yet been taken, but its population was certainly no greater than forty thousand, and of those almost thirty thousand were native Indians. (The total population would not reach a hundred thousand until the 1890s, and white colonists would not form the majority until the 1880s.) The native population was falling, but so was the white population, and in many ways the colony looked like a declining society in comparison with the high gold rush days when people had flocked in their tens of thousands to Victoria and the Cariboo. Victoria, the largest nucleus of population, had shrunk by 1871 to four thousand inhabitants, and farther north on Vancouver Island, in the coal-mining areas of Nanaimo, there were now perhaps seven hundred people. Despite its spell as a provincial capital, New Westminster could not muster many more than a thousand inhabitants, while now that the easy placer mining of the early days had come to an end, there were fewer than two thousand people remaining in Barkerville and the Cariboo. In the earlier mining region of the Fraser Canyon, about a thousand people remained between Hope and Lytton, and around Lillooet was another small community of about three hundred. Isolated fur traders and, increasingly, missionaries, were scattered over the province, and little nodules of miners formed and dispersed in the Kootenays and in the wilderness north of the Cariboo, concentrated largely around the Omineca goldfield, where miners wandered individually or in small parties, prospecting and starting occasional minor and transitory rushes.

The towns and villages—even Victoria—were tenuous outposts clinging precariously to the fringes of a wilderness whose resources had scarcely begun to be exploited. Nothing had yet replaced gold as an effective stimulus to the economy or a sure means of attracting and keeping population. Those who obstinately remained in British Columbia were sustained by a hope inspired by its untapped wealth and depressed by a sense of their lack of resources in manpower and money. More than one traveller to Victoria was reminded of classic Athens or Sparta, and the comparison was not as far-fetched as it might seem. There was no Phidias or Sophocles, no Plato or Epicurus or Pericles, yet in the political ferment of tiny communities like Victoria and New Westminster and Barkerville, where a few hundred or a few thousand people thrust up folk leaders like De Cosmos and Robson and produced an incessant political controversy, there was something that resembled those ancient Greek states with their small, turbulent populations. They too had been trapped between unfriendly mountains and an indifferent sea.

Yet the skeleton of a settled society was already beginning to form and its characteristic industries to develop. The visitor arriving by sea or across the mountains from the bare prairies was impressed by the vast forests of giant trees still hardly touched by the loggers, yet sawmills were already working on the shores of sheltered saltwater inlets and exporting their lumber far and wide. It might still be the Indians who benefited mostly from the numerous shoals of salmon that surged into the rivers in successive waves, yet the great migrations were already being turned to commercial ends by white entrepreneurs who not only caught fish for local consumption but were exporting salted salmon and had started in a rudimentary way the canning industry that would eventually send British Columbian salmon to world markets. The prosperous collieries around Nanaimo were the precursors of a more stable mining industry than that of the colonial era, and the wandering prospectors were accumulating a geological knowledge of the terrain that would be put to use from the 1880s onwards, when the search for metals like silver and copper and lead, zinc and nickel, assumed greater importance than that for gold.

Farming was also changing and spreading, and by 1870, as well as the cattle ranches of the Cariboo, the Thompson River area and the north end of the Okanagan Valley, no less than three hundred mixed and dairy farms had been started in the lower Fraser Valley, and settlers were establishing themselves not only in the parklands around Victoria but also on the Gulf Islands. In 1862 the first settler in what is now Vancouver, Fitzgerald McCleery, started his farm on the escarpment running down to the north arm of the Fraser; in an old house on the land he claimed, this book is being written.

But perhaps the most important development of the 1860s, in view of the later importance of Vancouver, was the emergence of Burrard Inlet as a harbour whose activities began already to rival those of Victoria and New Westminster. The inlet's trade was then based entirely on logging. On the south shore Edward Stamp in 1865 began to build his Hastings Mill, and two years later "Gassy Jack" Deighton founded the Deighton Hotel in the first urban nucleus of Vancouver, Gastown, whose respectable name was Granville. Farther west, Jeremiah Rogers began a spar-cutting operation at Jerry's Cove, which later became Jericho Beach. On the north shore, at Moodyville, which later became North Vancouver, "Sue" Moody had already built a steam-driven mill. From both Hastings and Moodyville, sailing ships carried sawn lumber and spars to San Francisco and Latin America, to Australia and China, and even to Britain. The Burrard Inlet mills and their tiny settlements still seemed appendages to New Westminster, to which the inlet was linked by overland trails. Only a few foresightful people yet envisaged the inlet's future as one of Canada's great seaports.

This development of a modest but solid and steady economic foundation for the life of British Columbia meant that the towns of the province, many of which were not much larger than English villages, were already taking on the look of established communities, with regular townsites (usually in the standard American grid form) and with solid architect-designed buildings beginning to take the place of the more makeshift structures of an early era. Many of the buildings that are familiar ornaments of the older towns like Victoria date from this transition period when the colony of British Columbia became a province of Canada.

XI

The Decline and Fall of the Native Societies

Triumph and Lament

In the spring of 1847 on 8 April the Canadian painter Paul Kane arrived at Fort Victoria, having crossed the prairies and the Rockies and descended the Columbia River to Fort Vancouver. Roderick Finlayson provided "a comfortable room, which I made my headquarters during the months I was occupied in sketching excursions among the Indians of the neighbourhood and the surrounding coasts." Not only did Kane do a series of those vivid *plein air* oil sketches that are now generally recognized as superior to the elaborate studio paintings of Indian subjects he concocted back in Toronto but he left a vivid record in his diary of what he saw of the native cultures in a place where the white men had established themselves so recently that some of the fort buildings were still being completed when he arrived.

Kane had a purpose that gave his account a certain bias, for, like George Catlin in the United States, he was urgently recording the traditional features of native cultures doomed to irreparable change, if not to extinction, as the frontiers of white settlement moved inexorably westward. As he observed the Salish Indians in the Songhees village close to Fort Victoria and wandered among the camps that visiting northern tribal people were already establishing along the foreshore, he did in fact see groups of Indians who were still living vigorously according to their traditions. He made drawings of the exteriors and interiors of the long, pitch-roofed Salish houses, with the women weaving at their looms under the racks of drying salmon and the now extinct little white dogs they bred for wool playing around them. He sketched war parties returning in their great canoes with the heads of enemies hung from the prows, and men dancing in the strange blind Xwaihwe masks of the Salish. He described the institution of slavery on the coast and some of its more horrifying excesses, and also the great giving feasts that took place from time to time.

He conveyed the idea of a culture that was still strong even if it was threatened, and this was not a false impression, for the local Indians did not accept the presence of the traders on their territory without hostile activity. In 1844, for example, they began killing the horses and oxen that were put to graze outside the fort, and when Finlayson demanded compensation, the Songhees band called on the reputedly bellicose Cowichan people, led by the famous war chief Tzuhalem, to assist them. The allied bands surrounded the fort, harmlessly peppering the palisades with musketshot. Finlayson kept his men from shooting in retaliation but instead fired grapeshot from one of his nine-pounder cannon at the largest house in the Songhees village, "and the effect of which was that it was completely demolished," as he reported, "and splinters of the cedar boards flying in fragments in the air." This was war conducted as it had always been between the fur trade men and the Indians; swift and dramatic retaliation, and equally swift reconciliation, with the Indians making compensation for the slaughtered cattle, a whiff of the pipe of peace to wipe out the memory of the whiff of grapeshot, "and so we parted good friends, trade was resumed as formerly & after this no more of our animals were killed."

Already, though it was Kane's purpose to minimize this, trading had notably affected certain aspects of Indian life, as was shown by the weight of musket fire, rather than arrows, that Finlayson experienced only a year after Fort Victoria was established. Even the painter found it timely to record the ways in which trade goods had been adopted into the native cultures. He portrayed chiefs proudly wearing English or American uniforms, and in describing potlatches, he showed the prestige that trade goods had acquired in comparison with Indian products. He talked of one chief who had gathered together for his feast as many as

> twelve bales of blankets, with numberless pots, kettles and pans, knives and other articles and cutlery, and great quantities of beads, and other trinkets, as well as numerous beautiful Chinese boxes, which find their way here from the Sandwich Islands.

The Perils of Dependence

The Indians and the fur traders represented two entirely different societies that had found a common interest; in their pursuit of that interest, something very near to a symbiotic relationship in the natural world had emerged. The fur traders depended for their commerce on the existence of an untamed wilderness with a native population whose desire for the superior weapons and tools and other goods that could be acquired in trade would induce them to provide a steady and sufficient supply of furs. But the symbiosis was not quite a true one, since the dependence of the trapper had profound and lasting effects on his life and his culture, whereas the trader merely moved on when the supply of furs dried up. Some of the traders were quite frank about their intent to create a dependence, and though such dependence might be less harmful among the coastal tribes with their rich supplies of fish and other marine foods, it could have a disastrous effect among groups who had abandoned a subsistence hunting economy and a neolithic technology for a life dominated by trapping to secure trade goods.

An example of what could happen is offered by the consequences of the Fort St. John "massacre" in 1823. The Beaver Indians were angered by the Company's proposal to close the post and replace it by one in Sekani territory at Rocky Mountain Portage; this would be too distant for the Beaver, and they were expected now to go to Fort Dunvegan on the Peace River. The stock was being evacuated to the new post, and the clerk in charge at Fort St. John was on his own. Some Beaver killed him and then four voyageurs on their way back to the fort.

The Company's usual policy in such a case was to apply the *lex talionis*, so well understood by the Indians, of sending in a party to wreak vengeance or obtain compensation. This time, perhaps because there were not enough men available to send in a punitive expedition, the Company chose a crueller way to teach the Indians a lesson. It closed not only Fort St. John but also the only other posts the Indians could have used, Fort Dunvegan and the Rocky Mountain Portage post. The closure, it was calculated, would have the added advantage of acting as a kind of conservationist measure, allowing the population of fur-bearing animals to build up by the time the Company was willing to resume trading. The effect was disastrous, for the Indians were unable to obtain the guns and ammunition that had changed their way of hunting, yet they found it difficult to resume their traditional skills, so that they now starved in an area where life had always been difficult or meagre. When John McLean went through the country four years after the massacre, he reported that many Indians had starved to death, and Governor George Simpson, with the chilly smugness to which he was so prone, remarked that closing the forts had brought "the whole population of the upper parts of the river to the utmost distress."

Dependence on trade might not incur the same dire possibilities among the coastal Indians as in the meagre forest economies of the interior of British Columbia. Nevertheless, it resulted in profound changes in the native economy, as well as in the cultural and social life of the coastal peoples. Whole areas of native craftsmanship were abandoned as trade goods took the place of native manufactures. Even as early as the 1790s travellers were remarking on the extent to which, except for ceremonial purposes, Indians of chiefly class were abandon ing their native garments of cedar bark and goat's wool for the ornamental European garments that the British and American traders brought to tempt their vanity. Claret Fleurieu, writing the account of Etienne Marchand's world voyage in 1791, recorded that the Haida chiefs were already discarding their sea otter capes, so valuable to the traders, for jackets and greatcoats, and the Spanish sailor Jacintho Caamano, reaching the same area, observed one chief who wore two frockcoats, one over the other, and had decorated the coats and the trousers with Chinese cash, "so that he sounded like a carriage mule, as he walked."

Because they controlled the trade, the chiefs had the first choice of trade goods, but before long the potlatch system had spread these widely through society, and a rapid technological evolution took place: items that had been slowly and painstakingly made by native methods were replaced by items obtained in trade, which were usually more practical and durable even if not artistically so appealing. With an abundant supply of blankets—Hudson's Bay and the lesser kinds—there was no longer any need to prepare cedar fibre and weave it. Items like fishing hooks, which took so much time to devise out of wood and antler, fishing nets carefully woven out of nettle fibres, as well as cables and fishing lines made of kelp, were all replaced by manufactured substitutes that were more convenient and more robust. It became pointless to spend many hours cutting and bending and grooving a piece of cedar and sewing it into a watertight box for cooking with red-hot stones immersed in water, when an iron pot could be got for a beaver skin and would boil the food more efficiently. The tools and weapons that had been made of stones of many kinds became slowly obsolete. This meant that a whole section of the native economy vanished almost overnight, with its quarries celebrated for various forms of flint and chert and obsidian, its long trade routes, and its specialist craftsmen. A whole series of practical crafts was abandoned in this way; the skills were lost, and they have not been revived in the resurgence in recent years of the more ceremonial arts.

Even in the potlatches, which grew increasingly lavish during the middle years of the nineteenth century, gifts of trade goods took the place of gifts of traditional commodities, and photographs show the decks in front of the longhouses covered with commercially made enamel ware and pottery, with pieces of furniture, with piles of manufactured blankets, with sacks of flour and sugar. European objects seemed to have an almost irresistible attraction, and the coastal peoples, who had such splendid sea-going craft of their own, began to acquire dinghies and shallops and whaleboats and even to make them. The Kwakiutl village of Cape Mudge, long a notorious stronghold of Euclataw pirates, started to build European-style fishing boats, and very soon these became greatly in demand up and down the coast for their superior quality. But at the same time the carving of the great war canoes dwindled rapidly even among the Haida, and before the end of the nineteenth century it had come to an end.

Something different happened in the case of the artifacts used among the Coast Indian peoples for ceremonial and social purposes. There the forms remained the same, and so for the most part did the techniques and the materials, though all were modified by the metal tools brought in by trade. Most of the remarkable examples by which today we judge the art of the Coast Indians were made after the fur trade began on the coast in the 1780s and the newly acquired tools allowed more precise and more rapid carving. Though cedar and alderwood remained the materials most generally used, there was in later years a tendency to use store-bought paint for colouring because of its more vivid tints, and a development in ceremonial costume was the button blanket, made of pearl buttons sewn in traditional patterns onto trade blankets; the button blankets gradually replaced the woven Chilkat blankets of the past.

From the precontact period we have little evidence of the character of the coastal art but that provided by the finds at Ozette, the portable items Cook's associates took back to Europe, and the drawings John Webber made of the Nootka houses with their carvings. These speak of a vigorous tradition already existing, but not of work so ingenious, varied and original as appeared in the mid-nineteenth century, especially among the Tsimshian, Haida and Kwakiutl. If the tools the Europeans brought vitalized the art to an unprecedented degree, it was the wealth the trade injected into the native economies that made it possible to sustain the artists and to give the feasts in which the use of artifacts was validated.

There were other ways in which trade affected the arts of the Coast Indians and especially of the Haida. A trade in "curios" began relatively soon, and in the first half of the nineteenth century the Indian craftsmen found two original ways to satisfy it. Some of their young men went as hunters and hands on whaling and sealing vessels, and watched the English seamen carving bits of wood with their knives into scrimshaw work, which they would later sell. Around 1810 or perhaps a little later, a Haida discovered near Skidegate a quarry of argillite, a clay stone also called black slate, soft enough to be worked easily and in close detail, and began to make small sculptures with European as well as Indian motifs which looked enough like jet carvings to impress the Victorians and sell easily. About the same time the craft of silverwork, which the Russians had taught some of the Tlingit, found its way southward and was taken up by Haida craftsmen who used silver dollars to make bracelets on which native designs were shown in low relief. Ironically, though the high arts of the Coast Indians, tied to their own ceremonial life, almost died out by the end of the nineteenth century except on the upper Skeena (the last of the great Haida poles being carved before the end of the 1880s), these arts for tourists survived and a small number of carvers continued to make a living from them.

The Coming of the Miners

The end of the symbiosis between the two cultures represented by traders and trappers came abruptly in April 1858, when the fur economy was shattered as men intent on exploiting the land directly came in their thousands by sea and overland, and began the great transformation of property relations that would be complete by the end of the century. The fur traders had come to sojourn in the land, the miners in their turn came to enrich themselves and then pass on, but the settlers who quickly followed them came to live on and off the land, to own it and to exploit it; they would transform human habitat into a commodity. Accompanying them—sometimes preceding them—were the administrators who would turn British Columbia into a political society dominated by a ruling race; the men of war—both human and figurative—who would enforce their authority; and the missionaries who would transform not only the beliefs of the Indians but also reshape their social patterns.

The fur trade relationship between trader and trapper, with its implied recognition of the parallelism and mutual autonomy of Indian and white societies, could not survive. The Indians found themselves facing white men who were not unlike the Boston Men of the coast, men who had no sense of the land as the home of its native population or the domicile of its wild life, and who in any case were infected by the American contempt for the native peoples that had developed through generations of Indian wars.

In some parts of Canada native rights of possession, rather than ownership, were recognized in the colonial period and also under the dominion, and they were cleared by a series of treaties in which the Indians abandoned claims to what had formerly been their domain in exchange for reserves and miserly gifts. In British Columbia this did not take place. During the 1850s Sir James Douglas started on his own process of treaty making on a very small scale, acting on behalf of the HBC, which at this time still held the title to the land under the grant of Vancouver Island. There were fourteen such treaties, and they covered land used for farming and mining as well as for the actual forts of the Company's establishments at Victoria, Nanaimo and Fort Rupert.

The treaties provided for the village sites and small areas of ground around them to become reserves. There were modest payments of money, and the Indians were allowed to hunt over unoccupied land and to continue their fishing. The last of Douglas's treaties was completed in 1854, and after that there were no treaties between the crown and the Indians of British Columbia, except for a few bands in the Peace River country who in 1898 were included in the dominion government's Treaty No. 8. Otherwise, no Indian in British Columbia has ever been included in a treaty, since successive provincial administrations have refused or neglected to recognize aboriginal title.

When the miners began to work in the sandbars of the Fraser River in 1858, Sir James Douglas was faced by the question of establishing some kind of order even before the mainland had been subjected to any political authority. His licensing system, later developed by the gold commissioners who registered the areas staked out by the miners, had no reference to Indian rights over the land. It assumed everything, above and below the surface of the earth, was the crown's to give or withhold. This was a situation that might have led to serious conflict, and there were indeed some early clashes between miners and Indians in the relatively thickly populated lower Fraser Valley, but both sides responded surprisingly passively to the presence of the Royal Engineers and of Brew's constabulary. The records are not entirely clear. A few Indians appear to have been killed; there were certainly no deaths among the miners, though the cattle and horses of parties coming north by land were stolen.

The Great Plague of 1862
The unlikely place where the miners and the Indians met in most fatal contact was not in fact the goldfields or the long roads that led to them, but Victoria, which from 1858 onward became a kind of mecca for the northern native peoples. The fur traders had provided vast quantities of unaccustomed wealth, and the miners, whose requirements were somewhat different, in their own way continued the process. Each autumn, when the fishing ended and the miners left the freezing

streams of the interior for milder climes, the great canoes would come down from the north, filled, not with warriors but with women. For though the Indians brought furs and curios for sale, they probably earned more from the prostitution of their women; the chiefs would offer their slaves, and lesser men their wives and daughters, who do not appear to have been especially unwilling. Their customers included not only the miners but also merchant seamen and sailors from the naval vessels that now anchored at Esquimalt, who paid them either in cash or in trinkets (gilt buttons from uniforms were particular favourites) and in the alcohol which, since the elimination of competition from the sea-trading Boston Men, the HBC traders no longer dispensed. There were also illicit whisky dealers, including, according to the *Colonist*, some of Victoria's most outwardly pious citizens.

Each year until 1862 the Indians arrived, in growing numbers. A head count in April 1859 showed that 1,545 were encamped within musket-range of the fort, and the next day, apparently, a large group of almost seven hundred arrived from the northern areas, with Haida and Tsimshian in the majority. Even larger numbers came in the following years, and with the hundreds of Salish in the Songhees village, the small white town of Victoria with its five thousand inhabitants would have upwards of three thousand Indians living on its doorstep for months on end. They were not only a threat to peace, as the *Colonist* pointed out in frequent heated editorials, but also, in the crowded and insanitary camp life they lived, a danger to public health. Governor Douglas was alarmed enough to organize a volunteer corps of former HBC men.

The Indians themselves soon began to show the effects of these annual jaunts. Alcoholism, with its attendant problems, was increasing among them, and they contracted various venereal diseases, which resulted in death and widespread infertility among the women. Then, in 1862, smallpox was carried by a white man from San Francisco, and though it had comparatively little effect on the immunized inhabitants of the town, it spread rapidly in the less immunized Indian encampments where, as the *Colonist* had prophesied, people began to die in large numbers. Governor Douglas and the other British officials were alarmed and took rapid panic action. They ordered the Indians to leave and used naval vessels to chivvy them northward, while their camps were burned.

Dispersing the Indians may have cleared out a dangerous plague centre so far as the people of Victoria were concerned, but it resulted in a full-scale epidemic. As the northern peoples sailed home, they left the sickness at every place they touched, and those who attacked the fleeing people, like the pirates of Cape Mudge, suffered the same fate as their victims. The epidemic also spread into the interior, and by the time it had burnt itself out in 1863, the Indian population of the colony had been reduced by more than a third. There were a few places where isolated doctors or priests, or even fur traders, vaccinated the people and in this way saved many of them, and William Duncan, the famous missionary of Metlakatla, gained an undeserved repute for miracle-making because he had taken his converts to Metlakatla from Port Simpson shortly before the sickness arrived. On the whole the smallpox was less lethal in the interior, where the Indians were fewer, than in the populous little villages along the coast. The Haida were perhaps the worst hit of all. There may have been eight thousand of them before the white men came, and even in the 1830s the appearance of their war canoes still created dread among the more southerly peoples. After the great sickness of 1862, only about eight hundred Haida were left, and they were further reduced to less than six hundred by 1915, when their population reached its lower ebb.

The Tsimshian and the Kwakiutl were also badly affected, and the Bella Coola almost as severely as the Haida, so that the balance of forces shifted radically among the populations of the coast, and the slaving raids of the northern groups came to an end. There were also, as a consequence of the epidemic, striking changes among the local Indian societies. Many villages that had once been populous and prosperous, with their fine poles and painted housefronts lined above the beaches, were abandoned by the few survivors, until in the end the Haida were gathered in two villages, Skidegate and Masset.

The consequence of this concentration and of the deaths of many chiefly men and women was an extraordinary disruption of what had once been a stable if elaborate ranking system. To begin with, when villages coalesced, the amalgamation of various communities meant that the local remembrancers had to create new ladders of precedence, establishing the correct order between freshly united lineages. To complicate matters, the deaths of numerous title holders meant that many people regarded as commoners and never dreaming of being anything better unexpectedly became the heirs to names and titles, to crests and songs and dances held within their lineages, and might even become house chiefs. All they had to do was to validate their pretensions by generous potlatches, and this introduction of a new contingent of givers added to the ostentation and extravagance of such occasions, as men made newly rich by trade sought to establish themselves—not unlike nineteenth-century English millowners and coal magnates—among the aristocracy. The gradual cessation of actual warfare among Indian groups turned the potlatches into the principal way of expressing hostility as well as rivalry among lineages and individuals, and there were times when the Indians themselves would somewhat sardonically refer to the potlatch, in its somewhat fevered final phase, as a kind of warfare.

Unequal Contests

We shall probably never have any complete record of the real warfare, forays and clashes between various groups of Indians that took place between the 1780s and the 1870s when something like a *pax canadica* was established among the native peoples of the West and the Far West. One gets a glimpse, through the recollections of fur traders, through traditions picked up by anthropologists, through Paul Kane's sketches of war parties, of a simmering state of warfare among the tribes that gradually came to an end as the arm's length policies of the fur traders towards native affairs was replaced by the interested paternalism and gunboat methods of a settlement-oriented society.

The 1860s were a transition period during which Indian violence gained notoriety on the occasions when it was directed towards whites and was met by dramatic counterviolence. In hindsight, it is the connection between the violence of the 1860s and the new form of white penetration, with its organized patterns of government and increasing demands on the land, that seems particularly significant. Much if not most of the antiwhite violence of the 1860s seems to have been connected with that enduring dispute over land rights which continues more than a century afterwards.

The interracial clashes during the 1860s have never been listed completely. What is clear in all of them is an increasing awareness among the Indians that their situation had become more desperate, and a resolution on the part of the ruling race to use all its resources to sustain its domination. I offer some instances.

The first is the so-called Chilcotin War, which we have already observed from the white viewpoint as a police operation seeking alleged murderers (who happened to be Indians) and trying and executing them with a triple purpose—to establish an unquestioning recognition of British domination over the land and its people, to apply the punishment—already understood in Indian custom—of a life for a life, and to establish the role of the Indians as wards of the imperial power.

A procedure was worked out by Seymour, advised by Brew and Begbie, by which an appearance of acquiescence could be given to the surrender of the Indians. The governor, the judge and the policeman did not raise the question of rebellion. There was not an Indian nation, so that loyalty to an entity larger than the tribe was an idea neither Chief Alexis nor any of his people would have understood. But they well understood the crime of murder, and the idea that it must be repaid by either death or compensation. It was because they themselves recognized the *lex talionis* that the chiefs were able to persuade their culpable followers to surrender and that later their execution was accepted so passively by the whole Chilcotin people. They did not even show their resentment of the trickery practised by magistrate William George Cox, who without authority promised an amnesty that induced some of the fugitives to give themselves up. Ruse, after all, was perhaps the most admired element in Indian warfare.

At the time, people involved in the affair had various explanations to offer for the attack on Waddington's labourers, which Margaret Ormsby well summarized in her *British Columbia: A History*:

Waddington blamed the white man's introduction of smallpox; others, including the artist Frederick Whymper, attached to his party, attributed it more directly to his action in supplying the Chilcotins with arms while keeping them so short of food that they "disputed with their wretched Cayota dogs anything we threw out of the house in the shape of bones, bacon rinds, tea leaves and other such like luxuries." Judge Begbie later concluded that concern over Indian title to land was a more important factor than either plunder or revenge.

The judge, I suggest, was right. Begbie was unusual among British Columbian officials of his time in his sympathy for the groups whom today we would call the visible minorities. He showed a considerable sympathy for the Chinese and concerned himself with the wider implications, in terms of human liberties, of attempts to exclude or harass them. He set out very deliberately to make sure that Indians who came into his court shared the same benefits of doubt as English or Canadian or American offenders.

By 1860, however, land was indeed becoming an issue. In the interior of British Columbia the miners had for several years been taking land where they wished (and having their claims recognized by the gold commissioners without any reference to possible prior Indian rights). When the Chilcotin, a fairly cohesive group with a good hunting territory, saw the white men impinging on it from the west as well as the east, and even establishing townsites, it seems reasonable to assume they feared the loss of their lands, as during the same decade other local Indians did.

Sporadic incidents began in 1861, when the first of the important gunboat actions took place. A party of Haida, led by a chief who had adopted the name of a trader and was called Captain Jefferson, decided that the whisky they bought in Victoria had been adulterated with sea water, and in revenge they stole a great quantity of goods in the city, including surveying equipment, carpenters' tools, blankets, cloth, flour and of course rum. They landed on Saltspring Island and plundered and terrorized the newly arrived settlers, and took goods from the *Laurel* and a number of other small vessels they encountered on the way. The gunboat *Forward*, commanded by Lieut. Charles Rufus Robson, went in pursuit and overtook the marauders encamped near Cape Mudge. The usual unequal contest ensued. The *Forward* fired its two cannon at the encampment; the Indians replied with musket fire. One crewman was wounded and four Indians were killed before the five chiefs surrendered and were taken to Victoria to be tried for plundering the *Laurel*.

The attacks on Saltspring Island settlers were part of a growing pattern. Settlement was now beginning to spread around Victoria, up the Fraser Valley and on the Gulf Islands, which were not only fertile and idyllic but also somewhat isolated from the larger European communities. Land, it must be remembered, was far more precious in British Columbia than on the prairies, since so little of the mountainous and forested colony was fit for farming or even for grazing. Seeing white men put down their roots without permission on lands the Indians had always regarded as their own, the latter became anxious of the effect on their fishing and hunting, and began to react with resentment and even hatred. They resorted almost automatically to the violence with which their ancestors had always re-acted to encroachments on their rights. A glance through the pages of the *British Colonist* for the years between 1858 and 1865 shows a sharp rise in the number of violent incidents. Attacks on trading boats continued sporadically, but settlers and travellers were also being killed.

In November 1862 a settler named Frederick Marks and his married daughter Caroline Harvey were travelling from Waldron Island to Mayne Island. Because of bad weather, they landed on Saturna Island, where Marks was shot by a small band of Cowichan Indians. His daughter was chased along the shore and hacked to death. Marks's body was never found, and only a few months later were his daughter's remains discovered, stuffed into a rock crevice and covered with stones. She was identified by a comb. When the news of her discovery reached Victoria, the alarmed and angry citizens called for action, and a small fleet steamed out of Esquimalt towards Kuper Island and the Lamalchi village whose inhabitants were suspected of harbouring the murderers. The *Forward* was again in evidence, with its fellow gunboat the *Grappler*, as well as the paddle sloop *Devastation* and the cor-vette *Chameleon*. There followed a typical example of gunboat rule. The four boats cruised the waters picking up evidence. Then, on 20 April, they converged on the Lamalchi village, and the *Forward* and the *Grappler* returned on 2 May, landed parties of seamen and marines, and burnt the village. Four murderers were caught and subsequently hanged, while a fifth was killed by his own people, who took the body on board the *Devastation*. The surviving people of Lamalchi fled across Juan de Fuca Strait and found refuge among the Salish in American territory.

In the same month of April 1863, William Brady, travelling through the Gulf Islands in a whaleboat with a Cherokee Indian as his companion, was killed on Pender Island by some Cowichan to whom he had just made a present of tea, sugar and bread. Once again the *Forward* was ordered out and caught up with the assail-ants at Kulleet Bay near Chemainus. Three men and a woman were sentenced to death; in all these cases the *lex talionis* was being applied in multiple ratio. The woman was reprieved and committed to prison for life, but forced to witness the hanging, where the three men declared she was the most guilty of all, having in-cited them to the killing by mocking their manhood.

Raids on ships continued into the late 1860s, and the most spectacular show of naval force they provoked followed the attack on the small sloop *Kingfisher* by the Ahousat in Clayoquot Sound. The crew of three was killed and the boat pillaged and burnt. When the news reached Victoria, Rear Admiral Denman decided to lead the expedition in the Esquimalt flagship HMS *Sutlej*, accompanied by the *Devastation*, which on this occasion lived up to its name. Boats were sent from the two ships, equipped with rockets they fired indiscriminately at dwellings and boats, so that at the end of the firing nine villages had been burnt down and sixty-four canoes had been sunk. A shore party fought a miniature pitched battle in which fifteen Indians were killed, including some of the supposed murderers. Several other presumed culprits escaped and were never captured, and the jury in Victoria provided an unexpected anticlimax to the glorious imperial occasion when it acquitted the prisoners Admiral Denman did take back with him.

The *Kingfisher* itself had been in trouble with the navy shortly before its destruction. Under a previous owner, it had been one of the small boats rounded up by the *Devastation* in April 1863 on an expedition to control the illicit whisky trade. The boats were seized and towed to New Westminster, where they were confiscated, their cargoes poured away and their captains fined. This kind of operation the navy added regularly to its pursuit of Indian criminals.

Thus, from the time the Royal Navy established itself at Esquimalt, colonial authorities and imperial forces co-operated to make the turbulent Indians of the coast aware of the white man's mastery. It was gunboat government in its crudest form. The less bellicose peoples of the interior, on the rare occasions when they did turn violent, could be overawed by hastily organized volunteer groups. But still, with the Indians in the majority and their social organization largely intact, subordination was not complete. The Indians were still feared, were seen as dangerous rivals for the land, and were equal to the extent that they were dangerous. As sickness sapped their numbers, and as immigration increased the white population, the Indian menace grew less. But the final stage of subordination, when all the Indian claims to their lands could be safely disregarded, was that of total dependence. The traders had already started that process; it was to be continued in a different way by the missionaries and to be completed after 1871 by the federal bureaucrats, who finally set out to turn the native peoples into wards of the state as helpless, rightless, voiceless and voteless as lunatics or convicts.

Villages of God

If there was anything that united the missionaries of various Christian churches who found their way to British Columbia during the nineteenth century, it was their conviction that the secular as well as the spiritual patterns of Indian life must be changed if conversion were to be true and lasting. Even Indian languages were often regarded as impediments to Christianization.

This is why the history of missionary endeavours in British Columbia is marked by the creation of model villages, ecclesiastical utopias that entirely transformed social as well as religious patterns. There are examples not only among the more active of the larger churches—the Catholics, Anglicans and Methodists—but even among the Salvationists, who established a beachhead on the Skeena in the 1890s.

The Catholics were first in the mission field, with Father Bolduc reaching Victoria with James Douglas in 1843; Fathers De Smet and Demers had entered the Okanagan and New Caledonia even earlier. But the first missionary to attempt the founding of a religious utopia on the coast, and perhaps the most famous, was William Duncan, an Anglican lay worker. Duncan's story shows the close links that existed between the missionaries and the secular authorities during the colonial period in British Columbia. He was sent there on the initiative of Capt. James Charles Prevost, who had been in command of HMS *Virago* on the Pacific coast between 1852 and 1854 and had seen a wide open field for conversion among the native peoples. He persuaded the Church Missionary Society to send a mission worker. The society picked William Duncan, a former north country leather merchant, and Prevost took him out in 1857 on the newly commissioned *Satellite*.

When Duncan arrived and announced his intention to start work among the 2,300 Tsimshian gathered around Port Simpson, he found that Governor Douglas and the HBC traders were far from pleased with his plans. However, he made a close friend of Edward Cridge, the aggressively Low Church HBC chaplain at Fort Victoria, and Cridge's pleas, together with Prevost's urgings, removed Douglas's objections, and Duncan soon went north. He learnt Tsimshian, and then, not without risk, took to preaching in the clan houses. Some of the chiefs supported him, but he quickly saw that it was a matter of rivalry in terms of prestige and that the pagan way of life, with its shamanism and its ritual cannibal ceremonies (which particularly appalled him), was little changed. He decided that the Indians were victims of their own past but equally the victims of the white men who exploited them.

Accordingly, he decided to make a clear break with both the pagan past and the trading present. In 1862 he led his congregation in establishing a model mission village on the site of deserted Indian settlements along the shore of the protected channel of Metlakatla. When the smallpox passed over Metlakatla in its great sweep north, Duncan's prestige rose, and in the end about a thousand people were assembled in the village. It was probably the most complete and for a time the most successful experiment of its kind on the coast. The people were induced to live in individual and identical small houses with gardens and picket fences rather than in the old large clan homes. A large school and a huge carpenter's gothic church were built by Indian workers, the wood for church, houses and furniture being prepared at the village sawmill. There were rope-making and net-making shops, a co-operative store and eventually a trading schooner, so that—with its crops and its fish—the community was almost self-supporting. Its people dressed like respectable English workingmen, and Bishop Bompas, visiting the village, was amazed at their neatness and how well they kept their clothes. There was a police force, and a lockup under the bandstand, for Duncan was also busily substituting western forms of leisure activity for native ones, and the Tsimshian quickly showed a predilection for brass bands. No winter dances were performed, at least openly, at Metlakatla, and other native celebrations—all of which Duncan regarded as games of the devil—were forbidden.

The community at Metlakatla came to an end through a theological point that arose over Duncan's strictness about pre-Christian ceremonial. He came to the conclusion that the Indians should not receive holy communion because the symbolic eating of the body of Christ would appear to them a form of the ritual cannibalism he was trying to root out. When a High Anglican bishop, William Ridley, arrived, conflict was inevitable; and rather than give in, Duncan departed in 1887 with 850 of his followers to found another industrial village, New Metlakatla, in Alaska. After his departure, the original Metlakatla was no longer self-sufficient, for there was nobody with the personal drive to keep it so.

Other Christian villages modelled on Metlakatla followed in the 1870s. The Anglican priest Robert Tomlinson founded such a community, called Aiyansh, among the Nishga on the Nass River in 1878. Round about the same time, at Sechelt, the Roman Catholics organized their own model village on a system developed by Bishop Durieu of New Westminster. Like the people of Metlakatla, the Salish of Sechelt built a new village of small houses for themselves, with a splendid church, and like William Duncan, the Catholics forbade potlatches, native dances, gambling and shamanism. But, unlike him, they introduced the Indians to the traditional theatricality of Catholicism, with pageants and processions and passion plays. In a similar way the Methodist preacher Thomas Crosby succeeded with the Tsimshian clans Duncan had left behind at Port Simpson. A group of high-ranking Tsimshian chiefs had gone down to Victoria and been converted in a Methodist meeting hall. They asked for a missionary to be sent to them, and when they received Crosby as their teacher, they seem to have been delighted by the noisy emotionalism of the revivalist Christianity that Methodists were practising at the time. In a few years the old communal houses at Port Simpson, with their poles and handsome house fronts, had been abandoned, and the place had become, like Metlakatla, an industrial village of small houses dominated by a vast church, a school and a girls' home.

No mission village was permanently successful, though by the end of the nineteenth century virtually all the Indians of British Columbia had been at least nominally converted. Perhaps more important in their lasting influence were the residential schools, which all the major sects, Catholics and Anglicans, Methodists and Presbyterians, operated in eventual co-operation with the various federal agencies dealing with Indians. Taking the children at the ages when they would be most impressionable and in most circumstances be learning from their parents how to live traditionally off the land, the residential schools not only attempted to instil the occupational patterns of modern European society but also tried to root out all vestiges of traditional living, so that there were many schools where only English was allowed as a language of conversation and children were punished for speaking to each other in Haida or Salish or whatever their real language might be.

Yet there was a notable ambivalence to the position of the missionaries. Most of the whites in British Columbia in the 1860s, whether American or other, were racists in the sense that they believed Caucasians were intrinsically superior to Blacks, Chinese or Indians. Central to the missionary outlook was the idea of redemption, which proclaimed that any person—of whatever race—was eligible for salvation and hence potentially the equal of other Christians. The impediments to that equality were those of belief and custom, and once the Indian had given up pagan ways and accepted the ways of the Christian world, all distinction vanished; the convert became the brother or sister of all other Christians. Some of the most interesting passages of the life of a man like Duncan are those in which we see him standing as champion for the rights of the Indians who had shown their trust in him.

Like Begbie, Duncan recognized that the land question lay at the heart of the Indians' predicament as they moved from their old life—the prosperous, primitive world of fishing or hunting—into an uncertain future dominated by land-hungry whites who had no understanding of the native peoples and their needs. He argued that the lands over which the Indians had in the past hunted and gathered berries, the waters in which they had fished, were God-given; they belonged to the native peoples by a kind of divine right and should not be alienated. He found white men difficult to persuade. He did recruit the Marquess of Dufferin on his side, when the latter—as governor general—visited Metlakatla in 1876. At a banquet in Victoria, Dufferin reproached the British Columbians for their lack of sympathy for the Indians, and he was quickly shown that his intervention was unwelcome.

After Duncan's departure to Alaska, other missionaries encouraged the Indians in demanding their lands and rights, and one of the most militant land rights movements in Canada emerged on the remote Nass River at this time, largely owing to the influence of early Anglican missionaries like Robert Tomlinson and J. B. McCullagh.

Apartheid—Canadian Style

The entry of British Columbia into Confederation brought a new element, that of bureaucratic organization, into the relations between the native peoples and the white intruders. It took a decade and a half, until the mid-1880s, for the Indian and the non-Indian populations to balance each other as the native peoples steadily declined. The transfer from colonial to dominion government meant a change in the status of the Indians and in the administration of their affairs, which was complicated by the rival jurisdictions and somewhat different aims of the federal and provincial governments.

Except for Manitoba, several times smaller than its present extent, the vast area of Rupert's Land was formed into the Northwestern Territories and ruled from Ottawa by the Department of the Interior as if it were a colony. The land was regarded as belonging to the dominion, and the Indians became dominion wards after a series of treaties in which they gave up aboriginal title to their lands and agreed to live on reserves: it was an early form of *apartheid*. A branch of the Department of the Interior dealt with Indian affairs from 1873 to 1880, when it became a separate Department of Indian Affairs, which dealt so inefficiently with the problems of Indian distress caused by the death of the bison herds that it helped to provoke the rebellion of the prairie Indians and the Métis in 1885.

In British Columbia, the situation at the time of the colony's entry into Confederation was complicated by the fact that crown lands belonged to the province and not to the federal government. The treaties made by the dominion authorities in the prairies had proceeded on the assumption that, though the land in theory belonged to the crown, an aboriginal title existed which had to be wiped out by treaty. In spite of Governor Douglas's few small treaties in the 1850s, the colonial authorities in British Columbia had gone on the assumption that no such thing as aboriginal right existed. There was no colonial legislation regarding Indian affairs, and no treaty was made since the 1850s, though in practice the Indian possession of the small areas around their villages was respected.

Under the British North America Act, once British Columbia had entered Confederation, the administration of the Indians became the responsibility of the dominion government; eight Indian agencies were established on the coast and in the southern part of the province, and British Columbia became the only province with a commissioner of Indian affairs, a post given to Dr. I. W. Powell, who had been one of Macdonald's local contacts during the pre-Confederation period.

Almost immediately the federal authorities and their provincial counterparts fell out over the question of Indian lands. In finally marking out the reserves, the federal representatives wished to give the Indians more land than they already had, and the provincial representatives wanted to reduce even the small existing reserves. A Joint Commission on Indian Reserves was appointed in 1876, but it made such slow progress that David Mills, then the minister of the interior, telegraphed to Powell in August 1877:

> Indian rights to soil in British Columbia have never been extinguished. Should any difficulty occur, steps will be taken to maintain the Indian claims to all the country where rights have not been extinguished by treaty. Don't desire to raise the question at present but Local Government must instruct Commissioners to make reserves as large as to completely satisfy Indians.

The Indians would never be completely satisfied. The federal government during the 1870s and 1880s had too many other problems with its new province to press very hard on Indian rights, and only in 1924 did both governments ratify the last of a series of commission reports; the land question was settled so far as the two levels of government were concerned. It left the 189 bands of Indians in the province with 1,620 small reserves totalling about 840,000 acres (340 000 ha), roughly one three-hundredths of the province's area.

The largest single blow to the traditional native cultures of British Columbia came with the amendments to the Indian Act in 1884. Impressed by the missionaries and the Indian agents who represented the various kinds of Indian feasts as profligate occasions that prevented the Indians from learning the Victorian virtues of thrift and frugality, the federal government introduced a clause outlawing these vitally important ceremonies, the potlatches and winter dances of the northern peoples, the spirit dances of the Salish. The Indians protested, and Judge Begbie did his best by disallowing the law as it was first drafted. But the bureaucrats made a revised law that Begbie could not overthrow, and it remained on the statute books until 1951, when it was quietly dropped for a new Indian Act. The law was never completely successful. Clandestine potlatches and dance gatherings were held in out-of-the-way places, but they were mostly small, furtive affairs, and these evasions or defiances could not halt the decline of ceremonial life and the decay of the social order that followed it. Before the end of the nineteenth century the great Coast Indian tradition seemed dead.

It was at this point—the last quarter of the century—that a new wave of white intruders entered the scene: the ethnologists, half-scholars and half-plunderers, began to haunt the Indian villages, putting into their notes and books the detritus of a declining culture as old men told it haltingly through interpreters, and acquiring the surviving artifacts for transfer to museums and private collections around the world. Some of them stooped to theft, others misunderstood what they were told, yet they preserved fine works of art that would otherwise have been destroyed or have decayed, and they delineated—like Homer writing when Mycenae and Troy were mere memories—the traditions of an extraordinary civilization blossoming briefly out of the stone age. For that we must be thankful to the great travelling scholars like Franz Boas and Marius Barbeau, to whom we owe so much we know about this dying splendid culture.

XII

From Canada to the Pacific

A Political Breach of Promise

British Columbians entered the confederation of Canada with an eye to the main chance. They were members of a community in crisis; the prosperity flowing from the gold rushes had dwindled, and a diminishing white population hung on in the surviving but shrinking communities. The undulating pattern of mining, rush followed by recession, had led to chronic business instability. And nothing by 1871 had yet replaced gold as an effective stimulus to the nascent economy or as a lasting means of attracting population. In 1867 Governor Seymour had correctly seen the widespread British Columbian interest in Confederation as "the expression of a despondent community looking for change," and the despondence was hardly diminished by the news of the celebrations with which the new dominion was being hailed in Ontario, and to a lesser extent in Quebec.

What British Columbia needed, to solve both the fiscal problems of the government and the economic difficulties of the colony in general, was the means of emerging from an isolation in which its principal trading partners were California, the Oregon Territory and the Sandwich Islands. Such emergence required the development of better means of transportation than the sea routes around Cape Horn and the primitive land routes that then existed into Washington Territory. And it was for the possibility of linking up with a larger economy which would activate their own that the British Columbians grasped at the straw of a union with Canada, which would offer them merely a wagon road on which traffic might move slowly to Lake Superior.

All this was expressed by the level-headed Dr. Helmcken during the legislative council's 1870 debate on Confederation, when he said that sentiment should not enter into the argument, for "love of Canada has to be acquired by the prosperity of the country." By "the country" he meant British Columbia. And he added, in tones that were to echo for decades afterwards: "No union between this Colony and Canada can permanently exist, unless it be to the material and pecuniary advantage of this Colony to remain in the Union."

As much was understood by Anthony Musgrave, the new governor, who soon formed the opinion that "the matter of communication" was the crucial question, since that would relieve the colonists' sense of isolation and hold out a promise of economic growth. In the spring of 1870, after he had finally won over the legislative council to considering entry into Canada, but before discussions opened between the colonial delegates and the dominion ministers, he wrote to the colonial secretary, Lord Granville:

> If a Railway would be promised, scarcely any other question would be allowed to be a difficulty. Without the certainty of overland communications through British territory within a reasonable time, I am not confident that even if all other stipulations are conceded, the Community will decide upon Union.

Granville must have passed this opinion to Macdonald, for, as we have seen, the appropriate gift was offered at the appropriate time, with what degree of sincerity we shall never know. Certainly before that promise of a transcontinental railway was made, it was only with misgivings that the legislative council drew its debate on Confederation to a close in May 1870. Dr. J. S. Helmcken reflected the opinions of many of his fellow citizens when he discussed the prospect of a taxation system directed from central Canada and applied to the Pacific coast colony.

> Anything that deprives this Colony of the power of protecting the local industries and interests of the Colony, and of regulating and fostering its commerce and trade, cannot be otherwise than dangerous and injurious to the country.

De Cosmos, the leading popular advocate of Confederation, had by now developed enough distrust of the way events were shaping to make his celebrated remark:

> I would not object to a little revolution now and again in British Columbia, after Confederation, if we were treated unfairly; for I am one of those who believe that political hatreds attest the vitality of the state.

And, indeed, if British Columbia never broke into revolution, it came very near to rebellion in the first years of its participation in the experiment of Canadian federation.

The terms of the union, as tentatively agreed on by the British Columbian delegation and the Canadian ministers, included a provision for the dominion to take over the colony's debt, and for the new province to be granted an annual subsidy of $216,000, which included $100,000 per annum for the grant "in trust" of the equivalent of a 20-mile (32-km) belt on each side of a proposed railway. But it was the promise of a railway that really decided the British Columbians to accept the terms of Confederation. True, Dr. Helmcken, who had an inclination to brood uneasily over the future, remarked that if the railway were not in fact completed within ten years, the people of British Columbia might not only have reason to complain and ask for compensation; they might even think they had a reason to secede.

In that moment of euphoria, nobody listened to him. But in fact the next decade and more were to be occupied politically with the difficulties caused by that extraordinary undertaking on the part of a new nation with about three and a half million people, to build a railway line through thousands of miles of virtually uninhabited muskeg, mountain and prairie, so as to link up with a community of barely more than ten thousand white people. Economically, socially, demographically, British Columbia would virtually stagnate over the first decade and a half of its life in Canada. The fluctuations of the mining economy would continue, other extractive industries would grow slowly for lack of easily available markets, towns would vegetate, and the population by the census of 1881 would be (Indians included) a mere 49,000, just over a third more than in 1871.

But if other things went slowly, the political passions of white British Columbians ran high in these years after entry into the dominion. Signs of trouble first appeared when the agreement on Confederation, which the colony had already accepted, went for ratification to the Canadian Parliament. Its terms—and particularly the railway clause—were repudiated by the Liberal opposition, but there were also Ontario Tory MPs who rather realistically were anxious about being trapped into a commitment to build the railway in a set period.

The debate in Ottawa began on 1 April 1871, and Joseph Trutch returned to Ottawa, ostensibly to make sure that the terms of union went through without alteration as the British Columbians had passed them. But when Trutch met the members of the Tory caucus in a closed meeting, he apparently set their minds at rest. What Trutch said in the closed caucus can be inferred from the speech he made as guest of honour at the Ottawa banquet held on 10 April to celebrate the entry of British Columbia into the Canadian union. He assured his audience the British Columbians were such a reasonable people that, although they had been promised a railway in ten years' time, it would be a "fallacy which cannot bear the mark of common sense" to assume that they would expect the railway promise "to be carried out in the exact interpretation of the words themselves, regardless of all circumstances."

Trutch's act of weakness, folly or self-interest was received angrily in British Columbia, and the incident made it obvious to many people on the West Coast that, while the Canadians had accepted the letter of the terms of union, they had not committed themselves to the spirit. But the old office-holder got the reward he expected when he was appointed lieutenant-governor of British Columbia, for it was he who was given the post that many thought should have gone to Amor De Cosmos.

Later in 1871 the province of British Columbia elected the six members who would represent it in the House of Commons, and the twenty-five members of the provincial legislative assembly, which now became an entirely representative body. There were as yet no political parties, though in practice the six British Columbian MPs began by supporting Macdonald and his Conservatives. In the provincial assembly, the old division between appointed officials and elected representatives was replaced by a shifting pattern of factions, in which Vancouver Island interests (particularly in matters such as the terminus of the new railway) competed with mainland interests, while up-island Nanaimo showed the same kind of difference in viewpoint from Victoria as interior Cariboo did from river-mouth New Westminster.

At first it seemed doubtful whether responsible government was yet really recognized. Trutch used his prerogative as lieutenant-governor in 1871 to pick as the first premier of British Columbia an obscure and uninspired lawyer, John Foster McCreight, and during McCreight's brief incumbency, Trutch insisted on sitting in on the cabinet meetings. When McCreight ceased to be premier at the end of 1872, Trutch had no alternative but to call on De Cosmos to form a government. De Cosmos refused to carry on cabinet business until the lieutenant-governor left the room, and at this point British Columbia gained effective responsible government.

After being the most passionate British Columbian advocate of entry into the Dominion of Canada, it was the ironic fate of Amor De Cosmos to find himself, once that union had been achieved, becoming the spokesman for provincial discontent. British Columbia had been waiting since the summer of 1871 for some sign that work on the railway really would start within two years of the union. The railway was important to the province's citizens not merely in ultimate terms as a means of communication with central and eastern Canada; long before a train ran through the Rockies to the coast, construction work would immediately revive the sagging economy. But July 1873 came and went, and all British Columbia received from Ottawa were the annual subsidies and the Tory political appointees sent out to take over the posts of former colonial officials. A sod lifted symbolically at Esquimalt had been the only evidence of railway construction.

De Cosmos realized that the commencement of the railway was the province's first priority, and for this reason he considered it important to apply as much pressure as possible on Ottawa. He became virtually an absentee premier, with the attorney general, his old associate George Anthony Walkem, carrying on the actual business of provincial government, while De Cosmos tried to further British Columbia's interests in Ottawa. The province protested in the summer of 1873 over the delays in construction, but by now Macdonald was in deep political trouble over the Pacific Scandal, which drove him temporarily from office.

In November 1873 the province renewed its protest, and Alexander Mackenzie, now prime minister, replied by expressing a desire to change the terms of union so far as the railway clause was concerned. Any talk of changing the terms of union seemed to the increasingly restive British Columbians a betrayal of their interests, and De Cosmos himself would soon become the undeserving victim of their passionate feelings.

For some time in Ottawa he had been trying to get a better deal on several items in the terms that had no relation to the railroad. He had worked out with Macdonald's government an arrangement by which, instead of a guarantee of the cost of the graving dock at Esquimalt, the province would receive a cash grant, and by which a slight adjustment of the clause relating to the province's public debt would enable it to obtain an immediate loan of $1,000,000. Both arrangements favoured British Columbia, and Alexander Mackenzie, after coming into office, agreed to stand by them. In addition, De Cosmos had been in London, and while the prime minister and the colonial secretary had evaded seeing him for fear of being involved in the railway controversy, he had met Goschen, the first lord of the Admiralty, and had come away with a promise of $30,000 in cash towards the graving dock.

De Cosmos returned to Victoria to find that in January 1874 the assembly had passed a further resolution calling on the dominion government to honour the terms of Confederation. Nevertheless, on 3 February, Walkem introduced into the assembly a bill providing for changes in the terms as they affected the graving dock and the public debt. But the suggestion of changing the terms of union in any way now enraged the citizens of Victoria, and while the assembly was still debating the bill on 7 February, a public meeting passed resolutions declaring it inadvisable to enter into undertakings regarding the graving dock and the provincial debt until the Mackenzie government made clear its intention regarding the railway, and expressing opposition to any amendment of the terms of union by the provincial government "until the same shall have been submitted to the people for adoption."

Then the news reached the meeting that at this moment the debate in the assembly was reaching a crucial point. Speakers suggested that the popular resolutions should be presented immediately at the bar of the house, and the audience, some eight hundred people, surged excitedly from the hall. They gathered supporters on the way until (according to some reports) two thousand people, led by local dignitaries, marched over the James Street Bridge and invaded the Birdcages. Though Helmcken later declared that he had accompanied the mob merely in the hope of tempering its anger, there were witnesses who claimed that it was he who led the demonstrators in the chant "We'll hang old De Cosmos on a sour apple-tree" with which they thundered into the chamber. While the organizers of the meeting attempted to present their resolutions to the house, their followers jostled the members and the speaker, hurled insults at De Cosmos, calling him "tyrant" and "traitor," and, according to one report, "pistols were drawn and clubs flourished, but no one was injured."

The speaker left his chair, thereby adjourning the sitting of the house, and De Cosmos took refuge in his room until the demonstrators had departed. Had he been a man of ironic humour—which he was not—he might well have recollected his own fiery statement on the eve of the province's entry into Confederation. For he himself was now experiencing something that might well be called "a little revolution" in which he might see "political hatreds attest the vitality of the state."

British Columbians were in revolt because they felt they were being treated unfairly, but, of all people, it was against De Cosmos that they performed their "little revolution."

Two days later the assembly passed a resolution that was a virtual surrender to the mob. It declared that no change would be made in the railway clause without reference to the electorate. As for De Cosmos, he took advantage of a new law that prevented individuals from being members of the House of Commons and of a provincial assembly at the same time. He chose Ottawa, and George Anthony Walkem succeeded him as premier and leader of what had by now become a crusade against central Canadian perfidy. But it was a divided crusade, since two routes were still being considered: one to Bute Inlet, by connecting boat to Nanaimo, and thence by railway to Victoria; and another route through the Fraser Valley to a terminus on Burrard Inlet. Walkem allied himself with the Victoria merchants advocating the Bute Inlet route. A railway from Esquimalt to Nanaimo figured in both schemes, but the Vancouver Islanders were particularly concerned over whether it would really be the final stage of the transcontinental railway leading to a Victoria terminus, or whether it would be merely a local feeder line for a mainland railway.

At this point the imperial government ineffectually entered the scene. Gilbert Sproat, the agent-general for British Columbia in London, convinced Lord Carnarvon of the seriousness of the dispute between the dominion and the province. Carnarvon telegraphed Mackenzie on 17 July 1874, offering to arbitrate the dispute. At first Mackenzie refused to accept his offer, and even British Columbia delayed until 3 August to allow Walkem to make a final effort in Ottawa to resolve the impasse. Finally, Mackenzie intimated that, even if he would not accept binding arbitration because that would represent undue imperial interference, he would accept terms suggested by Carnarvon as the basis for an agreement. The result was the egregious compromise known as the Carnarvon Terms, a travesty of the original terms of union.

The Carnarvon Terms provided for an immediate start on the Esquimalt to Nanaimo Railway on Vancouver Island as a gesture of good will, and for active surveys to begin on the mainland. A wagon road and telegraph line were to be built rapidly from Red River to the Pacific coast, and no less than $2,000,000 a year was to be spent on railway construction. But the Carnarvon Terms did not contemplate the railway being built even as far west as Fort William on Lake Superior before 1890, and no date was even suggested for the completion of the line as far as western salt water.

At first Mackenzie seemed inclined to accept, and at this point British Columbia might have done so. But the prime minister was in fact facing a double opposition: the reinvigorated Tories outside his party, and within it the faction headed by the mercurial and eloquent Edward Blake, which opposed any work, for the time being, on the transcontinental railway and was willing to accept British Columbia's secession if that were the consequence. And so, though he gave an ap-

pearance of accepting the terms, Mackenzie imperilled their achievement by in-
sisting that there must be no increase in taxation as a result of railway work. Still,
he did bring special legislation to the House of Commons in March 1875 providing for the construction of the Esquimalt and Nanaimo Railway, but couched in
such a way that it would be regarded as local work and not necessarily as part of
the transcontinental railroad. He managed to get the bill past the Commons in
spite of Blake's heated protests, but the Senate took what Blake said to heart and
rejected it; Mackenzie had too much fear for the unity of his party to reintroduce
the bill. Instead, he accepted an order in council drafted by Blake and dated 20
September 1875, which provided for a cash bonus of $750,000 to be paid to the
province for the delay in building the transcontinental railway.

It was never stated, when the minute containing the order in council belatedly
reached British Columbia on 10 November, whether the compensation would be
for past or future delay, but Walkem and his government were shrewd enough to
realize that if they accepted the grant it would be interpreted as meaning that the
dominion's responsibility was liquidated. Accordingly, in January 1876 the assembly rejected the proposition; on 10 January a resolution was passed calling for the
province's secession from Canada.

Shortly afterwards, in March, De Cosmos kept the fires of controversy burning
by proposing in the Commons an amendment to the motion to go into the committee of supply; he moved that, since in 1871 Canada had pledged to British Columbia to start on the railway by 1873, and in 1874 Mackenzie had agreed in principle to the Carnarvon Terms, and neither undertaking had been filled, the house
was of the opinion that in 1876 work must begin on the railway in the West, by
which he meant the Esquimalt and Nanaimo. Apart from the six British Columbian MPs, only four members voted for the resolution; it was a sign of how little
importance was attached by the central Canadian MPs to an apparently binding
obligation to a weak and remote community on an ocean few of them had ever
seen.

By this time Walkem's frustrated administration had been defeated at the polls,
to be replaced in 1876 by that of Andrew Charles Elliott, a former stipendiary
magistrate. Elliott was no more successful than his predecessor in gaining better
terms from Ottawa, and when the Marquess of Dufferin visited the province in the
spring of 1876, on the first viceregal visit west of the Rockies, he found the mood
of the people desperate and truculent. More than once he refused to proceed under welcoming arches that carried messages threatening secession. But his efforts
to smooth over the situation were fruitless, since Mackenzie was too aware of
Blake's rising power in the Liberal party to make any of the concessions that would
satisfy the British Columbian voters.

The situation continued through 1877, but in the spring of 1878 the growing
desperation of people beyond the Rockies demanded expression, and found it in
various ways. On 10 May, De Cosmos rose in the House of Commons to reproach
the government for ignoring the economic potentialities of British Columbia; he
declared that if the transcontinental railway were not started quickly, there would

be no alternative for British Columbia but to seek annexation to the United States. Since De Cosmos detested the Americans, this dramatic statement was clearly meant to mirror the anger stirring in British Columbian minds, an anger that in the following month would lead to the voters' rejection of the Elliott government and its replacement by a new Walkem administration pledged to a hard line towards the federal government. The hard line quickly softened.

On 9 August 1878, Walkem rose in the assembly and moved an address to the queen, which listed the breaches of the terms of union on the part of the Canadian government. The motion asked that, in view of such flagrant breaches of contract, "British Columbia should hereafter have the right to exclusively control her Customs and Excise and to withdraw from the union," as well as the right to compensation from the defaulting dominion.

The motion was passed by 14 votes to 9. But, having made their defiant gesture, Walkem and his associates did not appear to know what they should do to implement it. Instead of making sure the address to the queen was transmitted directly to the imperial government, which would have assured action by an alarmed Colonial Office, they sent it to the federal secretary of state in Ottawa for transmission to Westminster. It arrived in the interval between the defeat of Mackenzie's government in the elections of October 1878, and Macdonald's resumption of power and his launching of the National Policy, in which the railway to the Pacific was a major plank. It was mislaid, perhaps deliberately, and surfaced only some months later; in the meantime Walkem's government did nothing to reinforce its gesture. Clearly these gentlemen were little more than political posturers with none of the spirit of "a little revolution now and again" that De Cosmos had once evoked, and none of the militancy the Victoria protesters had shown when they invaded the legislature in 1873 and stopped the government agreeing to any changes in the terms of union. Walkem and his associates had a just cause; they did nothing to sustain it, or, more likely, they were unwilling to match their actions with their words.

By the time the secession resolution came to the surface in Ottawa, it could safely be ignored on all sides, since the Macdonald government had decided to start work on the railway and to proceed with it as quickly as possible. It was left for De Cosmos to provide a suitably bizarre coda to the frustrating early years of British Columbia's existence as a province of Canada. In April 1879 he rose to move in the House of Commons a resolution providing for the province to be severed from the dominion.

He must have arranged the quixotic little drama beforehand, since none of his fellow members from the province rose to second his motion. Thus he was able facetiously to express his pleasure at being unsupported by those hostile members who in the past had been so free in expressing their willingness to get rid of the Pacific province.

That province has been called an excrescence, an incubus, has been accused of endeavouring to gain something from this Dominion without any equivalent. I ask the

honourable members to say they wish to get rid of this province, to second the
motion.

And he added bitterly: "The people of British Columbia have as little faith in one
side as they had in the other."

At Home in the 1870s

The matter of the railway promises that did not materialize occupied the minds of
British Columbian politicians in the 1870s, yet there were political developments
in other directions that were largely a consequence of the entry of British Columbia into Canada. This was not an age when governmental intervention, except in
terms of railway subsidies, was greatly favoured, and the changeover from a colonial to a provincial status was marked mainly by alteration in the means of government control and in the way such control was implemented. For the first years,
the court system remained very close to that which Begbie and Cameron had established in British Columbia and on Vancouver Island respectively, and the provincial police derived from that which Chartres Brew had originally organized,
though in the realm of law administration the federal presence was dramatically
declared by the fortresslike penitentiary erected in 1878, overlooking the Fraser
River at New Westminster. The customs and excise duties were now collected by
federal officials, and as yet there was no income tax for anybody to collect. As in
colonial days, road construction and maintenance remained a major concern of
the local government, not only because communication had to be established
with new mining areas (particularly those near the American border) but also because it was a good source of employment in hard times and of patronage always.
Even so, nothing as ambitious as the Cariboo Road was built during the 1870s,
since so much was being expected of the new railway.

The welfare state was still, of course, far away, except in the minds of the province's few early socialists. The one area in which the social responsibility of government did receive some attention was education. In the first colonial days, the
responsibility of the state to provide schools was acknowledged in the establishment with public funds of Craigflower School in 1854 and of the Colonial School
in Victoria shortly after. The idea of creating a universal education system for the
colony, with some kind of centralized control, had emerged already in the colonial
legislation of 1865 and 1869 which vested authority in the governor-in-council.
After Confederation the trend towards complete regulation of local education was
accelerated by the appointment of a board of education and of John Jessop as first
provincial superintendent of schools. Jessop, who would fall a prey to political
intrigues and lose his job by 1878, was a man of notable vision, who in 1872
brought in a public education act that has influenced the British Columbian
school system ever since; it was modelled on the School Act with which in the
preceding year Egerton Ryerson had created in Ontario at least the promise of free
universal education.

Jessop's aims ran high, and in 1877, just after the province's first high school (the Central School) had been established in Victoria, he was already looking forward, in a province of about 45,000 people of all origins, towards a more ambitious goal:

> A provincial University also will speedily become a necessity if British Columbia youth are to be prepared for the various avocations of youth without going to the other Provinces for the purpose of graduating in Arts, Law and Science.

The reality of the educational situation was that schools and schooling were subject to the succession of depressions and booms that marked an economy so much dependent on mining; in 1872 the public schools of Victoria had actually closed down for lack of ready funds. In 1876, when the economic situation seemed brighter, the construction of the Central School, with its enrolment of seven hundred students, was regarded as heralding the end of the era of one-room schools, but by 1878 the Central School was itself running out of funds and a special poll tax had to be levied to keep it going.

The situation of the schools reflected the economic insecurity of the province during its first years of existence while it awaited the railway, which would provide immediate employment and stimulate the industrial life of a province that as yet had scanty connection with the potential markets for its products.

But there were some significant shifts in the industrial pattern during the 1870s. Mining had already declined by the time the province was founded, and its exports in 1871 were a mere $1,400,000 in comparison with the $4,000,000 officially reported as being exported in 1867, and there would not be an appreciable increase in earnings or the number of people it employed until the discovery in 1882 of the Blue Bell lead and silver mine opened the base metal rush to the Kootenays. In 1871 about 2,300 people were engaged in mining, and about 2,500 in 1882; they included the colliers of Vancouver Island.

Agriculture developed slowly during the decade up to 1881, and though the Oblate fathers had already started the first orchard in the Okanagan Valley in 1862, fruit growing did not become important until the late years of the nineteenth century. Farming in the 1870s was still mainly concentrated in the lower Fraser Valley and the southern end of Vancouver Island, where dairying and mixed farming flourished, and in the Kamloops area and the southern Cariboo, where ranching was slowly expanding. Markets in the interior had shrunk with the decline of Barkerville, but an export trade persisted with Alaska, the Sandwich Islands and the western United States. In 1871 the number of people engaged in various kinds of farming was about 2,800, somewhat more than in mining.

William Hankey, a fur trader with the HBC, recognized the farming possibilities of the valleys of the Skeena, Nass and Stikine, where the summer is short but hot and admirable for growing potatoes, hay, vegetables and small fruit, and where the grazing lands are extensive. Shortly after his arrival, he left the Hudson's Bay Company to break land in the place he called Hazelton, where in 1871 Thomas Dewdney laid out a townsite. Hazelton sprang into life at the end of the 1890s when the Yukon Telegraph was being built and operated through northern British Columbia to Dawson City. It was the head of steam navigation on the Skeena and served as a depot where the paddleboats deposited their cargoes, which pack trains would distribute to the telegraph constructors and operators, and also to the scattered mines that still operated in the Omineca region.

Logging, which would become the dominant staple of British Columbian industry, still operated on a relatively minor scale, with little demand for lumber in the stagnating local towns, though there was already an export trade on which the Burrard Inlet mills depended; in all there were twenty-seven sawmills, employing about four hundred people.

The industry that had moved forward surprisingly was commercial fishing. From Confederation until 1923 the Indians were forbidden to fish commercially, and this meant that a white man's industry, which the Japanese would later penetrate, developed; it was largely linked to the appearance of the fish canneries. Farmers living in the Fraser delta began experimenting with canning late in the 1860s, and the first actual canneries, like that operated by Thomas Ladner near the community that bears his name, were in operation by the mid-1870s. Since the Fraser was the major route for the migration of the various species of Pacific salmon, it remained the principal centre of commercial fishing and canning, but by the end of the 1870s the first canneries were being established on the inlets and the salmon rivers of northern British Columbia, and particularly on the Skeena and Nass, which were navigable a good way up from their estuaries. In the beginning most of the fishing was done close to the canneries, by oared skiffs dragging gillnets across the stream. Later, steam tenders picked up catches and towed the skiffs out to fishing grounds farther away. It was a primitive, labour-intensive operation, but no more so than the process of canning itself, where everything from the butchering of the fish to the making of cans was done by hand. The mechanization of the industry would come later, under the stimulus of international demand for Canadian salmon in the 1890s. According to the figures of the time, about 2,800 workers were employed, but this did not include the cannery workers, of whom over 1,000 were included among the 2,900 industrial workers noted in the 1881 census.

It was a very mixed labour force that operated these early industries. In 1881 there were 25,981 Indians in a population of 49,459; still a majority, but by now a passive one. There were 19,548 Caucasians and blacks, including women and children, as against 4,350 Chinese, almost entirely male. The Chinese worked on farms and ranches and in mining—particularly the coal mines around Nanaimo. Some became cooks and domestic servants and others ran small businesses like laundries, but the merchants of any consequence were to be found within the Chinese communities, mainly in Victoria. Many of these Chinese belonged to a new wave of immigrants brought in by labour contractors from Kwang Tung in the

1870s. The Indians were less adaptable than the Chinese and slower to abandon their traditional way of life or find a place for themselves in the white industrial world, but by the end of the 1870s some of them were working in sawmills or as cowboys on ranches, and many were taking seasonal employment in fish canneries, which for a long time remained a customary Indian occupation.

For the rest, there were the slowly growing white-collar occupations followed by the whites—and occasionally blacks—who inhabited the residential areas appearing around Victoria and New Westminster. A province-wide scattering of clergymen and missionaries; a small medical profession with links to the new hospitals in Victoria and New Westminster; a growing legal profession hanging shingles even in the smaller towns. Entry into Canada had meant an immediate increase in that business of government which was to become such an important staple of Victoria's economy, particularly as British Columbians began to learn the fine art of patronage from their federal counterparts. The Birdcages began to fill with provincial bureaucrats and clerks, so that by the 1890s the need for more elaborate governmental installations would make itself felt. And there was already, in a Victoria that by 1881 had grown again to a population of seven thousand, a considerable commercial element in which, as in all imperial possessions, the line of social acceptability was sharply drawn between wholesale commerce and retail trade. Only wholesale merchants and professional people with the right racial credentials were likely to be invited to Government House or to be elected to the Union Club, which was founded in 1879. As the nomadic democracy of the gold rush era faded out, the social structure defined itself in ways that would have been acceptable in Cape Town or Calcutta, in Singapore or Sydney, but were already outdated in a London where the Prince of Wales was letting the bounders in.

The Railway Achieved

In the elections of 1878, which his party won without difficulty, Sir John A. Macdonald was surprisingly defeated in his home town of Kingston, and the people of Victoria found him a safe seat in their city, with the evident hope that this would improve the chances of a transcontinental railway being built quickly and of Victoria becoming its terminus.

But Macdonald and his government were committed to nothing but building the railway as quickly as possible. A great many of the preparatory surveys had in fact been carried out under the supervision of Sandford Fleming, who had been appointed chief engineer for the dominion in 1871, and in 1872 had taken an initial journey across the continent, with the Rev. George Monro Grant in his entourage, who wrote that classical description of western Canada in the 1870s, *Ocean to Ocean.*

Even so, the route had not been finally decided, nor had the syndicate that would build the main part of the Canadian Pacific Railway and finally operate it been formed, when work began at Yale on 14 May 1880, as the American contractor Andrew Onderdonk began to blast a railbed through the difficult stretches of the Fraser Canyon. Onderdonk had been given a contract to build merely 128 miles (206 km) of track from Emory's Bar near Yale to Savona near Kamloops, but the resources needed were immense and the effect on the local economy was immediate.

Yale, which had lived in near hibernation as a way station on the Cariboo Road, suddenly sprang awake as workers streamed into the community, and hotels, restaurants, stores and brothels were quickly established. Not merely was it the transshipment point for men and large quantities of goods coming upriver by steamboat; Onderdonk also manufactured his explosives there.

Onderdonk's bold and ruthless methods of construction needed vast supplies of manpower, and the pool of local unemployed merely filled the edge of his demand. The wharves and backstreets of San Francisco were combed clear of possible workers, and a fine collection of semiderelicts was shipped northward, but Onderdonk's needs remained unsatisfied, and in the spring of 1881 he brought in two thousand labourers from China. Eventually, out of the thirteen thousand men who worked on the line between Yale and Savona, nine thousand were Chinese, and their presence would become a sore political issue.

Of more immediate significance was the controversy that blew up in British Columbia over the place where the railway, so long desired, was actually under construction. For the choice of Yale as the starting point for construction meant that the Fraser Valley had finally been picked as the route by which the new railway would reach the Pacific.

It was the conclusion of a debate that had been going on for most of the 1870s over the possible western terminus of the transcontinental railway. Port Simpson, near the site of Prince Rupert (which later became the terminus of the Grand Trunk Pacific), was considered, but rejected because it might be vulnerable to growing Russian naval strength in the Pacific. Commercial interests in Victoria favoured a route that would follow the way planned for Alfred Waddington's ill-fated wagon road in the 1860s over the Chilcotin plateau to Bute Inlet. From Bute Inlet either a ferry, or possibly even an audaciously designed bridge, could carry trains to Vancouver Island, and the Esquimalt and Nanaimo Railway would lead them to a terminus near Victoria. But it was finally the Fraser Valley route, with a terminus at Burrard Inlet, that was chosen, largely to compete with the Northern Pacific Railway being built on American territory to Puget Sound. Even after Onderdonk began his initial work, the route it would take through the Rockies was uncertain. Sandford Fleming had picked the northerly Yellowhead Pass, with its relatively low grades, that would later be used by the Canadian Northern as well as the Grand Trunk Pacific. It was only later, after William Van Horne was appointed general manager of the Canadian Pacific Railway, that the more audacious route through Kicking Horse Pass and Rogers Pass, was chosen as a result of the surveying work by Major Rogers in 1881 and 1882; it would be completed not by Onderdonk or another contractor but by the Canadian Pacific syndicate itself.

Macdonald disappointed the expectations of his Victoria constituents by withdrawing his half-promise to make the Esquimalt and Nanaimo Railway a terminal link in the Canadian Pacific, and the beginning of construction at Yale angered the provincial assembly, with its dominant combination of Vancouver Island and Cariboo interests. Walkem himself went to Ottawa in the summer and again in the winter of 1880 to try and get assurances over the island railway. He failed completely and returned to Victoria to renew the separatist strategy. In March 1881 he introduced into the assembly yet another petition to the queen, demanding as a minimum the fulfilment of the Carnarvon Terms; it was passed by an unaccustomed majority of 20 to 4. This time Amor De Cosmos was deputed to take it to London, and the new governor general, the Marquess of Lorne, was sufficiently impressed by the urgency of the situation and the reality of the threat of secession to urge on the incumbent colonial secretary, Lord Kimberley, the need to find a way of ensuring that no difficulty would occur in the completion of such a vital artery of the empire.

De Cosmos arrived in London, where he seemed to Kimberley "a fearfully tedious man"; nevertheless he gained some concessions. The dominion government would provide at least a light railway on the island, the main railway would be extended to tidewater at the head of Burrard Inlet, and the $750,000 promised as compensation would indeed be paid. The $750,000 was duly paid, together with a further federal grant of $250,000 towards the dry dock at Esquimalt, but the railway on Vancouver Island fell into trouble on both sides. George Stephen, on behalf of the Canadian Pacific Railway, refused to undertake any railway building on Vancouver Island, though the stretch down the Fraser Valley from Yale to Port Moody was started. The Vancouver Islanders, considering that a light railway was below the dignity of the province's capital city, were so angry at this suggestion that later in 1882 the legislature committed what a delighted Macdonald described as "the insane action" of cancelling the arrangement by which the dominion would build the island railway. The Esquimalt and Nanaimo would finally be built between 1884 and 1886 by a consortium headed by Robert Dunsmuir, the Nanaimo coal magnate. To have a railway served Dunsmuir's mining interests, and at the same time he and his associates received not only as a cash bonus the $750,000 paid by the federal government in compensation for the lack of an island railroad, but also 2,000,000 acres (477 800 ha) of land in southwestern Vancouver Island. In the meantime, as part of a general settlement of differences in 1884, Macdonald picked as the dominion's railway land grant from the province the 3,500,000 rich farming acres (1 416 450 ha) of the Peace River Block; Macdonald had learnt how rough was the country through which the railway would pass in British Columbia, and he had no scruples about appropriating the province's only large area of good wheat-growing land.

The making of peace, mostly to the advantages of Ottawa and of the railroad and mining interests, was made possible by the removal from the scene of the two most obstinate advocates of regional interests. In May 1882, Macdonald adroitly elevated Walkem, a smalltown advocate of no great legal competence, to a seat in the supreme court. Two months later the electors of Victoria defeated De Cosmos, who was so shaken by the disloyalty of his fellow citizens that he never attempted to re-enter public life.

A new administration began in the province, under the premiership of Robert Beaven, the first of a series of politically weak leaders who would act as servants rather than as restrainers of the economic and political predators about to descend on the vast storehouse of natural resources that was British Columbia.

Meanwhile the construction of the railway went ahead, under the direction of that American expatriate of many talents, William Cornelius Van Horne, and did so with surprising speed in view of the recurrent financial crises that George Stephen and Donald Smith, as the railway's financial managers, had somehow to overcome. The need to suppress Gabriel Dumont's guerrillas during the Northwest Rebellion of 1885 led the government to offer a final life-saving guarantee when the Canadian Pacific consortium was on the edge of bankruptcy, and the work on the prairies and through the mountains continued with such speed that in August 1885 the new governor general, the Marquess of Lansdowne, travelled by rail to a spot 18 miles (29 km) east of Revelstoke; 47 miles (76 km) farther on, on the other side of the gap, he boarded a train that took him to the new settlement of Port Moody at the head of Burrard Inlet. Port Moody was only one of the communities the railway seeded as it traced its way southwestward across the province. Van Horne's choice of key railroad centres created towns in the heart of the wilderness, like Kamloops and Revelstoke and Golden, where before there had been only Indian villages, Hudson's Bay posts or mere trappers' cabins.

In November 1885 a special train of two coaches loaded with directors and officials of the CPR left Montreal bound for the Pacific. At Eagle Pass in the heart of the Monashee range between Revelstoke and Kamloops, they stopped to watch the last rail being laid on a wet autumnal day, after which Donald Smith, later Lord Strathcona, drove the last spike. A famous photograph survives and records the modesty of the occasion; a small crowd of workers gathers around a group of prosperous-looking men in top hats and bowlers, and a white-haired Donald Smith fragilely lifts a gandy dancer's hammer. No political dignitaries were invited, because Smith had made a lifelong enemy of Macdonald by voting against him in 1875 over the Pacific Scandal. Van Horne celebrated the occasion with a speech of lapidary brevity: "All that I have got to say is that the work was well done in every way." Afterwards the train continued to the coast and arrived quietly at Port Moody.

The celebrations were reserved for the arrival, more than six months later, of the first scheduled passenger train from Montreal, which reached Port Moody at a minute past noon on 4 July 1886. It was a Sunday, but sabbatarian scruples did not trouble the thousand people who had come from Victoria and New Westminster and Nanaimo to welcome a new era for the West. The Victoria Brass Band played, the members of a travelling Italian opera company rendered some arias, and William Smithe, the most recent in a series of short-term premiers, gave the welcoming speech. It seemed as though the future of the newly created city of Port Moody was assured as a major transport centre.

The Western Metropolis

In fact, by the time the first train drew into Port Moody, the future of the ambitious little community was already in doubt. Port Moody lay at the far, narrow end of Burrard Inlet, with not much level land around it, and the Canadian Pacific directors decided that they needed a large deep-sea port to receive vessels from Asia and thus fulfil the potentialities of their railway as an imperial route.

In 1884, Van Horne had declared his preference for Coal Harbour, adjacent to the First Narrows and named after the modest veins of lignite that had been found there, and already a busy spot. During the early 1860s, not long after Fitzgerald McCleery began to farm near the Fraser, three Englishmen (John Martin, William Hailstone and Sam Brighouse, later known as "the Three Greenhorns"), had registered a mining claim to the whole area south of Coal Harbour between present-day Burrard Street on the east and Stanley Park on the west; it became known as the Brickmakers' Claim, since instead of digging coal they dug clay and made the first bricks on the mainland.

A few years later there were developments eastward along the inlet. A corduroy trail called the Douglas Road was made in 1865 from New Westminster to Burrard Inlet, and beside the beach at the end of it, summer cottages were built and a Brighton Hotel with a steamboat landing. At the same time, close by, Edward Stamp began to build his Hastings Mill, which opened in 1867, with the Fraser River pilot Jack Deighton following not long after with his hotel and the little community called Gastown until it was politely renamed Granville. Meanwhile, Morton and Brighouse, the two Greenhorns still on the ground at Coal Harbour, laid out a plan for a "City of Liverpool." Neither Granville nor Liverpool seemed distinctive enough for Van Horne, and once he had decided on Coal Harbour as the site for his terminus and instructed CPR surveyor L. A. Hamilton to lay out a townsite in 1885, he decided to name it Vancouver, perhaps because in an oblique way this reflected his own Dutch ancestry and subtly commemorated him as well.

Vancouver Islanders were naturally annoyed, and Americans from Washington Territory were perplexed, since they had already their own Vancouver on the site of the old Hudson's Bay Company fort beside the Columbia. But neither of these considerations concerned Van Horne so much as the anger of the Port Moody speculators, who took action in the Supreme Court of British Columbia against the provincial government's grant of a right-of-way that would enable tracks to be laid to the new terminus. The British Columbia court rejected the plea, which Port Moody then carried to the Supreme Court of Canada, while Van Horne, confident of a favourable decision there, quietly laid track and began to construct a railway wharf. When a verdict favourable to the railway came down from the court, he speeded construction, and on 23 May 1887, the very eve of Queen Victoria's golden jubilee, the garlanded Engine 374 (which still survives in a Vancouver park) drew the first transcontinental train into the terminus.

Plenty of people were there to greet it, for no sooner had the townsite been laid out than land speculators, land buyers and businessmen began to move in. David and Isaac Oppenheimer, the San Francisco merchants who had already established themselves in Victoria and at Yale, bought land around the Hastings Mill. The two remaining Greenhorns still retained their 550-acre (223-ha) claim though their City of Liverpool had not begun to develop, and both Dr. Isaac Powell of Victoria and the New Westminster politician John Robson had bought up considerable lands in the area. Still, there was enough unpre-empted land for William Smithe's government to present 6,000 acres (2428 ha) adjacent to Coal Harbour to the willing CPR. Not be to outdone in gratitude, the Oppenheimer brothers, John Robson and other local speculators donated a third of their holdings to the railway that was about to make their fortunes.

The city was incorporated on 6 April 1886. Within two months a clapboard settlement of almost eight hundred buildings had sprung up, most of them business establishments, as well as residences, with a population of two thousand. Then, on 15 June, a land-clearing fire ran out of control, leapt from building to building, and burnt the new city to the ground in forty minutes with a loss of thirteen lives. The survivors found refuge in wells and in the Hastings Mill, on boats and rafts in the harbour, and next morning emerged to start rebuilding their young city. By the next year when the first train arrived, there were already five thousand inhabitants.

Three weeks later Vancouver's future as a great seaport began to take shape as the liner *Abyssinia* arrived on 14 June from Yokohama with a cargo of tea and silk and a complement of first-class passengers. The CPR had hired the ship and two other small liners from the Cunard Company to start its trans-Pacific route, but in 1891 the first of its own elegant clipper-lined Orient ships, *The Empress of Japan*, entered the harbour.

The growth of Vancouver was rapid and steady, and by 1889 it already had eight thousand inhabitants. Its first two mayors—the real estate agent M. A. McLean from 1886 to 1887 and David Oppenheimer from 1887 to 1892—worked energetically at providing the necessary facilities for a new city with metropolitan ambitions. Under McLean the city fathers had the foresight to petition the federal government for a lease of Coal Peninsula, the local military reserve. The request was granted in the form of a lease in perpetuity at $1 a year, and under Oppenheimer the decision was made to turn it into a park that would combine sea walks, gardens and natural forest. It was opened in 1888 by the incumbent governor general, Lord Stanley, after whom it was named. In a gesture quite exceptional in those imperial days, it was dedicated for the enjoyment of people of all races, colours and creeds.

Vancouver quickly developed the features of a modern city. Within two years it had waterworks and a sewage system and 36 miles (58 km) of roads had been made, many of them provided with sidewalks. There was a system of electric trams (the Vancouver Street Railway), and the Vancouver Transport Company built to New Westminster the first interurban railroad in Canada. Apart from the dozens of other hostelries that went up, the CPR built the first Hotel Vancouver (a mere four storeys in height), and the new Vancouver Opera House provided a setting for both local amateurs and visiting professionals in the musical and dramatic arts. With tax concessions and in other ways, the city set out to attract commerce and industry, and warehouses and factories, like the B.C. Sugar Refinery, were built on the waterfront. Entrepreneurs who had made money on the Fraser River paddleboats started freight and passenger lines like the Canadian Steam Navigation Company, which sent its boats up to the canneries and logging camps that were appearing all the way up the coast to the Alaskan border.

In a few years, by the end of the century, Vancouver would displace Victoria as the transport and commercial centre of Canada's west coast. The commercial materialism of the city impressed many visitors who arrived in those early days, like the English writer and economist J. A. Hobson.

It is a purely business town, a thing of stores and banks and meagre wooden houses, with no public buildings of account. . . . The stranger was amazed at the profusion of solid banking houses; it would almost seem as if the inhabitants must be a race of financiers, concerned mainly with money and stocks and shares. . . . And, in point of fact, this is a land of speculation, in mining properties, lumber lands, fruit lands, and, above all, in city lots, the price of which has doubled in the last two years.

XIII

Progress, Profits, Plunder

The Rush to the Kootenays

The effect on British Columbia of the joining of rails in 1885 up in Eagle Pass can be seen both in demographic figures and on the map. The population almost exactly doubled between the 1881 and 1891 census (most of the increase after the completion of the railroad); it almost doubled again to 178,657 by the 1901 census, with the balance of population now decisively tipping in favour of the Caucasian immigrants and their descendants.

But this did not herald a province-wide development, as had been expected by many of those who were eager for the railroad to reach the coast quickly. Vancouver, as the terminal city, benefited most, drawing on the trade of the coast, and so, to a lesser extent, did Victoria, as the commercial centre of the island and the centre of provincial government. But otherwise the route of the CPR split the province into two, with an increasingly prosperous and populated triangle to the south, between the main line and the American border, and a neglected region to the north, as far as the Yukon, which actually formed the greater part of the province and had to wait decades for development. While there would be a considerable railway development south of the CPR during the late years of the century, northern British Columbia would in no way be served by railways until the second decade of the twentieth century.

The main reason for this pattern of transport development was the change in the nature of mining so that base metals replaced gold as its principal staple; base metals were discovered extensively in the south of the province, particularly in the Kootenay area and perilously close to the American border.

The Kootenays and the so-called Boundary area farther west formed a closely knit triangle of mountains and narrow valleys, with long deep lakes in their folds, between the Okanagan region and the Rocky Mountains. Gold was found at Rock Creek in 1860 and shortly afterwards at Big Bend on the Columbia River, but never in quantities that made the area a rival of the Cariboo. Small rushes continued for the next twenty years and hurried camps would arise, not even substantial enough to become ghost towns, without the placer miners recognizing the real wealth that lay in the region.

When the rich silver and lead lodes were discovered at the Blue Bell Mine in 1882, followed by the Silver King not long afterwards, the city of Nelson came into being, and quickly developed into the administrative and commercial centre of the area. Early in the 1890s there were silver and lead finds on Slocan Lake, where famous mines like the Slocan Star and instant settlements like Sandon, Slocan City and New Denver came into existence. In 1892 the founding of the unruly community of Rossland followed on the discovery of the Le Roi and other mines on Red Mountain, and the finding of copper in the Boundary district led to the establishment of Phoenix. The Silver Plate mine was opened at Hedley in 1898 and continued in operation for many years. By this time the price of silver had risen dramatically on world markets, and from 1895 onward the movement in the Kootenays developed into a rush, the peak of which was the discovery of the great Sullivan mine of Kimberley, a veritable mountain of ores that has been producing lead, zinc and silver in large quantities, and smaller amounts of tin and antimony, cadmium and bismuth, ever since.

Again, like the Fraser River rush, this was dominated by the Americans, coming overland from the Washington Territory. But this time there were considerable differences from the old gold rush days. In the Kootenays no overnight fortunes waited to be made by individual operators as in the placer-mining era. A few prospectors might make lucky finds, but these could be exploited only by combines with large capital. Consequently, most of the population of the new and boisterous towns that sprang up, and often wasted away so quickly, were wage earners, and it was their cash rather than the gold dust of placer miners' pokes that passed over the counters of the saloons or into the stockings of the red-light quarters. This new generation of miners brought with them the militant unionism of such American-born labour organizations as the Western Federation of Miners and the Industrial Workers of the World, and added industrial strife to the normal turbulence of a mining centre.

The new style of mining, involving the extraction of the metal from the ore, led to the partial industrialization of the region. At first the ore from the Kootenay mines was taken south into the United States for smelting, but in the 1890s smelters were established at Nelson, and at Grand Forks and Greenwood farther west in the Boundary area, and in 1895 F. Augustus Heinze, an American entrepreneur, built the great smelter at Trail. With the coming of the smelters and their noxious emissions began the serious pollution of the British Columbian landscape, so that for long periods the hillsides beside the Columbia near Trail were virtually denuded of vegetation.

The appearance of the smelters coincided with the second wave of British Columbian railway building. By the 1880s the Dewdney Trail over the mountains from Hope to Similkameen and eventually to Rock Creek had fallen out of use and become impassable, and there was no other route out of southeastern British Columbia to the coast. When the Canadian Pacific was linked up in 1885, wagon trails were started southward from Golden and Revelstoke to link up with East and

West Kootenay respectively, but transport by such routes was slow and expensive; it was obvious that whoever could provide an effective railway connection to the mines and the smelters would be able to profit greatly. The profit lay not only in what might be reaped from passengers and freight but even more in what the provincial politicians might be persuaded to give in terms of land grants.

One's inclination is to condemn immediately the prodigality with which the vast acres were dispensed by the early administrators of British Columbia and often appropriated for their own profit, but, in explanation rather than justification, two considerations have to be stressed. Firstly, British Columbia politicians had been set a bad example by their earlier counterparts in eastern Canada; spoils and patronage had been built into the Canadian system at the time of the Family Compact and the Chateau Clique, and they were not quickly shed as Canada moved into responsible government and towards nationhood. Secondly, land—and what it grew as forests or concealed as minerals—seemed the one commodity that British Columbia had in abundance. There was not much cash in the public coffers, but there was an abundance of mostly unused land—more than 3 1/2 square miles (5.6 km^2) of it for every inhabitant in 1891—and, at the very time when the Indian chiefs were forbidden to hold their native potlatches, the British Columbian politicians organized virtual giving feasts of their own, distributing enormous largesse and expecting appropriate rewards in good time.

In the early political development of British Columbia, the scanty numbers of the ruling race meant that politicians, land speculators, railway magnates and merchants were less differentiated among the small elite than they later became. Businessmen of one kind of another succeeded the fur traders as leaders of the community, and often combined the roles of land speculators, pioneer industrialists, and legislators or even ministers.

The most striking examples of rich and powerful industrialists who actively participated in shaping the colony's political as well as economic directions were the members of the Dunsmuir family. Robert Dunsmuir, the Nanaimo coal magnate who made an immense fortune out of the mines on Vancouver Island and built the Esquimalt to Nanaimo railroad on a vast grant, was elected to the legislative assembly in 1882 and joined the cabinet as president of the council in 1886. His son and successor, James Dunsmuir, became an unwilling and not very effective premier of the province in 1900.

The coming of the railway gave an impetus to the exploitation of every kind of natural resource, and land offered either freely or at small charge to entrepreneurs of various kinds was the politicians' expected and willing contribution. The fish canners were allowed to pre-empt the sites on rivers and inlets that seemed to them most advantageous. The emergence of ranching as a major industry was largely encouraged by the fact that until the late 1880s land could be pre-empted in the interior of the province at $1 an acre (0.4 ha) and grazing land could be leased at an annual rent of six cents an acre. It was at this period that many of the great ranches, which still operate a century later, were established in the Cariboo, Chilcotin and Nicola regions.

Timber was already enjoying a small early boom in the late 1860s when the large mills were built on Burrard Inlet, and during the next two decades successive governments did everything they could to encourage the timber magnates. The timber leases up to 1888 varied between one and ten cents an acre per annum, and mostly they were towards the low end of the scale. The Moody Sawmill leased about 11,000 acres (4450 ha) and the Hastings Mill some 18,500 acres (7490 ha) of timberland on Burrard Inlet at one cent, and the Victoria magnate R. P. Rithet got similar terms for 15,000 acres (6070 ha) on Vancouver Island. In addition the logging interests paid a royalty of 20 to 25 cents per 1000 board feet (2.4 m³).

Nor were the railways backward in acquiring benefits. Apart from the gift of 6,000 acres (2428 ha) in the heart of Vancouver, whose manipulation in the 1990s still contributes to the company's prosperity, the CPR eventually benefited greatly from developments in the southeast of the province. There it seemed at first that its hegemony might be threatened by American railway interests from Spokane and Tacoma, anxious to divert the trade of this rich region into their own systems. But in the end it was the Canadian Pacific that emerged triumphant. It built a line, with a subsidy from the province of 20,000 acres per mile (5059 ha per kilometre), through the recently opened Crowsnest coalfield as far as Kootenay Lake, and thence its branches probed to Spokane Lake and other mining regions. It acquired the small railway that Augustus Heinze had built to his smelter at Trail and with it the Trail smelter, which became the core of the CPR's great mining subsidiary, Cominco. And it quietly mopped up the other small lines that had appeared in the region, acquiring another 750,000 acres (303 525 ha) of land, with which it helped attract new settlers to develop the agricultural life of the region as a complement to its mining and allied industrial activities.

Loose Fish Swimming in Troubled Waters

A symbiosis of a different kind from that between the Indians and the fur traders developed between provincial politicians and the increasingly powerful industrial and financial interests that moved in after the completion of the Canadian Pacific Railway. It was an equilibrium of interests that during the 1880s and 1890s began to be threatened by three factors.

One was the appearance, after the demise of the placer-mining era, of a genuine working class operating the mines, the sawmills, the railways and the first factories. Out of this began to emerge the radical labour trend that eventually produced both labour unions and socialist parties and resulted in a populist political style.

The second and more immediately important factor was the replacement, by the early Edwardian era, of faction politics by party politics. Faction politics had meant a shifting pattern of deals between groups determined by interest and locality, none of which was powerful enough to make a government of its own. Every government began with a compromise in order to produce a majority, and such deals were always insecure because of the lack of any kind of organizational or ideological discipline within the alliances that resulted. For always, apart from those who were committed to certain interests, there were the "loose fish" who were liable to change their allegiance as whim or profit might dictate.

Another factor in the instability of political life was the strange mortality that at this period afflicted provincial premiers, three of whom died in office in quite rapid progression. William Smithe, who had become premier in 1883 and welcomed the first CPR train at Port Moody in 1886, died a couple of weeks before Locomotive 374 drew its train into the final terminus of Vancouver in 1887. He was succeeded by A. E. B. Davie, who at least made a modest stand against the logging interests, changing the timber rights legislation so that rentals were raised to a minimum of five cents an acre (0.4 ha) and royalties to 50 cents per 1000 board feet (2.4 m^3), before he died in July 1889.

The shifting pattern of factions now threw up John Robson, the confederationalist radical, who had now himself become a rich man. By this time criticism of the government giveaways to the great vested interests had become so loud that Robson had to initiate the first effective legislation relating to resources in 1892, when he amended the land and mineral acts. Mineral and water resources were vested in the crown; mineral rights were separated from railway land grants; limits were placed on the sale of timber lands; and no more than a square mile (1.6 km^2) of surveyed crown lands could be sold to any one individual. Having completed this task, Robson succumbed to the fate of his predecessors.

He had been rather passionately involved in a colonization scheme for Scottish crofters who were to be settled in British Columbia with the aim of developing the province's deep-sea fisheries. He went to London to gain the blessing and the financial support of the imperial authorities. Hurrying about the city, he caught his finger in the door of a cab, and, though the injury seemed insignificant, he died quickly of blood poisoning in the summer of 1892.

Robson was succeeded by Theodore Davie, a brother of A. E. B. Davie and a fellow lawyer. Davie took office in boom time, for railway building and mining were flourishing, and building was continuing apace in Vancouver, while its importance as a port was increased by the inauguration of a Canadian-Australian line that provided passenger and freight service between Canada and its fellow dominion in the southern hemisphere. Though most of this prosperity originated on the mainland, Davie was a devoted islander, and it was during his regime that the decision was taken to abandon the historic but shabby Birdcages and to employ the young architect Francis Mawson Rattenbury to design the grandiose new parliament buildings that still stand beside the harbour of Victoria and that symbolically confirmed that city's political dominance over the province, even if commercial dominance had passed decisively to Vancouver.

Very soon Rattenbury's extravagant buildings seemed a reminder of a prosperity already gone, since by the time they were completed the Vancouver boom had collapsed and the great flood of 1894 had turned the farmlands of the Fraser Valley into a disaster area. The only people to profit from the depression were large companies that bought up failing ventures in the canning and timber industries and helped consolidate corporate power in the province. At the end of the 1890s a dozen firms controlled well over half the canning plants scattered up the coast, but perhaps the most spectacular example of the epidemic of amalgamation was the formation of the powerful British Columbia Electric Company, which originally combined the tramway and electric power systems of Vancouver, North Vancouver and Victoria, and steadily spread its influence through the province. In time B.C. Electric, as it was generally called, would become for British Columbians the quintessential corporate octopus, and populists of all kinds detested it until finally it was nationalized by the Social Credit government in 1961.

For the first time there was significant unemployment in Vancouver, and during the stark summer of 1894 the city was filled with agrarian refugees from the ruined Fraser Valley farms, and workless men queued up outside the soup kitchens the churches had organized. The growing activity in the mines of the Kootenays helped to prevent a total economic collapse. But it was not until 1898 that the situation in Vancouver and Victoria was saved, ironically by the last great stampede of the almost obsolete placer miners to the Klondike in 1898. Tens of thousands of men and not a few women passed through the two cities on their way north; the local merchants profited from outfitting the miners and the steamship lines from transporting them to Skagway.

The desire to attract railway and other capital to the province in order to mitigate the economic crises meant that in the latter part of Davie's regime, Robson's reformist inclinations were modified in favour of good terms to those who would provide employment. Eventually Davie managed to escape from the situation, being abstracted from the political scene in a different way from his three predecessors. He benefited from the death of Matthew Baillie Begbie, whose unworthy successor he became as chief justice of the Supreme Court of British Columbia in 1895.

With his departure, the succession of lawyer premiers came to an end, and appropriately enough, with one exception, the next five premiers were linked to the powerful primary industries of the province. John Herbert Turner was a gentlemanly wholesale merchant who made much money out of salmon canning. During his premiership, the province began seriously to coax in immigrants by advertising the southern valleys as good farming country. Lord Aberdeen had already established his extensive Coldstream Ranch at the north end of Okanagan Lake in 1891, and during the succeeding years genteel English settlers and retired businessmen with a taste for the open-air life began to establish the fruit industry, first around Vernon and Kelowna, then moving down the valley towards the American frontier. But generally speaking Turner operated on an old-style spoils system, and even a contemporary historian, R. E. Gosnell, far from a radical, remarked on the characteristics of this period in British Columbian history when he noted that "Turnerism" was a new word that had come to mean

favouritism, a lax civil service, extravagance in the expenditure of public money, looseness of administration, increasing indebtedness, encouragement of speculators and promoters at the expense of public assets, recklessness in railway charters and subventions, lack of definite and comprehensive policies, non-sympathy with labour aspirations, and everything else that might be chargeable against a government which had been a long time in power.

Eventually a disorganized opposition built up among honest opponents and disappointed place seekers, and during the elections of 1898 it became clear that Turner had lost his necessary basis of support, even though there was no well defined alternative alliance ready to take control.

But a new actor had entered the British Columbian political scene in the person of a New Westminster physician, Thomas R. McInnes, who had served his time as an independent MP and a senator in Ottawa, and in 1897 was sent back to his native heath as lieutenant-governor of British Columbia. McInnes declared that Turner's government had lost his confidence and also the confidence of the people of British Columbia. With dubious constitutionality, he refused to call upon him to form a government and picked the figurehead leader of the opposition in the last house, a Cariboo rancher named Charles Augustus Semlin with a taste for studying history rather than making it.

Semlin had at least the natural diplomacy of a shy and aloof man, and he was able rather precariously to reconcile the two other important opposition leaders, the maverick lawyer Joseph Martin and his enemy, Vancouver newspaperman Francis Carter-Cotton. Martin called himself a Liberal and Carter-Cotton called himself a Conservative because of their allegiances in federal politics, but in comparison with Turner and his business-oriented policies, both of them seemed radical. The precarious accord did not last. Semlin quarrelled with Martin, whom he had appointed attorney general, Martin gathered enough of his loose fish friends to defeat the government, and McInnes appeared again to dismiss Semlin and call on Martin.

The assembly had already rejected by 22 votes to 15 the dismissal of Semlin, and now, by a vote of 28 to 1 declared its lack of confidence in Martin. Almost immediately afterwards McInnes arrived in his role of lieutenant-governor to prorogue the house. Led by James Dunsmuir, the whole of the representatives except for Martin and the speaker rose and walked out, and it was to the hostile spectators, jeering from the gallery, that McInnes made his speech.

It was the political end of the road for both Martin and McInnes. Martin did put together the semblance of a ministry formed of men of no consequence, which lasted for three months. When it was inevitably defeated, McInnes in desperation called on James Dunsmuir to become premier. The legislators were implacable in their resentment towards the queen's representative, and in ratifying the choice of Dunsmuir as premier, they called for the lieutenant-governor's dismissal. Sir Wilfrid Laurier, appraised of the state of West Coast politics, agreed and appointed as the new incumbent Sir Henri Joly de Lotbinière, head of a leading Québécois seigneurial clan and well removed from British Columbian factions and feuds.

When he came into office in the summer of 1900, James Dunsmuir seemed the kind of bold and decisive businessman who might organize the province as efficiently as he organized his industrial empire. But Dunsmuir had been put into the premier's seat not because of his personal ambition, nor even because of any proven political competence, but because he was about the only member of any standing who had not been discredited by failure.

When Dunsmuir took over, the depression had come to an end, but New Westminster was only beginning to recover from the effects of a great fire that had burnt down its business district in 1898. The Boer War was in full swing and helped a little to reduce unemployment by inducing small parties of adventurous or patriotic young men from the larger cities, the Okanagan and the mining areas to offer themselves as recruits. James Dunsmuir made his personal statement in March 1900 at the time of the relief of Ladysmith from siege by the Boers, when he adopted the South African city's name for a new mining town on Vancouver Island. The war became a test for patriotism, and that patriotism, the people and the legislators left in no doubt, was British rather than Canadian, reflecting the fact that up to the end of the nineteenth century immigration into the province had been overwhelmingly English. "British Columbia is British," resolved the legislative assembly in February 1900. "We desire the Home Government and the Government of Canada to know that we, an integral part of the British Empire, can be depended upon to assist, both by men and means, to uphold our Empire." The assembly as well as many private individuals talked of raising and financing a local regiment of rough riders, and when Prime Minister Laurier, trapped by his disagreements with Québec over participation in the war, replied lukewarmly, there was great local indignation in the English-style private schools and gentlemen's clubs that had recently sprung up and at the garden parties and cricket matches that were still much the vogue.

Yet despite all these patriotic fervours, it was an increasingly disunited province. The pattern of factional alliances had placed a special importance on the mining areas of Vancouver Island and the southern interior of the province, where there were concentrations of voters with a special interest in labour problems. This meant that even coalitions that appeared to be conservative in general outlook were inclined to pay at least lip service to labour's demands. The Semlin government had passed a law imposing an eight-hour day in the metal mines, and Dunsmuir's government in 1900 introduced taxes on coal and coal products and also a 2 per cent tax on the gross output of the metal mines.

Whatever these measures might have gained in conciliating the workers was entirely negated by the attitude of the employers, who actively resented not only the recent provincial legislation but also a federal Conciliation Act, which for the first time established some kind of rudimentary procedure for settling labour disputes. The mine owners denounced the Conciliation Act and refused to implement the eight-hour law; Dunsmuir's government neglected to proceed against them, which incensed the workers, so that the turn of the century was a time of massive strikes

in the Nanaimo coalfields and the Kootenay metal mines. The discontent spread
to other industries, and there were also strikes among the Fraser Valley fishermen
and the maintenance workers on the Canadian Pacific Railway.

Once again the railway interests asked for and got support from the government, which included a large loan to build a railway bridge across the Fraser; but
to make sure of these measures Dunsmuir had to fragment the opposition, which
he did by striking a deal with Martin and two of his followers for their support. At
this point the young New Westminster lawyer Richard McBride, whom Dunsmuir
had made his minister of mines and who despised Martin, decided it was time
to move into the wilderness, and he became the acknowledged leader of the
opposition.

Dunsmuir stayed on only long enough to represent British Columbia at the cor-
onation of Edward VII, and then he resigned, disgusted with the disturbance politics created in the kind of life he felt a man of wealth should live. He was succeeded by his minister of mines, a mining engineer and colonel of militia, Edward
Gawler Prior, who had formerly been a Tory MP but was unseated for corrupt electoral practices. Prior was an even stronger advocate of railway interests than his
predecessors, and he won the next election on a plan that was popular on the island and in the Cariboo; he proposed to assist Mackenzie and Mann, the builders
of the Canadian Northern Railway that was being laid across the prairies to Yellowhead Pass, to extend their line to the coast using the route considered and
abandoned for the CPR, via Cariboo to Bute Inlet, with Victoria as the ultimate
terminus.

It was in these years that British Columbian factional politics collapsed in an atmosphere of tawdry farce. The most ludicrous incident came out of the bitter rivalry between Martin and McBride, whom the older Martin regarded as a political
upstart. McBride had been accepted by the opposition caucus as their leader, but
Martin, who had begun to play hard-to-get with the government, hoped to usurp
the position. At the beginning of the 1902 session, the session at which Dunsmuir
resigned, the two men quarrelled over the symbolic matter of the seat that was
used by the leader of the opposition. McBride occupied it, as of right, and Martin
screamed insults at him. Later, at prayers, Martin slipped in behind McBride, who
sat down to find himself in Martin's lap. There was a scuffle in which several
members used their fists, until the principals withdrew from the chamber in response to the pleas of the speaker and the chaplain, and the house voted McBride
the leader of the opposition.

Prior's government came to an end with scandals of another kind in the summer
of 1903. Two of the ministers had already been dismissed in April over a scam in
the Kootenays connected with land subsidies given to the Columbia & Western
Railway, a subsidiary of the CPR. In June the premier himself was deeply involved
in another unsavoury affair. He still owned an engineering company, but when
the government called for tenders for the cables of the Chimney Creek suspension
bridge on the Cariboo Road, his manager did not submit a tender because he

thought the premier would not want his firm involved. The premier thought otherwise, and E. G. Prior & Co. submitted the lowest bid. This was not surprising
because Prior, as acting commissioner of lands and works, had already seen the
other bids. When he was challenged by a house committee, Prior declared that his
company, being incorporated, had a legal right to submit a tender. Pressed about
the appropriateness of the premier's firm doing business with the government, he
answered that he was not more to blame than "a member who is a lawyer, or is
Attorney-General, and his partner takes charge of looking after a Private Bill for
anybody and lobbying it through the house." Nobody was more shocked by this
statement than the lieutenant-governor, who refused to grant Prior a dissolution,
but instead demanded his resignation. On the first of June, Joly de Lotbinière
called on Richard McBride to form a government.

It was a caretaker government, preparing for the provincial elections that would
take place in the beginning of October. It was also the end of a political era, the
era of a factional and informal type of government appropriate to a society small in
numbers, where the inhabitants of little communities knew each other much as
the inhabitants of small Greek cities must have done.

The Arts and Their Patrons

We always associate the Greek cities, and the mediaeval Italian cities as well, with
resurgences of culture under the patronage of wealthy individuals and sometimes
of the community. And British Columbia, in the later decades of the nineteenth
century and the Edwardian era, was the setting for a movement in the visual arts
that can be fairly correctly called a renaissance, since it consisted mainly of the re-
birth of genres and formal idioms that had already enjoyed their first lives elsewhere. These manifestations were almost entirely visual, so that it was the artists
and architects and a few photographers, rather than the writers or the musicians,
who flourished.

Whether amateurs or touring professionals, actors who performed in Vancouver
or Victoria produced either tired classics or trite New York or London comedies,
though James Anderson did write some farces for the Theatre Royal at Barkerville.
Anderson's example as a vernacular poet was not followed, though the American
Wobbly poet Joe Hill composed some of his most catching songs about the labour
struggles in the province.

The first good prose writers in British Columbia were those who reacted directly
rather than imaginatively to the land, and the best books to come out of it before
World War I were narratives of discovery and travel, the journals of earlier mariners and fur traders, like Cook and Vancouver, Caamano and Thompson, Fraser
and Harmon, and travel narratives like Paul Kane's *Wanderings of an Artist Among
the Indians of North America* (1859), Dr. Cheadle's *The North-West Passage by Land*
(1865) and Morley Roberts's *The Western Avernus* (1888). It was the land, primary subject of most significant British Columbian literature and art, that these
writers confronted, and Simon Fraser spoke for them all when he said, at Hell's

Gate in the Fraser Canyon: "It is so wild that I cannot find words to describe our situation at times." It is this stunned hesitation of the voice or eye that explains the prime importance of the explorer in early British Columbia: the land, so strange, so overpowering, had to be described before it could be encompassed by the imagination.

Life in British Columbia—the fur trade and the gold rushes and the scuffles with Indians—must have seemed often so much stranger than fiction that novelists rarely tackled it and never successfully until the first decade of the twentieth century. Even then, their works ranged on the wrong side of sensationalism, as in Jack London's *The Call of the Wild* (1903) and Morley Roberts's *The Prey of the Strongest* (1908); the only novel of true originality and character was Martin Allerdale Grainger's *Woodsmen of the West* (1908), a fine autobiographical tale (full of documentary meat and outspoken for its time) about logging communities and camps on the coast and their muscle-bound and booze-befuddled inhabitants. The first actual professional novelist with any name did not arrive until 1920. He was Frederick Niven, who then set down temporary roots in the Nelson locality.

Similar problems faced the painters, though they confronted them directly and visually without having to translate into the different language of words. But the directness—despite the awe that sometimes paralysed painters on first reaching the "sea of mountains"—was in their favour. They found, long before the writers, the means to create authentic art out of their experience with the wilderness, to go beyond the documentary insight into the imaginative construct.

Patronage was important from the beginning. John Webber arrived as the official artist on Cook's expedition, and his fellow painter, William Ellis, was the surgeon's mate. Their sketches are invaluable as documentation of Coast Indian life and culture at the point of first contact, and Webber's impressive large watercolour, *Resolution and Discovery in Nootka Sound*, is our first notable work of West Coast landscape art, in which the great rock walls and the forest towering above them push into insignificance the ships that represent human achievement. There were Spanish artists too, and one of them, José Cardero, who accompanied Malaspina's expedition in 1791, made some sombre paintings that emphasized the difference of the Northwest Pacific area from the kindlier landscapes of warmer climes he had already visited.

The struggle with the landscape would preoccupy the artists who found their way to British Columbia in the early nineteenth century. During the fur-trading period, independent travellers of any kind were not encouraged, nor, indeed, was there much eagerness among painters to find their way to the margins of civilization the fur-trading posts represented. Paul Kane was exceptional in the 1840s when he expressed a desire to paint among the Indians of the West and Far West, and Sir George Simpson was equally exceptional among fur traders by exercising a kind of patronage through providing Kane with transport and lodging all the way to the Pacific and back.

Kane's work was an unusual combination of the academically romantic and the humanitarian documentary. His original documentary urge kept him from being entirely absorbed by landscape, as later painters on the West Coast were, and during his time on the Pacific resulted in the fresh and immediate sketches of Indian life out of which, eventually, he made his rather preposterous studio paintings of the heroic and vanishing Indian. At the same period Lieut. Henry James Warre, on his secret war office mission to the Pacific coast in 1845, was producing modest sketches of Fort Victoria life and some sensitive and picturesque monochrome watercolours of the Cordillera. Like Kane, Warre kept a journal, which emphasized the desolation of the scene and the sense of solitude it induced in the traveller: "Not a vestige of human life to be seen, nay! so far as we knew existed for miles around. . . . The trackless vallies were smooth with unbroken snow. No living thing dared to brave the awful loneliness." No living thing but the artist! Here is foreshadowed the spirit of excitement and adventure that from the 1840s onward increasingly tempted Canadian artists to journey into the remoteness of their great land. By the time the next wave of artists came during the gold rush period, it had becoome an area where white nomadic populations scurried over the landscape in their search for gold and sometimes came together in large and usually temporary communities.

Almost all artists of any consequence who arrived during this period were English, with some kind of earlier training in the arts. William G2. R. Hind, for example, was Canada's only true neo-Pre-Raphaelite, born in England and trained in London and the painting schools of Paris. He applied the Pre-Raphaelite love for luminous detail and William Morris's ideals of nordic manliness to his sketches of the mining camps he reached after crossing Canada in 1862–63 with the Overlanders. Hind settled down for a while as a professional painter in Victoria, executing everything from inn signs to topographic drawings of mining claims, and killed his spare time painting an extraordinary series of self-portraits. His intimate landscape paintings, often inhabited by labouring or travelling miners, were exquisite in their vividness and clarity, but he had no real power to depict the more massive shapes that haunt the British Columbian landscape; this limitation is shown in the unbearable fussiness with which the snowpeaks are rendered in his often reproduced painting from the Overlander journey, *At the Foot of the Rocky Mountains.*

Other painters drawn by the gold rush dealt more effectively with the larger landscapes. Frederick Whymper was not only the brother of the famous mountaineer and Alpine artist Edward Whymper but also a son of the well-known London wood engraver Joseph Wood Whymper, from whom he learnt both drawing and engraving. In British Columbia he lived mainly by serving as artist for various expeditions: he took part in Waddington's disastrous venture inland from Bute Inlet and accompanied the 1864 expedition that explored the interior of Vancouver Island. He left many interesting sketches of gold rush settlements and Indian camps and graveyards. Often his landscape drawings did not go much beyond the topographical, but he knew his craft, and at times he could combine fine drawing with the use of watercolour in tiny haunting scenes of small settlements with their flags flying and their chimneys smoking under the implacable walls and the diaphanous clouds of the mountains. His sketches convey the delight and the occasional dread of stepping out for a moment from one's cabin and seeing anew the world that dwarfs one with its stern or glittering splendour.

I suspect Whymper inherited a touch of the true craftsman's humility from his father. He did not display the artistic pretensions of his rivals, Edmund Coleman and E. M. Richardson. Coleman had actually exhibited at the Royal Academy in London and was a mountaineer of almost equal stature to Whymper's brother, having climbed Mont Blanc twice. He reached British Columbia in 1863, but like most sensible men of the time did not try his fortune in the goldfields. Instead, he found a patron in Joseph Trutch, then a contractor with political pretensions, and one of his few known works is a meticulous pencil sketch of the Alexandra Bridge, which Trutch built over the Fraser Canyon as part of the Cariboo Road. It is a strangely still and static picture, a world trapped in time as in a photograph, the imagination never lifting the concept out of the prisoning lines of the artist's skill.

Much more lastingly evocative were the watercolours E. M. Richardson painted around Victoria in the middle 1860s. Richardson had been trained at the Royal Academy school in London and had reached British Columbia after working three years as a surveyor on the Great Northern in the United States. Somewhere—perhaps in England, perhaps in San Francisco—he had come into contact with the nineteenth-century cult of *chinoiserie* and had adopted an Asian idiom, so that some of his sketches of local scenes, like *Inner Harbour, Victoria*, look as if they might have been done by a visiting Chinese painter of the Ching dynasty.

The next wave of artists to reach British Columbia came with the advent of the railway and of such new technologies as photography. In the 1870s, when the first surveys for the CPR began, photographers replaced topographical artists in Sandford Fleming's expeditions to find a suitable route through the Rockies. Benjamin Baltzy, who went in 1871, and Charles Horetsky, who went first in 1872, were the earliest visual artists of any kind to bring back significant images of the great mountain chains of B.C. The nature of their assignments meant that their photographs were mainly topographical in intent, but both men had strong aesthetic judgement and an appropriate sense of awe towards the mountain country through which they separately passed.

William Van Horne of the CPR saw the possibilities of the Rockies and the other British Columbian mountain ranges as a terrain for artists. His patronage was modest. The mystique of the land was dawning on the artists themselves; eager to enter the new realm of possibilities, they were content to accept the free passes that Van Horne offered them. Some of them—already established painters in central Canada like John Fraser, Lucius O'Brien, Edward Roper, F. W. Bell-Smith and Thomas Mower Martin—came regularly year after year to the region, and sometimes Van Horne would join them with his easel and paints. Most of them were at first stunned by the sheer scale and starkness of the landscape, though eventually almost all of them felt what Martin described as a mission "to interpret the beauties of nature into a language that all can understand."

When the artists had finally adjusted their sights to the splendour of the western mountains, these years of the 1880s and 1890s formed the most productive era of Victorian landscape painting in Canada. The finest artists of the period did their best work in the Cordillera: the evocative mountain distances of Lucius O'Brien, the bolder and more direct scapes of John Fraser, and Mower Martin's extraordinary *jeu d'esprit*, a masterpiece of luminous and intricate colour, *The Interior of the Great Illecillewaet Glacier*. Some of these painters spent most of their time in the mountains; others continued to the coast and revived Paul Kane's interest in the Indian peoples there, whose culture in the 1880s was undergoing its final flowering.

Like most of the inhabitants of British Columbia except for the native peoples, the nineteenth-century artists whose names we remember were British or eastern Canadian by birth. During the Edwardian decade, the scene began to change. Sophie Pemberton, native-born daughter of Vancouver Island's first surveyor-general, went to study in France in 1890, and by the turn of the century was back painting vibrant and vivid Vancouver Island scenes that showed a remarkable sensitivity as a colourist. By 1908 Emily Carr returned from England, painting her first stiff and gloomy woodland scenes, which gave little promise of her future work.

Another native-born painter who emerged before World War I was Samuel Maclure, but he is much less known for his watercolour sketches of the countryside around Victoria than for the buildings that still survive in Victoria and Vancouver as monuments to the wealth and ambition of the age. Together with his rival and occasional collaborator, the young English immigrant Francis Mawson Rattenbury who arrived in 1893, he changed the look of British Columbian cities and established a heritage of notable buildings. Both Rattenbury and Maclure can best be described as brilliant eclectics. They borrowed and mingled stylistic elements of every kind from the Renaissance onward, and the result, with its echoes of past periods of conspicuous wealth, was pleasing to businessmen and politicians alike in the quickly developing communities of a province that could only barely afford such symbols of pride.

Rattenbury is best remembered for his public buildings, which set the architectural shape of downtown Victoria and contributed notable elements to other cities. Stage by stage he transformed the setting of Victoria's Inner Harbour, the true heart of the city, with his parliament buildings in the 1890s and later with the Empress Hotel. The result was and remains spectacular: the modified chateau style of the hotel contrasts with the parliament complex, whose romanesque elements save it from the dead classicism of American public buildings, while the more purely classical ferry terminal and the Crystal Garden with its echoes of Paxton complete an imperial ensemble appropriate to the time and its sentiments. Rattenbury helped to shape the public scapes of other British Columbian cities, particularly with his series of courthouses, ranging from the stark and sombre Vancouver example to those he designed for the new railway and mining cities like Revelstoke, Rossland and Nelson, the last of which is perhaps the most extravagantly decorative of his buildings. Rattenbury also planned many of the substantial homes of the era, including his own lavish neo-tudor dwelling, Glenlyon, at Oak Bay. He returned to England in the 1920s, rich and well known; in 1935 his fame was given an unwelcome twist when he was murdered by his chauffeur, the lover of his young second wife, who herself committed suicide after the murder.

There was no such sensation in Maclure's life; a sick heart kept him from the effort of the painting trips in the mountains which he longed to undertake. And he is remembered mainly as a domestic architect, though very often he designed private houses for public display. His favourite style was a neo-gothic adapted to coastal weather, and his large half-timbered houses with their granite foundations and their great shingled roofs made resourceful use of local materials and satisfied the pride of their rich owners.

The richest of all Maclure's patrons was James Dunsmuir, heir to the Nanaimo coal mines. His father Robert had already built Craigdarroch, a granite mansion constructed by Scottish masons, which he did not live to inhabit. James competed with Hatley Park, a great fortresslike building, in the late mediaeval style, looking over Esquimalt Harbour and designed by Maclure. With its 700 acres (283 ha) of grounds and its hundred Chinese servants and gardeners, it was an almost perfect expression of the pride and prosperity and imperial loyalties of British Columbia's entrepreneurs, and it remains, now converted into Royal Roads naval college, as the most striking local monument to the age.

XIV

Party Politics

The Rise of the Parties

On 3 October 1903 the first election on party lines was fought in British Columbia. It resulted in a Conservative victory and a government presided over by Richard McBride, who would act as premier until 1915, the longest incumbency in British Columbia until the twenty-year reign of W. A. C. Bennett half a century later. The 1903 election was fought by the Socialist party of British Columbia, which at this time was a local party, the Conservative and Liberal parties, which were allied to the federal parties of the same name, and a scattering of unattached labour candidates.

The Socialists were first in the field. The idea of legislators who specifically represented the workers was an old one in Canada. Immigrant British workingmen had started to establish their craft unions in Victoria not long after the beginning of the Fraser Valley gold rush in 1858. The bakers had organized in 1859, and the shipyard workers and printing workers not long afterwards. But there was no organization among the highly individualistic placer miners, and even the bitter strikes of the 1870s against the Dunsmuir coal interests at Nanaimo had only the most rudimentary organization.

With the construction of the Canadian Pacific, unionization on a substantial scale appeared in British Columbia. The Knights of Labor spread north from the United States and for a decade were active throughout Canada, founding twelve locals in British Columbia. They were an industrial union, disregarding the narrow interests of the craft unions, and professed their willingness to gather in workers of all crafts and races, though, like other unions of the period, they drew the line at Chinese. In a similar spirit to that of the workingmen who were creating the Independent Labour party in Britain, they insisted that it was necessary to get involved in the great social issues beyond "mere unionism." Like those later and much more militant unionists, the International Workers of the World, the Knights believed that they would usher in a new society where the great exploiters would be swept away.

It took a decade and the arrival of working-class militants from Britain before such feelings found any real political expression. The earliest representatives of the workers in Canadian legislative bodies operated under the aegis of the established parties. The first of them, Henry Buckingham Whitton, was a railway shop foreman elected at Hamilton on a Conservative ticket in 1873. In British Columbia a short-lived Workingmen's party was formed in 1886; its platform was Henry Georgian and populist, calling for a single tax, referendum and recall, more safety regulations in industry and, inevitably at the time, the exclusion of Chinese. The first group to take actual political action was the Nanaimo Reform Club, which in 1894 ran three candidates; none of them was successful, but one—Ralph Smith— not only became president of the Trades and Labour Congress of Canada, the fledgling national labour union organization of the period, but in 1898 was elected to the British Columbia legislature. However, if he was a genuine working-class legislator, he was by no means a genuine socialist, and in 1900, when he was elected to the House of Commons, he supported Laurier and the Liberals faithfully until he lost his seat in the great Liberal debâcle of 1911.

By 1900 a new militancy had entered the province. That year the Fraser River fishermen, including many of the recently arrived Japanese, went on strike to gain better terms from the canners, and the coal miners of Vancouver Island became increasingly militant in reacting against the ruthless anti-union policies of the Dunsmuirs and their reluctance to adopt adequate safety measures in the mines. The situation was ready for the appearance of a socialism more sharply defined than that of the Knights of Labor, and in 1899 branches of the populist-inclined Socialist League were founded in British Columbia. Various other small socialist groups appeared, and in 1901 they came together to form the Socialist party of British Columbia. Parallel to it, a more extreme Revolutionary Socialist party, aiming at the immediate overthrow of the capitalist system, was organized in Nanaimo, and by 1902 the two groups had united to pursue a radical socialist policy. By this time a loosely formed Nationalist party consisting of liberal radicals had appeared and vanished, and in April 1901 a heterogenous collection of socialists, single taxers, union men and farmers' representatives (not unlike the CCF of later years), gathered in Kamloops to form the Provincial Progressive party, which veered towards the political centre and did not survive the almost immediate secession of the Socialist party and the militant Western Federation of Miners.

Meanwhile the fever of partisan regrouping had infected the regular politicians of British Columbia, loose fish and faction leaders alike, and they followed the patterns established by the existing federal political parties, to one or other of which most of them already offered allegiance. The provincial Liberal party was founded at a convention in February 1902, electing Joseph Martin by a close-shave vote to a leadership he did not hold for very long. In September the Conservatives held their own convention. Both parties, responding to the anticapitalist mood of the times, adopted platforms that at a distance of almost a century seem to reek of collective hypocrisy. The Tories called for state-owned coal mines and railways, for reforestation clauses in timber leases and for the control of freight rates on railways built with cash or land bonuses. The Liberals were all for the pub-

Many new railways were built through the mountains during the 1890s to serve the new mines. This view at Payne Bluff on the line between Kaslo on Kootenay Lake and Slocan Lake is typical of the kind of construction work involved. B.C. ARCHIVES AND RECORDS SERVICE/HP5235

Swaihwe dancers, performing on the Songhees Reserve near Victoria, 1895. B.C. ARCHIVES AND
RECORDS SERVICE/HP15784

Rossland, founded in 1892, was probably the wildest of the Kootenay mining centres. The Strand
was one of its many saloons. B.C. ARCHIVES AND RECORDS SERVICE/HP36631, COURTESY ROSSLAND
HISTORICAL MUSEUM

Premechanical loggers working with saw and axe to fell the first-growth giants. B.C. ARCHIVES
AND RECORDS SERVICE/HP67870

Steamboats preceded the railway in the north. The *Inlander* in 1911, steaming into the difficult Kitselas Canyon on the Skeena River. B.C. ARCHIVES AND RECORDS SERVICE/HP29365.

The fishing fleet in the estuary of the Fraser River during the great salmon run of 1905. NATIONAL ARCHIVES OF CANADA/C 4677.

A Tsimshian shaman performing his cure at Kitwanga, c. 1910. VANCOUVER MUSEUM, G. T.
EMMONS PHOTO/276

The *Komagata Maru*, full of Sikh would-be immigrants, which the Canadian navy, as its first action, escorted out of Vancouver harbour on 23 July 1914. VANCOUVER PUBLIC LIBRARY/6232

Helen Gregory MacGill became the first woman judge in British Columbia in 1919. UNIVERSITY OF BRITISH COLUMBIA/9729

University of British Columbia students on their Great Trek in 1922. UNIVERSITY OF BRITISH COLUMBIA/1437

Simon Gun-an-noot, the Gitksan outlaw. B.C. ARCHIVES AND RECORDS SERVICE/HP12931

Unemployed men boarding a train at Kamloops in June 1935 as part of the On-to-Ottawa march.
NATIONAL ARCHIVES OF CANADA/C 29399

Cowboys in northern British Columbia, 1934. B.C. ARCHIVES AND RECORDS SERVICE/HP82089

Duff Pattullo was premier of British Columbia from 1933 to 1941. VANCOUVER CITY ARCHIVES/ 94-13

Shipbuilding flourished during World War II. A corvette is launched at Esquimalt in 1941.
NATIONAL ARCHIVES OF CANADA/PA170287

A wartime resettlement camp for Japanese and Japanese Canadians in the interior of British Columbia. UNIVERSITY OF BRITISH COLUMBIA/1474-9

The Indian Advisory Committee of the Province of British Columbia, 1949–50. *Top row, l to r:* George Bruce, Reginald Kelley (Haida), Capt. Charles Cates, Ed Bolton (Tsimshian). *Bottom row, l to r:* Lawrence Guichon, the Hon. John Cates, Chief William Scow, Ernest Brewer.
VANCOUVER CITY ARCHIVES/PORT.P.1210

Women workers at a factory during World War II. VANCOUVER PUBLIC LIBRARY/26804

Frank Calder, Nishga chief and first native Indian MLA. UNIVERSITY OF BRITISH COLUMBIA/
14851-116

Ethel Wilson, British Columbia's best noveslist. UNIVERSITY OF BRITISH COLUMBIA/14-9

A labour union protest rally in the 1950s. UNIVERSITY OF BRITISH COLUMBIA/1844-57

Premier W. A. C. Bennett presents the budget as his own finance minister, in 1962.
B.C. ARCHIVES AND RECORDS SERVICE/HP64718

lic ownership of utilities and even of smelters and refineries, and for compulsory arbitration to prevent strikes. Both parties came out in favour of the exclusion of Chinese, and so, inevitably, did the Socialists.

The weaker Nationalist and Progressive parties having fallen by the wayside, it was the Conservatives, the Liberals and the Socialists who contested the 1903 election, and the Tories, under Richard McBride, won with a slim majority of 22 out of 42 seats. This placed the two successful Socialists, James Hurst Hawthornthwaite of Nanaimo City and the Welshman Parker Williams of Newcastle, and the Independent Labour representative from Slocan, William Davenport, in a favourable situation. Hawthornthwaite was a veteran of the assembly. He had been elected for Nanaimo when Ralph Smith ascended to the House of Commons. Already he had used the tactics of the crucial minority, which J. S. Woodsworth was to manipulate nationally to such effect in later years. Playing on the insecurities of the Prior government, he had induced it to pass a Workmen's Compensation Act, the first legislation of its kind in Canada. Shortly afterwards he was involved with Joe Martin and Martin's associate Smith Curtis in virtually blackmailing a reluctant administration into accepting a mild trade union bill.

The Reign of Glad-Hand Dick

McBride in 1903 was the youngest British Columbian premier on record, and at the age of thirty-three fully prepared for the lengthy term of office he would eventually enjoy. "Glad-Hand Dick," as his critics called him, was a good-looking, affable and courtly man, and something of a dandy. He made friends easily, in politics and outside; lieutenant-governors always liked him, and even the politicians in Ottawa found his manners impeccable when he raised the ghost of De Cosmos with the kind of demands for better terms and the hints of separatist inclinations that in partisan as well as pre-partisan days have regularly been offered by active British Columbian premiers with an eye to an issue that will unite all classes. Within the province McBride managed to manipulate a difficult employer-labour situation in such a way that a large number of workingmen long believed he had their interests at heart without a large number of employers appearing greatly alarmed.

Though he was destined to rule through his first term with a precarious majority and was faced by an alarming debt and deficit situation inherited from previous administrations, McBride started off with two palpable advantages.

The first was that on 20 October, seventeen days after his election victory, the international tribunal judging the Alaska boundary dispute presented an award supporting the American claim to the control of the whole of the inlets on the Alaska Panhandle, to some of whose heads Canada had laid claim. Canadians were particularly incensed by the fact that the British representative, Lord Chief Justice Alverstone, had voted with the Americans. The two Canadian members of the tribunal refused to sign the award, and indignation ran high in Canada and particularly in British Columbia. It has been said that while British Columbians still considered themselves Britons until October 1903, after that date they finally began to see themselves as Canadians. McBride united himself with his fellow British Columbians in condemning the award, which robbed the province of important territory just as the Oregon boundary award had done in 1846.

McBride was also fortunate in choosing, as his minister of finance, Capt. Robert Garnett Tatlow. Tatlow was a man for the moment, capable financially and of startling public integrity in a province where that quality had long been conspicuous by its absence.

When Tatlow took over his portfolio, he found that the province was near to bankruptcy. The public debt amounted to $12,000,000, the deficit for the previous year was $1,500,000, the province was carrying guarantees for various railways to the extent of another $10,000,000, and it was deep in hock with the Bank of Commerce. In the present era of deficit financing and vast public debts, these seem pathetically small sums to threaten the stability of a government, but money was worth much more in those days, and though gentlemen might bilk their tailors, Victorian codes of prudence generally dictated that one must live within one's means. This was certainly what the Bank of Commerce meant when it loaned Captain Tatlow another million dollars on the strict condition that all highway and other public works projects be halted for the time being.

Tatlow chiselled at the resources of municipalities by shifting some of the school costs on to them, and at corporations and individuals by increasing income levies and taxing railway property; he even doubled the claims fees for prospecting. In two years, by 1905, he was able to show a surplus.

And from this point McBride was helped by the upsurge in the economy, as people and promoters flowed into the province from all over the world. By 1911 the population had more than doubled in ten years since the last census, to a total of 392,480. Vancouver had become a major commercial and industrial centre with a population of 110,000, and urbanization was proceeding up the Fraser Valley as British Columbia Electric pushed its interurban tramways as far as Chilliwack.

Encouraged by the new abundance of manpower and the wealth of natural resources, which then seemed inexhaustible, industries like fishing and lumbering kept pace with mining. The sockeye salmon runs of 1901 and 1905 were phenomenally large—the largest in recorded history—and the fishing industry was assisted by technological advances, such as the invention of gasoline engines that would be used on gillnetters, the introduction of new machinery to make cans and an automatic butchering machine popularly called the "Iron Chink." Cartels of the larger canning companies dominated the industry with agreements that fixed both purchase and selling prices for fish and, in a primitive attempt at conservation, the amount of fish to be caught and processed each year.

By 1910, mainly through the expansion of fishing and the phenomenal growth of the timber industry, British Columbia had changed from a debtor-and-beggar province into an affluent one. That year there was a budget surplus of $8,000,000, which placed McBride and Tatlow in the position of being able to declare that, alone in Canada, the provincial government had enough money in the bank to pay off its debts.

But this favourable position had been attained at the cost of establishing a pattern of exploitation, whose ultimate consequences were probably evident to few at the time. Among that few Premier McBride could certainly not be included, for the carefree geniality that made him so many friends also made him responsive to the approaches of anyone who seemed willing to sink capital in the province and provide employment. And this was especially evident in the relations between his government and the timber and railway interests.

Until the twentieth century the logging industry in British Columbia was operated mainly by local entrepreneurs and largely for local consumption as the population began to grow in geometric progression and the towns and cities expanded. From the 1840s, when the Hudson's Bay Company established the first mill, there had been a small but growing export trade, mainly to Pacific markets and mainly by sailing ship, and about the turn of the century the settlement of the prairies created a new demand as the farmers grew prosperous enough to move from shacks of sods or poplar logs to frame houses.

Meanwhile in the United States the loggers had virtually exhausted their own pine forests in Minnesota, Michigan and Wisconsin, and were attacking the first-growth stands of their northwestern territories. The great untouched forests of the southern interior of British Columbia lay just off their paths, and after their cruisers had combed the area, the American companies moved in to buy up timber licences. Between 1904 and 1911, in the southern interior and along the coastal inlets, no less than 11,000,000 acres (4 451 700 ha) of prime forest land were handed over to foreign and domestic enterprises. Employment grew, and great profit was gained by the exchequer; by 1908 more than 40 per cent of the government's revenue came from timber licences. By 1910 American investment in timber enterprises had reached $65,000,000, not counting considerable investments by German and other European interests. Baron Alvo von Alvensleben, later interned and accused of acting as a secret agent for the imperial government in Berlin, acquired several logging operations, and altogether more than $5,000,000 in German money was invested in timber and in real estate, which was booming in Vancouver and in the North.

McBride's term coincided with the real development of the Okanagan, as the dry hillsides were bought and irrigated by speculators and by greenhorn gentlemen farmers from Britain and many European countries. In the Kootenays and the Boundary country the original population of miners was now leavened by settlers on the land, notable among them the six thousand Doukhobors who arrived from the prairies in 1908. These Russian pacifist sectarians had abandoned their homestead lands in Saskatchewan because they wanted to farm their lands communally. Now, under their spiritual leader, Peter the Lordly Verigin, they came with cash in hand to establish a great community on land they had bought near Nelson and

Grand Forks, and set about establishing not only orchards and wheat fields but also industries adapted to local resources, such as sawmills, brickworks and a factory that made jams famous through the Canadian West for their quality.

As a result of his good fortune, McBride became more than a mere provincial politician. He was well regarded in Ottawa, and when he visited London in 1907, he won the confidence of politicians as varied as Earl Grey and Winston Churchill. In 1912 he appeared in the birthday honours list as Sir Richard McBride, KCMG, the only British Columbian premier ever to achieve knighthood. At one time, Robert Borden, leader of the federal Conservative party, was prepared to step down in favour of McBride.

McBride's popularity was enhanced by the benefits a booming economy allowed him—like W. A. C. Bennett in a later era—to offer the province: some good public health and labour regulations, stricter laws to conserve water and other resources, and at least the tentative beginnings—but only the beginnings—of a university.

British Columbia, caught up in the torrent of industrial growth, had been extremely dilatory in developing higher as distinct from elementary and secondary education. Though John Jessop had floated the idea of a provincial university as early as 1877, and an "Act Respecting the University of British Columbia" had been passed in 1890, the proposal had been allowed to founder in disputes between island and mainland about the site of the campus.

Meanwhile the school boards in Vancouver and Victoria had decided without government help to establish Vancouver College and Victoria College as institutions of higher education. In the absence of a functioning local university, the two colleges appealed to McGill in Montreal, which in 1906 incorporated a Royal Institution for the Advancement of Learning in British Columbia and took over the existing establishments in Victoria and Vancouver as two-year colleges.

Students still had to go elsewhere to complete their degrees; local pride suffered from such dependence, and Dr. Henry Esson Young, McBride's minister of education, accepted his appointment on the express condition that he be enabled to establish a university. A new University Act was passed in 1908, but by now the promised funds had vanished, used to subsidize a network of new railways, for in the second part of his time in office McBride also fell victim to the mania that afflicted so many British Columbian premiers, who saw in transport, however costly, the key to the rapid opening and development of the province. No money was left for education, and so British Columbia fell behind even Alberta and Saskatchewan, the prairie provinces established in 1905, in actually establishing a university. Though land at Point Grey, adjoining Vancouver, was earmarked for a campus and plans were made to open the university there in 1915, the year of its charter, it would be another decade before anything better than a makeshift institution inhabiting overcrowded temporary buildings represented higher education in British Columbia.

Approach to the North

The second great railway boom was linked with a premature attempt to open the north of the province to settlement and exploitation. The success of the Canadian Pacific, which was not only making profits from freight, passengers and steamships but was also earning a great deal selling the land it had picked up from various governments, aroused competitive ambitions, and two new railroads emerged, which planned to open the area of the northern parklands and prairies the Canadian Pacific did not serve and to make use of some of the routes in British Columbia that the pioneer railroad surveyors had explored and abandoned. The Grand Trunk Pacific was planned to extend an existing railroad, the Grand Trunk, from Winnipeg to the coast of British Columbia.

In 1909 McBride surprised the people of the province and antagonized Captain Tatlow, who resigned over the issue, by announcing the approval of a third transcontinental railroad, the Canadian Northern, which also would use the Yellowhead Pass and proceed via the North Thompson River to Kamloops, whence its track would more or less parallel that of the Canadian Pacific through the Fraser Canyon to Vancouver. The government guaranteed 4 per cent interest on bonds for the estimated construction cost of $21,000,000, a figure so inflated that Mackenzie and Mann, the promoters of the Canadian Northern, were able to buy the Dominion Coal Company with the surplus.

An electorate hypnotized by boom propaganda returned McBride to office with yet another large majority, and in 1912 a third new railroad was announced, also to be built in territory north of the CPR main line. This was the Pacific Great Eastern, planned to link up with the Grand Trunk Pacific at Fort George and reach salt water at North Vancouver, thereby providing the Cariboo with the railway link its people had long desired.

The northern parts of British Columbia, which these new railways were intended to open up, had remained virtually unsettled. Even the Cariboo, so populous and so world renowned in the 1860s, had shrunk vastly in population and importance. The ranchers in the region were suffering from the lack of accessible markets. Miners had passed northward through the country, some of them on their way to the Klondike, and had gathered temporarily in the Omineca, Cassiar and Atlin areas, but had created no lasting settlements of any importance. The Collins Telegraph Line, designed to link Europe to the United States by way of Siberia, had been strung into this territory in the early 1860s and had reached the Skeena River by 1866, when the news arrived that the Atlantic cable had been successfully completed. Work immediately stopped on the Collins Telegraph, the engineers and telegraphers and labourers departed, and the unused material was left in the wilderness. The Carrier Indians who lived beside the Bulkley River used the copper wire to build an ingenious swing footbridge over the Hagwilget Canyon which survived there for many years.

In general the pattern established by the North Westers in their New Caledonia posts in the early nineteenth century persisted well into the twentieth century. The scanty white population consisted of a few Hudson's Bay Company employees who traded with Indians following a fairly traditional hunting and fishing life, a few prospectors who hoped to discover another Klondike, and some missionaries. In the interior, the Oblate father Adrien Gabriel Morice, who served from 1885 to 1905 at Fort St. James among the Carrier, was a man of many parts, loved by the Indians, distrusted by his fellow clergy, and admired by historians and linguists. He laid the foundations for scholarship in the region by writing a *History of the Northern Interior of British Columbia* (1904), still read with trust and respect, and the first dictionary-cum-grammar of local tongues, *The Carrier Language* (1932). He also compiled, based on his own careful surveys, the first true map of the north-central region of the province, published in 1907.

In the far north of the province and on the Skeena, Nass and Stikine rivers, the fur traders did not penetrate far beyond the coast until the latter part of the nineteenth century, since the inland trade was mainly cornered by powerful Tlingit and Tsimshian middlemen chiefs. Only after the great epidemics of the 1860s had weakened the Indian grip on local trade did the white traders move in. William Hankey, for example, did not reach the Upper Skeena until 1868 to start direct trading for the Hudson's Bay Company.

The Gitksan people of this region, with their adapted coastal culture of splendid carving and rich ceremonial, clung more obstinately to their traditions than any other British Columbian group of Indians, carrying on the potlatch in secret after it was forbidden in 1884, and raising heraldic poles (many of which still stand in their villages) well into the twentieth century. One of their places, the remote settlement of Kitwancool with its splendid grove of poles, was so hostile to strangers that for decades even in the present century it was regarded as a kind of forbidden village. The great modern hero of the Gitksan was the outlaw Simon Gun-an-noot, who in 1906 fled into the wilderness after he had been accused of murder. Assisted by his fellow tribesmen, who sold his furs and left him food and ammunition, Simon and his family remained at large for thirteen years. Then he walked into a police station in 1919 to surrender himself voluntarily, and the white jury acquitted him partly for lack of evidence and partly out of admiration.

To most of the yet unoccupied northern region, modern times were brought by the coming of the Grand Trunk Pacific Railway, making its way across the province from Yellowhead Pass to the junction of the Nechako and Fraser rivers, and thence across country to the Skeena, beside which it ran down to the sea near Port Simpson. Almost immediately after construction began in 1906, a great speculative boom developed, not only along the route of the Grand Trunk Pacific but also around Kamloops, where the Canadian Northern would enter the populated parts of the province, and after 1912 along the proposed route of the Pacific Great Eastern. Where it had not been secured by the railways in free grants from the province, the land was mostly owned by syndicates, which had acquired it for small prices before the boom began. More than a hundred such groups were in operation along the routes of the various new railways. According to John Oliver, leader of the Liberal opposition in the assembly, "the speculators sometimes got their land for a dollar and a drink, and sometimes for a drink without the dollar." At the same time timber licences were being taken out freely in this area, which was still *terra incognita* to most British Columbians.

The real centres of speculative activity were the junction of the Fraser and Nechako rivers around the old HBC post of Fort George, and Kaien Island, where the railway company set out to establish a brand-new town with a name—that of Prince Rupert, the first governor of the Hudson's Bay Company—chosen through a public competition.

However cheaply they had got the land, they all sold, railways and syndicates alike, at high prices. In the Fort George area three competing townsites were laid out: Central Fort George and South Fort George as well as Fort George proper. Promoters touted the resources of the region and the transport possibilities of the site as a great railway junction, with "ten railroads building or chartered—some surveyed—all headed for Fort George." Land at Fort George was selling in 1910 for as much as $10,000 an acre (0.4 ha).

It was through Fort George that the railway—which held most of the land there—eventually ran. Renamed Prince George, it became the commercial centre of the northern interior of British Columbia, though after the boom receded it remained a relatively small town until well after World War II. At the rival sites, Central Fort George and South Fort George, those who bought land lost their money. Hazelton too suffered when the railway passed along the other shore of the Skeena and brought the era of paddle steamers to an end. Prince Rupert became not only the terminus of the railroad but also the only site for a viable port in northern British Columbia.

The inflated speculators' prophecies of northern development were realized only in a very limited degree. Far from ten railways converging on Prince George, the Grand Trunk Pacific—later the Canadian National—remained for more than forty years the only line to pass through the town. The Pacific Great Eastern quickly ran into financial difficulties, despite the generous government funding; less than 200 miles (322 km) of track were laid between the small town of Quesnel on the western verge of the Cariboo district and the equally small town of Squamish at the head of Howe Sound, whence a ferry boat provided a link with Vancouver. In 1918 the situation of this railroad from nowhere to nowhere was so precarious that the provincial government finally took it over, the first crown enterprise in British Columbia. It remained a minor line, chuffing through the forests and ranchland at such a leisurely pace that its acronym was reinterpreted as "Please Go Easy," and serving scattered ranches and mines, logging camps and Indian villages.

At the same time the PGE's two major rivals fell into the kind of trouble that might have been foreseen if Premier McBride had kept a map of Canada in his hand when he was weaving his visions of an immediate and rapid development of the north country of British Columbia. All the way from Winnipeg to the Yellowhead Pass, the two new railways were competing for traffic, while they both had to suffer the rivalry of the CPR, which was pushing up branch feeder lines from the south. The Canadian Northern suffered similar competition on the southwestern end of its route, where it virtually parallelled the CPR from Kamloops to the coast and often served the same communities. Only on the North Thompson stretch between Yellowhead Pass and Vancouver did it have some country to itself, and the steep rocky valleys it ran through there sustained a few mines and logging outfits but offered virtually no scope for agriculture.

The Grand Trunk Pacific had a more promising stretch from Yellowhead Pass to the sea, but its climate made it unsuitable for wheat farming, while the trees, rarely large enough for forest exploitation on a wide scale, had to wait for the introduction of pulp and paper plants after World War II. Though there was good pasture land around Prince George and Vanderhoof, markets were too far away for a dairy industry of any size to develop, and similar circumstances aborted a fruit industry. Even the full development of a fishing industry at Prince Rupert had to wait until adequate freezing techniques were developed. So the open north, from which so much had been expected, became in effect a thin line of settlement along the railway tracks between two relatively small towns, with the hinterland still unexploited; it remained a half-forgotten land without even a paved road linking it to Vancouver until the middle of the present century.

The railroads themselves never made a profit. In fact the Grand Trunk Pacific dragged its parent line, the Grand Trunk, into bankruptcy with it. Yet, once they were in existence, political as well as economic circumstances made it impossible to allow the trains to stop and the rails to rust. The federal government now appeared on the scene, subsidizing the Great Northern until finally it took over the railway in 1918 in payment for its accumulated debt, and buying up the Grand Trunk and the Grand Trunk Pacific after they had gone into receivership in 1919. Out of the two bankrupt concerns, the Canadian National Railways was formed.

The Polarization of Labour and Capital

Sir Richard McBride's reign had begun in a dawn of hope, when every circumstance seemed to be moving in favour of him and his new administration. It ended in disorder just over a year into World War I, during which McBride displayed his imperial loyalties to the full. He resigned, tired and perhaps more dispirited than he would admit, on 15 December 1915, and arranged for himself the post of British Columbia's agent-general in London. There he was welcomed by the many friends he had made in high places and sought treatment for Bright's disease; it proved ineffectual, and he died in 1917, less than forty-seven years old. The Conservative government he had led so long came to an end in 1916.

By the time he resigned, the circumstances that had favoured McBride when he came into office had largely evaporated. His own railway policies had strained the provincial finances, and now, after providing an artificial stimulus to the economy, the new lines were depressing it because the end of construction on all three of them caused a quick increase in unemployment, which the developing wartime economy did not immediately absorb.

The years of office and popularity had led to a gradual abandonment of McBride's early dependence on working-class legislators, and his government seemed to take negative attitudes on the great progressive issues of the day, such as women's suffrage and prohibition. His lukewarmness to prohibition came, as events showed, from sensing the general feeling within his province, for in 1920 British Columbia would be the first province outside Québec to recoil from the temperance hysteria of the war years and vote itself "wet" again. But on women's suffrage he was in tune with neither the present nor the future. In 1913, when the Women's Suffrage League presented a petition asking for votes for women, general support for the movement was growing rapidly; both the British Columbia Federation of Labour and the opposition Liberal party adopted the women's cause. McBride stood out stubbornly against such a change in his secure Edwardian world, and when a bill favouring extension of the suffrage was introduced by the Socialists, he killed it by wielding his Tory majority. He lived just long enough to see the vote given to women in British Columbia, after his government had fallen.

But the most striking aspect of the latter part of McBride's reign was the increase in labour unrest. The clear-cut divisions between capital and labour and between political right and left that even today distinguish British Columbia from other Canadian provinces came into existence in this era.

While in the early 1900s there had been a number of hard-fought strikes, particularly in the metal-mining south of the province, by the time McBride took power the industrial scene had settled down into an uneasy peace that lasted until 1910, the year of the foundation of the British Columbia Federation of Labour. The strikes that broke out in that year alone resulted in the loss of 312,791 working days, twice as much as for the whole five years from 1905 to 1910, during which a mere 151,385 days had been lost. The year 1912 was even more contentious; no less than 490,726 working days were lost, a record for the period before military warfare eclipsed industrial warfare in 1914.

Railways under construction and coal mines were the main locales of these strikes. The strikers were largely unskilled European immigrants whom the entrepreneurs thought they could easily exploit, and the activists were mostly American in origin; it was not the British-trained doctrinaire socialists who played the leading role in these disputes but the Industrial Workers of the World (IWW) and the militant miners' unions that originated south of the border.

The American-based Western Federation of Miners had already been active at the turn of the century in hard-fought strikes in the metal-mining region of the Kootenays. But by 1911 the initiative had fallen into the hands of the IWW (Wobblies), which had been founded in Chicago in 1905. The Wobblies were a purely North American phenomenon, bred of the plight of the many thousands of immigrant workers. Because their problems were in many ways identical, the

Wobblies shared with the revolutionary syndicalists of turn-of-the-century France and Spain a distrust of political methods and a philosophy of direct action that attracted with its grand simplicity the unorganized masses of immigrant workers. In the early 1910s they quickly gained influence in British Columbia among loggers, hardrock miners, fishermen and railway workers, particularly those involved in construction. Apart from their industrial activities, they were great fighters for freedom of speech, and in 1912 they successfully defied Vancouver city council when it tried to impose a ban on street demonstrations.

The first important IWW strike in British Columbia was in Prince Rupert, terminus of the Grand Trunk Pacific, where the Wobblies led a labourers' strike that became so militant that sailors from HMCS *Rainbow* were called upon to keep order in the first action of the newly constituted Royal Canadian Navy. Later in the same year the Wobblies led a strike of seven thousand labourers who were laying the Canadian Northern lines through the Fraser Canyon.

Joe Hill, the famous American Wobbly poet, came north to give his support, and one of his best-remembered songs, "Where the Fraser River Flows," was written about this strike:

Where the Fraser River flows, each fellow worker knows,
They have bullied and oppressed us, but still our Union grows,
And we're going to find a way, boys, for shorter hours and better pay, boys,
And we're going to win the day, boys, where the Fraser River flows.

The boys did not win the day on the Fraser River; they were defeated by the employment of large numbers of scabs protected by special police and by the arrest of strike leaders who were either imprisoned or deported. But these harsh measures did not discourage militant activity, for in the same year the miners in the Crowsnest coalfields struck for six months, and later there was a strike of three thousand construction workers on the Grand Trunk Pacific.

But the epic strike of the period was undoubtedly that in the Nanaimo area, where the local miners protested in 1913 about unsafe working conditions and about the dismissal of a man who had complained of particularly dangerous concentrations of gas in a mine at Cumberland, one of the outlying mining communities. After a walkout at the Cumberland mine, the owners locked out workers in all the pits of the area and attempted to keep the mines going by importing large numbers of Chinese, Japanese and other labourers. Following the pattern used in the railway disputes, McBride's government sided with the employers and sent in special constables to protect strikebreakers and company property.

This time the miners refused to accept the situation, and in August 1913, following the syndicalist tradition of direct action, a thousand of them rioted and took possession of Nanaimo. They burnt and looted buildings, attacked the strikebreakers and the special constables, one of whom was shot dead, and stoned the police chief until he ignominiously retreated. For a couple of days a genuine popular rebellion, which the authorities mistook for a revolution, was on foot, and the government reacted as governments do. McBride was away in England, but William Bowser, the attorney general and acting premier, called up the 72nd regiment of militia (the Seaforth Highlanders) and dispatched it from Victoria. Nanaimo was an occupied town for a whole year until the declaration of war in August 1914, when the militia was taken away for other uses. By that time the solidarity of the workers had largely broken down, many of them had returned to work, and the strike was collapsing.

Nobody won in this most spectacular British Columbia example of working-class militancy. The mine owners gained their shabby victory only at the cost of production losses that ran into millions. The workers in the end were demoralized and disorganized, and more than fifty of them—among the hundreds arrested—received savage prison sentences of up to four years. The legacy of labour bitterness that survived the strike has not yet dissipated. The taxpayers paid the bill for a thousand young men to waste a year of their lives serving in the militia. And the government of Sir Richard McBride, which at first won a great deal of approval for its decisive handling of "alien agitators," accumulated local disapproval and international derision as the military occupation of Nanaimo continued. In the end it was probably the Liberal opposition that profited most, for there is no doubt that McBride's growing unpopularity in many directions told against William Bowser when he succeeded McBride as premier and went down to defeat in the elections of September 1916.

The Racist Era

In British Columbia up to the middle of the present century, racism and labour militancy were closely linked, and their common target was the Chinese. In the volatile times of the early gold rushes when populations fluctuated according to the fortunes of the mines, the Chinese were probably the most stable group; peoples of other origins might depart when prosperity declined, but they remained. Frugal in their habits, they were able to extract enough to live on and to save some money for their relatives at home by working gravel deposits white miners thought too meagre, or even by repanning the piles of tailings left behind by other miners. They established the nucleus of a Chinatown in Victoria, and small exotic enclaves in other settlements. They worked for low pay as farmhands, navvies on public works and domestic servants, meeting a labour shortage at the time. In the 1860s, as Dr. J. S. Helmcken remembered, "The Chinese were believed by all to be an advantage and an improvement," since these "heathen" soon

> monopolized the market garden and the washing trade. . . . Previous to their advent the supply of vegetables had been scant, for Indians never took to this business, excepting in so far as they grew potatoes in small quantities.

Hostility towards the Chinese began to emerge among the unorganized white workers during the later 1860s as the Cariboo boom was deflating, but did not gain momentum until the 1870s and 1880s with the arrival of new Chinese immigrants to work on the CPR, and then it was directed by the earliest labour militants in British Columbia, the Knights of Labor. The Knights modified their boast of working for the benefit of all workers without regard for skill, sex or race by denouncing the use of Chinese labour, claiming that their own aim was to "elevate the working man, to keep his broad heritage for our sons and not for a race of aliens." The explicit racism of such a statement would be echoed in the exclusionist statements of British Columbian labour organizations for many decades.

In all, more than ten thousand Chinese arrived at British Columbian ports between 1881 and 1884, and another four thousand by way of American ports. Only the few merchants among them brought women—wives and concubines: the rest intended to return home and become big men in their villages when they had earned enough money. Many of them did so, but enough remained to provide competition for white workers in the period of unemployment that followed the completion of the railway.

At this period British Columbian attitudes towards the Chinese differed according to class. The presence of the Chinese enabled the well-to-do to live a taipan-like life surrounded by Chinese servants as they might have done in Shanghai. The Chinese provided employers—especially mineowners—with cheap and reliable labour, particularly useful when strikes had to be broken.

Thus the defenders of the Chinese came, in general, from among the better-off and more educated, and often their defences were reasonable and humane, if sometimes self-interested. When he appeared before one of the several Royal Commissions that investigated Asian immigration, Matthew Baillie Begbie spoke with unusual fairness, defending the Chinese from charges of excessive immorality or criminality:

> Their religion, notions of honour and rank, mode of thought, dress, amusements, sense of beauty are not to our taste. Their language appears to us ridiculous. Yet they as evidently despise all our attainments and they come here and beat us on our own ground in supplying our own wants. They are inferior in weight and size of muscle and yet they work more steadily and with better success on the average than white men.

Anti-Asian racism found its strongest support among workers who, struggling against ruthless employers, transferred much of their resentment to competitors even more ruthlessly exploited than they. The workers felt threatened in their very livelihood; they were vociferous about it and successful in influencing policy.

They did so because politicians of all parties were anxious not to alienate the growing labour vote, and on this issue there was not much difference between Conservatives, Liberals and Socialists. In 1879, forgetting the universalist implications of his adopted name, Amor De Cosmos supported in the House of Commons a petition of fifteen hundred British Columbia workingmen asking for an end to Chinese immigration; in 1880 he presented another. A different kind of ambivalence, completer in its cynicism, was displayed in 1882 by Sir John A. Macdonald, who replied to critics in Parliament of Onderdonk's hiring of Chinese labour for work in the Fraser Canyon; he admitted that in his view the Chinese "could not assimilate with our Arian population." Thus, it was a matter of expediency: "Either you have this labour, or you can't have the railway." In 1897 the provincial government yielded to pressure and banned the employment of Chinese as labourers on public works. The belief that cultures called Oriental were incompatible with the European ones from which Canadian society took its origins were particularly useful to politicians. Sir Richard McBride expressed the attitude succinctly when he remarked in 1914: "We realize that Western and Oriental civilizations are so different that there could never be an amalgamation of the two." McBride was mild in his views in comparison with a Royal Commission that at the same time declared that Asians were "unfit for full citizenship" because they were "obnoxious to a free community and dangerous to the state."

Early in the 1880s the provincial government adopted a series of entry regulations, based on those imposed in the colony of Natal in South Africa against immigrants from India; these made language proficiency the test for entry. The federal government disallowed the regulations as impinging on the dominion's prerogatives of controlling the entrance of immigrants. Ottawa substituted a series of head taxes specifically aimed at the Chinese; the tax began in 1885 at $50, rose to $100 in 1901 (by which time there were almost fourteen thousand Chinese in the province), and to $500 in 1903. These measures temporarily discouraged the flow of immigrants. Eventually in 1923 the federal government would pass a Chinese Immigration Act, openly discriminatory, which in practice excluded all Chinese except diplomatic personnel.

Meanwhile, immigrants from Japan had begun to arrive during the 1890s and to establish themselves in the fishing industry, where they competed for licences with white fishermen, which meant that they too became objects of popular resentment.

Throughout this period anti-Asiatic feeling remained strong in the labour movement; there were protests on Vancouver Island in 1883 when James Dunsmuir began employing Chinese in large numbers, and in 1887 the first anti-Chinese riots took place in Vancouver. In 1907 a rabidly racist Asian Exclusion League was formed in Vancouver, with the support of many labour union leaders. In September 1907 a march of the league through Vancouver's Chinatown and the adjoining Japanese quarter around Powell Street developed into a destructive riot that was halted only when the Japanese armed themselves, turned on their attackers and routed them.

Such incidents were pregnant with international implications in the tense later years of the Edwardian era. Whatever interest China may have had in the fate of its citizens overseas could perhaps be safely ignored, since it was already evident that the Manchu Empire was lurching towards its collapse in 1911, and the country had virtually no international presence. Japan, on the other hand, did have international presence and prestige as the one Asian country that had taken on a European power and emerged victorious, in the Russo-Japanese war of 1904–5. Besides, it was then Britain's valued ally in the Pacific, and Lord Grey, the incumbent governor general, was angry at the embarrassment the incident might cause.

William Lyon Mackenzie King, still a fledgling politician, was sent out to enquire specifically into the Japanese situation. A commission assessed and awarded damages to both Chinese and Japanese merchants who had suffered losses in the riots. And the Japanese government was enabled to save face by being persuaded to frame its own restrictions on Japanese emigration; from this time onward until World War II the Japanese were left relatively unmolested. There was little change in the situation of the Chinese, except that they were less threatened by mob violence as they withdrew into their Chinatown ghettoes and were gradually reduced by the attrition inevitable in a mainly bachelor society.

A new group of Asian immigrants were early faced with discriminatory measures, even though they were actually British subjects and, in any strict definition of that much abused term, as "Arian" as Sir John A. Macdonald himself. These were the Sikhs, who began to arrive in British Columbia early in the twentieth century, directly from India and also north over the border from the United States where they had found themselves unwelcome. They were not much more welcome in Canada where, largely as a result of Mackenzie King's investigation of Asian minorities, their entry into Canada was eventually banned, except on boats sailing from India to Canada, of which none existed at the time. Many of the five thousand who had first arrived departed, and by World War I only a hard core of two thousand remained, who devotedly sustained their religion and built their gurudwaras, while working in lumber camps and sawmills and as firewood merchants.

A famous attempt by militant Sikhs to promote further immigration, on the grounds that they were British by citizenship—the old *civis Romanus sum* argument—began when the Japanese ship *Komagata Maru* set out from Hong Kong with 376 Punjabis, mostly Sikhs, aboard. They arrived in Vancouver harbour in May, but most of them were not allowed to land. They obstinately remained, repelling boarding parties of immigration officers and police with fusillades of coal until finally, all court manoeuvres having been played out, HMCS *Rainbow* arrived from Esquimalt, trained its guns on the Japanese ship, and escorted it out to the high seas. This happened on 23 July 1914, not many days before the war began, and it was ironical that the Royal Canadian Navy's first maritime action should have been against British—not against German—subjects. The episode of the *Komagata Maru* did not have any wide-ranging effects in Canada itself, but it was an imperial incident of prime importance, strongly influencing the formerly loyal Sikhs of the Punjab itself to struggle against the British in India.

XV

War in a Land of Plenty

Distant Patriotism

In British Columbia, as in most parts of Canada, the most striking response to World War I lay in the reactions of thousands of individuals to the news of war and its effect on their strongly held loyalties. During the four years of war, British Columbia, with a population of somewhat over 400,000, contributed 55,000 men to the armed forces. More than 43,000 served overseas, and these were mostly voluntary enlisters, recruited before conscription was imposed at the end of August 1917; 6,223 were killed, and more than 13,000 were wounded. Most of these men went east by rail across Canada and then by ship to the killing grounds of France, but during 1918, after the war had ended in Europe, some of them sailed across the Pacific west from Vancouver in the Siberian Expeditionary Force, which remained in Vladivostok until Canada's interference in the internal affairs of a revolutionary country came to an end in 1919.

The earliest men called up were those of the active militia regiments, the first of whom left Vancouver by rail on 26 August 1914. Others followed quickly, including the Gordon Highlanders from Victoria, commanded by Lt.-Col. Arthur W. Currie, the Sidney real estate agent and land speculator who eventually succeeded Sir Julian Byng in command of the Canadian Corps on the European front. There had actually been a considerable buildup in militia activity in British Columbia, as in the rest of the Canada, during the internationally difficult years preceding the outbreak of war. Since 1910 there was a 50 per cent increase in militia enrolment across the country and an even greater increase in the militia budget.

Apart from the militiamen, most of the first recruits were Britishers by birth, stirred by the plight of the land they had left, which most of them considered in danger of invasion. The remittance men—those reprehensible young English who had been "sent out to the colonies" for the benefit of their disapproving families—volunteered almost to a man to defend the land that had expelled them. Other more purposeful Englishmen who had already put down roots in their new country were equally eager; the tale told of Walhachin, the fruit-rearing settlement of genteel English people established under Lord Aberdeen's patronage, where all the 43 younger men in the little group of 150 people left their new orchards and young wives and their children and never returned, is not an exceptional one. A fifth of the students in the newly opened University of British Columbia left immediately after registering, and four members of the legislative assembly exchanged their comfortable benches for dugouts in Flanders. Throughout the Okanagan there was an exodus of the male population, which was swelled by the hundreds of adventurous young men who had been finding themselves in logging camps and mining settlements, and were ready for what seemed, until they were engulfed in the stinking mudfields of Flanders, the greatest adventure of all.

More than three thousand men from British Columbia were in the first Canadian contingent, which sailed early in October from Montreal to England, and by the spring of 1915 they were deployed in the Yypres Salient. The British Columbia government made a gift of 25,000 cases of canned salmon on the strength of which Sir Richard McBride got a large order for fish from the British government. And the Doukhobor women of Brilliant in the Kootenays, perhaps more disinterestedly, sent a gift of jams and preserved fruit from their factory, expressing their "mournfulness" that the war was still going on.

Recruiting and supplying men for the imperial endeavour was the leading preoccupation of British Columbians for the first months of the war, and, as everywhere, it went on at the cost of dislocating family lives and the general economy. The requirements of war took away shipping needed for the essential export trades in fish and lumber. The price of copper and other base metals fell sharply and then rose just as quickly as the wartime demand speeded up, so that some mines were exhausted and busy little metal-mining centres like Greenwood and Phoenix and Sandon withered into ghost towns. Construction on the railways was ended by early 1913, and after that there were no major public works projects for the duration. There was nobody in search of real estate, which had been booming shortly beforehand, and the province's income from the sale of crown lands dwindled almost to nothing. Population fell sharply; some journalists claimed so many people left, owing to the enlistment of men and the exodus of unemployed workers, that a quarter of the province's population had gone by 1916.

The Threat to the Coast

Yet it was only later that their economic troubles rose into prominence in the minds of British Columbians. At first they were much more concerned with the possible dangers the war might bring, as it spread over the earth, to their province almost 7,000 miles (11 265 km) away from the main seat of conflict.

Fears were of two kinds: of actual attacks by German ships like the *Leipzig* and the *Nürnberg*, which were known to be prowling and raiding commercial shipping in the Pacific, and by submarines entering the local channels and harbours; and of betrayal by some or all of the many Germans who had recently been settling or buying land along the coast.

Many Germans and Austrians had already departed when the call came for men of military age to return to the fatherlands, and others were interned almost immediately after hostilities began. The sinking of the *Lusitania* in the Atlantic on 8 May 1915 was the signal for a xenophobic orgy in Victoria, inspired largely by the fear that even the island ferries were not immune from submarine attack. A mob led by recruits attacked a long-established German beer garden and a brewery for German-style beer whose owner had long been naturalized as a British subject. It was with difficulty diverted from Government House, where the first lady of British Columbia happened to belong to a greatly respected German family that had been in Victoria since 1858. German subjects were swept in far and wide, and the prisons of Nanaimo and Vernon and Saanich, having been emptied of their criminal populations, were well filled until 1918 with the victims of paranoia and racial hatred.

Apart from the presence of suspect aliens, the question of the safety of British Columbia involved the meagre defences of a distant corner of Canada and of the British Empire. Unlike European countries, Canada as a whole was not organized to meet the threat of invasion from the sea, though there were indeed contingency plans in the Department of Militia in Ottawa (and continued to be until World War II) to deal with possible invasion from the United States.

Between 1895 and 1900, when the growing naval power of both Germany and Japan were rousing anxieties among British strategists, the imperial government had built modern fortifications outside Esquimalt, equipped with what were then the latest in disappearing guns. Meanwhile Canada itself had entered the field of coastal defence in 1887 by establishing a regular artillery battery on Beacon Hill, and from 1897 the Canadian government had begun to share in the cost of the Esquimalt garrison.

The Anglo-Japanese alliance of 1904 resulted in a rearrangement of Royal Navy fleet arrangements, so that in 1905 Esquimalt ceased to be the headquarters of the Pacific station, with disastrous effects on the social life of Victoria. There were no more naval balls, no more officer escorts to elegant parties; only the dockyard and bunkering facilities remained. In 1906 even the British soldiers departed as Canadian troops took over. In 1910 when the Liberal government of Sir Wilfrid Laurier created a separate Royal Canadian Navy, the dockyard was finally handed to Canada, and Esquimalt became the base for the cruiser *Rainbow*, already somewhat antiquated, and lesser craft. During the years up to the Great War the defences were allowed to deteriorate. Guns that had been up to date in the 1890s had become obsolete by 1914, and some of those intended for the Vancouver Island defences had not even been installed. And even for the outdated guns that were in place, there was not sufficient ammunition.

It was the anxiety over this situation that led to one of the more curious episodes of the Great War in British Columbia—the three-day existence of a provincial navy. Anxious for his province, full of imperial zeal, and impatient at the weakness of the defences prepared by the dominion government, Sir Richard McBride heard that two submarines were being completed in a Seattle shipyard for the Chilean government. On that day, 29 July, the Admiralty had already sent out a telegram to naval stations all over the world warning of the likelihood of war, and McBride decided he must lay hands on these boats. Exactly how he managed to buy the submarines out from under the nose of the Chilean government has never been made quite clear, but there was certainly a dramatic race against time, for it was likely that the American government would apply its neutrality laws and impound the submarines if they were not acquired before the expiry of the British government's ultimatum to Germany at midnight on 4 August. McBride could not wait for a reply to the telegram he had sent to Ottawa and dispatched his agent, Captain Logan, to Seattle to complete the purchase. This was done on the afternoon of 4 August, and the submarines were taken out secretly to a rendezvous outside American territorial waters, where they were met by a ship with retired Commander Bertram Jones on board.

Meanwhile a provincial cheque, issued without authority of cabinet or assembly, was handed over to the builders, and on the morning of 5 August, the first actual day of the war, submarines cc. 1 and cc. 2, as they were designated, sailed into Esquimalt harbour. That morning a telegram arrived from Canadian naval headquarters telling McBride to buy the submarines and asking the price. He wired back, "Have purchased submarines." For three days this tiny modern navy remained the property of the province. Then the dominion government took them over; they remained for a considerable time on the West Coast, escorting troopships and other craft between the island and Vancouver. By the end of 1914 the *Leipzig* and the *Nürnberg* had been sunk in the Battle of the Falkland Islands, and the threats to the coast and its shipping grew less evident. British Columbia was not invaded.

Political Victory and Defeat

Though no military battles were fought during the Great War on British Columbian soil, it was the scene of a notable political battle, which resulted in a reverse of fortunes astonishing even in a province well known for its political surprises. During their years in office, the Conservatives had built up a powerful political machine, and in the elections of 1912 had won the largest majority in the province's history. They held forty seats, two socialist parties held two, and the Liberals none at all. Yet in the elections of September 1916, after McBride had resigned, the Liberals leapt from two seats they had won in recent by-elections to thirty-seven seats in an enlarged house; the Tories were left with nine, the Socialists with one.

The Conservative reverse in fortunes was not due merely to the replacement of the bland McBride by the abrasive, ruthless and rather capable Bowser. It was partly due to the fact that the great railway bonanza, which had redounded so much to McBride's credit in 1912 when construction was under way and land values were still booming, had turned sour over the years. The railways were completed—except for the Pacific Great Eastern—but neither showing a profit nor bringing about the great transformation of the hinterland that had been expected. Meanwhile, the province was running a deficit budget once again, with the provincial debt running above $10,000,000 and $80,000,000 looming in railway bonds. The Pacific Great Eastern had swallowed money without much to show for it, and the Liberals were accusing the government of having paid out $7,000,000 illegally to the promoters. The two larger railroads were lurching towards the bankruptcy that would shortly overtake them, and their completion had released on the labour market a horde of casual workers.

The McBride-Bowser government was looking at its worst just at the time when a surge of reformatory zeal, part idealist and part puritanical, was sweeping the province. The mission to protect soldiers who did not want to be protected (they voted consistently against prohibition) had taken hold of the temperance fanatics and swept a goodly number of otherwise sensible people with it. At one end of the social ladder in August 1915 a People's Prohibition League held in Vancouver its first rally, attended by almost a thousand people. At the other end, sugar magnate Jonathan Rogers formed a committee of a hundred temperance-minded businessmen committed to gaining legislation against drink.

The women, undeterred by McBride's rebuff of their petition in 1913, were again on the march, with the female intellectuals of the Vancouver-based University Women's Club in the lead and the thousands marshalled by the Christian Endeavour movement in strong support. Bowser gained no credit when he turned populist in the hope of evading both these issues, proposing to submit them to referenda rather than to make them the subjects of votes in the assembly.

Bowser's refusal to be decisive on the prohibition issue led to accusations of moral laxity from the puritans. The evangelical clergy moved from criticism into action when the Rev. A. E. Cooke headed a committee of six clerical activists calling themselves the Ministerial Union of the Lower Mainland. In April 1915, Cooke and his associates, giving themselves the title of "moral leaders of the people," sponsored the publication of *The Crisis in British Columbia,* a pamphlet in the classic muckraking strain, written by Moses B. Cotsworth, an accountant and actuary who was nimble with his statistics. His text was filled with tables that supported his arguments that public lands and timber licences had been swallowed up by speculative syndicates without the government having tried to protect the public interest—or any other interests but those of its friends and followers. The government was corrupt and partisan in its actions, and, in the view of at least one zealous clergyman, it teetered "on the very brink of an abyss of moral damnation."

A vast public meeting in Vancouver on 1 June, which called for a public commission into Cotsworth's accusations, was the beginning of a campaign in which the "moral leaders" toured the province, addressing large and excited meetings and distributing copies of *The Crisis in British Columbia* freely wherever they went.

The effect of these campaigns of opposition were shown when Bowser, now premier, tried to put together a new cabinet after McBride's resignation and those of two other ministers. His new minister of finance, the able A. C. Flumerfelt, and his minister of public works, C. E. Tisdall, had to stand in by-elections before they could assume office. Both were defeated, Tisdall in Vancouver and Flumer-felt in Victoria; Bowser had received virtual votes of no confidence in the two principal cities where more than half of British Columbia's population lived. Harlan C. Brewster, the fish canner who had been chosen as the leader of the party, was one of the two Liberals voted in to join the two Socialists in a tiny but vocal minority.

Bowser had no alternative but to call an election, which he eventually did for September 1916, and to prepare the best programme he could offer. It suggested the work of a more precise and capable mind than that with which Sir Richard McBride had floated so smoothly on the waves of good fortune and floundered so hopelessly when the weather turned bad. Hoping that the long expected war orders for fish and metals and silver spruce for the fuselages of aeroplanes and munitions, which were at last reaching British Columbia, would not only improve the revenue but also revive public confidence in his government, he devised a plan that would give something to many groups in the province. Seaports were to be developed—doubtless with a special eye to Prince Rupert, and shipbuilding was to be encouraged, no doubt with Victoria and Burrard Inlet enterprises in mind; farmers were to be helped under an Agricultural Credits Act and returning soldiers were to be offered free land; mining ventures were to be assisted, but at the same time the lot of the workers was to be bettered by improved Workmen's Compensation and Factory acts. But he stood his ground on the questions of prohibition and women's votes; a good drinking man and a male supremacist at heart, he insisted they must go to a popular vote, and so he assured that both the militant women and the militant temperance propagandists would work against him.

Yet perhaps it was the defection of the Tory dynast Sir Charles Hibbert Tupper that in the end guaranteed Bowser's downfall. Son of Sir Charles Tupper, who had been briefly prime minister of Canada, and himself a member of several federal cabinets, Tupper had settled in Vancouver to practise law when he retired from politics in 1904. Like many of the oldtime British Columbia Tories, he developed an intense personal hatred for Bowser. He referred to him habitually as a "little Kaiser," and claimed that he was the "Judas Iscariot who sold" Sir Richard McBride. And, in a statement that sounds strange coming from a man who had been one of the federal masters of patronage when the Tories reigned in Ottawa, he claimed that "the real, fundamental issue between the people of British Columbia and the government and Mr. Bowser is the question of patronage." On the other side of the political spectrum, the former Labour representative Ralph Smith abandoned federal politics and stood as a Liberal candidate in the election. The result of all these adverse circumstances was a political landslide, which left the Liberals with a majority of twenty-five seats over the combined opposition and began a long period of Liberal rule.

Harlan C. Brewster became premier and picked a cabinet that contained many men of talent and frustrated ambition, like Minister of Agriculture and Railways John Oliver, and Minister of Lands Thomas Dufferin Pattullo, both of whom would eventually rank among the more able premiers of the province. Ralph

Smith received his reward as minister of finance, but he died soon afterwards and was replaced by John Hart, yet another future premier.

If anything, the difficulties of governing the province increased during Brewster's period in office. He tried to attack the financial situation with sharp retrenchments in government spending, but this got him into trouble with his Liberal supporters who, however self-righteous they may have been over patronage when the Conservatives were in office, expected the spoils for themselves when their party came to power. He gave the women the vote, and after Ralph Smith's death, his wife, Mary Ellen, was elected the first woman legislator in Canada. But though the Prohibition Act was passed after a majority had voted for it in the referendum, the soldiers had cast their ballots against it, and Brewster delayed its implementation, to the annoyance of the temperance ladies who, now they had the vote, became more influential than ever.

Inevitably, as the seasons of war dragged on, British Columbia became more intimately involved. Local industries were being favoured with orders for war supplies, and because manpower was short, many women went to work in the munitions factories and older men returned from retirement. After the generals had poured their millions of men into the campaigns of 1917, many badly wounded soldiers returned to remind British Columbians of the realities of the distant conflict. And, like all of Canada, British Columbia became involved in the great 1917 debate over conscription. Although the federal Liberal party and its leader, Sir Wilfrid Laurier, had their power base in Québec and therefore were bound to oppose conscription, Brewster and the rest of the British Columbia Liberals were in favour of it and also of the Union Government, which the prime minister, Sir Robert Borden, was busily organizing, and from which Laurier and his associates stood aloof. Borden, who thought highly of Brewster, consulted him over the composition of the government, and rumours circulated that he was being considered for a federal cabinet post. Certainly, when a federal election took place in 1917, British Columbians returned entirely Union candidates.

With such matters, and with a series of reform-minded commissions investigating political corruption and influence peddling, Brewster's first years of office were largely consumed, and the few positive measures he undertook were based on initiatives already sketched out by Bowser. Then, like so many of the province's premiers, Harlan C. Brewster departed from the political scene by dying in office.

Four days later that true man of the people, John Oliver, who had been acting premier during Brewster's absence, was re-elected leader by the Liberal caucus and became premier pending the next election. It was Oliver who presided over the difficult last months of war and the equally difficult period of entering a different kind of peacetime from that which had been broken by the events of 1914.

Dissent on the Left

While patriotism—both national and imperial—flourished in the government and among the population of British Columbia, with army recruits and returned soldiers forming an unofficial storm troop prepared to attack opponents of the war, there were still considerable and even powerful forces of dissent.

The federal government, to the annoyance of many bellicose British Columbians, dealt tactfully and generously with those who objected to participating in the war on religious grounds. Provisions in the Militia Act exempted members of certain specified sects from service, and the inhabitants of the great Doukhobor settlements in the Boundary and Kootenay districts were left unmolested, as were numbers of Quakers and Mennonites. Pacifists of this kind tended to withdraw from rather than resist the war.

Working-class resistance, on the other hand, was widespread in areas like the Kootenays and the Vancouver Island coalfields, where left-wing miners' unions spearheaded opposition to conscription. However, it was not merely the miners who were opposed. A British Columbia Federation of Labour made its appearance and denounced the conscription of manpower, and so did the Trades and Labour Councils in both Vancouver and Victoria. The labour leaders came together to form an Anti-Conscription League, and the tones of Canadian nationalism and class war sounded in their statements as they criticized a war that had emerged from treaties in which Canada had no part and which bred the profiteers who grew fat on the blood and tears of the people. That men were being conscripted but not wealth was one of their regular themes.

Rhetoric was reinforced by action as workers began to feel the effect of quickly rising prices grinding against slowly rising wages; the cost of living rose 30 per cent in 1916 and 1917. A strike in the Crowsnest area, the province's most important coalfield, caused such disruption that the federal government took over control of the mines and dragooned the workers back to the coalfaces. Sporadic strikes broke out all over the province, and the Trail smelter—producing valuable war materials—was closed by a work stoppage. Vancouver by 1918 was in a positive ferment of labour discontent: longshoremen, city workers, bakers, shipyard workers and metal workers all went on strike.

Then, on 2 August 1918, the first general strike in Canada—a twenty-four-hour one—was called in protest against the police killing of the militant labour leader "Ginger" Albert Goodwin, a young Yorkshireman who had migrated to Cumberland on Vancouver Island and played an active role in the 1913–14 miners' strike there. Afterwards Goodwin moved to the Kootenays and in 1917 was elected president of District 6 of the International Union of Mine, Mill and Smelter Workers; he quarrelled with his associates and went to Trail, where he organized the strike for an eight-hour day. When conscription came, it was obvious that his enemies in management and government meant to use it to get rid of Goodwin; though he had been diagnosed as having tuberculosis, he was classified fit for military service, and two appeals against the classification were turned down. Accordingly, Goodwin returned to Cumberland, where he knew the country and the people, and went on the run there, hiding out in the hills and being supplied by the local people, until a provincial policeman, Dan Campbell, tracked him down and shot him. Campbell was charged with manslaughter and exonerated by a grand jury; the jury met *in camera* and the evidence presented before it was never revealed. Ever since, it has been believed in the labour movement that Campbell, probably paid by the mineowners, murdered Goodwin in cold blood. The day of Goodwin's funeral, the Trades and Labour Council of Vancouver issued a call for a twenty-four-hour general strike, and the response was so wide that in the city itself and throughout the mining areas transport was stopped and industry brought to a halt. It was a prelude to the bitter industrial conflicts of postwar days, and it revealed British Columbia as one of the main battlefields of the class war in Canada.

XVI

Doldrums and Depression

Awakening from the Nightmare

There was an undercurrent of apprehension to the exuberant rejoicing that greeted the Armistice on 11 November 1918. The crowds that surged and danced in the cities and the villages on that day were united more in their relief that the ordeal was over than in their triumph over the victory that had been won. But once the rejoicings were ended, they returned to their conflicts—especially returning soldiers against militant workers—and to a radically changed world.

There is a popularly held impression that the world changed suddenly in 1914, and then the modern age began. In fact, all the war did was to hasten and precipitate processes of change that had begun long before. Technologically the nineteenth century had been a time of constant progress that transformed industry and that in Canada, with its vast distances, was most strikingly expressed in methods of transport, with the railroads leaping across the country, and eventually the pioneer automobile. Vancouver's first horseless carriage was made in the city in 1898, and experimental aeroplanes followed not long afterwards in British Columbia. Transport in turn laid out the patterns of human occupation; by 1914 the fur trade travellers and the railway makers had between them determined the sites of almost all the important communities in the province.

In social terms, the Edwardian age had already been one of considerable ferment, with the enfranchisement of women a major issue and concepts of the power of workers changing as labour unions evolved from craft societies with narrow interests to organizations that demanded a say, and sometimes a revolutionary one, in the way society should operate. The years of the war and those immediately afterwards were only bringing these trends to a kind of fruition when women gained the provincial vote in 1917 (they won it federally the following year) and when in 1919 the militant unions of western Canada came together in that ambitious, menacing but ultimately doomed syndicalist organization, the One Big Union.

Even culturally, modernism in both writing and the visual arts had emerged during the Edwardian decade in Europe and the United States, and though British Columbia itself would not for many years produce painters or writers in the mod-

ernist vein, conceptions of the role of the arts were already shifting away from Victorian didacticism.

Into this world of accelerated change, the peace projected problems as profound
as those the war had created. Immediately after the armistice, the economy was
jolted by the sudden fall in the demand for raw materials, particularly metals,
which had been stimulated by the war. The demobilization of the tens of thousands of soldiers combined with the constriction of industry to produce widespread
unemployment. The population began to climb again because of the returning survivors, natural increase and the slow revival of immigration, but instead of more
than doubling as it had done between 1901 and 1911, the number of inhabitants
increased by a mere third between 1911 and 1921.

It was only slowly that Vancouver, the lower Fraser Valley and parts of the
mainland interior emerged into a modest economic upswing that continued from
1922 until the end of the 1920s; this was stimulated by the increased exports of
forest products by way of the Panama Canal, opened in August 1914, and also by
the development of Vancouver as a port, used largely for shipping prairie wheat;
all through the 1920s the long grain trains laboured one after another through the
mountains to the coast. By the middle of the decade Greater Vancouver had
passed the quarter-million mark in population and was competing with Winnipeg
for the position of third-largest city in Canada.

Other places were less fortunate than Vancouver. The smelter at Greenwood
was closed during the war for lack of ore, and that at Grand Forks in 1919; the
town kept alive thanks to the presence of the local Doukhobor community and of
other farmers and ranchers. Rossland survived by becoming a dormitory town for
Trail, where the great smelter kept going because of the seeming inexhaustibility
of the vast mountain of ore into which the Sullivan mine ate its way in Kimberley.
Victoria survived largely because it was the capital of the province, for its industry
languished, and it became economically so stagnant that between the two
censuses of 1921 and 1931 the city's population had grown by only three hundred.

Yet, stagnating or modestly booming, the cities changed. Building went on,
and around Vancouver the suburbs of new houses spread into districts like Kerris-
dale and Burnaby that up to 1918 had remained woodland or had been used by the
Chinese as truck gardens. On 1 January 1920 the city boundaries were broadened,
and the municipalities of South Vancouver and Point Grey were absorbed, so that
Vancouver now stretched from Burrard Inlet south to the Fraser, and west to the
boundary of the Endowment Lands that were still awaiting the building of a university. The university would eventually start operations there in 1925, after agitations by students returned from the war culminated in a march from downtown
Vancouver to Point Grey, which has gone down in academic annals as the Great
Trek, as a result of which in 1923 the provincial government granted funds that
enabled construction to be taken up again from the point at which it had been
abandoned in 1915.

Even around Victoria new houses were rising slowly in satellite communities like Saanich, and it was during the 1920s that the original Christ Church Cathedral was replaced by a fine gothic revival structure built of granite by Scottish masons; the tides of faith, ebbing around the world, paused briefly here.

The postwar age brought changes in habits that helped transform the look and life of the towns and cities. The department store chains—Hudson's Bay and the locally founded Spencer's (later absorbed by Eaton's) and Woodward's stores—extended their premises and dominated the retail trade. Their main stores—like the large neoclassical building the Hudson's Bay Company built in Victoria on the site of the old Driard hotel—became major landmarks, and even in small communities they were represented by mail order operations like that of Eaton's, whose voluminous catalogue became a classic record of Canadian popular taste. Styles of life tended to be dominated not only by the department stores and the increasingly varied goods they offered but also by the movie theatres. For better and usually for worse, the vulgarized cosmopolitanism projected by Hollywood films permeated the aspirations of people even in remote communities. World War I saw the beginning of the automobile's final triumph over the roads (and of the cult of speed); horse traffic virtually disappeared from the streets of cities, though not yet from those of smaller towns. And the mood of the twenties, here as elsewhere, was manifest in the extremities of fashion, in the desire for more amusement and more leisure, in the elaborate devices by which the strict liquor sale regulations that replaced prohibition in the 1920s were evaded to preserve social amenities (so that the bootlegger long remained a feature of the British Columbian scene).

The gradual spread of political rights for women was accompanied by liberation in another direction. Such developments as the spread of refrigeration, the invention of new labour-saving devices, and the increased availability of birth control information, eased the housewife's task. On the one hand, it lessened the need for domestic servants and slowly eliminated a class that already seemed out of place in an increasingly egalitarian society. On the other hand, it encouraged many women who had already held jobs in wartime to continue seeking work outside the home. In this they were encouraged by the manifest success in making public lives for themselves of women like Mary Ellen Smith, MLA, and Helen Gregory Mac-Gill, who became a judge in Vancouver Juvenile Court.

The search for a political alternative to the established pattern of two major political parties was already emerging strongly in the West by the end of World War I. In its beginnings, it consisted of disunited movements among farmers, returned soldiers, and wage earners. The farmers' movement in British Columbia inevitably differed from those in the prairie provinces and in Ontario. While in the provinces east of the Rockies the farmers represented a high proportion of the population, and farming in the prairies was still the major industry, the twenty thousand farmers of British Columbia made up only 4 per cent of the population, and farming was only one of at least four major primary industries. Moreover, the farmers were a much more varied group in class terms than their counterparts elsewhere in Canada, for the Cariboo ranchers and the Okanagan fruit farmers were largely upper-class Englishmen who still thought of themselves as forming a kind of gentry. The United Farmers of British Columbia, founded in 1917, never recruited more than a small minority of the province's farmers (in 1922 it had no more than 1,332 members), and though a resolution at the UFBC convention in 1920 calling for independent political action passed without debate, nothing came of it. The agrarian populism that swept the rest of the West found little echo at the time in the agricultural districts of British Columbia, and the province played little part in the extraordinarily rapid rise of the Progressive party, inspired by similar agrarian populist movements in the American Midwest, which in the federal elections of 1921 won sixty-five seats, to become the second party in the House of Commons and to be manoeuvred into extinction by Mackenzie King.

Nor did the B.C. farmers seem greatly inspired by the provincial successes of United Farmers' organizations elsewhere in the country. The United Farmers of Ontario gained enough seats in their province's 1919 elections to form a government of farmer-labour representatives, which ruled until 1923. The United Farmers of Alberta won the provincial election of 1921 and continued as its government until 1935, when they were defeated by another Western populist movement, Social Credit. But in the 1920 election, the United Farmers of British Columbia refused to endorse officially any of the farmer candidates who appeared in various constituencies and none of whom was successful. At their 1922 convention the UFBC, among whom the fruit farmers of the Okanagan and the dairy farmers of the Fraser Valley became dominant, decided not to become involved as an organization in political activity, though they did set up a committee to study independently the possibilities of a third party, an idea that found a response among some at least of their rank and file.

Another group that believed they had a special political interest to defend were the returning soldiers, who by 1917 were a quickly growing group in the community. The soldiers often had genuine reasons for grievance; they came back to find their own jobs either vanished or occupied by others. Politically, they tended to operate in the right field: the Great War Veterans' Association campaigned on behalf of the Union Government and of conscription, and less official soldier groups attacked union halls during the 1918 general strike provoked by the killing of Ginger Goodwin. But as the soldiers sank back into everyday civilian life, their special identity and special interests tended to fade.

The radical trends that emerged in the labour movement in British Columbia and indeed in the whole West at the end of the Great War were to have important long-term consequences, though in the short term they might have seemed to end in defeat. The Russian Revolution of October 1917 gave a stimulus to the movement. The revolutionary syndicalism of the Wobblies and the western miners' unions, which was essentially an anti-authoritarian movement aiming at the replacement of the state by a network of workers' syndicates, mistakenly sought an affinity in the authoritarian revolutionism of the Bolsheviks, and the identification created a dynamic upsurge in the western Canadian labour movement. Even veteran socialists like J. H. Hawthornethwaite moved perceptibly towards the communist position, and union members began to regard the Socialist party of Canada, revolutionary though its voice had become, inadequately attached to the workers' class interest, and in 1918 founded a Federated Labour party.

The Federated Labour party declared its aim to be "the complete overthrow of the present system of property and wealth production," and this position was reflected within the union movement, where the old-style craft unions were in temporary retreat before the new wave of revolutionary industrial unionism. The industrial unionists had become bemused by the old syndicalist idea of the general strike, which many of them regarded as a direct way to workers' control of production in a stateless society without going through political action and its electoral rituals, and so a split developed not only between craft unionists wishing to restrict the movement to the skilled and privileged trades and the industrial unionists wishing to open it to the unskilled masses, but also between revolutionary direct actionists and those who believed society could be changed and the worker's interests best served through political action, with workers' representatives sitting on the benches of the legislature. The syndicalists now dominated the British Columbia Federation of Labour, the Vancouver Trades and Labour Council, and even the Victoria Trades and Labour Council, all of which expressed their support of the Soviet Union and in principle favoured the idea of a general strike.

On the 13 March 1919 the delegates of the British Columbia Federation of Labour gathered with other labour representatives in the Western Labour Conference in Calgary, and there they decided to hold a referendum on the question of leaving the crafts-oriented Trades and Labour Congress of Canada, which was affiliated to the reformist American Federation of Labour, and forming an all-embracing revolutionary industrial organization they would call the One Big Union—an idea already launched in somewhat different form before the war by the iww.

Before the referendum vote was completed, a general strike had been declared by the Winnipeg Trades and Labour Council over the matters of collective bargaining and fair wages. The Winnipeg workers came out in force on 15 May, and this fact undoubtedly influenced the heavy referendum vote in favour of the One Big Union and gave the movement an initial impetus. Late in May the general strike spread over the mountains, and workers in Vancouver, Victoria and Prince Rupert came out and stayed out for three weeks. The strike was so complete that the Vancouver newspapers ceased publication because the printers refused to set up editorials and articles that were critical of the general strike in Winnipeg, an odd stance for men who shortly beforehand had voted for a general strike in favour of free speech. But though the enthusiasm generated by the Winnipeg General Strike gave an initial impetus to the One Big Union, the strike's defeat tended to weaken the appeal of its deceptively simple teaching that downing tools and folding arms would save the world. Within four years the One Big Union would be reduced to a tenth of its peak 1919 strength, and it would survive only as a rump organization until industrial unionism became a force again in the middle 1930s.

Such failed efforts as the Winnipeg General Strike dissipated the energy of the labour radicals, and as the 1920s continued and more prosperous times returned, the signs of class conflict became less evident, and the number of strikes declined, though the provincial legislature was never without its small group of socialist and labour representatives.

"Honest John," the Farmer's Friend

Politically this transitional period was presided over by John Oliver, who took over as Liberal premier in March 1918 after the death of Harlan C. Brewster. Oliver was the first of a series of populist premiers who revived the spirit of the pre-Confederation era personified by Amor De Cosmos and the early John Robson. He was as true a man of the people as any of the labour leaders who at times competed with him. His father had been a coal miner in pits owned by the Duke of Devonshire in the Pennines, and he kept the flat Derbyshire accent throughout his life. John Oliver had worked as a pit-boy before his family migrated to Ontario, where his father started farming in 1870. In 1877 he moved west to British Columbia and worked as an axeman with the survey parties of the CPR and as a labourer with the construction crews. Proud of his plebeian origin, Oliver arrived at official receptions in a rough tweed suit and saved money for the province by staying at cheap hotels and eating in popular restaurants when he travelled on public business.

Despite his simple lifestyle and his creed of hard work and honesty, John Oliver was not a poor man by the time he became premier. He had settled in Delta as what he called a "dirt farmer," and by mastering the arts of draining and dyking he had made his farm in the marshy estuary one of the best in the locality, rearing large flocks of pigs for the Vancouver market. He had little education but much common sense, about which he was far from modest. He was assiduous about his duties, and often when citizens lodged complaints against public departments, he would go out personally to investigate rather than trusting an intermediary, and for this he gained great popularity.

Oliver had waited long in the wings of British Columbian politics. He was first elected to represent the farmers of Delta in 1900, and during the Liberal party's years in the wilderness, he was its leader from 1905 to 1909, when he lost his seat. He retired from political activity for seven years, but then, in the great 1916 surge of anger against the Tories, he stood again and joined Brewster's cabinet. It was a sign of the populism that characterized the reform-minded Liberals that this capable and energetic but unpretentious farmer should be chosen in the 1918 ballot for the premiership, over his socially more presentable rivals, the Cranbrook physician James Horace King and the powerful Vancouver lawyer J. Wallace de Becque Farris, then attorney general.

Oliver believed that the economy of British Columbia was too closely dependent on the major extractive industries that remained susceptible to world markets and the caprices of nature. Circumstances immediately after the war seemed to confirm his assessment, for only logging was prospering, aided by a building boom in Australia and a general overhaul of the railways in Britain.

The fishing industry was in poor shape, from causes largely attributable to lack of human foresight. The great Fraser River runs had fallen away largely because construction on the Canadian Northern caused slides that partially blocked the Fraser at Hell's Gate in 1913 and drastically reduced for many years the number of sockeye ascending the river to spawn. As for the mining industry, the sudden and drastic fall in the demand for metals not only affected the mines and smelters but harmed the coal trade, since the demand for coke to fire the smelters also diminished. These circumstances aggravated unemployment by narrowing the job opportunities of demobilized soldiers, many of whom picked British Columbia as their destination even if they had not lived there before.

Farming, it seemed to Oliver, offered a way for returning soldiers to establish themselves in the community. His immediate efforts were directed of necessity to tidying up the fiscal affairs of the province, as he inherited a public debt exceeding $20,000,000 and outstanding railway guarantees of more than $60,000,000. It was a situation Oliver never completely solved, though he was helped by a pickup in the economy during the 1920s.

One of his most ambitious undertakings was the draining of Sumas Lake in the Fraser Valley south of Chilliwack and the great marshes surrounding it. Prosperous dairy farms replaced the reedbeds, and among the first settlers of this rich reclaimed land were Mennonite farmers, who in the early 1920s had fled from the Ukraine where the Bolsheviks and Anarchists were battling each other and making the land unlivable for pacifist sectarians. Shortly afterwards Oliver embarked on the irrigation of the southern end of the Okanagan Valley, where desert conditions prevailed near the American border, and his name was given to the little fruit-rearing community of Oliver that sprang up there. He also introduced a Produce Marketing Act to protect the prices of fruit, the first legislation of its kind in British Columbia.

An important feature of Oliver's programme for the agrarian redemption of the province was the resettlement of soldiers in undeveloped areas. He saw no reason, if the poor of Europe had been glad to settle on the prairies in the decades before the war, why returning soldiers should not be eager to start independent and healthy lives for themselves in British Columbia, where, after all, the climate was kinder and the scenery better than on the prairies. Government-sponsored settlements were planned at Merville on Vancouver Island, at Creston on Kootenay Lake, and at Telkwa in the northerly Bulkley Valley. But—to Oliver's chagrin—comparatively few men decided to avail themselves of the land offered in what were then rather remote situations.

Oliver was conscious that some of the richest farmland in British Columbia lay east of the continental divide in the Peace River area, which was really an extension of the prairie parkland. And there he negotiated the return to the province of the rich square of land known as the Peace River Block, which had been transferred to the federal government in 1884 as part of the terms for the completion of the Canadian Pacific Railway. Settlers had begun to arrive there before the war, and they continued to do so through the 1920s and even into the Depression era, when many people came as refugees from the drought-stricken farmlands of southern Saskatchewan. The sale of land in the Peace River area provided a welcome supplement to the province's income. This was the one really successful feature of Oliver's attempts to open the northland of British Columbia.

Even the public works programmes on which Oliver prided himself were mainly directed towards the farmers and the rural population. He realized that, largely because of the topography, the railways had left great areas of the province deprived of adequate transportation, and that something more than rough cart trails were needed. So, from 1920 onward, he replaced the railway building of the McBride era by road building, which had the added advantage that it provided work for farmers in the idle season, and men who earned a little money from a Liberal government might become or remain good Liberal voters. Even so, John Oliver's government never had enough money to build a really adequate system, and outside the lower Fraser Valley and southeastern Vancouver Island, there were as yet few paved roads. New highways in the Okanagan and the Kootenays remained local and fragmentary; no major artery united the province from east to west.

The inadequacy of the Cariboo Road to serve the requirements of ranchers, miners and loggers in the Cariboo and Chilcotin regions—the historic heart of the province's interior—led Oliver and his government to become involved in one of the failing railway schemes of the McBride era. While the federal government was struggling with the failure of the Grand Trunk Pacific and the Canadian Northern in a way that would lead to their eventual expropriation, the province was faced with the lamentable condition of the Pacific Great Eastern, on which millions had been wasted without any train running. Since the line was planned to operate only within British Columbian boundaries, it presented a problem for the province to solve alone; though Oliver tried hard, there was no help to be got from Ottawa. In 1918 Oliver decided that the line must be taken over and drove a hard bargain with the promoters, but this did not mean a complete solution, for whole stretches of the railway had still to be built before it could be put into effective operation.

The provincial government eventually took over loans amounting to $18,000,000 and completed the line from Quesnel to Squamish, the little port at the head of Howe Sound that provided water connection to Vancouver and Victoria, all in defiance of the opinion of three transportation experts hired in 1921 who unanimously reported that for many years the area would not provide enough traffic to justify the line's existence. Their pessimism was justified, and the Pacific Great Eastern was long a running sore on the province's budget, and puffed away at public expense through the forest and the bunch grass country, linking rough western cattle towns like Williams Lake and forlorn little places with Zane Grey names like Lone Butte.

But it would be unjust to John Oliver, whose populism was broad and generous, to concentrate entirely on his promotion of the farming industry and of the roads and railways that seemed to favour it. It was his government that finally granted the money for the University of British Columbia to move out of the obsolete sheds in downtown Vancouver to new buildings on its splendid campus overlooking the sea and the mountains at the tip of Point Grey. In 1925 he extended the benefits under the Workmen's Compensation Act and passed an Industrial Disputes Act tied in with new federal legislation. Early in 1927, with the province's prosperity recovering sharply and a surplus in the budget, he induced his legislature to introduce in British Columbia the first Old Age Pensions programme. It was a beginning, though a meagre one, for the pension was a mere $20 a month for people over seventy, with a strict means test.

It was the peak of his career, to which he and the Liberals had come through economic and political vicissitudes, but they were discontented times, when the balanced budgets and the public confidence—even euphoria—of McBride's high years were no longer consistently sustainable.

Even the reform policy with which Brewster and Oliver had leapt into power told against them in the end; they were never progressive enough for some voters, and particularly for those who were drawn towards the rapidly growing and evolving labour movement. Already, in the 1920 elections, Oliver's majority had fallen. His Liberals won twenty-six seats against the fifteen Conservatives, but perhaps the most significant development was the growth of the smaller groups. Four labour candidates and three independents were returned; together they made up almost a sixth of the house.

Though it was probably not recognized at the time, this was the beginning of a further major shift in the British Columbian political pattern. The turn of the century had seen the supercession of the old factional pattern in the legislature by that of parties sharing the names and in general terms the policies of the two federal parties, the Liberals and the Conservatives. But federal and provincial governments tended to have varying interests, the first directed towards overall national policies, and the latter towards the more specific needs of the regions. The period between the wars was to see British Columbians beginning to reject the federal party system, or even localized versions of it, as inapplicable to the provincial context. Quite apart from the largely western-based socialist and labour parties founded on economic and class issues, there appeared a series of movements based more specifically on regional discontents and stressing local interests. It was one such movement that almost put John Oliver out of office in his last election of 1924, when the great Liberal majority of 1916 melted entirely away.

The new movement was the Provincial party, established by a variety of local interests that wanted to get rid of Oliver's Liberals without letting Bowser and his Tories back in again. It was founded at a Vancouver convention held at the end of 1923, and Vancouver remained the epicentre of this short-lived but briefly powerful party. Its membership swept in representatives of all those groups outside labour and socialist circles who were unhappy, for good or bad reasons, with the governments that had held power in British Columbia since the turn of the century. There were discontented farmers from the United Farmers of British Columbia, and the last supporters of the short-lived postwar Soldiers' party. There were populist radicals who ironically saw the creation of a new party as the way out of the party system, there were dissident Tories and Liberals whose quarrels were with the personalities rather than the principles or practices of their party leaders. Sir Charles Hibbert Tupper, ancient, irascible and about to die, hovered over the party's genesis, but the leadership of the Provincials fell to Alexander Duncan McRae, an armchair general during the war—"the unscarred hero" as John Oliver called him—who had become a millionaire through his speculations in logging and fishing and had ridden high on the local boom of the mid-1920s, so that the great mansion of Hycroft he had built on the northern ridge of Shaughnessy in Vancouver was the site of parties that were the talk of the province and the goal of the socially aspirant.

The Provincial party fought a bitter campaign, accusing Oliver and the Bowser indiscriminately of corruption. It was financed at first mainly by McRae, and later by other Vancouver industrialists and speculators, but it uncovered a genuine popular distrust of party politicians, and it gathered enough votes to deprive the Liberals of a majority in many constituencies. In the end Oliver's party was reduced to twenty-three members in a house of forty-eight, though the Provincial party itself, in spite of its comparatively high popular vote, won only three seats. Ironically, all three party leaders, Oliver, Bowser and McRae, were defeated in their own constituencies. Oliver returned to the house through a by-election, and then he ruled with the support of the labour group and a few independents.

Like so many British Columbia premiers before him, John Oliver fell mortally ill while in office. The Liberal caucus out of loyalty refused to name a premier in his place, but it did nominate John D. MacLean, a Greenwood doctor who had become minister of finance, as acting premier and his eventual successor.

Dr. Tolmie Tries to Treat an Ailing World

MacLean took office on Oliver's death in August 1927 and carried on a policy geared towards the coming election, a policy whose caution was fatal in such volatile times. He abandoned Oliver's social assistance proposals and concentrated on strengthening earlier popular schemes like building yet more roads, helping agricultural interests by strengthening marketing regulations, subsidizing fruit growers in the Okanagan and dairy farmers at Sumas, talking about extending the rump of the PGE to Prince George and North Vancouver, and demanding further restrictions on the entry of Chinese and Japanese and the repatriation of those already in the province. (As late as the 1920s *all* parties in British Columbia were ardently racist.)

It was a lacklustre programme by a dull "safe" man, but not a safe enough man to take advantage of the notable improvement in the province's economy. Mining, logging and fishing were prospering as never before, and pulp and paper, made in great company towns like Powell River and Ocean Falls on the coast, was proving a vigorous new industry. Building was booming in the areas (Point Grey and South Vancouver) recently incorporated into Vancouver, now indisputably the third of Canada's great cities. It was a rare time of industrial peace, and wages throughout the province were higher than they had ever been before.

But none of this saved the Liberals from defeat at the hands of a man whose antecedents reached back to the very first years of British Columbia's existence. Bowser had at last resigned from the Conservative leadership in November 1926, and the call had gone out to Dr. Simon Fraser Tolmie. Tolmie was a veterinarian but also an experienced politician who had been representing Victoria in the House of Commons since 1917. He had served in two Tory cabinets and had been appointed minister of agriculture under Arthur Meighen in the same year as he was elected leader of the British Columbia Conservatives. Tolmie was the son of Factor William Fraser Tolmie, who had arrived to serve the Hudson's Bay Company at Fort Vancouver in 1833. His mother was Jane Work, the daughter of Chief Factor John Work, who had reached the coast in 1823, ten years before the elder Tolmie, and Jane's mother, Susette Legace, was a *métisse* from Fort Spokane. Simon Fraser Tolmie would be the only premier of British Columbia with native blood in his veins; he was a "native son" on two counts, but there is no evidence that he was ever interested in improving the lot of his Indian brethren.

For two years after being chosen as leader of the Provincial party, Tolmie remained in Ottawa, awaiting his call. It came when MacLean announced the election day as 18 July 1928; Tolmie immediately resigned from the House of Commons and the cabinet to return and travel by automobile more than 4,000 miles (6437 km) back and forth across British Columbia, introducing himself to the populace in remote settlements as well as large towns, and being introduced to the Liberals' patchwork of good and bad roads.

Liberal roadwork patronage and the unwonted prosperity of the province in 1929 did not sway the electors to give their support to MacLean's unexciting and unoriginal government. They voted on personality rather than programme or record, for Tolmie was a genial, expansive man with the comfortable look of a horse doctor turned prosperous cattle breeder. Farmers thought him one of their own, and the businessmen who had supported the Provincial party thought him more likely to be sympathetic to their interests than the Liberals—and particularly John Oliver—had seemed. In such circumstances the trouble Tolmie took to woo his voters paid off well, and there was another landslide victory, this time for the Tories: thirty-five Conservatives were elected against twelve Liberals and one labour member; MacLean was among the defeated.

Tolmie had just over a year left of the good times of the 1920s, and it turned out to be a banner year in economic terms and a lost year in political ones. Industrialists, stockbrokers, bankers and lawyers prospered in the hectic atmosphere of the last of the good times for many years to come. Conspicuous spending was more widely spread among the population than ever before, for the age of buying on credit had arrived, and people were busily equipping themselves with homes and

motor cars, with the latest appliances and clothes made from the first new synthetic fibres, all on the glad-and-sorry system, to the great benefit of department
stores and car dealers, real estate agents and builders and, above all, banks.

People traded frenziedly in shares of all kinds, but especially in risky mining
stocks, for which the Vancouver Stock Exchange had acquired a lasting and dubious fame. In 1929 there were eighty-three admitted millionaires in the city, which
might be represented on the map as a kind of giant squid sending out its tentacles
and sucking in the wealth of the province, much of it in the way of raw materials
to be used in local factories, but even more to be exported elsewhere, for Vancouver was not only the great entrepôt for heavy exports like metals and lumber but
also for the fruit of the Okanagan, the tinned fish of the upcoast canneries, the
dairy products of the Fraser Valley, the cheese of Armstrong, even the preserves of
Doukhobor jam makers. The hinterland depended on Vancouver to use or sell its
products, and in early 1929 the hinterland was prospering at the same time as the
commercial capital.

Dr. Tolmie and his associates seem to have imagined that the good days would
last forever. And like the industrialists and the financiers of Vancouver, and the
small people who had been riding on the illusory tide of prosperity, they were
taken by surprise on Black Thursday, 29 October 1929, when the New York stock
market collapsed because of the overextension of the credit markets by which all
of them had been living. Almost imperceptibly, economic developments since the
end of World War I had crossed political boundaries, and now the ripples of a crisis in Wall Street rocked the world. Demand fell immediately below supply and
continued to do so, and every region dependent on primary production, like British Columbia, felt the effect at once. People whose resources had melted away
overnight in the stock market no longer wanted new houses; they were too busy
trying to sell the homes they had. And so the demand for British Columbian lumber fell across the subcontinent. Nobody wanted to buy new cars or new appliances, even on credit, and so the market for metals declined, while even salmon
became a threatened commodity as the income of English workers fell away and
they could no longer afford high tea with tinned sockeye. Finally, the general economic decline meant a glut on the world grain market, and this—combined with
drought conditions in wheat-growing Saskatchewan—meant in turn that less
grain came to the ports of Vancouver and Prince Rupert for shipment. Even the
demand for Crowsnest coal and Okanagan apples fell away sharply.

All classes suffered, some more than others. People in general were trapped by
the debts they had incurred in the days when credit was granted recklessly, but
even when the credit institutions—trust companies and banks—foreclosed, they
found it hard to recoup their money, for the repossessed property was sold with difficulty and at low prices.

A classic case was the bankruptcy of the Doukhobor Christian Community of
Universal Brotherhood with its properties at Grand Forks and in the East
Kootenay. The Depression robbed the community of its cash income, and in the
mid-thirties, when the Bank of Commerce and Sun Life Insurance foreclosed on a

total debt of less than $400,000, they took over improved properties that in normal times would have been worth between $3,000,000 and $4,000,000. But the land was still occupied by thousands of malcontent Doukhobors, and both the financial institutions and the provincial government were apprehensive of the effects of an attempt to evict them, so that in the end the bank got no profit. After Dr. Tolmie had departed, the province bought the mortgage at cost and the Doukhobors remained as tolerated squatters.

Other proprietors were less fortunate; all over the province businessmen went into bankruptcy and middle-class people lost their jobs and homes, and in all this the towns of the interior, where production began, were even more deeply affected than Vancouver.

Yet it was in Vancouver, the industrial centre of the province, that the workers suffered most. In the summer of 1929 the average weekly wage had reached a record high of $29.20, but employment declined sharply after October, and in January 1930 alone the number of unemployed increased three times, far more than the usual winter seasonal increase. As the months went by the numbers were swollen by the fact the unemployed men began to filter in from outside the province, riding the rods, and almost all of them heading for Vancouver, to which they were attracted by the fact that the climate was more clement than in central Canada or in the prairie provinces. Once over the mountains, they set up their rough encampments—the famous "hobo jungles"—on the edges of the interior towns and lived as best they could on begging and casual labour and whatever relief the communities could offer them.

Before 1929 ended the breadlines were forming in Vancouver, and by the spring of 1930 some 7,000 men were on relief in that city alone. By February 1932 there were more than 67,000 unemployed in a province whose population according to the 1931 census was 694,000. In 1933, the year of Tolmie's departure, the figure reached 100,000, or somewhat more than an eighth of the population. The atmosphere of the cities volatilized as the communists, hitherto a tiny fringe radical movement that emerged in the early 1920s, came into prominence as militant leaders of the unemployed. Over the winter of 1929–30 there were persistent manifestations, mainly by single itinerant unemployed. The Central Relief Office in Vancouver was occupied by them, and they organized marches through the streets which the police habitually broke up.

The initial burden lay on the municipalities, for Tolmie was slow to involve the province. He raised a loan of $7,000,000, with which he provided 7,200 men with work on road construction, but he went no farther until he saw how the federal election of August 1930 would swing. In the meantime, he set on foot a programme of budgetary restraint to counter falling revenue. Among other economies, the closing down of the university was recommended by an advisory committee of businessmen Tolmie had appointed at the suggestion of the timber magnate H. R. MacMillan, but the institution managed to survive with a 43 per cent cut in its appropriation.

The federal election was won by Tolmie's fellow Conservative, R. B. Bennett, but Bennett was reluctant to become too deeply involved in the problems of the provinces, so it was only a year afterwards, in the fall of 1931, that he agreed to provide federal contributions towards public works.

Then the two higher levels of government decided to relieve the burden on the municipalities by setting up relief camps for the single men in the remote parts of the province where better communications were needed. Eventually, there were 237 such camps, containing more than eighteen thousand men. They were breeding grounds for discontent as the men tried to live on scanty provisions in primitive lodgings far away from ordinary communities; there were accusations that the relief officials were pilfering the food, and in some cases this was proved. For the communists, it was their hour of glory—the only time in Canadian history when they had even a small mass movement to lead, which they did with a curious mixture of concern and calculation, genuinely angry at the plight of the workless, yet eager to turn it to partisan advantage.

In February 1932, led by communist militants and imitating the unemployed in Britain, many of the men in the camps set off for Vancouver on a hunger march; there were violent clashes between them and their supporters, and the police. In the end, on 1 June 1933, when the province had found it impossible to sustain them, the camps passed under the control of the Ministry of National Defence and, unimaginatively disciplined in what became rural barracks, the unemployed became an increasingly explosive force.

The only way Tolmie could envisage out of the situation was an all-party coalition, like that of wartime, which he seems to have regarded as a kind of magic panacea. But Thomas Dufferin Pattullo (more generally known as "Duff") contemptuously rejected the proposal now that he was Liberal leader, and even Tolmie's own caucus was split over the question. Hanging on desperately, Tolmie waited before calling an election until the end of August 1933, a few days before his term of office ended.

Few British Columbians, even among Tolmie's supporters, were surprised when the political pendulum swung wildly and Tolmie went to a defeat even more sensational than his 1928 victory. The Conservative party was reduced to one member; Tolmie himself was defeated. Dissident Tories under William Bowser had created a non-partisan movement, but Bowser himself died of a heart attack on the eve of the election, and only two of his supporters were returned. The Liberals won thirty-four seats, enough for Pattullo to rule with a comfortable majority. But the great surprise of the election was that, apart from the usual small clutch of independents and dogmatic socialists, a party entirely new on the scene had gained seven seats, scooped up over 31 per cent of the popular vote, and deprived the Tories even of the satisfaction of becoming the official opposition.

Populism on the Left

The new party was the Co-operative Commonwealth Federation—the CCF—a movement so far apart from the old-line political trends that it did not call itself a party. The CCF, which became a lasting feature of the British Columbian scene and as the New Democratic party survived the Liberals and the Conservatives as a stable British Columbia provincial party, was founded in 1932 as an alliance of western agrarian populists, academic radicals, social gospel clergymen, urban socialists and trade unionists.

The CCF was like no previous political party in Canada. Its highly revered leader was the former Methodist minister James Shaver Woodsworth, who had come to left-wing politics through the social gospel movement, which also inspired T. C. Douglas and other early CCF activists. Woodsworth had lived in British Columbia, where he had run a mission before he left the church and worked on the docks. The more leftist members of the farmer-dominated Progressive party found their way into the CCF, and so did some members of the United Farmers of British Columbia. Most Canadian socialists eventually joined, yet the party's socialism was in fact undogmatic enough for small businessmen as well to find their way in under its wings. Some of Canada's brightest intellectuals had taken part in framing the Regina Manifesto, in which the party defined itself in August 1933, just over a year after a Western Conference of Labour Parties in Calgary decided in July 1932 to form a party that would bring together both farmer and labour groups. It was the Depression that brought the farmers in, just as it brought in the unemployed.

Immediately the CCF was formed, a Vancouver physician, Dr. Lyle Telford, became a kind of missionary for the new party and travelled over the province, speaking in town halls and village schoolrooms and setting up literally hundreds of CCF clubs. The party fielded forty-six candidates, almost a full slate, and scooped up over 31 per cent of the popular vote; while it won only seven of the seats, its presence contributed in other constituencies to the dramatic defeat of the Tories. With its emergence as the official opposition, the CCF became a lasting factor in British Columbian politics, and one of growing importance. Though it was born in the middle of the Depression and its immediate appeal was that of a movement that might show a way out of the troubles of the times, it was not merely a depression party but one that gained its local strength and lasting influence from the emergence among the people of a profound resentment of corporate outsiders who exploited their province and a profound distrust of political parties like the Liberals and the Conservatives that had their roots and origins in central Canada.

Mr. Pattullo's Little New Deal

Quite apart from the emergence of the CCF on the left, the elections of 1933 and 1937 represented a marked reformist shift in the provincial political style. The Liberal leader, Thomas Dufferin Pattullo, uncompromisingly rejected the proposal of a coalition government that Tolmie had advanced as a panacea for the province's ills, and the reasons why became evident as his innovative policies were quickly unfolded.

Pattullo stands among the most interesting of British Columbia's premiers as a personality and among the more successful ones as a politician responding to his time. He was a dandy who spent hours with his tailor and considered carefully the appropriateness of his buttonholes, yet he was also a man of notable kindness who by his courtesies won over even the parliamentary journalists. He was a personally reticent and in some moods an unapproachable man, yet his concern for the sufferings of others was genuine—particularly for those who had been deprived of their means to live in dignity by their own work because of a depression that had made others prosperous.

He brought to his task a considerable intelligence and a notable power to learn from experience, and his experience in political life had been a long and varied one. Born of a strongly Liberal family in Ontario, he had started off as a reporter on the Woodstock *Sentinel.* At the age of twenty-three he was editor of the *Galt Reformer.* But he ended what looked like a promising journalistic career when his father got him a patronage appointment as secretary to J. M. Walsh, the Mountie who had so famously dealt with Sitting Bull and who was now commissioner for the Yukon. Walsh departed under a cloud in 1898, but Pattullo stayed on in the Yukon government service to become assistant gold commissioner before he resigned in 1901 to join a brokerage and financial business. It was during this period that he first entered politics on the municipal level by becoming a member of the Dawson City council. When he moved to Prince Rupert in 1908 to sell real estate in the brand-new city, he continued his political side career, becoming an alderman and then the mayor of the town, a position he used as a stepping stone into provincial politics; in 1916 he was elected member of the legislative assembly for Prince Rupert.

Pattullo's political experience and obvious talents appealed to the Liberal leader Harlan C. Brewster, who could see ability in others even if he did not possess much himself; without any back bench interlude Pattullo was appointed minister of lands and continued in the role under John Oliver and under MacLean at a time when the profligate land policies of the McBride regime were being reversed and a less accommodating attitude towards speculators and exploiters was being developed. He strongly supported Oliver in his reclamation and irrigation schemes at Sumas Prairie and in the Okanagan, and indeed through his ministry was mainly responsible for their implementation; he was also responsible for the comparative failure of the various soldiers' land settlement schemes. He ran a good department and looked after his constituents without raising scandals, and in normal times one could perhaps expect nothing more from a provincial minister of the crown.

But these were not normal times, as Pattullo discovered after John Oliver died in 1927 and the Liberal party was defeated in 1928. As he performed his critic's duties as leader of the opposition, he was not content with merely exposing the government's weakness. He assiduously prepared himself to tackle the problems that Tolmie with his defensive budget-balancing approach had left unsolved; he read widely and observed the measures that in other countries were being taken to deal with the Depression, assessing their success. In particular he was encouraged by the New Deal, which Franklin D. Roosevelt had introduced early in 1933, with its bold advocacy of state intervention in an ailing economy whose failure was destroying the lives of millions of people. But, in justice to Pattullo, it must be said that it was the similarity of Roosevelt's proposals to ideas he had already developed that most impressed him. In opposition he had come independently to the conclusion that economies, even if they remained predominantly capitalist in terms of ownership, must be planned so as to avoid unforeseen crises. Governments, without being scared by the possibility of immediate deficits, should extend what he called "socialized credit" in order to create jobs and pay wages, and must be willing to keep private industry from collapse as well as to subsidize public works.

By the time Pattullo took over power in 1933, it was evident there was ample need for bolder measures than Tolmie had ever considered: 100,000 people—one person in seven of the province's population—were out of work, and the provincial debt stood at $165,000,000. There was no sign of the Depression lifting, and in fact it would be nearly three years before there would be a noticeable improvement in the economy. Alarmed by Pattullo's unorthodox economic views, the Bank of Commerce, which was the province's banker, cut off credit; and the dominion government of R. B. Bennett, probably for the same reason, was slow to act on Pattullo's requests for aid, which was a major setback, since he had always thought federal-provincial co-operation was necessary if his proposals were to be effective. It was not until the Liberals under Mackenzie King came into power in Ottawa in 1935 that the province was able to receive any substantial aid from the federal government, and then mainly in loans rather than grants, so that the old grievances against Ottawa began to rise up once more, and in British Columbia the word "separation" began to be spoken again in something more than a whisper.

With the assistance of the stockbroker John Hart, whom he made his minister of finance, Pattullo set about doing what he could with the means and resources available. They began, in what they called "The People's Budget," a series of measures aimed to take the pressure off the more desperately afflicted of the population. The poorer people were exempted from the minuscule 1 per cent income tax Tolmie had introduced in 1931. Unemployment relief funds were voted for municipalities, and a mortgage moratorium law relieved the pressure on the heavily indebted. Attention was given to schools at the insistence of Dr. George Weir, the minister of education, who raised the age limit for free education from twelve to fifteen, and increased teachers' salaries and grants to schools. The minister of labour was empowered to establish minimum wage rates and maximum hours of work in all industries. The pattern of social legislation was completed by a referendum in which the government eventually secured the people's approval of a controversial medicare scheme.

During his second session, Pattullo embarked on a programme of public works, mainly—like that of his Liberal predecessor John Oliver—devoted to the improvement of the road system. Existing roads were paved, $3,000,000 were devoted to constructing new roads, while $4,000,000 went into the construction of an ambitious bridge over the Fraser at New Westminster, which began in 1935 and was completed in 1937, providing much employment and greatly improving the transport links between Greater Vancouver, the Fraser Valley and the American border. Named the Pattullo Bridge after its originator, it remains his most visible monument.

In spite of Pattullo's efforts, it was a time of sharply rising discontent, for his measures, enlightened though they were and important in establishing a precedent in terms of government care for the unfortunate (whether or not one approved of the welfare state), merely scratched the surface of existing problems.

In 1935 the discontent of the unemployed was fanned into activism, largely through the efforts of the communists, who had failed in their attempt to elect members in British Columbia for either the provincial legislature or the federal House of Commons, but found a better response among the radical industrial unionists and especially among the workless single men who had been enrolled in the Unemployment Relief Camps. In the spartan setting of the camps, the men were given uncomfortable bunkhouse accommodation, food, medical care and 20 cents a day for a forty-four-hour work week, clearing bush, making roads, and reforesting. They were free to leave when they wished, but there was nowhere they could go to get work. In 1935, seventeen hundred of them, organized by the communist-front Workers' Unity League, went on strike and staged a hunger march to Vancouver, where they stayed for two months, occupying the Hudson's Bay department store and the public library, and clashing sporadically with the police, once so severely that Mayor Gerry McGeer read the Riot Act, in an undertone as the legend goes. Early in June the strikers decided to organize an On-to-Ottawa Trek, so that they could lay their case before R. B. Bennett and his ministers. They rode the roofs of freight cars as far as Regina, where on Bennett's orders the railway refused to take them any farther; the RCMP moved in to arrest the leaders, and this provoked the Regina Riot of 1 July, in which a policeman was killed, many people were injured, and 130 of the unemployed were arrested. The incident did not diminish the militancy of the protesters; many of those who took part on the On-to-Ottawa Trek eventually went to Spain and fought against Franco in the Mackenzie-Papineau Battalion of the International Brigade.

The plight of the strikers aroused sympathy among the general population, but many people even of liberal inclinations—Pattullo and Gerry McGeer among them—were pushed into a harder attitude by the violence not merely among the unemployed but also among the employed, for in the summer of 1935 there was a bitter longshoremen's strike in Vancouver and also a colliers' strike in the interior, both of which led to riots with mass arrests and many injuries.

By the next year, 1936, the general upswing that was beginning in the Canadian economy made itself especially felt in British Columbia. According to figures Finance Minister John Hart offered the legislature late in that year, the lumbering industry had gone up 69 per cent since 1933, fishing 45 per cent, farming 30 per cent and tourism had more than doubled, while capital had begun flowing in through the creation of more than sixteen hundred new businesses with a total capital of more than $314 million.

On the strength of the recovery of the economy and of his bold sounds of defiance against the federal government, which stirred the regional passions that lay
lightly concealed in the minds of most British Columbians, Pattullo called an
election in 1937, adding to his platform a proposal resurrected by later regionalist
premiers of British Columbia—the annexation of the Yukon, so that his province
might sweep majestically northward to the Arctic Sea, a proposal that—needless
to say—came to nothing.

He won an election with the still comfortable tally of thirty-one seats, including
those of his whole cabinet. The Conservatives showed a modest comeback with
eight seats, while the CCF retained its seven seats, though its popular vote fell to
28 per cent. Perhaps the most interesting feature of the election was the appearance for the first time of Social Credit, as yet a very minor factor in the province's
politics. The British Columbia Social Credit League was a group of orthodox followers of Major C. H. Douglas, who saw "Bible Bill" Aberhart's Social Credit
government in Alberta as a heretical group distorting the doctrines of the master.
The Social Credit League ran eighteen candidates in thirteen constituencies,
where many finished last, and gleaned about 1 per cent of the popular vote. Another minority party, the British Columbia Constructionist (or Constructive)
party, was a breakaway from the CCF organized by a social-gospelling Anglican
clergyman, the Rev. Robert Connell, and it did somewhat better than Social
Credit, gathering less than 2 per cent of the popular vote but no seats. However,
the Constructivist party quickly vanished, while Social Credit clung precariously
to life and survived.

Pattullo was never at a loss for ideas, and in his second term he turned towards
the great and still mostly empty north of the province of which the Yukon had
seemed to him the natural extension. He was fascinated by the possibilities of better northern communications offered by the development of local aviation
through the appearance of the bush pilots. He was encouraged by developments in
gold mining—the discoveries at Bridge River and the renewed activity at Wells
outside Barkerville—and he grubstaked placer miners to explore and find more deposits. The discovery of oil in Turner Valley in Alberta stirred his imagination; he
talked in terms of a government-assisted search for petroleum deposits in British
Columbia, and he had plans to establish a Coal and Petroleum Control Board. He
became particularly excited over news that the American government was considering building a highway to Alaska; he foresaw unlimited benefits to the province
if it were routed through British Columbia, and this subject was doubtless high
among the topics of conversation when Pattullo's hero, Franklin D. Roosevelt,
visited Victoria in September 1937 and invited the premier to be his guest at Hyde
Park the following month.

But not many of these aims were to be achieved, and Pattullo found his second
term far less easy than his first, partly because people were ceasing to be cowed by
the Depression and were anxious to show their reviving confidence. Business, particularly mining, was definitely on the upgrade, and the number of people on relief

in the province was steadily declining. Yet there remained the hardcore of militant single unemployed men who tended, since the federal government began to close down the Unemployment Relief Camps, to gravitate to Vancouver, where they survived largely by rattling tin cans under the noses of timid citizens.

By the summer of 1938 there was a concentration of such men in the city, augmented by some sixteen hundred prairie men whom the federal government had supported over the winter in British Columbia reforestation projects, and whom the province now wanted to get rid of, offering them free transport home. But the men refused to move, and at various levels the authorities exacerbated the situation by their actions. The provincial government had already reduced its relief loans to municipalities, arguing that single men should now be able to find work in the summer months. Then the ministry of labour announced that no relief at all would be given to the prairie men, and the mayor of Vancouver complicated the situation by banning begging under the guise of tagdays. Both these announcements were made on 10 May, and on the next day nearly sixteen hundred of the unemployed, in well-disciplined columns, marched to the Vancouver Art Gallery, the General Post Office and the Hotel Georgia, all of which they occupied with the intent of staging an indefinite sit-in strike. The group in the Hotel Georgia moved out, as ordered as a small army, when the Vancouver city council offered them some money as temporary relief; clearing the hotel was regarded as a priority, with the tourist season coming on. But those who occupied the art gallery and the post office stayed put, nonplussing the authorities, who knew that in the volatile situation rough methods were as likely to arouse anger as approval among the general population of the city.

Eventually Mackenzie King broke the deadlock by ordering the RCMP to clear the post office, which was a federal building and hence outside Pattullo's jurisdiction. Early on the morning of 20 June, the Mounties arrived at the post office and the police chief of Vancouver appeared at the art gallery with his own men. In each place the unemployed were given twenty minutes to evacuate the building, and then warning tear gas bombs were released. At the Vancouver Art Gallery, the radical CCF leader Harold Winch persuaded the men not to damage the paintings and to leave peacefully. But at the post office, Steve Brodie made a fiery speech, after which the sit-in strikers smashed the windows, which gave the RCMP the excuse to attack the strikers with whips and nightsticks. The men poured out down Hastings Street, smashing the windows of Spencer's and Woodward's department stores on their way, until they were finally dispersed by police attacks.

Extreme reactions followed. Pattullo appeared in the city and argued that by refusing his demands for further aid, Ottawa must bear most of the blame for what had happened. The CCF, trying to make capital out of the incident and steal the communist thunder, condemned the eviction of the sitdown strikers as "a ghastly, inhuman, brutal course of action," and demanded the resignation of the whole legislature, secure in the knowledge that they would never in fact be called on to put their own seats at peril. There was a big protest meeting in Oppenheimer

Square, from which a crowd of thousands proceeded to the police station, smashed a few more windows and shouted for the release of the strikers who had been arrested. Businessmen—except for the fortunate glaziers—were particularly indignant because of the property damage, and they decided it was time Pattullo made his peace with Ottawa, while it was among them that the idea of a coalition government arose once again. The sympathy which the CCF had somewhat self-righteously shown the demonstrators, mainly in order to secure their own core of voters from leftward erosion, was interpreted by everyone on the right as a sign of the party's incorrigible radicalism, and no longer would the aim of the proposed coalition be to deal with the Depression, which the balance sheets showed was retreating, but to keep the CCF from winning an election.

Pattullo remained strongly opposed to the idea of a coalition, though increasingly after the declaration of war in September 1939, he felt himself isolated even within his own party. The other cause in which Pattullo remained constant was in his uncompromising defence of the province's financial autonomy, which seemed to be threatened by the Ottawa-appointed Rowell-Sirois Commission, which in 1937 began to enquire into the relationship between federal and provincial sources of revenue, and between the respective responsibilities of the two levels of government for solving social and economic problems. The province presented a brief clearly aimed at getting as much as possible while surrendering as little as possible, and at any other time than the late 1930s, when people were still scarred by the Depression and at the same time anxiously anticipating involvement in a second great war, the regional sentiments in favour of it might have been considerable.

It was in many ways a traditional British Columbian request for "better terms" of the kind that premiers like De Cosmos and McBride had presented in the past, based on the province's exceptional needs. The dominion government was asked not merely to assume the entire financial responsibility for relief payments but also to pay all the cost for old-age pensions and to make grants in aid of the provincial health services. It was also asked to absorb the Pacific Great Eastern Railway into the national railway system, and to adjust freight rates and tariffs to suit local needs. At the same time, the province wanted the right to raise income tax to be amended in its favour and called for authority to raise revenue in any way it thought fit. Finally, and ominously in view of what would happen shortly afterwards in the province, it called for the stricter exclusion and repatriation of orientals. British Columbian politicians and labour leaders were never at a loss to find plausible reasons for their ingrained racism.

By the time the federal government called the provinces to a federal-provincial conference in January 1941 to discuss the report of the Rowell-Sirois Commission, Pattullo—who saw in the commission's recommendations nothing else than an attempt to restrict the rights of the provinces in favour of the centre—was already out of touch with most British Columbians, who in wartime circumstances were willing to accept a much greater degree of centralization than they would have been at any other time. At the conference he found two equally intransigent allies in William Aberhart, the Social Credit premier of Alberta, and Mitchell Hepburn, the maverick Liberal premier of Ontario, and so the occasion ended in a deadlock, which Mackenzie King typically smoothed over with appropriately neutral vaguenesses in his concluding speech.

Pattullo returned to British Columbia to fight his last election battle in October 1941. The times had vastly improved, and war industries had already closed the employment gap. In spite of his differences with Ottawa, Pattullo was full of patriotic afflatus; he put forward a good public works programme and extended at least half an olive branch to the dominion government by offering full co-operation in the war effort.

But it was obvious his charisma no longer swayed the people of the province. Even within his own party there was talk of the need for a coalition with the Tories, and he suspected that it was led secretly by his old and close associate, John Hart. The election was a narrow but humiliating defeat. The Liberals emerged with twenty-one seats, four short of a majority, while the ccf raised their number to fourteen, and the Tories to twelve. It was the count of the popular vote that was most desolating for Pattullo. In spite of their greater number of seats, the Liberals had gained only 32.94 per cent, against 33.36 per cent for the ccf and 30.91 per cent for the Tories.

The coalitionists within the Liberal party came into the open, urging the obstinate premier not to try and rule with a partisan minority government, which was sure to be defeated quickly. Finally, in a special one-day province-wide convention in December 1941, the provincial Liberal party voted for coalition. Pattullo, intransigent to the end, resigned, and was followed as coalition premier by his colleague and nemesis, John Hart. At the next provincial election, in 1945, he would be rejected even by his old constituents of Prince Rupert and retire from politics. He was a man of foresight, and many of the ideas he offered and social services he proposed have become part of the fabric of British Columbian life today.

XVII

Once More unto the Breach

A Parade of Unity

At first glance it might seem that Canada's—and hence British Columbia's—
role in World War II was a repeat performance of its role in the Great War.
English Canada as a whole respected the imperial connection and went to war
over a European quarrel, which it had done nothing to incite and from which it
had nothing to gain and not much, at least directly, to fear. As in the previous
conflict, about one person in ten became involved directly in the armed services,
though more women in proportion served in the second war and the casualties
were far less; roughly 4 per cent died as against 10 per cent in the first war.

Yet there were significant differences, particularly in Canada's role as a nation,
between the two wars. As in the Great War, Canada's participation was quite deliberately used as a means of enhancing its national status, and indeed the war so
far as Canada was concerned began in what was an act of independence towards
Britain as much as an act of hostility towards Germany. Mackenzie King deliberately delayed a declaration of war until the matter had been duly discussed in a
special session of the Canadian Parliament, and in this democratic way the country went to war on 10 September 1939, a full nine days after Britain's declaration.

Meanwhile, days before the federal Parliament, Premier Pattullo had already
declared his support for Britain's going to war, and in doing so without challenge
he represented a British Columbian population still predominantly Anglo-Celtic
in composition and still sustaining imperial loyalties that were far less strongly
held either in the prairies with their largely central and eastern European population or in French-speaking Québec. The proportion of volunteers in British Columbia was roughly three times that in Québec, and though there were not so
many recent English immigrants at the end of the Depression decade as in 1914,
there was an immediate exodus of the last of the remittance men and those whose
loyalties to their new home had not yet outgrown their bonds to the old one. Even
in the labour movement the opposition to war and conscription was less than it
had been in the previous conflict, partly because the influence of the antimilitarist
syndicalist elements had diminished, but partly also because in World War II the
workers' efforts to organize did not encounter the same opposition as in the previ-

ous conflict. Another determining fact was that, unlike its pacifist leader, J. S. Woodsworth, the CCF overwhelmingly supported the war.

Under the paraded unity of the war effort, British Columbia was not lacking in conflict. The very character of the coalition government reflected the fear of socialism that was less only than the fear of foreign enemies. British Columbian conflicts were and would remain dominated by class politics rather than cultural politics, though there was to be one notable and appalling exception.

The Politics of Fear

Racial conflict in the anti-Asian form that had been endemic on British Columbia since early colonial days flared into extremity as a panic fear of invasion swept the province after 7 December 1941, when the Japanese attacked Pearl Harbor by surprise, catapulting the United States into the war.

Suddenly what the people of Victoria and Vancouver and the other coastal communities had begun to regard with some complacency as a Pacific Ocean true to its name became a place of danger. Hong Kong was overrun by the Japanese in the latter part of December, and the two battalions of Canadian soldiers there were either killed or made prisoner. Shortly afterwards, Singapore, long regarded as an impregnable fortress, fell to the swiftly moving Japanese. The fears that now developed among British Columbians would be given what seemed to be dramatic justification in June 1942, when the Japanese actually set foot on American soil by capturing the two remote Aleutian islands of Attu and Kiska. Shortly afterwards, on 20 June, for the first time in either world conflict, British Columbia became the scene of an act of war, when a Japanese ship shelled the lighthouse on Estevan Point on Vancouver Island.

It was to be an isolated incident, but on that excited summer day British Columbians were not to know this, and, seeing the Japanese enemy approaching Alaska, they began to remember the phrase recently made so familiar by the Spanish Civil War, and to seek out a possible Fifth Column.

The Fifth Column they imagined they had found consisted of the Japanese immigrants and children of immigrants who had established themselves as competent fishermen and farmers, contributing notably to the province's economy. Mostly they lived in or near the cities of Vancouver and Victoria, where they could find markets for their produce, or along the coast where they carried on their fishing, and this was interpreted as a special danger, since spies and saboteurs among them would be in ideal positions to strike in favour of an invading force. So fear was added to a resurgent racialism and economic jealousy in inspiring the provincial politicians to demand their removal from the coastal regions.

To their credit the senior military and police officers in the region reported that in their view the Japanese posed no threat at all to the security of Canada, and in the event not a single Japanese was charged with disloyal acts towards Canada. But for reasons of state and party, Mackenzie King and his cabinet decided to accede to provincial demands; elaborate arrangements were made, and on 27 February 1942 one of the worst official crimes in Canadian history was enacted when 23,000 people of Japanese race, men, women and children, were rounded up from their farms and businesses, from their boats and the canneries where many of them worked up the coast, and gathered in a holding camp in Vancouver. Almost two thirds of these people were either Canadian-born or naturalized, but their exclusion from the franchise had made them automatically second-class citizens, and as such—people without rights—they were treated.

Afterwards these people were sent into a kind of Siberian exile, settled in ghost towns from which the miners had gone, like Greenwood and Bridge River, and placed on sugar beet farms in the Alberta prairies. Their property—farms, boats, businesses and even personal belongings—was confiscated and sold at derisory prices, an operation from which a number of unscrupulous British Columbians in official positions became rich. Before any of the meagre proceeds were paid back to the original Japanese owners, deductions were made for the relief payments they received while they were unemployed and destitute in the jobless places to which they had been exiled.

This situation continued until the end of the war in Asia, the fall of 1945, when the federal government decided that the system of camps must be ended and arbitrarily offered their inhabitants the alternative of being deported to Japan or being dispersed over the country, so long as they went east of the Rockies. Only a few took the first alternative, and they experienced great difficulty fitting back into the tight community of Japan. The rest preferred Canada, despite all that Canadians had done to them, and began to rebuild their lives with patience and fortitude. They aroused the admiration of other Canadians and stirred their guilt to such a degree that in 1946, when the government proposed to deport another ten thousand of them willy-nilly to Japan, the protests were so vocal and countrywide that the plan was abandoned.

By now a general shift in Canadian attitudes towards visible ethnic minorities was taking place, largely because the racist policies of the Nazis had made Canadians, and British Columbians especially, uneasy about their own prejudices and their discriminatory policies in the past. The dignified acceptance of their lot by the Japanese, and the willingness of the Chinese and the Sikhs to play their part in the war effort, had also influenced public opinion, and in 1947 the Chinese and the Sikhs were brought back into the community by being given the franchise, and the same rectification of the law was made in relation to the Japanese in 1949, though it would take another forty years before, in the late 1980s, the survivors would receive some compensation for the financial losses that had been forced upon them.

Playing Political Second Fiddle
"War is the health of the state," said the American radical Randolph Bourne, and there is no doubt that in times of war, centralization and bureaucratic control flourish, and even the most democratic society edges closer to the total state of the

fascists and the communists as all interests are increasingly ruthlessly subordinated to the end of victory, which is seen as the only way to survival.

In some parts of Canada, Québec especially, there was a measure of resistance to this inevitability, but in patriotic British Columbia there was virtually none. From the Conservative right to the CCF left (who were centralizers by socialist conviction), there was almost universal agreement on this point. Harold Winch, the left-wing leader of the provincial CCF, could without any sense of incongruity exhort a gathering of local businessmen over their tough chicken lunch "to look at things from the standpoint of Canada first and British Columbia second." The kind of local patriotism that found expression in talk about separation or secession abruptly came to an end.

John Hart never left any doubt of his willingness to accept on behalf of the province a lesser and less independent role than was customary in peacetime. The principle of federal requirements temporarily preceding provincial ones was tacitly recognized and confirmed formally in December 1941, when Hart concluded an agreement with Ottawa that ceded to it income tax and corporation tax revenues in return for a fixed annual grant.

The virtues of Hart's government were those of a well-run small business; midway through its life, Bruce Hutchison, by this time the most influential journalist in British Columbia, remarked that it had been more "competent and honest" than any other government in his experience of twenty-five years as a reporter. Hart kept house well, and he kept books well, but he was fortunate in the era when he lived. By the time he assumed office, the armed forces and war industries between them had soaked up all the unemployed; the vast burden of relief payments that Tolmie and Pattullo had struggled so hard and ineffectively to control was no longer there. In addition, a number of important public works came as free gifts to the province through the war, providing employment and also facilities that would be useful to the province and its people in times of peace.

The most important was the actual building, in 1942–43, of the great highway to Alaska of which Pattullo had dreamed during the 1930s. Hastily planned under the threat of Japanese invasion, 1,430 miles (2301 km) of rough road were built by the U.S. Army in eight months, beginning at Dawson Creek in the Peace River country and ending at Big Delta in Alaska. It crossed the northwestern corner of British Columbia, transforming old fur-trade posts like Fort St. John and Fort Nelson, through which it passed, into modern communities. In 1943 this rough road was upgraded into an all-weather gravel highway and extended to Fairbanks in Alaska. Shortly afterwards the province built a road from Prince George across the relatively low Pine Pass in the Rockies to link up with the Alaska Highway at Dawson Creek. By this highway, named after John Hart, the isolation of the wheat-growing Peace River area from the rest of the province was ended, and access was opened to much of the mineral-rich north. No less important was the immediate postwar extension of the coalition government's road-building programme by the construction of the Hope-Princeton Highway, largely following the route of the Dewdney Trail of the 1860s through the wilderness of Manning Park, providing a more direct link than had existed before between Vancouver and the southern interior.

Perhaps the third most important achievement of the Hart government was the creation of the British Columbia Power Commission, whose purpose was to extend electricity—"a bulb in every barn" as the slogan went—in the rural areas. People in remote areas benefited, but nothing was done to meet the demands of the CCF that the existing power companies be socialized, so that 90 per cent of the production and distribution of electricity in the province remained in the hands of B.C. Electric and of the much more localized West Kootenay Power Company, which was a subsidiary of the CPR. However, as a result of this bill, the public ownership of power facilities did begin to seem a viable option.

Even though Hart had surrendered much of the taxation field to Ottawa, the wartime boom in production resulted in such revenue benefits to the province that the government was able to declare successive surpluses and also to make modest gifts to the population in other directions than highways and rural power grids.

Education and the farming community were particularly favoured. Teachers' salaries were raised, especially in rural areas, and teachers were encouraged to upgrade their qualifications with free summer school training. School buildings were improved, and the University of British Columbia, so long regarded as a luxury that could safely be neglected, was granted increased funds, though between 1930 and the end of the war the only new building there, the Brock Building (intended for the student union), was erected with funds collected by the students themselves. Apart from rural electrification, farmers were helped mainly by the reduction of taxes of various kinds, notably the school taxes, which in rural areas were largely borne by the province. And, pushing in the direction of the social legislation of later years, family courts were established and the scope of the Mothers' Allowance Act was broadened to include older dependents.

Inevitably, as the war drew near its end, the problems of adjustment to a peacetime situation began to draw the attention of the provincial as well as federal legislators, and already in 1942 a postwar rehabilitation programme was being developed in British Columbia. Once again the agrarian solution to the problem of the returning soldiers, which had failed after the Great War, was brought forward. The province offered considerable financial contributions towards the resettlement of soldiers under the Dominion Veterans' Land Act, though it did not contemplate embarking independently on the kind of soldiers' settlements that had failed so notably when John Oliver and Pattullo attempted them at the end of the Great War.

Holding an election in October 1945, after the war ended in both Europe and Asia, the coalition won a seemingly notable victory, with thirty-seven of its candidates elected while the CCF members were reduced from sixteen to ten. But more significant than the tally of seats was the popular vote. The coalition won 55.8 per cent, but the CCF, despite its loss in seats, still gathered 37.6 per cent, which meant that it was a power not likely to leave the political scene in the near future. The communists, through their front organization, the Labour Progressive party, won no seats but 3.5 per cent of the popular vote; the wartime alliance between the western powers and Russia had conferred on them a degree of respectability, and they were powerful in some of the more radical labour unions. The embryo Social Credit movement, with a mere 6,627 people giving it their votes, scored less than 0.5 per cent, a minuscule anticipation of the shape of things to come.

The Wartime Boom

If war tended to freeze local politics in British Columbia into a standoff between the defensive alliance of the old parties and the obstinately undiminished strength of social democracy represented by the CCF, the social and economic changes precipitated by the needs of pursuing the conflict were considerable. The Hart government had such easy surpluses and so much money to spend on public works and handouts of various kinds mainly because of the tax income brought in by the rapid increase in production. Gross industrial production more than doubled between 1941, when the wartime boom took off, and 1945. And this was no speculative boom directed by the unpredictable forces of the free market. It was part of the immense planned operation carried out by the federal government through C. D. Howe's formidably organized Ministry of Munitions and Supply and after 1944 by his new Department of Reconstruction, a virtual economic dictatorship within a democratic order.

Vancouver—with Victoria as its economic satellite—was chosen as one of the principal centres in Canada for building the great number and variety of ships and other craft needed by both the navy and the merchant marine. Apart from the shipyards where the boats were constructed, numerous factories grew up to manufacture various components used in shipbuilding, which at the peak of war production employed more than thirty thousand people. The aeroplane industry also took root, mainly on Sea Island where the Vancouver International Airport is now located. There was a ready supply of woods usable in plane construction, and once again many subsidiary factories and workshops arose, manufacturing parts of various kinds and employing labour forces that, even more than in World War I, included increasing numbers of women. After the war both shipbuilding and plane construction would diminish in importance locally, but they would leave behind them an infrastructure of secondary industry such as had not before existed on the West Coast.

The boom extended into the interior, where the surviving base-metal mines flourished and the smelters at Trail and elsewhere turned out large quantities of lead, zinc and other metals for war purposes, and in the process manufactured necessary wartime chemicals, as well as artificial fertilizers used to increase the agricultural production of the region. Cattle ranchers, fruit growers and farmers could sell all they produced at steadily increasing prices.

One result of all this productive activity was a rapid wartime increase in the population of the two main cities and of the province in general, despite the loss of the tens of thousands of people who had left to serve in the armed forces. Men and women flooded into the West Coast cities not only from the interior but also from the prairies and eastern Canada, to meet the need for workers. Before the war had ended, the population of the province was touching a million, and that of Vancouver had passed the 300,000 mark. Vancouver, Victoria and other communities rapidly became overcrowded, and there was a serious lack of housing, a need that could be addressed only when the war had ended.

One of the most striking developments as a result of this wartime boom was a revivification of labour unionism, and particularly industrial unionism, on a scale even greater than that of the mining and railway boom years at the turn of the century. Since the collapse of the One Big Union in the 1920s, the Trades and Labour Congress, with its basis of old-style craft unions, had dominated the labour movement of British Columbia. During the Depression years industrial unionism had revived in North America, and in 1938 the militant Congress for Industrial Organization (CIO) was founded in the United States. Canadian unions connected with the CIO united with the ACCL and other syndicalist groups in 1940 to form the Canadian Congress of Labour (CCL).

The thousands of people entering wartime industries proved an excellent field for recruitment, and within three years the CCL, encouraged by federal legislation favouring labour unions, had made rapid progress in recruiting members. In the logging industry, the International Woodworkers of America increased during that period from fifteen hundred to fifteen thousand members. In 1943 when it was founded, there were almost thirteen thousand workers in the Shipyard General Workers' Federation of British Columbia, while the Mine, Mill and Smelter Workers counted eight thousand members, largely concentrated at the Cominco smelter at Trail. In 1944 the local CCL unions revived the British Columbia Federation of Labour which, like a number of the unions comprising it, fell under the temporary control of communist union bosses. These were dedicated men and capable organizers; many of them were converted syndicalists who imagined they were finding a revolutionary role in the communist ranks. They were militants of the kind who would certainly have found themselves in the Gulags if they had made their way to Stalin's Russia. But in their role as union organizers they had an importance that was quite outside their political stances. They laid the foundations of the strong labour movement that has persisted ever since and provided a continuity, in their passionate devotion to industrial unionism, with the IWW of early days.

Even in the ranks of the Trades and Labour Congress, the generally conservative and reformist wing of the labour movement, there were communist-dominated organizations, such as the West Coast Seamen's Union and the five thousand members of the United Fishermen and Allied Workers' Union, formed in 1945 through an alliance of former fishermen's and cannery workers' organizations. But the Trades and Labour Congress was perhaps most striking for the unions of white-collar workers that began to flourish under its wing, including the Newspaper Guild of journalists and editorial workers (formed in 1942) and the British Columbia Teachers' Federation, which joined the Trades and Labour Congress in 1944.

The power of the communists in the labour movement tended to widen a gap that had existed from the beginning between the industrial and political wings of the left. While the national body of the Canadian Congress of Labour endorsed the CCF without qualification, the British Columbia Federation of Labour supported the current communist line of the United Front. In its founding convention the delegates called for unity between the CCF and the Labour Progressive party. Though there were some communist sympathizers in the CCF, most of its members wanted no truck with either communists or Liberals. They were content to remain as a strong opposition without ties to any other party, since they did not doubt that very soon, in the after-war period, they would be able to rout the dwindling Liberals and Tories.

XVIII

The Tides of Change

After the War

Wars are great agents of change, often for the worse, but sometimes for the better. True, there were some respects in which British Columbia seemed little changed as it shook free from World War II. The great steam locomotives of the past still toiled their way through the passes of the Rockies; the neat black-and-white Canadian Pacific ferry boats still plied between Vancouver and its namesake island. But the old wooden mansions of Edwardian days rotted beside the streets of Vancouver's West End, expecting a rapid demise, and the suburban middle-class housing that had been new in the 1920s was looking shabby from years of neglect. A decade and a half of municipal cheese-paring had left the cities with obsolete public transportation, inadequate sewage and water systems, old schools in need of repair, and parks in need of attention. Great highways like the Cariboo Road were still unpaved, and the shortest way from Vancouver to Calgary went through the Selkirk Range by a road around the Big Bend of the Columbia that was little more than a rough track; most motorists went by the better roads of the United States on their way from British Columbia to the rest of Canada.

The war, which had left so much in the cities to decay and had concentrated production on goods to be destroyed rather than to be consumed, had helped to create the transport links by which the province's postwar recovery would be developed. Not only had highways been built into the north but wartime developments in aviation had changed the pattern of transport, especially in the north of the province. Canadian Pacific Airlines, founded in 1942 from the amalgamation of a dozen competing local outfits, began flying DC-3s along the coast and among the offshore islands. By the early 1950s, though hampered by government regulations, it was aiming to compete with the publicly owned TransCanada Airlines and was turning Vancouver into a hub of international air transport by probing southward to Mexico, Peru and Argentina, and eastward to Japan.

Serious exploration for oil and natural gas began for the first time immediately following the war, and by the 1950s the first oil pipeline was being built over the mountains from the Peace River area; in 1957 Westcoast Transmission would complete a natural gas pipeline through the Rockies to the lower mainland. The era of large hydroelectrical projects began as British Columbia Electric and the British Columbia Power Commission competed to serve the new factories, suburbs and communities that were appearing in all parts of the province. As a symbol of the growing importance of electrical power, B.C. Electric built an architecturally advanced headquarters on Burrard Street in Vancouver, a tall double wedge of a building, designed by the avant-garde architect Ron Thom and decorated with mosaics designed by B. C. Binning, one of British Columbia's leading modernist painters.

A tendency emerged for industry to go to the source of power and raw materials in the interior rather than remain in the coastal cities. The presence of abundant hydro power led the Aluminum Company of Canada (Alcan) to establish a great plant at Kitimat on a remote inlet off the northern coast of British Columbia. To run its operations, Alcan built an entirely new town for 13,500 people, carved out of the wilderness, between 1951 and 1954. New sawmills and pulp mills on a large scale appeared on Vancouver Island, in the Kootenays and at Prince George, while the pulp mill at Powell River and the Cominco smelter at Trail were greatly enlarged to meet the call of expanding world markets. The rising scale of industry led to greater concentration as small sawmills were forced out of operation, and five major combines came to control most of the province's lumber industry, while the number of fish canneries declined to a sixth of those which had been in operation at the end of the Great War. Industrial parks appeared on the edges of towns and in former waste spaces, and they brought to the province a wide variety of secondary industries.

The rapidly developing industries were fed by influxes of labour as well as of capital, as many soldiers returning from the war, like their predecessors in 1918, chose British Columbia for their final destination. By 1951 the provincial population had reached 1,165,210, an increase of a third over the last census, partly due to the beginning of a new wave of immigration. British Columbia was naturally one of the favoured destinations of British immigrants, who began to arrive in growing numbers from 1947 onward; unlike previous generations of British, the workers among them tended to be skilled rather than unskilled, and they included many professionals and people involved in the arts. With their experience and abilities, these immigrants contributed notably to industrial development, the medical profession was strengthened by them, and hundreds of writers, artists and performers helped to prepare the cultural renaissance that took place during these decades.

The Dutch began to arrive in 1947, shortly after the British; they established many nurseries and greenhouse complexes in both the lower mainland and Vancouver Island. The first postwar German immigrants also began to arrive as early as 1947; these were *volksdeutsche*, ethnic Germans (the so-called displaced persons) who had lost their homelands as a result of the war. The postwar ban on the immigration of German nationals was lifted in 1950, and for about a decade a steady stream of German immigrants arrived. Unlike some earlier German groups like the Mennonites, who tended to remain aloof from the ambient Canadian culture, both the Germans and the Dutch who arrived after 1947 assimilated quickly into Canadian society.

The Germans, like the English and the Dutch, tended to contain a high proportion of skilled people and professionals, but postwar expansion quickly created a need for unskilled labour. In the early 1950s, after the preferred northern Europeans had arrived, the Mediterranean peoples, first Italians, then Greeks and Portuguese, began to appear in large numbers, radically changing the ethnic variety of British Columbia's population. The population of Italian birth and extraction tripled as a result of this postwar influx. The Italians became the first experts in "chain migration," the cumulative sponsorship of relatives so that whole families and clans would be reunited in Canada. Before World War II, the largest proportion of Italians in British Columbia lived in Trail, where many of them worked as labourers at the smelter, but the postwar migration created a concentration of them in east Vancouver. The Greeks, who came somewhat later, similarly established themselves on the west side of Vancouver.

The decades after World War II saw a dramatic change in Canadian policies relating to immigrants of Asian origin and other "visible" groups like Africans and Caribbeans. The first relaxations of restrictions on Chinese entry during the 1950s allowed only relatives of Chinese of Canadian citizenship to enter the country. This narrow concession merely taxed the ingenuity of Chinese anxious to leapfrog via Hong Kong into Canada, and many people entered illegally with the aid of a complex network of middlemen, fake relatives and forgers of documents. In 1960 the RCMP estimated that of the 23,000 Chinese who had arrived in Vancouver since 1946, 11,000 came with false papers. The Canadian government reacted in the only realistic way, by offering an amnesty to all those who would come forward, and 12,000 Chinese people in fact legalized their entry in this way in just over a year.

In 1962 a significant change took place in immigration policy when skill was accepted as the leading criterion for entry. A few years afterwards, the "points" system came into operation, by which prospective immigrants were judged, at least nominally, by a series of criteria other than that of race. For Asians and Caribbeans, this meant that they could enter Canada on the basis of their own excellence as well as their family connections, though the programmes for the reunification of families still continued to provide most of the increase in the "visible" minorities, which in British Columbia tended to be Asian: Chinese first, then South Asian (mainly Sikh) and to a much lesser extent—in view of the rapid recovery of their own country—Japanese. The policies under which the immigrants entered British Columbia were federal in origin, though they were encouraged by changes in local attitudes towards Asians.

In the period of revived Chinese immigration, a change in the nature of the Chinese population took place in British Columbia. In 1972 there were approximately 150,000 Chinese in greater Vancouver alone, and smaller groups in other towns of the province. Now the descendants of the nineteenth-century pioneers and the reunited families of the 1950s had become a minority. The majority were new immigrants, who for the most part had come from Hong Kong and were originally fugitives from a mainland China whose political inclinations they had rejected by flight. The more educated Chinese spilt out of the traditional Chinatown localities of Vancouver and Victoria, and began to set up house in areas hitherto uninhabited by Asians. They also moved out of the traditional Chinese occupations of labouring and market gardening and laundering, of restaurants and small stores, and into a wide variety of trades and into the professions, particularly medicine and law. More than any other of the visible minorities, the Chinese have succeeded in assimilating economically yet remaining culturally distinctive.

In addition to these waves of immigrants called in largely by Canada's own need to strengthen a slowly growing population in a vast area, there were the special groups of immigrants admitted through a more active compassion than had existed in the past, the result of a kind of collective guilt that had arisen over the previous racism and xenophobia, and particularly over the persecution of Japanese Canadians during the 1940s and the Canadian government's callous rejection of Jewish refugees immediately preceding and during World War II.

Now, from the mid-1950s onward, Canadians—and British Columbians high among them—showed an instant concern for refugees in times of political crisis abroad. This was notably the case in 1956, at the time of the Hungarian uprising against a tyrannical communist government. One of the most striking incidents locally in connection with that crisis was the arrival of the whole Sopron College of Forestry from Hungary; its faculty and student body went collectively into exile, and were accepted at the University of British Columbia by an unusual arrangement, as a university within a university, until all the students graduated under the guidance of the teachers who had accompanied them. Later, in 1968, many Czechs arrived as a result of the Russian invasion of their country to suppress Dubcek's "socialism with a human face."

In 1971–72 a few hundred Tibetan refugees from the Chinese invasion of their country came to Canada through an arrangement between the Dalai Lama and the Canadian government; many of them settled in the British Columbian communities of Surrey and White Rock, where they still form a closely knit community, retentive of their language and their lamaist traditions. Finally, creating a break in what had become a pattern of assistance to refugees from communism, Canada in 1972 gave refuge to many of the Asians (mainly of Indian extraction) whom Idi Amin had expelled from Uganda; many of them settled in British Columbia, where they not only contributed commercial skills but also raised the cultural level of the local Indian community. Many were Ismaili Moslems, and their mosque, like the Sikh gurudwara that Arthur Erickson designed in South Vancouver, is among the most striking religious buildings in the province.

By 1972 British Columbia was a multicultural complex of peoples of many origins, traditions and beliefs, and now only in name and in history was it *British Columbia*.

The Fall of the Old Parties

While the character of British Columbian demography was changing so radically, the political situation was transformed, largely by the growing class divisions that drove the province at the same time towards populist movements and a polarization of attitudes between the left and the right. In the process, a deep division took place between provincial and federal politics, as the old-line parties lost their power base on a regional level while paradoxically continuing to represent the province in the federal Parliament.

The situation by the end of the war was that the left, with the rapid withering of communist influence and the decline of the Labour Progressive party, became concentrated around the social democratic CCF. It still represented, as it had done for several elections, somewhat over a third of the voting population. The addition of Asian and, by 1949, of native voters did not materially change the situation, though the first Indian MLA, the Nishga Frank Calder, elected in 1949, adhered to the CCF. During the first years of reconstruction following the end of the war, the coalition of the older parties could command a comfortable majority as long as they stayed together, though each was individually weaker in terms of popular vote than the CCF.

Yet, despite the fact that safety lay in unity, the alliance began to show serious signs of postwar strain, particularly after John Hart resigned in 1947 because of exhaustion and sickness. His departure activated a struggle over leadership and representation. According to the coalition arrangement, the Tories were perpetually junior partners, for they had contributed fewer seats when the agreement was reached, and the Liberals, who retained their majority position within the alliance, felt entitled to name the premier in perpetuity.

In the interim between Hart's departure and the naming of a successor, the Tories, and particularly their vain and irascible leader Herbert Anscomb, made clear their discontent with the situation. However, the Liberals stood their ground and went ahead naming their own leader. It began as a hard fight between abrasive personalities, and as an eventual compromise a mild-mannered back bencher and builder's supply merchant of Icelandic descent, Bjorn Johnson, who had made no enemies and been involved in no scandals, was selected. Though he was a capable politician, Johnson was so undistinguished that people could not easily remember his name. He was more often called Byron than Bjorn, and people generally adapted his family nickname of "Bjosse" to "Boss"—"Boss" Johnson—which gave the false impression that he was a machine politician. In the tradeoff, Anscomb received the prestigious post of minister of finance, and Tory representation in the cabinet was increased.

The resentment that lingered within the coalition was temporarily contained, and Johnson's government went ahead adapting to peacetime conditions. So much had to be done to repair the neglect of Depression and wartime years, and to begin exploiting the resources whose extent had become even more evident during the search for war materials. Capitalists were once again eager to move in and profit, but it was a different and perhaps politically less damaging situation than governments had faced during earlier boom periods. Almost all the railways that might be needed had been built, and almost all the land and mineral and forest rights that could usefully be acquired were already in the hands of private enterprise. The aggressiveness that had once been turned against the land was now largely internalized within the capitalist system. It was a time of takeovers, and this increased the pattern of polarization within the province as growing forest industry corporations—like the MacMillan interests, Crown Zellerbach, Bloedel, Stewart and Welch Limited and the various enterprises connected with the Czech immigrant Koerner family—faced monolithic labour unions like the International Woodworkers of America, whose membership in British Columbia had reached thirty thousand and was growing.

In this situation the coalition government tended to become the guardian of the interests of corporate employers against the militant labour unionists, and nothing was contributed to the alleviation of class antagonisms when the government first initiated a new system of direct licences that favoured the logging companies and then passed a new Industrial Conciliation and Arbitration Act. This involved such a long and complex conciliation procedure before a government-supervised strike vote could take place that it seemed, as Eugene Forsey remarked, "a method of prohibiting strikes without saying so." Even many of the Liberals who otherwise supported the government were opposed to the legislation, and in 1948 the government was forced to amend the act.

Another measure that aroused widespread resentment was the first retail sales tax imposed in British Columbia, a 3 per cent levy called the Social Security and Municipal Aid Tax. It was associated with an almost equally unpopular measure, the introduction of the hospital plan Pattullo had already proposed. The tax was not sufficient to support the insurance scheme, and the people of the province were forced to pay contributory premiums. The result was a spate of civil disobedience, and in some of the rural areas of the province 50 per cent of the potential participants refused to pay.

At the same time the Johnson government was active in fostering, by public works and ambitious industrial undertakings, the expansion of the province's economy. The later Social Credit governments of W. A. C. Bennett have often been credited with all the great developments that took place in British Columbia during the 1950s, but the Johnson government in fact started the process. Even under John Hart there had been such ambitious road developments as the Hart Highway and the Hope-Princeton Highway, while fish ladders had been built at the site of the Hell's Gate slide in the Fraser Canyon, which proved so effective that the sockeye run in 1958 would be one of the largest in history. Now, under

Johnson, it was decided to start work extending the Pacific Great Eastern Railway from Quesnel to the north of the province, and to start construction of a highway along the difficult rocky shore of Howe Sound to Squamish and work on various land rehabitation and flood control schemes. At the same time, as an example of the kind of industrial development they planned for the province, the government announced with a great deal of pride the agreement reached with Alcan for the aluminum plant and the new town at Kitimat.

On the strength of these achievements, the coalition went to the polls in 1949 and won a victory of deceptive magnitude. The parties supporting the coalition ticket won thirty-nine of the forty-eight seats in the assembly and gleaned 61.35 per cent of the popular vote. The CCF, though they gained 35.1 per cent of the popular vote, won only seven seats. The communists, who put up only two Labour Progressive party candidates, were virtually eliminated. The supporters of Social Credit improved their situation by gaining 1.6 per cent of the popular vote; few people paid much attention to their emergence, and nobody can have foreseen the circumstances that would bring them to power within three years.

The old parties would slide down from triumph in 1949 to abject defeat in 1952 for two reasons, which can perhaps be brought together under the single charge of political insensitivity. The frustrations of sharing power ate away at any will towards solidarity that remained among the parties a decade after they had come together. Now the war emergency that had nominally brought them together was ended and the socialist threat had been held off even if it had not been eliminated. Many people in both the older parties believed the CCF had reached its limits of expansion, and the more aggressive among Liberals and Tories alike were becoming foolhardily convinced that their own party, in an open election, could take on all opponents and win. A victory of this kind would mean that the spoils of office need no longer be divided.

Internal dissension within the coalition and the government itself tended to paralyze the administration as the decade turned over. Johnson's fortunes might have been better if he had been in complete control of his government, for the economy was in good shape.

Yet on one issue after another, the government began to fall foul of the public and of an increasingly critical press. There was the hospital insurance scheme, to which opposition had become almost universal; there was the failure to rationalize the liquor laws in accordance with changing manners; there was Herbert Anscomb's refusal to spend more than a minimum from a well-filled treasury on welfare measures; there was labour's discontent with what it considered anti-union legislation. Battered from all sides and internally disunited, the government stumbled ahead as if it were sleepwalking, and the only important legislation brought forward was actually devised with its own breakup in mind.

This was a radical amendment to the Elections Act providing for a new system of alternative voting: the votes would rank the candidates in order of preference. This meant that if no candidate received an absolute majority, the one with the lowest number would be eliminated and the votes cast for him added to those of the other candidates according to the voter's preference, and so on until an absolute majority was achieved. Since the CCF did not often achieve an absolute majority, and since it was thought that Liberals could be expected to show a second preference for Tories and vice versa, a victory for the CCF would be impossible even if the coalition broke apart. It was a device that would turn against its initiators.

The coalition came to an end through what was obviously a calculated blunder on the part of the Conservative leader, Herbert Anscomb. Anscomb had gone to Ottawa in January 1952 to negotiate new tax arrangements with the federal government. He returned to Vancouver on 15 January, and, without informing Johnson or the cabinet or the legislative assembly, he telephoned the results of the negotiations to the press gallery in Victoria. On 18 January, Johnson demanded Anscomb's resignation for a breach of political ethics, and Anscomb, who had clearly been expecting this reaction, complied at once, taking with him the other Conservative ministers, while the eleven Tory members crossed the house and became the official opposition, since they were more numerous than the CCF. The coalition had foundered on the rocks of political ambition.

Anscomb demanded an immediate dissolution and a new election on the grounds that the government had been elected on a coalition programme; Johnson procrastinated long enough to vote the funds necessary for the various construction projects he had initiated and to pass the legislation authorizing the new method of voting. And then, on 12 June, the province went to the polls for the most surprising election in its history.

There were four principal contestants: the ruling Liberals, the Conservatives, the CCF and Social Credit. Both the Liberals and the Tories went in with a certain confidence, not understanding either how their unpopularity had grown over the past three years or how the Social Credit movement would be able to profit from such unpopularity. They faced a discontent that went beyond specific grievances like hospital insurance or anti-union legislation. It was a great upswell of resentment on the part of all those who in some way or another felt their views were ignored and their interests disregarded; it was anger against the party machines in the cities, Vancouver particularly, and the wealthy lawyers and businessmen who ran them. It was a revolt of country against city, and even within the cities, of the lower middle class against the patricians of industry, commerce and the professions. It was a discontent that called for and received a populist answer.

The central figure in Social Credit's emergence as a rural and suburban mass movement was a dissident Tory, William Andrew Cecil Bennett. Bennett—called "Cece" by his friends and "Wacky" by his enemies—was a migrant from the Maritimes who had succeeded as a hardware merchant in Kelowna and had been elected MLA for South Okanagan. Twice, in 1946 and 1950, he had run unsuccessfully against Herbert Anscomb for the leadership of the provincial Conservative party.

Despite his obvious abilities and his Okanagan power base, Bennett had been consistently passed over when appointments to the cabinet were made in Victoria. He felt he was being treated as an outsider, so he became one by leaving the coalition in 1951 and sitting as an independent. Once he entered the wilderness of the outsiders, he found it inhabited, indeed crowded. For during 1950 and 1951 the hinterlands of British Columbia were being swept by a political grassroots movement that had many of the features of a religious revival. It even contained among its leaders and their followers the kind of people who activate and participate in such revivals.

This was the Social Credit movement, which, after its modest showing in the 1949 elections, had been injected with new life not merely by the example set by the record of William Aberhart's Social Credit government in Alberta but also because of the active political evangelism of the Alberta party. The Alberta movement sent its emissaries into British Columbia, provided with funds for campaigning. Many of them were preachers of various kinds, which meant that they had links with the numerous fundamentalist groups in the British Columbian interior. In 1951 the movement spread like bushfire, and many new Social Credit groups appeared in Vancouver, the Fraser Valley and especially in the southeastern interior, the Okanagan, Boundary and Kootenay districts, and also the Cariboo. Nothing was heard any more of the monetary theories of Major C. H. Douglas, though the nascent British Columbia movement inherited from him a distrust of banks and of financial institutions in general. The stress was on responsible government that balanced budgets and listened to the voice of the people while protecting them from their natural enemies: big bureaucracies, big corporations and big unions. It was, essentially, a movement of the hundreds of thousands of little men and women who felt themselves abandoned, dispossessed and disregarded. It was a rebellion of pride rather than poverty, for the standard of living everywhere in the province was higher than it had been during the 1930s.

W. A. C. Bennett had nothing to do with the foundation of the British Columbia Social Credit movement or with its early development. Through most of 1951 he maintained his stance of independence while he wooed other maverick Tories and gathered a small dissident group around him. But he sensed, as the situation of the government so obviously disintegrated, that there must be a role in which, as an unattached malcontent experienced in politics yet unstained by power, he could shine. He watched Social Credit carefully, encouraged by its growing mass support but disturbed by the extent to which the movement in Alberta was trying to dominate it. So he joined the movement in December 1951 and quietly watched developments while he built a personal following and made his alliances with existing Social Credit leaders. At the end of April 1952, in preparation for the forthcoming election, the Social Credit movement—it still refused to call itself a party—gathered to elect a leader. Bennett was proposed but shrewdly decided to refuse the nomination and bide his time. The nominee of the Albertans, a fundamentalist preacher named Ernest Hansell, was picked for the role, and Bennett quietly made his plans for the election and its aftermath.

On 12 June the electors overturned all the calculations of the Liberals and Tories, for the alternative voting procedure did not work as neatly as they had imagined. In that precomputer age, the complex counting of the votes took several
weeks, and when it was complete, the political map of the province was entirely
changed. To begin, a great mass of voters, particularly on the mainland, deserted
the older parties and drifted to Social Credit, while the CCF maintained its core
vote. Then an unexpected common feeling emerged between the dissidents of the
left and of the right; CCF voters gave their second preference to Social Credit and
vice versa. Even many Tories were so embittered by the Liberals that they gave
their second preference to Social Credit, and some Liberals did the same for the
CCF rather than appearing to support the Tories. It was a voters' revolt; the outsiders had risen and manifested decisively against the old establishment. When the
dust had settled and the final counts had been made, the political innocents of Social Credit emerged as the victors, with nineteen seats and 30.2 per cent of the
popular vote. The CCF actually excelled them in the popular vote, gaining 34.3
per cent but winning only eighteen seats, while the Liberals were reduced to six
seats with 25.3 per cent of the vote, and the Tories to four seats with a wretched
9.7 per cent. Johnson and Anscomb were both defeated.

Never again would a Liberal or a Conservative hold political office in British
Columbia in his party's name. What had happened that June day may not have
been a violent revolution, but it resembled a revolution in bringing to power men
and women who had never held it before, and on 15 July, as on many other revolutionary occasions, a meeting took place of untried men and one woman, with
little in common but their zeal, intent on creating their mechanism of ruling.
They were the nineteen elected Social Credit members gathered to choose their
parliamentary leader. This was the moment for which Bennett had been waiting,
the moment he had anticipated when he cannily declined nomination at the leadership convention two months before. Now, as everyone in the room was aware,
they were picking the man who would not only be party leader but would also
probably be the next premier. Faced with such a situation, the newly created legislators had little choice. Bennett could point to ten years of experience in the legislature, while none of the others, apart from Tilly Rolston (another bolter from
Tory ranks), could boast a single day; he knew the ropes, and they did not. And,
with a comfortable majority of fourteen votes to five, they elected him on the first
ballot.

After pondering for days on what he should do in a situation where Social
Credit had more seats but the CCF had more votes, and after consulting high court
judges and Prime Minister Louis St. Laurent, Lieutenant-Governor Clarence
Wallace called on W. A. C. Bennett on the first of August to form a government.

The Favourite of Providence

It was a government that, through several elections, a number of scandals, and
many cabinet changes, would stay in power under Bennett's leadership for twenty
years, the longest incumbency of any British Columbian premier. It was first a mi-

nority government; one of the reasons why Wallace had called on Bennett rather than on Winch, his CCF rival, was that he felt reasonably sure the Liberals and Tories would be less likely to unseat a Social Credit administration than a CCF one; in fact, the rumps of the old parties did give their support during the few months when Bennett chose to run a minority administration.

He worked with a cabinet whose members had to learn the business of government, and who, because of the nature of the Social Credit movement itself, were much nearer the grassroots of common life than any previous British Columbian government. Among the elected Social Credit members, Bennett could call on nobody who had experience in the professions or had worked for a large industry or a large governmental agency. At best he could find an accountant to preside over health and welfare and a teacher to act as provincial secretary. Yet he made some whimsically appropriate choices that worked out well. As minister of labour, he picked Lyle Wicks, who had spent most of his life as a street railwayman, and—in the long run perhaps his most happy choice—he picked for his minister of public works a flamboyant pentecostal preacher of Italian descent, the Rev. Phil Gaglardi, whose principal qualification for his ministry seems to have been that he had seen the construction industry from the bottom up, as a road worker and a cat driver.

But for the key posts in his cabinet Bennett moved boldly out of the legislature and out of his movement. For his minister of finance he picked Einar Gunderson, who had worked for the Alberta government and was Bennett's own accountant. For his attorney general, he dipped into the ranks of his dissident Conservative friends and chose a capable and imperturbable young lawyer, Robert Bonner, who had supported him in his efforts to unseat Anscomb as leader of the party.

This cabinet set the pattern for later Social Credit governments in British Columbia, which have tended to be predominantly middle class and small town in composition, without the array of lawyers that the older parties tend to cultivate, but usually with two or three figures drawn from the professions or the academies. British Columbian Social Crediters may last long in politics, but they rarely become professionals in the same way as federal politicians, perhaps because they always work relatively close to their constituencies and do not become involved in the kind of exile from their people that Ottawa requires.

The people of British Columbia had to wait only a short time before passing judgement on the new government. With the provincial coffers in good shape, Bennett boldly seized on the initiatives taken by Boss Johnson and began to steer them to completion to his own credit. On 1 November 1952 he and his cabinet rode into Prince George on the first train over the Pacific Great Eastern extension, and the pace of construction on the railway and on new roads was sustained. Some of the fundamentalists in the caucus tried to Christianize the school system, but Bennett quietly downed them and gave the government a less eccentric image by narrowing the scope of the sales tax and by lowering the detested hospital premium, with a promise to eliminate it altogether. Then, in the spring of 1953, anger flared over legislation that would weight school subsidies in favour of rural rather than urban areas. All the opposition parties, including the Liberals, voted against it, and the government was defeated by twenty-eight votes to seventeen.

Nobody could have been more pleased than Bennett himself as he called an election, for the situation put his government in the victim position he knew how to exploit. ("This poor little government" was a phrase frequently on his lips.) He and his associates, he let it be known, were martyrs for the people. Social Credit was a widespread populist movement overriding class divisions and equally opposed to "the forces of monopolism and the forces of socialism." He promised public works and gifts for everyone. Perpetually grinning, his words tumbling over each other in eagerness, Bennett was a loud and aggressive campaigner, highly emotional in his utterance, able to burst into tears in public if the occasion required it, yet always sure that he was right. The story that he claimed to be "plugged into God" is apocryphal, yet it expresses the feeling he tried to induce among his audiences that he and Providence were moving in the same direction.

It was too soon after the last election victory for any revulsion of feeling to have built up against his government, and though he had achieved nothing more spectacular than some minor tax changes, the voters showed their confidence in him and his inexperienced colleagues by giving Social Credit a decisive victory. This time the movement completely swamped the older parties and, with the help of many working-class votes, pulled decisively ahead of the CCF. When all the counts were made, Social Credit had won twenty-eight seats and 45.54 per cent of the popular vote, as against 37.75 on the first count, which meant that many supporters of other parties considered Bennett's movement as second best. The CCF gained fourteen seats, with a marginally reduced popular vote of 29.48 per cent. The Liberals won four seats and 23.36 per cent of the vote, while the Conservatives humiliatingly ended with one seat and 1.1 per cent of the final vote; a single labour representative was elected, mainly through his personal popularity, in the coal-mining centre of Fernie.

This time it was more than a vote of the hinterland against the cities, for now the cities themselves had joined in the slide; it was rather a declaration of alliance of the small people of the towns and the countryside against the great vested interests that had so long ruled British Columbia. It was also a vote of no confidence against professional politicians in favour of men and women drawn directly from the ranks of the people. And it was one of those statements of their distinctiveness as a regional society that British Columbians have made from time to time ever since they became a part of Canada. In every way it was a populist vote, and however much in later years Social Credit may have compromised with large financial and industrial interests, the feeling that it is as much a movement of the people as the CCF, and perhaps more genuinely devoted to local interests, has persisted and has led to an ongoing gladiatorial contest between these two upstart parties.

Bennett now had the mandate he desired and proceeded with boldness and speed to keep the considerable promises he had made; in comparison with the in-

ertia and indecisiveness of the last term of the coalition, the activity of Social
Credit in its second year of office seemed spectacular. The election results were
not finally tabulated until late in October 1953, and by the spring of 1954 Bennett
and his colleagues were already starting on programmes that in a few years would
change the look and nature of the province, proceeding by what they called a "pay
as you go" philosophy.

A cluster of small tax reductions was more than offset by an increase of the sales
tax to 5 per cent, but this in turn was balanced not only by the complete elimination of the detested hospital premiums but also an increase in the taxes on mining
and logging enterprises, which seemed to justify Bennett's boasts that he would
keep the corporations in their place. But it was by financial legerdemain that Bennett, who became his own minister of finance in 1953, contrived to keep his
promise of running an increasingly debt-free province. The ambitious public
works programme on which the government embarked was largely vested in crown
corporations, like the British Columbia Railway, the B.C. Power Commission,
and the newly created Toll Bridges and Highway Authority, all of which were empowered to make borrowings that on the books did not appear as government indebtedness. In the same way, school districts were instructed to raise the funds
necessary for school construction, the government merely guaranteeing their bond
issues and making annual grants to cover half the payments of interest and principal. In this way the direct debt situation appeared to be steadily improving and the
province's credit with it, though the indirect debt grew hugely and would depend
largely for its reduction on the earning powers of the works carried out by the
crown corporations. Bennett was assisted in realizing his aim by the general buoy-
ancy of the economy and also by the recognition on the part of the industrial corporations that they had as much to gain as anybody else by the opening out of the
province.

Operations began roughly simultaneously on a number of fronts. The B.C.
Power Corporation expanded its programme of rural electrification and in anticipation of the growing needs of the province began to explore the great power resources of the Peace River. Work also began extending the Pacific Great Eastern
both northward from Prince George to Fort St. John in the Peace River region and
southward from Squamish to North Vancouver.

But if railways had been the centre of political action and local mythology in
the McBride era, roads took their place during Bennett's long reign. A new minister of highways was created independent of the public works ministry, and Phil
Gaglardi was installed as its head. The map of the province became a network of
projected new highways and modernized old roads. In 1954 a serious start was
made on the completion of the lagging British Columbian sector of the Trans-
Canada Highway, which included the modernization of the oldest highway of the
region, the Cariboo Road.

Bennett, Gaglardi and their colleagues have been described as "the new Romans," and in terms of their road-building achievements this is a fair description.

By the end of Bennett's rule in 1972, every British Columbian community of any size would be served by a paved highway, and the speed and comfort of travel were immeasurably increased. Industry profited from the new highways, so that major plants began to appear in what hitherto had been small inaccessible communities. The new roads attracted tourists and combined with the influx of European immigrants to spread cosmopolitan lifestyles into the hinterland, as establishments more sophisticated than the old smalltown general stores and greasy-spoon eating places began to appear. Goods that had been accessible in the past only through the Eaton's catalogue became available in greater variety and abundance when one could drive comfortably for an hour or so into the nearest large town.

The course of the Bennett government, despite the favourable economic circumstances it enjoyed, was not undisturbed by scandals; the overt moralism and personal incorruptibility of Bennett and other prominent ministers did not extend to all their associates, and in 1956 a scandal erupted around the minister of lands, forests and mines, a former schoolteacher named Robert Sommers. Sommers was alleged to have received gifts, loans and other favours from a petty fixer connected with the forest industry, H. Wilson Gray. Sommers filed suits for slander and libel against his accuser, who happened to be Gray's bookkeeper. He then resigned from the cabinet, and Attorney General Bonner, refusing a judicial commission, handed over the case to the RCMP for investigation.

Meanwhile, Bennett turned to face the storm of scorn and scandal initiated by the press, which was dominated by the two Liberal-owned Vancouver papers, the *Sun* and the *Province*. He did so by bringing down another bumper budget, with bonuses for pensioners, a raise in pay for civil servants, grants to municipalities, and yet more roads. Then he went to the province, having secured another change in the Elections Act so that a simple majority would once again name the successful candidate. This time Bennett broadened his appeal. Social Credit was no longer to be merely a movement of the outsiders. "We are a movement for the small man and the large man," said Bennett shortly after the election, "we need them all." And there is no doubt that the business operators, impressed by the boldness—even recklessness—that Bennett displayed, wanted their share of the brave new world of Social Credit.

The small men certainly did. Social Credit enjoyed its greatest victory yet, thirty-nine seats out of an enlarged house of fifty-two, and 45.84 per cent of the popular vote. The CCF won ten seats with a slightly decreased percentage of the popular vote, the Liberals won two, a labour independent won one. The Conservatives were eliminated from the house. Even Robert Sommers, stained by scandal, was returned with enthusiasm by the working-class electors of Rossland-Trail, with 5,097 votes against 2,839 for his CCF opponent.

Sommers let down those who had put their faith in him. He could not face his accusers, and withdrew his libel and slander cases. Bennett and Bonner had shielded him as best they could, but now there was no alternative but to agree to a commission of enquiry, which led to a prosecution, a conviction, and Sommers and Gray being sent to the penitentiary for five years. But by now the affair had become a kind of personal tragedy that had lost its connection with the political scene, and even before Sommers was sentenced at the end of April 1958, Bennett was involved in dealing with a minor recession, which lowered the pace of economic growth and reduced the amount of funds available.

In the beginning, Bennett remained confident that his policies of providing first the transport routes and then the power facilities represented the best that could be done for the province and constituted legitimate government intervention short of socialism. But by 1958 he was already entering that shadowy area of state capitalism not always easy to distinguish from genuine socialism.

It began with a desire to safeguard the vulnerable but vital sea link between Vancouver Island and the mainland. This was served in the 1950s by two lines: the CPR, which ran ferries as the final link in its transcontinental system, and the Black Ball Ferries. In the spring of 1958 Black Ball was struck by the Seafarers' International Union, and Bennett declared that in future the links between Vancouver and Victoria would no longer be subject to "the whim of union policy or the indifference of federal agencies." Yet another crown corporation, B.C. Ferry, was established to build and operate a fleet of ferries that would serve Vancouver Island, the mainland coast and the islands in between. The CPR was not reluctant to withdraw from what it had found to be an insufficiently profitable service, and the Black Ball Ferries were pushed aside to the American run from Victoria, which they retained while the government corporation exercised a virtual monopoly elsewhere on the British Columbian coasts.

During the 1960s, as the great road schemes began to near completion, hydroelectric power replaced transportation as the leading goal of the Social Credit government. Two rivers in the province, the Columbia and the Peace, held enormous potentialities of power production, and there was an urgent demand both from the burgeoning industrial network in British Columbia and from the American Pacific coast states. But before he could carry out his sweeping plans to harness this power and reap the rewards, Bennett had to contend with the obstructionism of the British Columbia Electric Company, the private monopoly that produced and distributed most of the electrical power in the province. Fortunately for him, BCE had made itself unpopular by neglecting the rural areas and by charging higher rates than those customary elsewhere in Canada or in the American northwestern states. Bennett decided to expropriate the private company and amalgamate it with the old B.C. Power Commission in yet another crown corporation, the British Columbia Hydro and Power Authority. The Liberal press in Vancouver raised an outcry that was echoed in financial papers as far afield as Wall Street and the City of London. But the opposition in the legislative assembly was uncharacteristically subdued since the CCF had long been advocating this very action, and when the vote came in the house in August 1961, it was unanimous, with the chagrined socialists giving their support.

Bennett now embarked on his final vast schemes, which the real Romans would have regarded with admiration, the great dams on the Columbia and the Peace.

The Columbia scheme was the first to materialize. A Columbia River Treaty was in fact signed between Canada and the United States on 17 January 1961, but implementation was delayed by disputes between Ottawa and Victoria over jurisdiction. British Columbia had entered into a tentative agreement with the United States that would give the Americans entitlement to half the power produced. The federal government protested that only an agreement between nation and nation, not one between province and nation, was valid. But it was a time of unusual weakness at the centre, when the failing Tory minority of John Diefenbaker was giving way to the untried minority Liberal government of Lester Pearson. Pearson needed support in the West and so, despite Liberal protests within the province, he let Bennett have his way, and British Columbia became obligated to supply power until 1994 at what over the years has turned out an unrealistically low price. But the scale of the undertaking was vast, with three great dams on the Columbia, which the province built, giving many contracts and much employment, and it was a high day in W. A. C. Bennett's political life when President Lyndon Johnson came to the Peace Arch on the international boundary at Blaine, Washington, on 16 September 1964, and handed him the cheque for $273,291,661.25 for the first thirty years of power, which enable the provincial government to start work almost immediately. The first of the dams, at Duncan Lake, was opened in 1967; the last, the Mica Dam, in 1973. In the process, much farmland settled in the late nineteenth century along the Arrow Lakes was submerged.

Having won a fifth election with an easy majority on 12 September 1963, Bennett authorized the beginning of the development on the Peace River which he regarded as the great monument to his years of achievement. By 1968 the Portage River Dam had been opened, and the largest structure of all, appropriately named the W. A. C. Bennett Dam in 1967, had been completed.

Bennett never gained his imperial ambition of annexing the Yukon Territory, but after a long battle with the federal authorities, he did establish the province's right to create a Bank of British Columbia. The original Bank of British Columbia had emerged in the Cariboo during the early 1860s and had failed long ago, but the revival of its title was a significant link with the days before the colony was a part of Canada, while the establishment of what was widely advertised as a bank of the people—and was in fact largely used by workers—echoed back to the teachings of Douglas and earlier monetary reformers like Proudhon, that credit must be taken out of the hands of big institutions and originate with the people. It was a sad irony that the Bank of British Columbia should be unable to sustain itself and in less than twenty years should be taken over by that amphibious entity, the Hongkong Bank of Canada.

The mid-sixties were a time of recovery from the minor recession of the late 1950s, and, primed by continuing road work and work on the dams, the province was booming again, with a steady industrial development, though little attempt was made to go beyond the primary forestry and mining industries and create a sound basis for manufacturing.

Bennett continued to keep the voters happy with a succession of benefits; medicare, tax relief and capital grants to homeowners, supplements to federal old-age pensions, increased educational facilities. All these carefully calculated gifts, and a still booming economy, brought Social Credit in 1969 its seventh consecutive election victory, and the largest of all, for the government won thirty-eight seats, with 46.8 per cent of the popular vote, while the New Democratic party (into which the CCF had metamorphosed in 1961) kept steady at 33.9 per cent of the votes but dropped to twelve seats, and the Liberals, with 19.03 per cent of the vote, kept five seats. The Conservatives made no showing, though the party, which had seemed moribund, would be revived during the next session of the legislative assembly, when two Social Credit malcontents crossed the house to sit as Tories on the opposition benches.

These departures were indicative of the sudden crises that led to the astonishing end of W. A. C. Bennett's reign; only three years after his greatest electoral victory, Social Credit was decisively routed in the elections of August 1972. Eleven cabinet ministers were defeated, and Bennett was left to lead a rump of ten members until his resignation in the house on 5 June 1973; the Tories and the Liberals sat beside him on the opposition benches with two and five seats respectively.

Bennett, in part, had been the victim of circumstances largely beyond his own or any local control. The period between 1969 and 1972 election was a time of suddenly rising inflation, which led to industrial unrest and many strikes, among white-collar workers like journalists as well as blue-collar workers like construction workers and longshoremen, teamsters and transit workers. The economic uncertainty of the times led to a slowdown in industrial growth, while the great public works projects were drawing to an end and there was no money to finance others, so that the unemployment rate rose sharply to 9.4 per cent in January 1971. The situation was worsened by the fact that the dominant and capital-intensive extractive industries were being increasingly automated, while the more labour-intensive manufacturing industries were developing far less rapidly.

If the Social Crediters resembled the Romans in their passion for roads and other monumental constructions, they began to resemble them also in losing a sense of the human scale of their operations. There is a danger of Bonapartism in all populist movements, of leaders who were once the voices of the people losing contact with their followers, and in the process losing their charisma while seeking to keep their power. There was certainly a great deal of the Napoleonic (Napoleon III rather than Napoleon I) about Wacky Bennett as he became magnified from the little man into the big leader, proudly dedicating his massive monuments and hobnobbing with American presidents (Kennedy as well as Johnson) and international bankers and entrepreneurs. He slowly lost the common touch, and with it in the end he lost the common people.

Bennett's downfall was due largely to his poor judgement in choosing the ministers who dealt most closely with the people and especially with popular grievances. They were all men who shared, on their own diminished scales, the Napoleonic disdain of lesser beings. Appointed to the Department of Rehabilitation,

Phil Gaglardi seemed more intent on saving money by weeding out "deadbeats" than on reducing real distress or discovering its causes. Education Minister Donald Brothers and Health Minister Ralph Loffmark spent much of their time in dispute with such important groups as teachers, doctors and hospital workers. Discontent accumulated like a great reservoir during the three last years of Social Credit rule. It only needed a reinvigorated opposition to break the dam.

And the NDP was reinvigorated at the right time to change the political map of British Columbia. By 1972 it and its predecessor, the CCF, had been the province's opposition for so long that it seemed the social democrats, under whatever name, would ossify into a permanent opposition. Their coming to power was largely through the personal vigour of Dave Barrett, the party's new leader, who, like Bennett before him, was also a loner who made a virtue out of having been badly treated by the establishment.

Barrett was a social worker who in 1959 had been sacked from the provincial prisons service because he ran for election as a CCF candidate. In 1969 he was beaten in a bid for leadership of the NDP because the labour bosses put their votes behind his rival, Tom Berger. Berger lost the 1969 election, resigning shortly afterwards, and in 1970 Barrett became leader in his place.

Barrett had learnt a great deal from watching Bennett in action, and he used it effectively against him. He did not allow socialist theorizing to blind him to the fact that his predecessor had held power for twenty years through a masterly manipulation of multiple interests. He realized that in a province like British Columbia the NDP would never be elected as a party representing labour alone. Labour was the one third of the popular vote beyond which the NDP had been unable to grow since the 1930s; to win the next election it had to find new areas of support. And with this in mind Barrett made his plans, treating labour as a captive vote because the union bosses had nowhere else to go. He devoted himself to wooing other groups—teachers, provincial government workers, intellectuals, even merchants and farmers. He took over Bennett's populist stance and insisted that the NDP was not the party of one class but the people as a whole. Beyond this political wisdom he relied mostly on his own personality and vigour, and these qualities appealed—as they had done with Bennett in his younger days—to a British Columbian electorate that treasured individualism. His victory was another of the spectacular dawns of British Columbian politics. An era of promise seemed about to begin.

Province of the Mind

The great physical changes that took place in British Columbia during the Bennett era were parallelled by cultural changes only partly linked with the political complexion of the era. Like those of every other province of Canada, the educational needs of British Columbia expanded because of a rapid growth in child population ("the baby boom" generation), a radical transformation in educational expectations, and great changes in society's technological and professional needs, as well as the steady influx of immigrants, many of whom spoke neither English nor French. If British Columbia were to compete industrially and commercially, it must have more educated people. On their side, a larger proportion of students expected to proceed from high school to university, and the range of knowledge available to them simultaneously increased.

The Bennett government recognized a situation had arisen that could not be met by the old system of school boards operating with local taxes. In 1954 the Public Schools Reconstruction Act committed the province to sharing the cost of new schools and led to the virtual extinction of the little white clapboard schoolhouses of the West, as primary and secondary education were consolidated but not necessarily improved in large establishments, supplied by widespread school bus services.

A few years later the pressure point reached the level of higher education. After World War II there had been a flood of returning veterans into the University of British Columbia, tripling the enrolment from three thousand students in 1944–45 to nine thousand in 1947–48. To accommodate them, fifteen abandoned army and air force camps in the province were dismantled and their huts brought to the campus to serve as classrooms, laboratories, offices, even residences for students and faculty. The malls were lined with them, and for almost two decades they gave a dismal, makeshift look to large parts of the university. At the same time a great deal of substantial and permanent building went on. By 1952 more than twenty structures had gone up, notable among them buildings for the School of Medicine (the only one in British Columbia) and for the Department of Physics, which housed a great Van de Graff atomic generator that symbolized the university's dedication to research and especially to work in atomic fields.

As the University of British Columbia developed into one of the three largest universities in Canada, with a faculty of three thousand, a student body eventually touching thirty thousand, and the second-largest library in the country, the Social Credit leaders began to look on it with a degree of alarm. Not only did it represent a great concentration of the kind of academics whom—as men themselves mostly lacking in university education—they distrusted. It also added to Vancouver's claims to primacy in the province which, as good hinterlanders, most of them resented.

Accordingly, when it became evident that the facilities for higher education still did not meet the demand, the government decided against spending its money on extending the existing provincial university. Instead it created three others outside the local metropolis, as well as a dozen community colleges scattered over the province, offering first- and second-year university courses. Of the three higher level establishments, the first was the University of Victoria, whose nucleus was Victoria College, which since 1961 had been giving degrees as a constituent of the University of British Columbia; it was elevated to independent status in 1963, and a new campus was created at Gordon Head, outside the city. An entirely new establishment, Simon Fraser University, was also chartered in 1963, and housed in a structure of unusual form, a whole campus within a single complex building on the top of Burnaby Mountain, designed by the young Vancouver architect Arthur Erickson at the beginning of a career that made him world famous. Simon Fraser was opened in 1965, and during the 1960s became—as the Social Crediters had certainly not intended when they founded it—a notable centre of New Left radicalism among students and faculty alike. The third university, an attempt to develop higher education in the interior of the province, was a privately funded Catholic college at Nelson, which was elevated to Notre Dame University. It failed after a few years, but the idea of a private university as well as the large provincially operated ones persisted, and afterwards a charter was given to Trinity Western, a former Methodist college close to Fort Langley.

Quite apart from formal education, the period from the late 1940s onward had been one of steadily expanding cultural activity in British Columbia. The series of centennials—of British Columbia in 1858, of Confederation in 1867, and of British Columbia's entry into the dominion in 1871—led to a widespread and enthusiastic interest in regional history, which not only laid the foundations for a local publishing industry but also resulted in the appearance of museums in all the important and many of the smaller communities. The most impressive were the new Provincial Museum in Vancouver, built during the 1960s to display the province's rich collection of Coast Indian artifacts formerly housed in small dark rooms in the basement of the parliament buildings, the Centennial Museum and the Maritime Museum in Vancouver, and the remarkable museum of 'Ksan at Hazelton on the Skeena, a reproduction of a traditional Gitksan village created by local native people with help from the federal and provincial governments; it contains craft workshops, communal houses (carved, painted and equipped as they would have been in the early nineteenth century), and a museum where the regalia of the local chiefs are housed until they are needed for the ceremonial feasts that have been revived in the area.

In the creative and performing arts, there has been a remarkable upsurge in the decades since World War II, and it has been largely self-generated, since although the provincial government established a Cultural Fund in 1967, it was a very faint echo of the Canada Council, supporting the arts so meagrely that British Columbia gives less per capita support for creative activities than any other province except Nova Scotia. The combination of rich talent and deep official philistinism is another of the self-perpetuating contrasts of British Columbian life.

Painting in British Columbia began as landscape work, with some genre painting, mostly of Indian subjects. The earlier painters—with a few notable exceptions like Sophie Pemberton—came from outside the province, in search of new material. Between the wars, however, painters more attached to the local environment, by birth and personal mythology, began to appear. Until the later 1940s, landscape remained the dominant direction, and it was most strongly represented by Emily Carr, with her extraordinary response to the rain forest and the decaying remnants of Coast Indian settlements on their remote beaches. In recent years Carr's repute has tended to obscure the merits of other sensitive and original landscapists of the period, influenced somewhat by the impressionists and sometimes by the Japanese, like Statira Frame, Walter J. Phillips and Charles John Collings, as well as Thomas Fripp, who during the 1920s refined in his mist-shrouded paintings the grandiose Rocky Mountain style of painting of the 1880s and 1890s. During this period there was still a flow of painters from central Canada intent on interpreting the spectacular scenery of British Columbia; they included members of the Group of Seven, like A. Y. Jackson, J. W. G. Macdonald, Lawren Harris (who eventually took up residence in West Vancouver), and F. H. Varley, who taught for a decade at the Vancouver School of Art.

The Vancouver School of Art was the centre of the transformation of Pacific coast art during the late 1940s and the 1950s, as landscape painting gave way to various forms of abstraction. It was an abstraction of a peculiarly British Columbian kind, which rarely detached itself from the insistent forms of the surrounding natural world, and over the decades it has produced some of the most remarkable painting in Canada. Immediately after World War II a group of fine and dynamic painters began to teach at the art school; most of them had served as war artists with the Canadian army. They included B. C. Binning, Jack Shadbolt, Molly Bobak and Bruno Bobak, and they inspired a generation of students, the most vital of whom have tended to dominate West Coast painting ever since. Among them were Gordon Smith, John Korner, Don Jarvis, Joe Plaskett and Peter Aspell. Other notable painters of the period drawn in other ways to the coast included Toni Onley, Alistair Bell (also a remarkable engraver), and the fine expressionist painter Maxwell Bates, who moved from Calgary to Victoria in 1961. A recognition of trans-Pacific influences appeared not only in the work of painters of Japanese and Chinese origin like Roy Kiyooka, Takao Tanabe and Paul Huang (who founded the leading gallery representing local modern artists, the Bau-Xi) but also painters of non-Asian origin like Jack Wise. The other visual arts flourished alongside painting, with such notable exponents of pottery as John Reeve, Wayne Ngan and Walter Dexter, while there has been a constant interflow between the most originative painters and the more remarkable modern architects, like Arthur Erickson, Geoffrey Massey and the late Ron Thom; B. C. Binning created abstract mosaic decorations for buildings designed by Thom, and Gordon Smith painted murals for some of Erickson's buildings.

Writing in British Columbia was slow to move out of the descriptive into the imaginative, but by the end of the 1930s a number of skilful, sensitive and original writers had begun to appear. They included the poets Earle Birney and Dorothy Livesay, while there were stirrings of fiction in such novels as Frederick Niven's *Wild Honey* and Howard O'Hagan's remarkable combination of myth and fiction, *Tay John*, whose publication in 1939 "ushered British Columbian fiction into the modern period," as Gary Geddes has remarked. Early in the war (1941) Emily Carr, forced by bad health to exchange the brush for the pen, published *Klee Wyck*, a charming memoir of experiences with Coast Indians that moves constantly between memory and fiction, and followed it with other vivid volumes of sketches.

Ethel Wilson had been publishing short stories in English journals in the late 1930s, but it was not until 1947 that her first novel, with a British Columbian setting, appeared. It was *Hetty Dorval*, published when the author was fifty-nine, the beginning of a brief but remarkable late flowering career that ended with the publication of *Mrs. Golightly and Other Stories* in 1961. Another writer who became a major figure in the postwar years was Roderick Haig-Brown, a nature writer and essayist whose *Measure of the Year* (1952) splendidly evoked the seasons of the Pacific coast. Other important fiction writers to emerge in British Columbia during the period up to the 1970s included Audrey Thomas, Robert Harlow, John Mills, Hubert Evans, Jane Rule, and, most original of all, Sheila Watson, with her haunting avant-garde fable of the dry interior lands, *The Double Hook*. Among the fine poets who originated in British Columbia or gravitated there during this period were P. K. Page, Phyllis Webb, Patrick Lane, Robin Skelton, Pat Lowther and Susan Musgrave, and the young poets associated with the local avant-garde magazine of the early 1960s, *Tish*, the most durable of them being George Bowering and Frank Davey. During the late 1950s and 1960s, Vancouver drew poets to it like a magnet, and as well as those I have named, poets from other regions like Al Purdy, Margaret Atwood and Milton Acorn lived there a while.

In that atmosphere a number of literary magazines of national status were founded in British Columbia, including *Canadian Literature* and *Prism International* in Vancouver, and the internationally oriented and respected *Malahat Review* in Victoria.

Like other parts of Canada, British Columbia experienced a revival of live theatre about the end of the 1950s. Interest in the theatre had persisted in an age oriented to the cinema through the presence of CBC radio, which virtually kept Canadian drama alive during the Depression and war years and the decade immediately afterwards. The CBC gave writers an opportunity to continue playwriting, and offered employment to actors, so that when propitious circumstances (including the foundation of the Canada Council in 1957) emerged for the stages to be opened again, the writers and the actors were there; under producers like Robert Allen and George Robertson, and later, Gerald Newman and Norman Newton, radio drama in British Columbia kept going at a high level well into the 1960s. By that decade professional theatres were beginning to emerge, like the Playhouse and the Arts Club Theatre in Vancouver, and the Bastion Theatre in Victoria. Some of them, like Vancouver's Tamahnous Theatre, were dedicated to Canadian plays and others, like the New Play Centre, to experimental drama. Around them clustered a variety of small theatres, professional, amateur and amphibious, and together they represented a sum of dramatic activity unexampled in earlier decades and supported by schools of drama at the various universities, often with their own theatres like the Frederick Wood at the University of British Columbia. In addition, a local publishing house, Talonbooks, had by dint of specialization become the leading publisher of contemporary drama texts in the whole of Canada. Many local writers at one time or another tried their hand at drama, for radio or the stage, including Earle Birney, Dorothy Livesay and George Woodcock; the most successful have probably been George Ryga (with his *The Ecstasy of Rita Joe*), Betty Lambert, Beverley Simons and Herschel Hardin.

The other performing arts have found increased expression in British Columbia during recent decades. Vancouver has never been a city sufficiently devoted to the classical ballet for a company resembling the Royal Winnipeg Ballet to spring up there. But modern dance groups have flourished, led by noted choreographers like Judith Marcuse, Karen Jamieson and Anna Wyman. The Anna Wyman Dance Theatre, which often performs its highly original works in Vancouver's public spaces but has also travelled as far as China, India and Australia, has perhaps been the most important.

In music British Columbia has been stronger in performance than in creation, though a number of the more distinguished Canadian composers have in fact worked in the province, including Barbara Pentland, Jean Coulthard, Murray Schafer and Murray Adaskin. The Vancouver Symphony Orchestra, surviving sometimes precariously since 1930, became one of the leading orchestras of its type in Canada, and rival groups appeared in Victoria and other larger towns in the province, while for many years the CBC ran its own Vancouver orchestra of high quality under the direction of John Avison. An opera association has presented a season every year for decades, but for lack of an opera house performs in the Queen Elizabeth Theatre, which was opened in 1959 as a belated commemoration of the British Columbia centennial. For a number of years after that centennial, from 1958 to 1968, Vancouver was the centre of an International Festival of the Arts, which at first earned the city a great deal of credit in the international arts community. Laudably elitist, during its first year under the direction of Nicholas Goldschmitt, it attracted Herbert von Karajan and Bruno Walter, staged a version of Mozart's *Don Giovanni* in which Joan Sutherland made her debut as a major operatic star, and hosted the Comédie Française. The fickleness of the Vancouver audience and the stinginess of the provincial government in giving supporting funds led to the decline of the festival, its disastrous popularization, and its termination in 1968.

XIX

Returning to the Equilibrium

The Native Peoples Enter the Twentieth Century

During the mid-twentieth century there was also a notable cultural resurgence among the native peoples of British Columbia. In some ways, because institutions like the Vancouver Art Gallery offered major exhibitions of Coast Indian artifacts and because such artifacts were keenly bought by collectors, the revived Indian arts and crafts seemed to become a kind of backwater of the mainstream of contemporary art, and it was easy to assume—as many did—that the rehabilitation of Coast Indian art was due to the increased perceptiveness of non-Indian critics who stood in the role of patrons. The situation was in fact more complex, for the re-emergence of artists adapting the traditional forms of Coast Indian art was the result of a series of events as much social and political as cultural in the narrow sense.

Perhaps the twenties was the crucial decade in the transformation of the Indians of British Columbia from the apparently dying remnants of once-proud peoples to a group of indigenous societies that had recovered their sense of identity and offered a viable alternative to the intruding majority society. In demographic terms, the most basic of all, it was the time when the numbers began to change direction. The year 1929 showed the lowest total Indian population of 22,605, and from that time, with the major killer diseases in control and a fertility rate twice that of the non-Indian population, the increase began, so that today there are probably as many native people in the province as when Pérez and the Haida first saw each other more than two centuries ago.

Seven years before that crucial demographic shift, an event had taken place that today assumes a strong symbolic importance. In 1922 one of the highest-ranking Kwakiutl chiefs, Dan Cranmer, defied the law by calling at Alert Bay a potlatch that may well have been the largest ever known. The chiefs came from islands and inlets far around, with their traditional regalia, to dance their dances, sing their songs and receive their splendid gifts. No photographs survive, but it was obviously a lavish occasion and a grand act of defiance, to which the local Indian agent reacted by calling in the RCMP. An infamous deal was forced upon the chiefs, by which those who surrendered their potlatch regalia would go free. Many complied, and most of the material went to the National Museum of Canada in Ottawa, though an American collector laid his hands on some choice pieces. Dan Cranmer refused to accept the bargain and went to prison, becoming in the process a hero around whose example Indian pride in their heritage and Indian resentment of interference began to build up.

Afterwards the fate of the regalia seized at Alert Bay mirrored the change in Canadian attitudes towards the art and culture of the Coast Indians. They were never exhibited but remained stored in a basement of the museum in Ottawa, out of danger of being sold off to the dealers who had plucked so much of their heritage from the demoralized Indians during the 1920s and 1930s. But during their sequestration, their status changed. In the eyes of non-Indians they metamorphosed from ethnographic curiosities into works of high art, and in the eyes of the Indians they began to be regarded as holy relics of a past and better time. All this created an agitation, and in 1980, after a great deal of persuasion by Indians and their friends, the National Museum finally agreed to return the regalia to the coast, provided they were preserved in local museums, and the native peoples of Cape Mudge and Alert Bay constructed two buildings dedicated to their heritage and undertook the custody of the artifacts.

By this time the attitudes of the majority culture had changed so much that, legally at least, Indians were the equals of other members of the Canadian community of peoples. They had been given the right to vote in provincial elections in 1949 and in federal elections in 1960; in 1951 the humiliating rules against the possession and use of liquor by Indians had been withdrawn. In the same year the prohibition against potlatches and spirit dances had lapsed and the native peoples were free to pursue their ceremonial life as they saw fit. Yet even today the Indian groups remain to some degree in a condition of tutelage, since the Indian Act still exists, and though politically the Indians are Canadian citizens like any others, the majority of them remain wards of the state, protected within their special status.

The revival of the artistic heritage and of other traditional cultural values has been comparatively recent, a matter of a generation. In the 1920s those who were prepared to pay a price to maintain their traditions, like Dan Cranmer, were few, and the majority had accepted profound cultural changes during the nineteenth century. By the end of that century, 90 per cent of British Columbian Indians had been converted to Christianity, which seemed to give a positive direction to their lives when indigenous spiritual values failed them. By the census of 1931 only twenty-eight people declared "aboriginal beliefs." The rest had joined a variety of churches ranging from the Catholics to the Salvat on Army, or one of the smaller groups like the Shaker Church, which combined Christian beliefs with native ecstatic practices. Similarly, where they could the Indians mingled economically with the order that had replaced theirs, adopting modern fishing methods and often prospering by them on the coast, and inland labouring—when they could get work—for local farmers, acting as seasonal field and orchard workers or, in the

Chilcotin especially, becoming—as cowboys—part of the new ranching economy.

Yet there are areas of life where even now they maintain their distinctiveness. Language is one of them. Except for groups that have become extinct, the languages survived in spite of the efforts of the notorious residential schools. The young people may speak less completely and less well, but there were always older people who acted as remembrancers until the linguists could start their task of recording, and now the languages are reviving as speaking the tongue of one's ancestors becomes not only a declaration of identity but also in its own way a badge of sophistication. The retention of language has always been the sign of a subject people determined to defend its identity, and in this respect the British Columbian native peoples have become the equivalent of the Welsh or the Estonians or the Tibetans.

Another recognized mark of cultural retentiveness is the continuation of traditions in eating and drinking. Many Indians also persist in preparing food in their traditional ways, gathering seaweed and herring roe in season, pressing oolichan grease and preparing sopalallie from soapberries, smoking and drying their fish in the old ways, so that their feasts are traditional even if they many of them live like the whites from day to day.

Land Claims and Indian Politics

But the most significant witness of the native peoples' sense of a difference from the rest of the population is to be found in the attitude to the land, which has remained remarkably persistent among them even if the strength and manner of their expressing it have varied. Here is the factor that decisively marks off the native peoples from the other minorities like the Doukhobors, who have struggled to sustain their traditional values against the hostility of the majority society. The Doukhobors had no original stake in the land; they acquired and eventually owned it, which is an act of alienation. The native peoples, either individually or collectively, never owned the land; they possessed it and used it, sharing it with the other members of the natural world. It is this situation of possession and use for which they have always fought; they did not traditionally seek to own, which was why Maquinna and Meares misunderstood each other, but they resisted those who sought to own land they had used and to exclude them from it.

Through this matter of land, and through the definition of aboriginal right to it, the Coast Indians first developed in the twentieth century a political dimension to their cultures. Their organization at the time of first contact was social rather than political, and their society, beyond the elaborate structures of rank and ceremony, was almost as amorphous as that of the Inuit. Quite unlike such politically minded peoples as the Blackfoot or the Iroquois, they formed no kind of common front, as tribe against tribe, or as natives against white intruders. Yet in the end, during their contests with provincial and federal governments over the matter of land rights, they became perhaps better organized and more sophisticated than native peoples in the rest of Canada.

This was because they had, particularly in the early period, the assistance and advice of members of the majority culture, and also because a number of capable British Columbian Indians, mainly through mission education, learnt the ways of the majority society and used their knowledge to help preserve the integrity of their peoples and their cultures.

It was among the people of the Nass River that the struggle for the retention of native lands began, as early as 1887, and here the encouragement of the Anglican missionaries, following William Duncan's example of supporting Indian land claims, was of prime importance. The Nishga protested and passively resisted the government surveyors who began to work in their country. When a provincial commission was sent to the Nass in 1887 to discuss their grievances, the chiefs who gathered to meet it behaved with exemplary unanimity. Their pleas were eloquent. They pointed out that they had once possessed all the land and had never signed a treaty giving it up, yet they were expected to live on the few small reserves arbitrarily granted to them. With dignity they told the commission:

> What we don't like about the Government is their saying: "We will give you this much land." How can they give it when it is our own? We cannot understand it. They have never bought it from us or our forefathers. They have never fought and conquered our people, and taken the land that way, and yet they now say that they will give us so much land—our own land.

Anticipating later Indian groups in the province, the Nishga chiefs asked for a treaty that would recognize their aboriginal title, give them larger reserves, and compensate them for the land they would be surrendering outside the reserves. The commission was merely one of enquiry; it could only gather facts and opinions, and when it returned to Victoria and reported what it had been told, nothing was done to redress the Nishga grievances.

The people of the Nass persisted with remarkable steadfastness, and in their activities over a century they have demonstrated the two directions in which Coast Indian activity over land claims has developed: the way through a strong development of a sense of identity among specific peoples with their separate language traditions, and the way through alliances of peoples who in the past had no sense of common interest, let alone a common identity.

By 1909 the sixteen ranking chiefs of the Nishga had formed themselves into a Land Committee to pursue their claims; their growing political sophistication was shown by the fact that the chairmanship of the committee rotated among the various villages. Its first aim was to raise funds to gain proper legal advice in plotting a campaign. By 1913 they had prepared what became known as "The Nishga Petition," laying out their claims; they submitted it to Ottawa, asking that it be considered by the Judicial Committee of the Privy Council in London, which was then the highest court of appeal for Canadian cases. Somewhere along the line the Nishga had been mistakenly promised that they would have a hearing before the

Judicial Committee, but now it was revealed that this body considered only cases tried first in lower courts in Canada. The Nishga refused to go before a lower court and persisted in their demand for a hearing, sending delegations to Ottawa in 1915 and 1916.

The Land Committee survived in vestigial form, but in 1955, largely through the initiative of Frank Calder, it was replaced by the Nishga Tribal Council, in which the villages were represented equally. The council has been described as "a blend of tradition and modernity," and certainly it marked a political step forward: a popular assembly created by the Nishga people and not by the government, in which all Nishga—but only Nishga—had an equal vote in the assemblies, though as before the Anglican clergy maintained a strong advisory role. Tradition tended to be maintained because the people were likely to elect the clan chiefs to executive posts, though major decisions were made by the popular assembly. By 1969 the Tribal Council brought the Nishga case before the courts, with Tom Berger, former leader of the NDP, as their counsel. The case went to the British Columbian courts and at each stage was rejected. In 1973 it finally reached the Supreme Court of Canada, whose conclusions were ambivalent and amounted to a technical defeat for the Nishga. A majority of the court indeed agreed that aboriginal right existed under common law, but the court split on the question of whether it was alienable. Three judges declared that aboriginal right could not in fact be alienated either by treaty or statute, thus supporting the Nishga claim. Three declared that it could be alienated. A seventh judge refused to decide either way, but dismissed the case on a petty procedural point: that the tribal council had not obtained permission from the attorney general of British Columbia before suing the province. With such a verdict, the judicial options of the Nishga were closed, at least for the time being, and the matter became an affair of governments again, a political affair, a matter of disagreement between a federal government that agreed in principle to negotiate on aboriginal claims but did nothing about it, and a provincial government that, whatever its political complexion, had always denied aboriginal right and refused to negotiate native land claims.

During this time the Nishga also took part in several of the intertribal organizations that appeared in British Columbia during the early twentieth century, participating in general agitations for the hearing of land claims. In 1909 the Nishga Land Committee called meetings with the chiefs of other northern peoples and formed the Allied Tribes of British Columbia. In the same year the well-known amateur anthropologist J. A. Teit gathered a group of Salish chiefs from the southern interior to form the Indian Rights Association, which afterwards became the Interior Tribes of B.C. In 1916 the two groups came together to form the Allied Tribes of British Columbia, mainly devoted to putting forward a general land claim. They were led by mission-trained Indians, prominent among them Andrew Paull of the Squamish and the Haida Anglican clergyman Peter Kelly, who failed to control the disagreements that arose between coastal and interior chiefs and led to the withdrawal of the Nishga in 1922. Nevertheless, the Allied Tribes existed long enough for their agitation to induce the federal government to appoint a Special Committee of the House of Commons and the Senate to look into the question of aboriginal title. The committee, reporting in 1927, declared that the Indians "have not established any claim to the lands of British Columbia based on aboriginal or other title," and went so far as to recommend a prohibition of fundraising to support land claims, which was incorporated into the Indian Act. As a meagre gesture of good will it recommended a grant of $100,000 a year to be distributed among British Columbia Indians in lieu of treaty payments. The Allied Tribes withered away from lack of moral and financial support.

Just as the morale of British Columbian Indians was upraised by their increase in population, so their prosperity, at least on the coast, was enhanced by their being allowed to take part in commercial fishing from 1923 onward. Out of this development emerged the next Indian association that attempted to bring together a number of peoples, the Native Brotherhood of British Columbia. It was an organization mainly based on the native fishermen along the coast and the defence of their special interests. The Indian fishermen had observed the role unionization played in the lives of their non-Indian counterparts, and in practice the Native Brotherhood was from the beginning a native labour movement. It was established by leading Haida and Tsimshian chiefs and modelled on the successful Alaska Native Brotherhood. In 1936 the Kwakiutl formed a similar organization called the Pacific Coast Native Fishermen's Association, and in 1942 this group joined the Brotherhood, which established itself in Vancouver and began to publish a monthly, *The Native Voice*, the first newspaper in British Columbia expressing the viewpoint of the Indians.

The Native Brotherhood depended for its support mainly on the coastal peoples, and except for Andrew Paull, its leaders were Protestant, so linked with the missionary churches that, though it worked closely with left-wing non-native fishermen's unions, its battle song was neither "Solidarity Forever" nor "The Red Flag" but "Onward Christian Soldiers." The preponderance of this Protestant element provoked Andrew Paull in 1945 to lead a secession of the Catholic groups among the Nootka and the Coast Salish to form the rival North American Indian Brotherhood, which claimed to be nationwide but had little visible presence except in the southern interior, where Paull organized a Confederacy of the Inland Tribes of British Columbia.

The relationship between the two organizations was less than harmonious, as was shown in 1947 when a Special Joint Parliamentary Committee was set up to consider amendments to the Indian Act. The Native Brotherhood had already established its credentials sufficiently to be invited to send a spokesman to Ottawa. The Confederacy of the Inland Tribes was annoyed to be passed over and declared that Guy Williams, the Native Brotherhood's representative, did not speak for all Indians: "And we refute everything he has said." The confederacy and the North American Indian Brotherhood established no lasting presence, while the Native Brotherhood, with its solid basis of fishermen support, survives to this day as the oldest established public Indian organization in British Columbia.

A later attempt in 1951 to weld the Indians into a united political movement was made when Guy Williams proposed an Indian Non-Partisan party that would represent specifically Indian interests both provincially and federally. A number of prominent chiefs from the northern tribes and the Kwakiutl attended a meeting to launch the party. But the Nishga, the most politically adept group, remained aloof, and the party failed to materialize, though Williams himself followed a modest political career and ended up a token Indian in the Senate.

A more promising attempt at forming a united organization was made at the end of the 1950s. The Shuswap George Manuel had taken up Andrew Paull's mission and was organizing inland groups to demand improvement in health services on the reserves. He made fraternal contact with the Native Brotherhood in 1958, trying to interest them in co-operation between coastal and inland groups. The Native Brotherhood decided to hold its 1959 convention in Kamloops, and encouraged Manuel to recruit delegates from the interior so that they could together prepare a brief for yet another Joint Parliamentary Committee that was looking into Indian problems. Manuel gathered together some of the Salish chiefs of coast and interior bands, including the remarkable Genevieve Mussel, the Scandinavian woman who had married into the Chilliwack band and become its chief; they formed an Aboriginal Rights Committee to counterbalance the Haida, Tsimshian and Kwakiutl majority in the Native Brotherhood.

In the event, the Kamloops Convention further disunited the Indians of British Columbia, for it underlined the profound cultural differences between the relatively well-off Indians of the northern coast and the poor Indians of the interior. Peter Kelly of the Native Brotherhood promised to consult with Manuel and his group before making a submission to the parliamentary committee in Ottawa, but failed to do so, and thus alienated them. The Nishga believed that they could expect no effective help from the Native Brotherhood in furthering their own claim and decided to rely on themselves, as in the past. The interior Indians, having been ignored by the Brotherhood, decided there was no future in unity, and Manuel set about building an organization of tribes outside the proud coastal tradition. The Brotherhood withdrew into itself as a Protestant fishermen's union.

Manuel continued the Aboriginal Native Rights Committee until 1960, when he revived Paull's North American Indian Brotherhood, which carried out the first effective organization of people in the interior, supported at its peak by more than 75 per cent of the inland bands, as well as those in the lower Fraser Valley as far west as the environs of Vancouver, where Gertrude Guérin, the capable woman chief of the Musqueam band, joined Genevieve Mussel on its executive. They were the first women publicly active in the native rights movement, and their example preluded a general rise in the militancy of Indian women, illustrated in the record of the Indian Homemakers' Association of British Columbia, composed of women's clubs originally sponsored in the villages by the Department of Indian Affairs. Breaking loose, the locals of the Homemakers' Association became active critics of education and health services.

During the 1960s groups organized on territorial or linguistic lines began to emerge. The West Coast Allied Tribes, founded in 1958, consisted entirely of Nootka-speaking bands. Six years later, in 1964, Salish bands speaking the Cowichan dialect founded the Southern Vancouver Island Allied Tribes Federation. In 1966 a last major attempt at unity was made when these organizations, as well as the Nishga Tribal Council, the Native Brotherhood and the North American Indian Brotherhood, came together to discuss the creation of a Confederation of Native Tribes of British Columbia. The first meetings concentrated on the land question, and the progress then made seemed so promising that the organizers issued a statement in *The Native Voice* in December 1966, saying:

> We have confidence that with the formation of the Confederation, the Indians of British Columbia have attained unity and are now in a position to speak with one voice on the main matters of concern starting with the land question.

But soon the differences between the comparatively powerful and prosperous coast peoples and the poor and scattered inland peoples emerged again, and by 1968 Gertrude Guérin was probably speaking for a majority when she said:

> My voice is not for organization, my voice speaks out for the people in little villages, unorganized people in isolated areas who must have area representation. The organizations here represent coastal areas. In other areas the needs are different, and they must have a voice.

Two years later the Confederation of Native Tribes of British Columbia died without a whimper.

Thus, though there was a great sense of the need for unity in the form of an organization that would include all the Indians of the province, the cultural and historic differences between the various peoples prevented it. Anyone who at the beginning of the century harboured the illusion that the Indians of Canada or even of British Columbia formed a real nation that could confront the nation state of the intruders was shown to be mistaken by the experience of the decades since the first attempts in 1909 to organize the Indian peoples of British Columbia.

The process of recovery from the nadir of Indian societies at the turn of the century has in fact been the difficult one of recreating a group identity—or rather a number of group identities—in a setting that has changed utterly. In the past the natural world was the background to Indian life; now the background is the materialistic society of the majority culture. It is like Adam recreating his life with Eden gone.

Something of the confusion the Indians of British Columbia have felt as change seemed to swing back in their favour was exemplified by the unexpected reaction, among them as much as anywhere else in Canada, to the White Paper on Indian Policy, presented by the federal government in 1969. Imbued with the populist idealism of the 1960s, Pierre Trudeau and his fellow simpletons, accepting the arguments of white radicals, offered a policy they believed would end paternalism and discrimination. The Indian Act must be repealed; Indians themselves must shed the advantages and disadvantages of their special status; they must rely on the good will of provincial governments rather than on the federal government for education, health and welfare. They must become not Canadian citizens with a special status but Canadian citizens equal in all respects, suffering no discrimination, enjoying no privileges, asserting no distinctiveness.

The proposal never reached the statute books because of the storm of anger that arose in Indian communities. It was not any mundane and material fact, such as the prospect that they would eventually have to pay income tax, that enraged the Indians. It was the fact that they would lose that very special status that the Liberal innocents had imagined they bore like fetters. To make them one with other Canadians would involve the abrogation of their special relationship with the crown, as sovereign entities treating with another sovereign entity; it would involve the abdication of their treaty and aboriginal rights, which would invalidate the land claims many of them had long pursued. As the Cree leader Harold Cardinal argued, the Liberal proposal was "a thinly disguised programme of extermination through assimilation." No longer forming separate communities on their own land, the Indians would be encouraged to merge with the majority society. Their languages would die in the city schools, the cultural identity they were rebuilding in the twentieth century would suddenly be made irrelevant. The Indian communities made it clear that they were unwilling to abandon the protection the Indian Act offered until their demands for a different status, involving recognition of aboriginal right and of political autonomy, were met. The government retreated, and the Indians, in Canada generally as well as in British Columbia, turned to what seemed to them the basic issues, land and sovereignty.

By sovereignty they did not mean the creation of an all-Canadian Indian nation. Canada-wide organizations of native peoples have been as fissiparous and inclined to dissension as the provincial organizations in British Columbia. Among the many reasons for this failure to agree were religious sectarianism (Indians still take their religion more seriously than other Canadians, and among them the differences between Catholics and Protestants still seem as important as they did in nineteenth-century England); pride of rank (the northern coastal tribes still consider themselves superior to the Salish, who formerly provided their slaves); differences in standard and style of living (the coast Indians are trying to re-enact the kind of rich ceremonial life in which the inland Indians never engaged). The result has been an increasing tendency for the various peoples to turn in upon themselves, to emphasize their different identities, and to act as bands or groups of bands representing particular languages.

The Nishga, fighting their own cause so vigorously by means of the Tribal Council even when they took part in attempts to create broader organizations of native peoples, set an example for the rest. Like them, the tribes have largely turned themselves into militant and vocal groups in which rank still retains its importance and the chiefs play a notable role, though they act now through elected bodies. Some, like the Council of the Haida Nation, emphasize in the title they chose a widespread tendency for each language group to seek sovereignty as an autonomous nation in treaty relationship with the larger society rather than as part of an impossible Indian nation. Similar tribal councils have emerged among the Nootka (the Nuu-chah-nulth Tribal Council) and among the Gitksan of the Skeena. Such groups are prepared to fight in the courts to support their land claims, and in recent years they have also shown a willingness to resort to non-violent direct action—blocking highways and other public demonstrations—to prevent the ravaging by loggers of their traditional lands over which title is undecided, as the Haida have done recently in the Queen Charlottes and the Lillooet people of Mount Currie have done to preserve the Stein Valley.

The land issue remains of prime importance and at present is not within sight of settlement. In British Columbia there were in 1972 (and still are today) more than 1,600 reserves out of the 2,284 in Canada as a whole, but they are usually minute, and today, with a changed living pattern, they have little economic value. But the native peoples are not merely seeking to acquire more economically viable land bases. There is also at least a spiritual if not a religious aspect to the situation, as the former animism of these often devout Christians emerges in their insistence on the sacredness of certain areas associated with spirit questing or in some other way with native traditions. This attitude has brought the native peoples unexpected allies in the majority community, among environmentalists and other nature lovers, who also seek to preserve much of the province of British Columbia, and especially its wilderness, in pristine form.

The Cultural Upsurge

The alliance of sentiment and convenience between the environmentalists and the Indians of British Columbia is one instance of the way in which the recovery of self-awareness is related to tendencies among people beyond the reserves. Another is the cultural resurgence, particularly among the coastal peoples, which arose partly from a desire to recreate their unique ceremonial patterns but also from changes in taste and appreciation by the arts community of the majority culture.

The appreciation of primitive arts that began among postimpressionist painters in Paris like Matisse and Picasso early in the twentieth century was slow to reach Canada. Not until after World War II did the writings of European art historians like Herbert Read, André Malraux and Claude Lévi-Strauss, with their efforts to establish a synthesis of world art that included the primitive traditions, lead Canadians to learn—so largely from outsiders—that there had been great artists on the Pacific coast.

The shift from ethnological interest to aesthetic appreciation on the part of Canadians may perhaps be said to start—as with African art in Europe—among the local artists, notably Emily Carr during the 1930s, and in the 1940s Jack Shadbolt. A broader sign of the change of attitudes was the crucial exhibition offered by the

Vancouver Art Gallery in 1956, *The People of the Potlatch*. Organized by art critic Jerrold Morris and anthropologist Audrey Hawthorn, this was the first major attempt in British Columbia to commemorate the artistic creativity of the coast peoples, particularly the Kwakiutl, the Tsimshian and the Haida.

This broader and deeper interest in the Coast Indian cultures, together with the renewal of traditional ceremonies after the legalization of potlatches and spirit dances, encouraged the re-emergence of the ancient crafts. Surviving carvers like the Kwakiutl Mungo Martin were brought out of neglect by institutions like the Provincial Museum to carve poles once again in the ancient style. The Haida Bill Reid not only carved new poles in the old style for the University of British Columbia but also developed into a kind of Indian Benvenuto Cellini, producing beautifully crafted jewellery using traditional Haida motifs, which sold to an international market. Here was a high level hybrid art, deriving from the jewellery native carvers like Charles Edenshaw had made from silver coins in the late nineteenth century. Like Edenshaw's work and the argillite carving developed in the nineteenth century, Reid's work not only applied ancient designs by new techniques to new materials; it also depended on markets outside native societies, and just as Haida carvers in the transitional period had worked largely for dealers serving the tourists, so contemporary Coast Indian artists have worked for art gallery shops and for stores specializing in such hybrid artifacts. Yet there has also been a more genuine revival on another level of the art associated with Indian ceremonial, the art of masks and rattles and other objects used once again in potlatching and the winter dances, which remain largely private and exclusive, outsiders rarely being invited.

The result of this double demand for Coast Indian artifacts has been a degeneration as well as a revival of the craft and, except for the more imaginative artists, a tendency to the mechanical repetition of older forms and images. The extraordinary ingenuity and variety that the arts of the northern peoples showed in the decades after first contact with the traders have not been repeated. Yet the role and dignity of the artist and particularly of the carver in tribal life have been reasserted, partly because the best known of the carvers have become prosperous, but partly because they have played such an important role in relinking the life of the northern peoples to its past, so that the seasons and the rites of passage again find their appropriate expression.

The inland hunting peoples and the Salish of the southern coast, who did not have the high traditions of ceremonial art that the northern peoples and the Kwakiutl developed, have enjoyed neither the profits nor the prestige that came from the elevation of Coast Indian art in the general community. Yet the spirit dances of the Salish, when the young initiates—female as well as male—perform the dances and sing the songs their tutelary spirits have given them, are occasions when one senses the strength a people, however small in numbers, can gain from having retained its spiritual identity, like the taproot of a plant that dies down in winter and emerges again in the spring of a changed world.

This does not mean that by 1972—or even today when I write—the problems of a century and a half of isolation and poverty in the more remote reserves in the interior have been solved. Health and educational services have improved, and voluntary agencies have helped to ameliorate the situation, so that, though there is much unemployment, nobody starves, even if hunting no longer serves as a reliable resource. But the anomie that life on welfare creates, particularly among the young, with its attendant consequences of drunkenness, crime and suicide, is still endemic in smaller Indian communities. Yet no group has lost the sense of its peculiar and special identity. Even here in these dejected villages, the great decline of the turn of the century has been halted, and there are individuals and groups seeking, with whatever help they can get from outside, to make their communities viable without abandoning their land or forgetting their traditions. The Indian peoples will never recover the freedom of the land that they retained long after Cook made his landfall; they will never again outnumber the intruders as they did until the late nineteenth century. But their sense of themselves and their pride in themselves is returning, and they are beginning to face the white men as Maquinna faced Cook, equal and distinct.

Epilogue

The role of the historian can be illuminated by devising a Canadian variant on the famous aphorism of the ancient Greek philosopher Heraclitus. To emphasize his doctrine of the universe involved in endless flux, Heraclitus declared: "You cannot step twice in the same river." The flow, he contended, is ever renewed, but the water is never the same, and for anyone who lived on the shores of the Aegean, where the rivers never freeze over, his intent was clear. What seems constant is always changing, and its apparent constancy (or flow) indeed seems to demand that it never remain the same.

Heraclitus lived before the art of history developed; he belonged to the generation preceding Herodotus. And while he had heard of those cold Hyperborean realms from which shamans and shamanism entered the Greek consciousness, he had never seen a frozen river, or considered the paradox of a river *into* which one can never step twice, but *on* which, once it is frozen, one can step often, without the surface below changing until the spring.

What the historian does is to walk on a magically frozen river, time frozen at his will, while far below, under the ice, time and change are continuing as the stream flows on. In self-protection he has to declare a point of observation, and if he is wise he will freeze his river not too near the time when he writes, so that the passions of the present will not prematurely thaw his view of the past. What goes on outside while he is writing he will, if he is wise, leave to those who write on current affairs, or whatever else one may call the difficult study of the present, and most of all he will avoid the future, where history has no place, except perhaps as the example invariably disregarded.

I have picked 1972 as the point to end this book largely because it gives a fair space—more than half a conventional generation—over which to look back at the past. But why do I choose 1972 rather than 1971 or 1973? Mainly because the date gives me a reason to reflect in these final pages on the continuities that environmental circumstances and people's response to them have imposed on British Columbian history.

In the last chapter I ended my account of British Columbian politics in the present century with the final arrival in power—in 1972—of the province's long-time opposition, the NDP. And I remarked, "An era of promise seemed about to begin."

That was a view held by many in 1972, who today would agree that the victory in the polls of Dave Barrett and his fellow social democrats in fact represented no greater change in the political, social and economic situation than any other exchange of power between parties. In terms of a real transformation in the state of the province, of a fulfilment of millennial expectations, its effect was no more than that of an electoral hiccup.

What was revealed, during the brief three years of Barrett's incumbency, was the close space within which the type of populist and confrontational politics British Columbia had developed allowed its practitioners to work. The virtual destruction of the old-line parties by the combined forces of the social democrats and Social Credit cleared away a great deal of debris to reveal the true fissures in provincial political and social life. But it established on those fissures the narrow boundaries within which British Columbians continued to conduct their political affairs even during the late 1980s.

How close these boundaries were is shown by the little Dave Barrett and his social democrats could achieve between 1972 and 1975, in comparison with their own hopes and the electorate's expectations. In fact, the brief NDP government did no more to shift British Columbia in the direction of a balanced socialist economy than its predecessor had done. As a symbolic gesture, Barrett had threatened a provincial takeover of the British Columbia Telephone Company, but had found it entrenched behind a federal charter. He did indeed establish a crown corporation to take over motor vehicle insurance in the province and acquired four failing pulp mills, which their owners had proposed to abandon. But the latter was a stopgap measure to save jobs and did not represent a permanent incursion of the province into the forest industries, while the socialization of car insurance was a slight achievement in comparison with Bennett's record of expropriating the powerful British Columbia Electric Company and his creation of a provincial bank and a provincial ferry fleet.

What Barrett's failures demonstrated was the difficulty of any government making a radical shift in the economic structure of British Columbia. Barrett did make welcome reforms in areas, like the legal system and the welfare system, that were especially important to him as a former social worker, and he tried, like the Czech leader Dubcek, to give the state a human face. He was approachable and responded often to valid appeals by action within the limits of his possibilities. But all this was a matter of style in government rather than the substance of radical economic action. And Barrett did nothing that appreciably changed the pattern by which British Columbia relied on the primary industries that depleted the environment and its resources. His government offered little encouragement to the secondary industries that might have given the province a more balanced and independent economy. Instead, he turned like his predecessors—Social Credit, Liberal, Tory—to the untapped resources of the northern areas and encouraged their development by capitalists from outside the province.

Inadvertently, he was in part responsible for a late twentieth-century repetition of the speculative land fevers of earlier generations. Alarmed by the spread of suburbia and the unrestricted alienation of farmland by real estate developers, he and his government introduced legislation withdrawing such properties into an "agricultural reserve" of land that could not be sold except for further farming. Unfortunately he did not accompany this measure with a freeze on prices of urban and other nonagricultural land. The result was a sudden inflationary rise in property values and a speculative market in real estate, so that for a decade and a half the property boom continued as a kind of undulating fever—and a corrupting one. It affected municipal as well as provincial politics, as developers with vast capital replaced the land speculators of the past, a trend that continued under the later Social Credit governments led by W. A. C. Bennett's son, Bill Bennett, and by William Vander Zalm.

The steady urbanization of the province continued during this period, and the drift to the cities encouraged the developers. Now more than 80 per cent of British Columbia's population live in communities of more than five thousand people, and round about 60 per cent of its inhabitants are concentrated in the commercial capital of Vancouver (Greater Vancouver's population approaches a million and a half) and the political capital of Victoria, which has more than a quarter of a million people. The smaller centres, with their fur trade and railway pasts, have grown more slowly, and only Kamloops (the ranching and railway centre), Prince George (the transport hub of the north and the pulp and paper centre), and Kelowna (the centre of the fruit-growing and tourist-ridden Okanagan) have populations between sixty and eighty thousand. For the rest, British Columbia remains a province of small and often still rustic towns where religious fundamentalism and right-wing populism tend to flourish.

The urban changes have given a new aspect to land booming, for just as the forests are now being exploited for their second growths, so the cities are undergoing a second reaping. Once it was trees that were felled to make way for buildings; now it is buildings that are felled as the land is bought again and the original fabrics of the cities are replaced by new and transforming structures. This is especially the case in Vancouver, where the business district is forested by glass and concrete towers that spread into the old residential district of the West End, while the former industrial heart of the city, around False Creek, has been transformed by events like Expo 86, and its maze of small workshops has been replaced by housing estates and the market and entertainment quarter of Granville Island.

The concentration of the province's industrial life in the primary areas of logging and farming, fish and minerals, continues, complemented by a rapidly growing tertiary complex of service industries in real estate, finance, bureaucracy, entertainment, communications and the retail trade, increasingly decentralized in suburban and small town malls. The continued importance of the primary industries has meant that behind British Columbian politics still lurks—exemplified most visibly in the logging companies and their restless workers—the old antagonism between ruthless bosses and militant unions, which continues whatever the regime in power; and occurred under the NDP government of Dave Barrett, voted out in 1975 largely because it legislated three striking unions back to work, Barrett using the populist argument that his party represented the people and not any special interest like labour.

A new factor entered the situation through the politicization of the environmental movement, which in recent years has grown increasingly militant, embracing not only the intellectual and artistic strata of society and the native peoples but also growing numbers of the general population alarmed by the threats to wildlife and to the natural environment. At this point one sees forming against the environmentalists a reactionary alliance of forest companies and big unions, trying to defend the rights they feel they established long ago to a free hand in the forests.

The rain forests are indeed threatened in British Columbia, and are dwindling as they are in other parts of the world. The cities clamber up the mountainsides in the communities of Vancouver's North Shore, or insidiously creep over the farmlands of the lower Fraser Valley and impinge on the wetlands that are a vital part of the flightpath of vast flocks of migratory birds. On the other hand, modernization and mechanization have made small farms uneconomic, and so, added to the ghost towns that commemorate the mining era, there are ghost valleys whose fields are returning to bush. Only the mountain tops seem unaffected by the cycle of expansion and its counterpart, decay. And even here there are examples of exploitation in the spreading centres for winter sports like Whistler in the Coast Mountains north of Vancouver.

As the province has changed within its narrow economic confines, its population has continued to grow and to vary, with the arrival of new groups of people, sometimes in sudden rushes like the thousands of Indochinese "boat people" at the end of the 1970s, but just as often by the slow accretion of families recreating themselves in a new home. These demographic changes have had important effects on British Columbian life. They have affected habits—particularly eating habits—so that restaurants representing many cuisines are to be found even in country towns, and the shelves of supermarkets and liquor stores contain a variety of food and drink unknown a generation ago. The practice of education, if not the curriculum, has been profoundly changed, since often, especially in certain Vancouver areas, most of the children in a school speak English as an acquired language. Racial barriers and prejudices have dissolved in ways that would have seemed impossible even in the 1950s. No districts are residentially exclusive any more, and the old prejudices against employing orientals have long ago vanished as people of Asian and Caribbean origins have moved into every profession and every trade, and into politics as well.

A new equality has thus emerged, but also, often appearing in oblique form, a new conservatism. It appears by definition in the urge towards conservation of the natural environment and even of older buildings that have a new land's fragile claims to be considered historical. It appears too in a retreat from the radical imperatives of the 1960s, a retreat largely motivated by the appearance of people from the more conservative cultures of Asia. But this is by no means only a matter of outside intrusion. It comes also from a sense of historical identity that is not merely provincial.

British Columbians are indeed deeply conscious still of their own local identity, even though they no longer see it as a matter of being especially British. They cannot ignore the natural barriers that detach them from other provinces, or the millennia of prehistory and the almost complete century of history that elapsed before their ancestors and predecessors somewhat unenthusiastically joined Canada. Now, though they sustain their unity with Canada, and in any foreseeable future seem likely to do so, they are also aware of other unities and loyalties in a narrowing world.

Historically, after all, they retain deep bonds with the Pacific coast of the United States. Washington State and some of Oregon were part of the Hudson's Bay Company domain and might have remained in British Columbia if the British government had been a little firmer at the time of the Oregon Boundary Treaty in 1846. Links with San Francisco have been strong ever since the merchants arriving from that city transformed Victoria from a trading post into a town in 1858.

In recent years the development of Vancouver's international airport has created not only direct links with the principal European countries but also a network of communications with the countries of the Asian littoral, which forms the western sector of the Pacific Rim, that collection of communities with different origins and cultures but of growing common interests. In that Pacific world, British Columbia realizes, much of its future lies.

The merit of regions conscious of their own identity, of their collective selfhood, is that they can overleap the limitations of nationality and take their own places in the broader world, as Québec has done and British Columbia undoubtedly will do. The next phase of its history—one of growing contact with the Asian world—will synthesize its Pacific and North American loyalties, as the loyalty to Britain implied in its name becomes a sentimental one, a matter of history rather than actuality.

Further Reading

This does not pretend to be a complete bibliography. It does not list more than a fraction of the books and articles I have read over the past forty years of involvement in British Columbian history, nor does it even acknowledge the hundreds of oral communications, and even of a traveller's visual impressions, that have shaped my image of British Columbia in past and present. It is a list that readers may pick over to find books that will broaden and deepen their knowledge of British Columbian history. But it is by no means exhaustive, for in recent years, particularly since the centennials of 1958, 1967 and 1971, much local history has been written, and British Columbians interested in the region as a whole or in their own localities may profit by talking to local librarians.

Adachi, Ken. *The Enemy That Never Was: A History of the Japanese Canadians.* Toronto, 1976.

Akrigg, G. P. V., and Helen B. Akrigg. *British Columbia Chronicle, 1778–1846.* Vancouver, 1975.

———. *1001 British Columbia Place Names.* Vancouver, 1969.

Allison, Susan. *A Pioneer Gentlewoman in British Columbia. The Recollections of Susan Allison.* Ed. Margaret A. Ormsby. Vancouver, 1976.

Anderson, James. *Sawney's Letters.* 2nd ed. Barkerville, 1869.

Bancroft, Hubert Howe. *History of British Columbia, 1792–1887.* San Francisco, 1890.

Barman, Jean. *Growing Up in British Columbia.* Vancouver, 1984.

Beaglehole, J. C., ed. *The Journals of Captain James Cook on His Voyages of Discovery.* Cambridge, 1968.

Begg, Alexander. *History of British Columbia from Its Earliest Discovery to the Present Time.* Toronto, 1894.

Bell, Michael. *Painters in a New Land: From Annapolis Royal to the Klondike.* Toronto, 1973.

Birney, Earle. *The Collected Poems of Earle Birney.* 2 vols. Toronto, 1975.

Blanchet, M. Wylie. *The Curve of Time.* 4th ed. Sidney, 1980

Bowen, Lynne. *Boss Whistle: The Coal Miners of Vancouver Island Remember.* Lantzville, 1982.

Brody, Hugh. *Maps and Dreams.* Vancouver, 1981.

Butler, William Francis. *The Great Lone Land.* London, 1872

———. *The Wild North Land.* London, 1873.

Carr, Emily. *Growing Pains: The Autobiography of Emily Carr.* Toronto, 1946.

———. *Hundreds and Thousands: The Journals of Emily Carr.* Toronto, 1966.

———. *The Book Of Small.* Toronto, 1942.

Dalzell, Kathleen E. *The Queen Charlotte Islands, 1774–1966.* Terrace, 1968.

———. *The Queen Charlotte Islands: Of Places and Names.* Prince Rupert, 1973.

Daniells, Roy. *Alexander Mackenzie and the North West.* London, 1969.

Davidson, Gordon Charles. *The North West Company.* Berkeley, 1918.

Dawson, George M. *The Journals of George M. Dawson, British Columbia, 1875–78.* Ed. Douglas Cole and Bradley Olckner. 2 vols. Toronto, 1989.

Dixon, George. *Voyage Round the World: But Most Particularly to the Northwest Coast of America.* London, 1789.

Drucker, Philip. *Indians of the Northwest Coast.* New York, 1955.

Duff, Wilson. *The Indian History of British Columbia, Vol I: The Impact of the White Man.* Victoria, 1964.

Dunae, Patrick. *Gentlemen Emigrants: From the British Public Schools to the Canadian Frontier.* Vancouver, 1981.

Elliott, Gordon R. *Barkerville, Quesnel and the Cariboo Gold Rush.* Vancouver, 1958.

Fraser, Simon. *The Letters and Journals of Simon Fraser, 1806–1808.* Ed. W. Kaye Lamb. Toronto, 1960.

Galbraith, John S. *The Hudson's Bay Company As an Imperial Factor, 1821–1890.* Berkeley, 1957.

Haig-Brown, Roderick. *Measure of the Year.* 2nd ed. Toronto, 1968.

Harmon, Daniel Williams. *A Journal of Voyages and Travels in the Interior of North America.* Andover, 1820.

———. *Sixteen Years in the Indian Country. The Journal of Daniel Williams Harmon 1800–1816.* Ed. W. Kaye Lamb. Toronto, 1957.

Harper, J. Russell. *Painting in Canada: A History.* Toronto, 1966.

———. *William G. R. Hind.* Ottawa, 1976.

Harris, R. Cole, ed. *Historical Atlas of Canada, from the Beginning to 1800.* Toronto, 1987.

Helmcken, John Sebastian. *The Reminiscences of Doctor John Sebastian Helmcken.* Ed. Dorothy Blakey Smith. Vancouver, 1975.

Hoagland, Edward. *Notes from the Century Before.* New York, 1969.

Howay, F. W. *The Work of the Royal Engineers in British Columbia 1858–1863.* Victoria, 1910.

Hutchison, Bruce. *The Fraser.* Toronto, 1950.

Innis, Harold A. *The Fur Trade in Canada: An Introduction to Canadian Economic*

History. Rev. ed. Toronto, 1956.

Jenness, Diamond. *The Indians of Canada.* 3rd ed. Ottawa, 1955.

Jewitt, John R. *The Adventures and Sufferings of John R. Jewitt, Captive Among the Nootka, 1803–1805.* Ed. Derek G. Smith. Toronto, 1974.

Johnston, Hugh. *The Voyage of the Komagata Maru: The Sikh Challenge to Canada's Colour Bar.* Delhi, 1979

Kane, Paul. *Wanderings of an Artist,* London, 1859.

Ledyard, John. *John Ledyard's Journal of Captain Cook's Last Voyage.* Hartford, 1783.

Lillard, Charles. *Seven Shillings a Year: The History of Vancouver Island.* Ganges, B.C., 1986.

Livesay, Dorothy. *Collected Poems: Two Seasons.* 2nd ed. Toronto, 1972.

Macfie, Matthew. *Vancouver Island and British Columbia, Their History, Resources and Prospects.* London, 1865.

McKelvie, B. A. *Fort Langley: Outpost of Empire.* Vancouver, 1947.

Mackenzie, Alexander. *Voyages from Montreal.* London, 1801.

MacLennan, Hugh. *Rivers of Canada.* Toronto, 1974.

McMillan. Alan D. *Native Peoples and Cultures of Canada.* Vancouver, 1988.

Marlatt, Daphne. *Steveston Recollected.* Victoria, 1975.

Mayne, R. C. *Four Years in British Columbia and Vancouver Island.* London, 1862.

Meares, John. *Voyages Made in the Years 1788 and 1789 . . .* London, 1790.

Milton, Viscount, and W. B. Cheadle. *The North-west Passage by Land.* London, 1865.

Morice, A. G. *The History of the Northern Interior of British Columbia.* Toronto, 1904.

Morton, Arthur S. *A History of the Canadian West to 1870–71.* London, 1939.

Murray, Peter. *The Devil and Mr. Duncan.* Victoria, 1985.

Nichol, Eric. *Vancouver.* Toronto, 1970.

Ormsby, Margaret. *British Columbia: A History.* Toronto, 1958.

Peake, Frank A. *History of the Anglican Church in British Columbia.* Vancouver, 1958.

Pemberton, J. Despard. *Facts and Figures Relating to Vancouver Island and British Columbia.* London, 1860.

Reid, Dennis. *"Our Own Country Canada": Being an Account of the National Aspirations of the Principal Landscape Artists in Montreal and Toronto 1860–1890.* Ottawa, 1970.

Rich, E. E., ed. *The Letters of John McLoughlin from Fort Vancouver to the Governor and Committee.* 3 vols (1825–46). Toronto, 1941–44.

Robin, Martin. The *Pillars of Profit: The Company Province, 1933–1972.* Toronto, 1973.

———. *Radical Politics and Canadian Labour: 1880–1930.* Kingston, 1968.

———. *The Rush for Spoils 1871–1833: The Company Province.* Toronto, 1972.

Roper, Edward. *By Track and Trail through Canada.* London, 1891.

Ross, Alexander. *The Fur Hunters of the Far West: A Narrative of Adventures in the Oregon and Rocky Mountains.* 2 vols. London, 1855.

Roy, Patricia E. *A White Man's Province: British Columbia Politicians and Chinese and Japanese Immigrants, 1858–1914.* Vancouver, 1989

Sage, Walter N. *Sir James Douglas and British Columbia.* Toronto, 1930.

Scholefield, E. O. S., and F. W. Howay. *British Columbia from the Earliest Times to the Present.* 4 vols., Vancouver, 1914.

Shadbolt, Doris. *The Art of Emily Carr.* Vancouver/Toronto, 1979.

Shelton, W. George, ed. *British Columbia and Confederation.* Victoria, 1967.

Simpson, Sir George. *An Overland Journey Round the World, during the Years 1841 and 1842.* Parts 1 and 2. Philadelphia, 1847.

Sunahara, Anne Gomer. *The Politics of Racism: The Uprooting of Japanese Canadians during the Second World War.* Toronto, 1981.

Thompson, David. *David Thompson's Travels in Western North America, 1784–1812.* Ed. Victor G. Hopwood. Toronto, 1971.

Tippett, Maria. *Emily Carr: A Biography.* Toronto, 1979.

———, and Douglas Cole. *From Desolation to Splendour: Changing Perceptions of the British Columbia Landscape.* Toronto, 1976.

Vancouver, George. *A Voyage of Discovery to the North Pacific Ocean And Round the World.* 3 vols. London, 1798.

Walbran, John T. *British Columbia Place Names, 1592–1906. Their Origin and History.* Ottawa, 1909.

Ward, W. Peter. *White Canada Forever: Popular Attitudes and Public Policy toward Orientals in British Columbia.* Montreal, 1978.

Warre, Henry. *Sketches of North America and the Oregon Territory.* London, 1848.

Watters, R. E., ed. *British Columbia: A Centennial Anthology.* Toronto, 1958.

Williams, David Ricardo. *"The Man for a New Country." Sir Matthew Baillie Begbie.* Sidney, 1977.

Woodcock, George. *Amor De Cosmos.* Toronto, 1975.

———. *Peoples of the Coast: The Indians of the Pacific Northwest.* Edmonton, 1977.

———. *A Social History of Canada,* Toronto, 1988.

———, ed. *British Columbia: A Celebration,* with photographs by Janis Kraulis. Edmonton, 1983.

———, and Ivan Avakumovic. *The Doukhobors.* Toronto, 1968.

Wilson, Ethel. *The Innocent Traveller.* London 1949.

Periodicals and Collections. There are two periodicals of great value to students of British Columbian history. *B.C. Studies* is a scholarly quarterly published by the University of British Columbia in Vancouver, and *Raincoast Chronicles* is a more popular occasional collection of articles and stories issued by Harbour Publishing at Madeira Park. That noble publication, the *Dictionary of Canadian Biography,* contains from Volume IV onward many articles on figures connected with British Columbian history.

Index

Aberdeen, Lord, 165
Aboriginal Native Rights Committee, 259
Abyssinia (ship), 158
Adaskin, Murray, 252
Adventure (ship), 57
aeroplane industry, 227
Africans, 232
agriculture. *See* farming
Ahousat, 135
Aiyansh, 138
Alaska, 25, 37, 53, 68, 74, 80, 107, 177, 218, 223
Alava, Brigadier General, 37
Alberni, Pedro, 35, 36
Alcan (Aluminum Company of Canada), 231, 236
Alert Bay, 253–54
Alexis, Chief, 116, 133
Allan, Captain, 60
Allen, Robert, 251
Allied Tribes of British Columbia, 257–58
Alvensleben, Baron Alvo von, 179
Alverstone, Lord Chief Justice, 177
Americans, 31, 32, 33–34, 37, 45–47, 53, 55, 56–60, 62, 64, 65, 69, 72, 74, 75–78, 98–101, 103, 110, 152, 153, 185
Anderson, James, 110, 169
Anglo-American, The. See Victoria Gazette
Anscomb, Herbert, 234, 236, 237, 239
Anti-Conscription League, 198
Antler Creek, 102
Argonaut (ship), 34, 58
arts: ceremonial, 6–7, 8, 9, 14, 16–20, 55, 128, 182, 254, 263; literary, 110, 169–70, 250–52; metalworking, 8, 11, 55, 263; performing, 101, 109–110, 159, 169, 251–52; stoneworking, 9, 11, 55; visual, 170–74, 249–50; woodworking, 6, 7, 8, 9, 11
Arts Club Theatre, 251
Ashcroft, 110
Asian Exclusion League, 189
Aspell, Peter, 250
Associated Merchants of London and India, 34
Astor, John Jacob, 44, 47
Atahualpa (ship), 58–59
Athapaskan language group, 4, 15, 16, 18, 20, 21, 22, 51, 52
Atrevida (ship), 35
Austrians, 192–93
Avison, John, 252
Ayres, G. W., 59

B.C. Electric. *See* British Columbia Electric Company
Baltzy, Benjamin, 172
Bank of British Columbia, 245
Barbeau, Marius, 55, 141
Barker, Billy, 109
Barkerville, 103, 109–111, 122. *See also* gold
Barkley, Capt. Charles, 32, 58
Barkley, Frances, 32
Barnard's Express, 110
Barrett, Dave, 247, 266–67, 268
Bartlett, 105–106

Bastion Theatre, 251
Bates, Maxwell, 250
Baynes, Rear Admiral Robert, 107
Beaven, Robert, 156
Beaver, 21, 127
Beaver (ship), 9, 71–72, 79, 80, 85, 96
Beaver Harbour, 80
Begbie, Matthew Baillie, 94–95, 96,
    101–104, 107, 109, 110, 133, 134,
    140–41, 165, 188
Bell, Alistair, 250
Bella Bella (Heiltsuk), 3, 4, 15, 16, 39,
    41–42, 52, 58–59
Bella Coola people, 3, 4, 132
Bella Coola River, 52
Belle Vue Point, 66
Bell-Smith, F. W., 172
Bengal Fur Company, 32
Bennett, Bill, 267
Bennett, R. B., 212–13, 216, 217
Bennett, W. A. C., 235, 237–48
Bennett (W. A. C.) Dam, 245
Berger, Tom, 247, 257
Bering, Vitus, 25
Big Bend, 160
Binning, B. C., 231, 250
"Birdcages." *See* parliament buildings
Birney, Earle, 250, 252
Bishop, Captain, 54
Black, Captain, 46
Black, Samuel, 63
Black Ball Ferries, 244
Blake, Edward, 147, 148
Blanchet, Father François, 88
Blanshard, Richard, 84–85
Bloedel, Stewart and Welch Ltd., 235
Blossom (ship), 46–47
Blue Bell Mine, 151, 161
Boas, Franz, 141
Boat Encampment, 44, 49, 64
Bobak, Bruno, 250
Bobak, Molly, 250
Bodega y Quadra, Juan Francisco de la, 27,
    35, 36–37, 56, 58
Boit, John, 57
Bolduc, Father Jean Baptiste, 88, 136
Bonner, Robert, 240, 243
Borden, Charles E., 7
Borden, Sir Robert, 180, 197
Boston (ship), 58

Boston Bar, 102
boundaries: British-Spanish disputes,
    34–35, 36–38; Russian, 47; American-
    British disputes, 47, 63, 68, 77–78,
    107–108, 112, 269; American-
    Canadian disputes, 177–78
Bowering, George, 251
Bowser, William, 187, 195, 196, 209, 210,
    213
Brady, William, 135
Brew, Chartres, 94, 95, 110, 116, 130, 133
Brewster, Harlan C., 196–97, 215
Brewster, Mary Ellen, 197
Bridge River, 218, 224
Brighouse, Sam, 157
Brilliant, 192
British Colonist, 105, 106, 118, 131, 135
British Columbia (crown colony): estab-
    lished, 93; colonial officers appointed,
    94; HBC licence to exclusive trade ends,
    96; capital city chosen, 96–97; growth
    of New Westminster, 101–102; roads,
    102; gold mining, 102–104, 108–111;
    opposition to Douglas, 104–107; depar-
    ture of Moody and Royal Engineers,
    111; Douglas retires, 112; first legislative
    council, 112
British Columbia (united colony):
    proclaimed, 1866, 117; legislative coun-
    cil, 117–18; Victoria named capital,
    118; enters Confederation, 122
British Columbia Constructionist (Con-
    structive) party, 218
British Columbia Electric Company (B.C.
    Electric), 165, 178, 226, 231, 244
British Columbia Federation of Labour,
    185, 198, 204, 228, 229
British Columbia Ferry Corporation, 244
British Columbia Hydro and Power Au-
    thority, 244
British Columbian, 106–107, 114
British Columbia Power Commission, 226,
    231, 242
British Columbia Power Corporation, 242
British Columbia Railway, 242
British Columbia Social Credit League, 218
British Columbia Teachers' Federation, 229
British North America Act, 119, 140
Brody, Hugh, 21
Brother Jonathan (ship), 105

Brothers, Donald, 247
Broughton, William, 36, 37
Buckingham, Duke of, 119
Bulwer Lytton, Sir Edward. *See* Lytton, Sir Edward Bulwer
Burdett-Coutts, Baroness, 110
Burrard Inlet, 36, 123, 154, 196

Caamano, Jacintho, 35, 127
Cadboro (ship), 70, 80
Calder, Frank, 234, 257
California, 80, 81, 88–89
Cameron, David, 85–86, 91
Cameron, John ("Cariboo Cameron"), 109
Camerontown, 109
Campbell, Dan, 198–99
Canadian Congress of Labour, 228, 229
Canadian Literature, 251
Canadian National Railways, 184
Canadian Northern Railway, 168, 181, 182, 184, 186
Canadian Pacific Airlines, 230
Canadian Pacific Railway: agreement with Ottawa, 121–22; and Confederation, 143–44, 145–46, 148–50; search for route, 147; work begins at Yale, 153–54; Burrard Inlet chosen as terminus, 154; refuses to build on Vancouver Island, 155; first train to Port Moody, 156; first passenger train to Port Moody, 156; first passenger train to Vancouver, 157; role in developing Vancouver as seaport, 158; impact on settlements and industry, 160–62; acquires Trail smelter and land in Vancouver, 163; maintenance workers' strike, 168; competition with other railways, 181, 184; ferries, 244
Cannibal Society (Hamatsa), 19
Cape Alava, 10–11
Cape Mudge, 51, 128, 134, 254
Cardero, José, 170
Cardinal, Harold, 261
Caribbeans, 232, 268
Cariboo, 102–3, 108–11
Cariboo Gold Escort, 110
Cariboo Road, 102, 108–109, 115, 168, 172, 207, 242
Cariboo Sentinel, 109
Carnarvon, Lord, 147
Carr, Emily, 173, 249, 250, 262

Carrall, Dr. R. W. W., 121
Carrier, 18, 22, 41, 42, 67, 182
Carter-Cotton, Francis, 166
Cartier, Sir George Etienne, 121
Cary, George Hunter, 114
Cary Castle (Cary Folly), 114
Cavendish, George, 24
CBC (Canadian Broadcasting Corporation), 251, 252
CCF (Co-operative Commonwealth Federation), 213–14, 218, 219, 220, 221, 223, 225, 226, 229, 234, 236, 239, 241, 243, 244
Chameleon (ship), 135
Che-wich-i-kan, Chief, 81
Cheadle, Dr. W. B., 169
Chilcotin people, 3, 41, 115–16, 133–34
Chilcotin War, 115–16, 133–134
Chilkat, 53
Chilliwack people, 259
Chinese, 33, 34, 100–101, 102, 110, 134, 152–53, 154, 175, 176, 177, 178, 186, 187–89, 209, 224, 232–33
Chinese Immigration Act, 189
Chinook, 52
clans, 15–16, 19, 22, 53, 56. *See also* arts, ceremonial
Clayoquot Sound, 45, 57, 59, 135
Clerke, Capt. Charles, 28, 30
Cloose, 9
Clover Point, 79
Coal Harbour, 157
Coast Salish, 4, 10, 22, 51, 52, 125, 131, 138, 140. *See also* Cowichan; Musqueam; Songhees
Coleman, Edmund, 172
Collings, Charles John, 250
Collins Telegraph Line, 181
Colnett, Capt. James, 34, 58
Colonial Office, 64, 83–84, 85, 86–87, 93, 105, 112, 114, 117, 119, 120, 143. *See also* British Columbia (crown colony); British Columbia (united colony); Vancouver Island (colony)
Columbia, 46, 49, 51, 61, 62, 63–66, 67, 73, 75–76, 77–78. *See also* Hudson's Bay Company; McLoughlin, John; New Caledonia; Simpson, George
Columbia (ship), 37, 57, 71
Columbia & Western Railway, 168
Columbia River, 44–45, 46, 74, 75, 244

Columbia River Treaty, 245
Colvile, Eden, 66
Colwood, 86, 88
Cominco, 163, 228, 231
Commodore (ship), 92, 98–99
Communist party, 213, 217, 228–29, 234
Confederacy of the Inland Tribes of British
    Columbia, 258
Confederation, 118–22, 139–41, 142–43
Confederation League, 120
Confederation of Native Tribes of British
    Columbia, 260
Connell, Reverend Robert, 218
conscription, 197, 198
Conservative party, 175, 176, 177, 194,
    209, 218, 221, 234, 236, 237, 239, 240,
    241, 243, 246
Constant Cove, 86
Cook, Capt. James, 28–30
Cooke, Reverend A. E., 195
Cooper, Capt. James, 85, 90, 91, 106
Cormorant (ship), 89
Cotsworth, Moses B., 195
Coulthard, Jean, 252
Council of the Haida Nation, 262
Cowichan, 43, 126, 135, 260
Cox, John Henry, 31, 33
Cox, William George, 116, 133
Craigflower, 86, 88
Cranmer, Dan, 253–54
Crease, Henry, 121
Cree, 261
Crespi, Fray Juan, 26
Creston, 206
Cridge, Edward, 88, 92, 137
Crisis in British Columbia, The, 195
Crosby, Thomas, 138
Crown Zellerbach, 235
Crowsnest coalfields, 186, 198, 211
Cumberland, 186
Cumshewa, Chief, 58
Currie, Lieut.-Col. Arthur W., 191
Curtis, Smith, 177
Czechoslovakians, 233

Daedalus (ship), 84
Davenport, William, 177
Davey, Frank, 251
Davie, A. E. B., 164, 165
Davie, Theodore, 164
De Cosmos, Amor (William Smith), 105,

106, 113–14, 117, 118–20, 121, 143,
    144, 145–47, 148–50, 155, 156
de Gallo, Count Paul, 105, 106
De Smet, Father, 136
Deighton, John ("Gassy Jack"), 123, 157
Demers, Father Modeste (later Bishop), 88,
    105, 136
Dené, 15
Denman, Rear Admiral Joseph, 135–36
Derby, 96, 97
Descubierta (ship), 35
Destruction Island, 56
Devastation (ship), 135, 136
Dewdney, Edgar, 102
Dewdney Trail, 102, 117, 161, 226
Dexter, Walter, 250
Dietz, "Dutch William," 102
Discovery (ship), 28, 30, 35, 36
Dixon, George, 31, 32
Dominion Coal Company, 181
Dominion Veterans' Land Act, 226
Douglas, Amelia, 82
Douglas, Captain, 33
Douglas, Major C. H., 218
Douglas, James (later Sir): fur trader,
    62–63, 68, 72, 74, 76, 79–80, 81–82,
    83–84; governor, 85–86, 87, 88,
    90–94, 95, 96, 97, 100, 103, 104, 105,
    107, 111–12, 115, 118, 130, 137
Douglas (town), 102
Douglas Road, 157
Douglas Trail, 102
Doukhobors, 179–80, 192, 198, 201,
    211–12
Drake, Capt. Francis, 23–24
Driard, Sosthenes, 101
Duff, Wilson, 54
Dufferin, Marquess of, 139, 148
Duncan, William, 114, 131–32, 136–38,
    139
Duncan Lake, 245
Dunsmuir, James, 162, 166, 167–68, 174,
    176, 189
Dunsmuir, Robert, 81, 155, 162
Durieu, Bishop, 138
Dutch, 231

East India Company, 31, 46, 69
East Indians, 190, 232, 233
Eaton's department store, 202
Edenshaw, Charles, 263

education, 88, 150–51, 180, 216, 226, 247–49. *See also* residential schools
Elections Act, 236–37, 243
Eliza, Francisco, 35
Elliott, Andrew Charles, 148
Ellis, William, 30, 170
Empress of Japan, The (ship), 158
environmental movement, 262, 268
Erickson, Arthur, 250
Esquimalt, 88, 89, 90, 91, 100, 107, 118, 136, 145, 193, 194
Esquimalt and Nanaimo Railway, 147–49, 154, 155, 162
Esquimalt harbour, 82, 89
Estevan Point, 223
Etolin, Adolph, 74
Euclataw, 51, 128
Europa (ship), 60
Evans, Hubert, 251
Experiment (ship), 32

farming: in 1790s, 35; first farm on lower mainland, 46; in 1820s, 69; HBC involvement, 72–73; ranching, 110, 123, 151, 162, 227; in 1870s, 123, 151–52; Fraser Valley flood, 164; Agricultural Credits Act, 196; agrarian populist movement, 202–203; resettlement of soldiers after World War I, 206; John Oliver's improvement program, 206–207; in 1936, 217; resettlement of soldiers after World War II, 226; 1940s tax reductions, 226; World War II boom, 227; agricultural reserve land, 267. *See also* fruit industry; Puget's Sound Agricultural Company
Farris, John Wallace de Becque, 205
Federated Labour party, 204
Felice (ship), 33
Fernie, 241
Finlayson, Duncan, 71
Finlayson, Roderick, 80, 81, 82, 125, 126
Fisgard (ship), 89
fishing, aboriginal (before arrival of Europeans), 2, 3, 4–5, 6, 7, 21
fishing industry: in 1820s, 69; HBC involvement, 80; in 1870s, 123, 152; canneries, 123, 152, 153, 162, 178, 231; technological advances, 178; Japanese immigrants, 189; impact of World War I, 192; impact of railways, 206; impact of

Depression, 211; in 1936, 217; Hell's Gate fish ladders, 235; aboriginal people permitted to take part, 258
Fleming, Sandford, 153, 154
Fletcher, Francis, 23
Fleurieu, Claret, 127
Florez, Antonio, 34
Flumerfelt, A. C., 195–96
Forsey, Eugene, 235
Fort Alexandria, 46, 49, 68
Fort Astoria (renamed Fort George in 1812, a NWC post), 45–46
Fort Babine (Fort Kilmaurs), 68
Fort Camosun. *See* Fort Victoria
Fort Chipewyan, 39, 41
Fort Colvile, 66, 73
Fort Connolly, 68
Fort Dunvegan, 127
Fort Durham, 74, 80
Fort Forks, 41
Fort Fraser, 42
Fort George (HBC post, later Prince George), 42. *See also* Prince George
Fort George (formerly Fort Astoria), 46–47, 64, 65
Fort George (HBC post founded 1824, later Fort Vancouver), 49, 66
Fort Hope, 81
Fort Kamloops, 45, 49, 66, 81, 93, 110
Fort Kilmaurs (Fort Babine), 68
Fort Langley, 68–69, 80, 81, 86, 93, 94, 96
Fort McLeod, 42, 67
Fort McLoughlin, 70, 80
Fort Nisqually, 70, 73
Fort Okanogan, 45, 49
Fort Rupert, 80, 81, 84, 87
Fort St. James, 42, 46, 49, 62, 67, 182
Fort St. John "massacre," 127
Fort Simpson, 5, 51, 70, 75
Fort Spokane, 64
Fort Stikine, 72, 75
Fort Taku, 71, 74
Fort Vancouver (formerly Fort George, later Vancouver, Washington), 49, 63, 66, 69, 70, 71, 72, 75, 76, 81, 157
Fort Victoria (Fort Camosun), 63, 79–80, 81–82, 83, 86, 87, 88, 105, 111, 125, 130. *See also* Victoria
Fort Walla Walla, 46, 49, 64
Fort William, 46

Fort Yale, 102
Forward (ship), 116, 134, 135
Frame, Statira, 250
Fraser, Donald, 91
Fraser, John, 172, 173
Fraser, Simon, 42–44, 169–70
Fraser River, 41, 42, 44, 117, 206. *See also*
  fishing industry; gold
Frederick Wood Theatre, 251
French, 25, 100
Fripp, Thomas, 250
fruit industry, 165, 206, 227
Fuca, Juan de (Apostolos Valerianos), 24
Fuca, Strait of Juan de, 4, 35, 37, 56, 58,
  75, 78
fur trade: in 1740s, 25; in 1780s, 30,
  31–32, 33; British traders unite against
  Spanish, 34; and War of 1812, 46; im-
  pact on aboriginal people, 49, 50–51,
  52, 53–57, 60 126–29; traders want
  schools, 88. *See also* HBC; North West
  Company; Pacific Fur Company; Russian American Company

Gaglardi, Phil, 240, 242, 246–47
Galiano, Dionisio Alcalá, 35
gas and oil industry, 230–31
Gastown (Granville), 123, 157. *See also*
  Vancouver
Georgia, Strait of, 35
Germans, 100, 192–93, 231–32
ghost dances, 14
Gibbs, Mifflin, 100
Gilford, Lord, 116
Gitksan, 4, 22, 52, 182, 262
Gitlaxdawk, 53
Gitsaex, 53
Gladstone, William Ewart, 90
gold: Antler Creek, 102; Barkerville, 103,
  109–11; Big Bend, 160; Bridge River,
  218; California, 80, 81, 88–89;
  Camerontown, 109; Cariboo, 102–3,
  108–11; Fraser River, 92–94, 98–99,
  102; Horsefly, 102; Keithley Creek, 102;
  Klondike, 165; Lightning Creek, 102;
  Lowhee Creek, 102; Queen Charlotte
  Islands, 92–93; Rock Creek, 160;
  Thompson River, 93; Wells, 218; Wild
  Horse Creek, 117; Williams Creek, 102,
  103. *See also* mining industry
Goldschmitt, Nicholas, 252

Goodwin, Albert ("Ginger"), 198
Gordon Highlanders, 191
Gore, Lieut. John, 30
Gosnell, R. E., 165–66
Government House, 114, 153
Grainger, Martin Allerdale, 170
Grand Forks, 161, 180, 201
Grand Trunk Pacific Railway, 181, 182,
  183, 184, 186. *See also* Canadian Na-
  tional Railways
Grand Trunk Railway, 181, 184
Grant, Cuthbert, 63
Grant, George Monro, 99, 153
Grant, Capt. Walter Colquhoun, 84, 87,
  96, 104, 108
Granville, Lord, 143
Granville (Gastown), 123, 157. *See also*
  Vancouver
Grappler (ship), 135
Gray, Capt. Robert, 37, 56–58
Gray, H. Wilson, 243, 244
Great Northern Railway, 184
Great War Veterans' Association, 203
Greeks, 24, 100, 232
Green, Jonathan, 50–51
Greenwood, 161, 192, 201, 224
Grey, Earl, 83, 86
Grey, Lord, 190
Guérin, Gertrude, 259, 260
Guichon, Lawrence
Gulf Islands, 123, 134
Gun-an-noot, Simon, 182
Gunderson, Einar, 240

Haida, 3, 4, 9, 10, 11, 15, 16, 26–27, 50,
  52, 53, 55, 57–58, 85, 92–93, 120,
  127, 128, 129, 131, 132, 134, 257, 258,
  259, 262, 263
Haig-Brown, Roderick, 251
Hailstone, William, 157
Hamatsa (Cannibal Society), 19
Hamilton, L. A., 157
Hamlyn, Dr. Richard Julian, 67
Hankey, William, 151–52, 182
Hanna, James, 31, 56
Hansell, Ernest, 238
Hanwell, Captain, 70
Hardin, Herschel, 252
Harlow, Robert, 251
Harmon, Daniel Williams, 46, 65
Harmon (ship), 31

Harpooner (ship), 87
Harris, Lawren, 250
Harris, Thomas, 114
Hart, John, 197, 216, 221, 225–26, 227, 234
Harvey, Caroline (née Marks), 135
Hastings Mill, 123, 157, 163
Hawthorn, Audrey, 263
Hawthornthwaite, James Hurst, 177, 204
Hazelton, 152, 183
health insurance, 236
Hedley, 161
Heiltsuk. *See* Bella Bella
Heinze, F. Augustus, 161
Helmcken, Cecelia (née Douglas), 87
Helmcken, Dr. John Sebastian, 71, 82, 84, 87, 91, 92, 113–14, 119–20, 121, 142, 143, 146, 187
Henday, Anthony, 40
Hezeta, Bruno de, 27
Hill, Joe, 169, 186
Hill's Bar, 104
Hind, William G. R., 108, 171
Hobson, J. A., 159
Hope, 68, 122
Hope (ship), 37
Hope-Princeton Highway, 102, 225–26
Horetsky, Charles, 172
Horsefly, 102
Howe, C. D., 227
Howe, Joseph, 105, 106
Howe Sound, 183
Huang, Paul, 250
Hudson, Captain, 34
Hudson's Bay Company: early fur trade, 39–40; merges with NWC, 46–49; economic warfare on aboriginal traders, 60; takes over New Caledonia and Columbia, 61; competition with Americans, 64–65, 70; establishes headquarters at Fort Vancouver, 66; diversifies and acquires ships, 69–71; agreement with Russian American Company, 72; establishes Puget's Sound Agricultural Company, 72–73; moves headquarters to Fort Victoria, 63, 79–80; initiates mining, 80–81; receives Royal Grant of Vancouver Island (colony), 83–84; colonization of Vancouver Island, 86–87; trading monopoly in Vancouver Island (colony), 87; taxes and licences

gold seekers, 94; licence to exclusive trade in New Caledonia ends, 96; opposed by colonists, 106; and San Juan Islands border dispute, 107; closes posts in response to aboriginal protests, 127; treaties with aboriginal people, 130; after World War II, 202. *See also* Columbia; McLoughlin, John; New Caledonia; Simpson, George
Hungarians, 233
hunting, aboriginal (before arrival of Europeans), 2–3, 6, 7
Hurdy Gurdies, 109–110
Hutchison, Bruce, 225
Hyack Fire Brigade, 116
hydroelectric power, 231, 244–45

Imperial Eagle (ship), 32
Indian Act, 140–41, 254, 261
Indian Advisory Committee
Indian Affairs, Department of, 139
Indian Homemakers' Association of British Columbia, 259
Indian Non-Partisan party, 259
Indian Rights Association, 257
Indochinese, 268
Industrial Conciliation and Arbitration Act, 235
Industrial Workers of the World (IWW) ("Wobblies"), 161, 185–86, 203
Ingraham, Joseph, 37
International Festival of the Arts, 252
International Union of Mine, Mill and Smelter Workers, 198
International Woodworkers of America, 228, 235
Interior Salish, 4, 6, 15, 22. *See also* Lillooet, Nicola, Okanagan, Thompson River people
Inuit, 12
Iphigenia (ship), 33
Isaac Todd (ship), 45, 46
Italians, 232

Jackson, A. Y., 250
Jamieson, Karen, 252
Japanese, 176, 186, 189–90, 209, 223–24
Jarvis, Don, 250
Jasper's House, 64
Jefferson, Captain, 134
Jericho Beach (Jerry's Cove), 123

Jessop, John, 150–51
Jewitt, John, 58, 59
Jews, 100, 233
Johnson, Bjorn (Byron), 234–37, 239
Joint Commission on Indian reserves, 140
Joly de Lotbinière, Sir Henri Gustave, 166, 169
Jones, Bertram, 194

Kaien Island, 183
Kalispell House, 44
Kamloops, 45, 267
Kanakas, 65, 82, 85, 87, 89, 110
Kane, Paul, 125, 169, 170–71
Keithley, William ("Doc"), 102
Keithley Creek, 102
Kelly, Peter, 257, 259
Kelowna, 267
Kendrick, Captain, 56–57
Kennedy, Alexander, 66
Kennedy, Arthur Edward, 113–14
Kennedy, Dr. John F., 91, 116, 117
Kimberley, Lord, 155
Kimberley, 161, 201
King, Captain, 28, 30
King, Mackenzie, 190, 203, 216, 219, 222, 223–24
Kingfisher (ship), 135, 136
King George (ship), 31
King George's Sound Company, 31
Kitimat, 231, 236
Kitwancool, 182
Kitwanga
Kiyooka, Roy, 250
Klondike, 165
Knights of Labour, 175, 188
Koerner family, 235
Komagata Maru, 190
Kootenae House, 44
Kootenay, 4, 15, 20, 21, 42
Korner, John, 250
Koya, Chief, 57
Kulleet Bay, 135
Kwakiutl, 3, 4, 9, 10, 13, 14, 15, 16, 18–20, 22, 42, 51, 53, 84, 85, 128, 129, 132, 253, 258, 259, 263. *See also* Bella Bella

Labouchère, Henry, 93
labour: unions, 161, 163, 175–76, 177, 185–86, 198–99, 200, 203–205, 227,

228–29, 235, 258, 268; strikes, 84, 95–96, 167–68, 176, 185–87, 198, 204, 217, 219–20, 235, 246, 268; farm-workers, 86, 87; Kanakas, 89; anti-Oriental activity, 187–89; Industrial Disputes Act, 208; impact of Depression, 212–13; relief camps, 213, 217; conscription, 222–23; influx after World War II, 231; aboriginal people, 254–55. *See also* CCF; Labour Progressive party; New Democratic party; Socialist party
Labour Progressive party, 227, 229, 234, 236
Ladner, Thomas, 152
Ladner, 152
Ladysmith, 167
La Gassi, 42
Lamalchi, 135
Lambert, Betty, 252
land claims, aboriginal, 133–34, 136, 139–40, 255–58, 261, 262
Lane, Patrick, 251
Langford, Capt. Edward Edwards, 86, 88, 90, 91, 112
Lansdowne, Marquess of, 156
Laurel (ship), 134
Laurier, Sir Wilfrid, 166, 167, 176, 193, 197
La Vérendrye, Sieur de, 25
Le Blanc, 42
Le Courrier de la Nouvelle Calédonie, 105
Ledyard, John, 11, 29, 30
Lee, Jason, 76
Legace, Susette, 210
Le Roi (mine), 161
Lester, Peter, 100
Liberal party, 175, 176, 185, 194, 195, 196–97, 197, 205, 209, 210, 221, 234, 236, 237, 239, 240, 241, 243, 244, 246
Lightning Creek, 102
Lillooet, 43, 102, 122, 262
Livesay, Dorothy, 250, 252
Llama (ship), 60, 71
Locarno Beach people, 6, 8
Loffmark, Ralph, 247
Logan, Capt. W. H., 194
Lok, Michael, 24
London, Jack, 170
López de Haro, Gonzalo, 34
Lorne, Marquess of, 155

Lowhee Creek, 102
Lowther, Pat, 251
Lulu Island, 96, 101
lumber industry: in 1820s, 69; first sawmill, 80; in 1870s, 123, 152; growth of mills, 163; U.S. acquisition of timber licences, 179; impact of World War I, 192; post-World War I boom, 206; pulp and paper, 209–10, 231; impact of Depression, 211; in 1936, 217; forestry corporations, 235
Lydia (ship), 58
Lytton, Sir Edward Bulwer, 93, 94, 96, 97
Lytton, 44, 102, 122

McBride, Richard (later Sir), 168, 169, 175, 177, 178, 179, 180, 181, 184–85, 186, 187, 189, 193
McCleery, Fitzgerald, 123
McCreight, John Foster, 145
McCullagh, J. B., 139
McDonald, Archibald, 67, 69
Macdonald, J. W. G., 250
Macdonald, Sir John A., 121, 145, 149, 153, 154–55, 189
Macfie, Reverend Matthew, 98
McGeer, Gerald Grattan ("Gerry"), 217
MacGill, Helen Gregory, 202
McGowan, Edward ("Ned"), 103–104
McInnes, Thomas R., 166
Mackay, Alexander, 41
McKay, J. W., 91
Mackay, John, 32
Mackenzie, Alexander (fur trader), 39–42
Mackenzie, Alexander (prime minister), 145, 146, 147–49
Mackenzie and Mann, 168, 181
McLean, John, 127
MacLean, John D., 209, 210
McLean, M. A., 158
MacLeod, Gregory, 40
McLeod Lake (Trout Lake), 42
McLoughlin, John, 62–64, 66, 69, 70–71, 72, 73–74, 75–77, 78–79
McLoughlin, John (son of John McLoughlin), 75
Maclure, Samuel, 173, 174
MacMillan, H. R., 212, 235
MacMillan (H. R.) Ltd., 235
McMillan, James, 64, 65
McNeill, W. H., 60, 71

McRae, Alexander Duncan, 209
Makah, 4,, 10–11, 23
Malahat Review, 251
Malaspina, Alejandro, 35
Manuel, George, 259
Maquinna, 29, 31, 32, 33, 34, 36, 53, 56, 58
Marchand, Etienne, 127
Marcuse, Judith, 252
Marks, Frederick, 135
Marpole people, 7–8, 9
Martin, John, 157
Martin, Joseph, 166, 168, 176, 177
Martin, Mungo, 263
Martin, Thomas Mower, 172, 173
Martínez, Esteban José, 27, 34, 37
Mason, George, 80
Masset, 132
Massey, Geoffrey, 250
Mayne, Charles, 89, 104
Meares, John, 32, 33–35, 58, 60
Mennonites, 198, 206
Mer de l'Ouest, 25, 40
Merville, 206
Metlakatla, 114, 131–32, 137–38
Mexicana (ship), 35, 36
Mica Dam, 245
Milbanke Sound, 58
Milliken, 3
Mills, David, 140
Mills, John, 251
Mine, Mill and Smelter Workers, 228
mining industry: in 1840s, 80–81; Kanakas, 89; licences, 92–93; shift to wage labour, 111; in 1870s, 123, 151; impact on aboriginal people, 130; Esquimalt and Nanaimo Railway, 155; base metals replace gold as staple, 160–61; anti-union policies of Dunsmuirs, 176; impact of World War I, 192; decline in metals markets, 206; impact of Depression, 211; World War II boom, 227. *See also* labour
Ministerial Union of the Lower Mainland, 195
missionaries, 26, 48, 88, 114, 122, 136–39, 182, 256
Modeste (ship), 78, 89
Monck, Governor General Lord, 119
Moody, Richard Clement, 94, 95–96, 97, 101, 104, 111

Moody, Sewell ("Sue"), 123
Moody Sawmill, 163
Moodyville (North Vancouver), 123
Morice, Adrien Gabriel, 182
Morris, Jerrold, 263
Moses, W. D., 110
Moslems, 233
Mount Currie, 262
Muir, John, 81, 87, 91
museums, 249
Musgrave, Anthony, 120, 121, 142–43
Musgrave, Susan, 251
Musqueam, 6, 9–10, 43, 259
Mussel, Genevieve, 259

Nanaimo, 81, 87, 89, 91, 122, 186–87
Nanaimo Reform Club, 176
Nass River, 52, 70, 138, 139, 152
Nationalist party, 176
Native Brotherhood of British Columbia,
    258, 259, 260
Native peoples:
    archaeological sites, 3, 5, 6–7, 9–11
    arts. *See* arts, ceremonial
    ceremonies. *See* potlatches; spirit
        dances; winter dances.
    cultural groups, coastal. *See* Bella Coola
        people; Coast Salish; Haida;
        Kwakiutl; Nootka; Tlingit; Tsim-
        shian
    cultural groups, interior. *See* Beaver;
        Carrier; Chilcotin; Kootenay; Lil-
        looet; Nicola; Okanagan; Sekani;
        Shuswap; Slave; Thompson River
        people; Tsetsaut
    cultural groups, other. *See* under indi-
        vidual names
    cultural resurgence, 253–255, 262–264
    decline, 51, 125–26, 136, 139–41,
        253. *See also* smallpox
    first contacts with Europeans, 11, 25,
        26, 28
    languages, 3–4, 15–20. *See also*
        Athapaskan language group; Salishan
        language group; Wakashan language
        group
    origins in prehistory, 2–11
    political activities, 257–260
    religion. *See* missionaries; spirit dances;
        spirit quests; winter dances
    social organization, 15–16, 21, 132

trade, 7–8, 21, 22, 52–53. *See also* fur
    trade
warfare: 4, 6, 7, 10, 16, 22; against
    Europeans, 56–60, 126–27,
    132–36. *See also* Chilcotin War
See also Indian Act; land claims; residen-
    tial schools; treaties; White Paper on
    Indian Policy
Native Voice, 258, 260
Nelson, 161, 170, 179
New Caledonia, 42, 46, 49, 51, 61, 62,
    65–66, 67, 77–78, 81. *See also* Colum-
    bia; HBC; McLoughlin, John; Simpson,
    George
New Democratic party, 246, 247, 266, 268.
    See also Barrett, Dave
New Denver, 161
New Metlakatla, 138
New Play Centre, 251
New Westminster (Queensborough), 97,
    101–102, 106–107, 107, 112, 117,
    118, 122, 167
New Westminster Rifle Corps, 116
Newcastle, Duke of, 112, 117
Newman, Gerald, 251
Newman, Peter C., 50
Newspaper Guild, 229
Newton, Norman, 251
Ngan, Wayne, 250
Nicola, 51
Nishga, 4, 51, 52, 120, 138, 256–57, 259,
    260, 261–62
Nisqually, 76
Niven, Frederick, 170, 250
Nootka, 4, 11, 15, 16, 27, 28–30, 31, 32,
    34, 53, 128–29, 258, 260, 262. *See also*
    Ahousat
Nootka (ship), 32
Nootka Convention, 34, 36, 37–38
Nootka Sound, 11, 27, 28–29, 31, 32,
    33–35, 36–37, 56, 57, 58, 70
Norman Morison (ship), 84, 87
North American Indian Brotherhood, 258,
    259, 260
North Vancouver (Moodyville), 123
North West America (ship), 33, 34, 37
North West Company, 40–41, 42, 44,
    45–47. *See also* Fraser, Simon; Macken-
    zie, Alexander; Thompson, David
Northwest Passage, 23, 27, 35
Notre Dame University, 249

Nuu-chah-nulth Tribal Council, 262

O'Brien, Lucius, 172, 173
O'Hagan, Howard, 250
O'Reilly, Peter, 103, 121
Ocean Falls, 210
Ogden, Peter Skene, 64, 70–71, 79
Okanagan Valley, 179, 192, 206
Okanogan River, 45
Old Age Pensions, 208
Oliver, John, 183, 196, 197, 205–209, 215
Oliver (town), 206
Omineca, 122
Onderdonk, Andrew, 153–54, 189
One Big Union, 204–205
Onley, Toni, 250
On-to-Ottawa Trek, 217
Oolichan, 8
Opitsaht, 57
Oppenheimer, David, 158
Oppenheimer, Isaac, 158
Oregon Boundary Treaty, 47, 63, 107, 269
Ormsby, Margaret, 84, 133
Otter (ship), 85, 96
Overlanders, 108, 171
Ozette, 10–11, 55

Pacific Coast Native Fishermen's Association, 258
Pacific Fur Company, 44, 45–47, 59
Pacific Great Eastern Railway, 181, 182, 183, 195, 207, 220, 236, 240, 242
Pacific Mail Steamship Company, 81
Page, P. K., 251
Pandora (ship), 89
parliament buildings, 111, 146, 153, 164
Parsons, Capt. Robert, 96
Pattullo, Thomas Dufferin ("Duff"), 196, 213, 214–21, 222
Pattullo Bridge, 216–17
Paull, Andrew, 257, 258
Peace River, 41, 206, 242, 244, 245
Peace River people, 130
Pearce, Thomas, 37
Pearson, Lester B., 245
Peigan, 21, 44
Pemberton, Joseph Despard, 87, 91
Pemberton, Sophie, 173, 249
Pena, Fray Tomas de la, 26
Pender Island, 135

Pentland, Barbara, 252
Pentlatch, 51
People's Prohibition League, 195
Pérez Hernández, Juan Josef, 26–27
Petroglyphs, 9
Phillips, Walter J., 250
Phoenix, 192
Phoenix (mine), 161
Plaskett, Joe, 250
Plumper (ship), 89, 95, 104
Pond, Peter, 40–41
Portage River Dam, 245
Portlock, Nathaniel, 31, 32, 50
Port Moody, 156–57
Port Simpson, 70, 132, 137, 138
Portuguese, 232
potlatch, 16–18, 22, 55, 126, 128, 132, 138, 140, 182, 253–54
Powell, Dr. Isaac W., 140, 158
Powell River, 210, 231
Prevost, Capt. James Charles, 137
Prince George (Fort George), 183, 231, 267
Prince Rupert, 4, 5, 52, 53, 183, 186, 196, 204, 211, 215
Princesa (ship), 34
Princess Royal (ship), 34
Prior, Edward Gawley, 168–69, 177
Prism International, 251
Produce Marketing Act, 206
Progressive party, 203, 214
prohibition, 185, 195, 196, 197
Provincial party, 208–209, 210
Provincial Progressive party, 176
Public Schools Reconstruction Act, 248
Puget Sound, 35–36, 69, 74, 107
Puget's Sound Agricultural Company, 73, 80, 84, 86, 90, 91. *See also* farming

Quadra Island, 51
Quadra y Bodega. *See* Bodega y Quadra
Quakers, 198
Queen Charlotte (ship), 31
Queen Charlotte Islands, 3, 4, 25, 26–27, 35, 52, 53, 57, 70, 92–93, 262
Queensborough. *See* New Westminster
Quesnel, Jules, 43
Quesnel, 183
Quimper, Eliza, 35
Quimper, Manuel, 35

Raccoon (ship), 46
Rainbow (ship), 186, 190, 193
Rainy Lake House, 44
ranching. *See* farming
Rattenbury, Francis Mawson, 164, 172–73
Reeve, John, 250
Reid, Bill, 263
relief camps, 213, 217
residential schools, 138, 255
Resolution (ship), 28, 58
Revolutionary Socialist party, 176
Richardson, E. M., 172
Richfield, 109
Rickman, Lieut. John, 30
Ridington, Robin, 21
Ridley, William, 137–38
Rithet, R. P., 163
roads and highways, 102, 108–109, 115,
    116–17, 157, 207, 216–17, 218,
    225–26, 230, 236, 242–43
Roberts, Morley, 169, 170
Robertson, George, 251
Robson, Charles Rufus, 134
Robson, John ("Honest John"), 106–107,
    112, 118, 120, 121, 158, 164, 165
Rock Creek, 160
Rocky Mountain House, 44
Rogers, Major A. B., 154
Rogers, Jeremiah, 123
Rogers, Jonathan, 195
Rolston, Tilly, 239
Roper, Edward, 172
Ross, Alexander, 64
Ross, Charles, 80
Rossland, 161, 201
Rowell-Sirois Commission, 220–21
Royal Canadian Navy, 186, 190
Royal Engineers, 95–96, 102, 104, 108,
    111, 116, 130
Royal Institution for the Advancement of
    Learning in British Columbia, 180
Royal Navy, 46, 70, 80, 85, 89–90, 107,
    136, 193
Rule, Jane, 251
Russian American Company, 25, 60, 70,
    72
Russians, 25, 31, 47, 72, 74–75. *See also*
    Doukhobors
Ryerson, Egerton, 150
Ryga, George, 252

Saanich, 202
St. Laurent, Louis, 239
Salish. *See* Coast Salish; Interior Salish
Salishan language group, 3, 4, 20, 21, 22
Salish House, 44
Salter, Captain, 58
Saltspring Island, 100, 134
San Carlos (ship), 34
Sandon, 161, 192
San Juan Islands, 107
Santiago (ship), 25–27
Sapperton, 112
Satellite (ship), 94, 104, 137
Saturna Island, 135
Schafer, Murray, 252
Schubert, Catherine, 108
Schubert, Rose, 108
Scott, Gen. Winfield, 107
Sea Island, 227
Seafarers' International Union, 244
Seaforth Highlanders, 187
seaport (Vancouver). *See* shipping
Sechelt, 138
Sekani, 21, 41, 127
Semlin, Charles Augustus, 166
Seymour, Frederick, 113, 114–19, 120,
    133, 142
Shadbolt, Jack, 250, 262
Shakes, Chief, 53, 54
shamanism, 6, 9, 12–14, 138
shipbuilding industry, 196, 227
shipping (seaport) industry, 123, 158, 192,
    196, 211
Shipyard General Workers' Federation of
    British Columbia, 228
Shuswap, 41, 43, 68
Siberian Expeditionary Force, 191
Sikhs. *See* East Indians
Silver King (mine), 161
Silver Plate (mine), 161
Simon Fraser University, 248–49
Simons, Beverley, 252
Simpson, Aemilius, 70
Simpson, George (later Sir), 48, 61–76,
    78–80, 127, 170
Skeena River, 52, 53, 152
Skelton, Robin, 251
Skidegate, 132
Skinner, Thomas James, 90, 91
Skoglund's Landing, 3

Slacum, William A., 78
Slave people, 21
slavery, 10, 16, 17, 22
Slocan City, 161
Slocan Star (mine), 161
smallpox, 50–51, 131–32, 137
Smith, Donald (later Lord Strathcona),
    156
Smith, Gordon, 250
Smith, Jedediah, 69, 75
Smith, Mary Ellen, 202
Smith, Ralph, 176, 177, 196–97
Smith, William. *See* De Cosmos, Amor
Smithe, William, 156, 158, 164
Smoky River, 41
Social Credit party, 218, 227, 235, 236,
    237–43. *See also* Bennett, W. A. C.
Socialist League, 176
Socialist party, 175, 176, 176, 185, 194,
    204
Soldiers' party, 203, 209
Sommers, Robert, 243–44
Songhees, 79–80, 85, 88, 125, 126, 131
Sonora (ship), 27, 35, 56
Sooke, 84, 87, 91, 92
Southern Vancouver Island Allied Tribes
    Federation, 260
South Sea Company, 31, 32
Spanish, 11, 25–27, 31, 33–38, 47,
    57–58
Spanish Banks, 36
Sparrowhawk (ship), 120
Spencer's department store, 202
spirit dances, 18, 138, 140, 263
spirit quest, 14, 22
Sproat, Gilbert, 113, 147
Squamish, 183, 257
Staines, Emma Frances, 88
Staines, Reverend R. J., 88, 90
Stamp, Edward, 123, 157
Stanley, Lord, 93, 158
Stanley Park, 158
Stein Valley, 262
Stephen, George, 155, 156
Stikine River, 52
Strange, James, 32
strikes. *See* labour
Stuart, David, 45
Stuart, John, 43, 45
Stuart Lake, 67
Sullivan (mine), 161, 201

Sumas Lake, 206
Surrey, 233
Sutil (ship), 35, 36
Sutlej (ship), 116, 135
Sweet, Lulu, 96, 101

Tahltan, 18, 22
Talonbooks, 251
Tamahnous Theatre, 251
Tanabe, Takao, 250
Tatlow, Capt. Robert Garnett, 178, 179,
    181
Tawnington, Captain, 58
Teit, J. A., 257
Telford, Dr. Lyle, 214
Telkwa, 206
Thom, Adam, 73
Thom, Ron, 231, 250
Thomas, Audrey, 251
Thompson, 58
Thompson, David, 44–45
Thompson River, 44, 93
Thompson River people, 16, 21, 43, 51
Thorn, Captain, 59
"Three Greenhorns," 157
Tibetans, 233
Tiedemann, Hermann Otto, 111
Tisdall, C. E., 195–96
Tlingit, 3, 4, 11, 15, 16, 17, 22, 25, 27,
    50, 52, 53, 70, 129, 182
Tod, John, 62, 67, 85, 91
Toll Bridges and Highway Authority, 242
Tolmie, Dr. Simon Fraser, 210, 212, 213
Tolmie, William Fraser, 210
Tomlinson, Robert, 138, 139
Tonquin (ship), 45, 59
Tory (ship), 87
tourism industry, 217, 243
trade, before arrival of Europeans, 4, 8,
    11–12, 21, 22, 52–54
Trades and Labour Congress of Canada,
    176, 228, 229
Trail, 161, 163, 198, 201, 227, 228, 231,
    232. *See also* Cominco
TransCanada Airlines, 230
TransCanada Highway, 242
treaties, 46, 108, 130, 139, 140
Treaty of Ghent, 46
Treaty of Washington 1871, 108
Trimble, James, 119
Trinity Western, 249

Trudeau, Pierre, 260–61
Trutch, Joseph W., 108, 121, 144, 145, 172
Tselax, 9–10
Tsetsaut, 22, 51
Tsimshian, 3, 4, 9, 10, 15, 16, 51, 52, 53, 54, 129, 131, 132, 137–38, 182, 258, 259, 263. *See also* Gitksan; Nishga
Tupper, Sir Charles Hibbert, 196, 209
Turner, John Herbert, 165, 166
Tzuhalem, Chief, 126

Ugandans, 233
Union Club, 153
Union Government, 197
unions. *See* labour
United Farmers of British Columbia, 203, 209, 214
United Fishermen and Allied Workers' Union, 228
United Front, 229
University of British Columbia, 192, 201, 208, 212, 233, 248
University of Victoria, 248
University Women's Club, 195

Valdéz, Cayetano, 35
Valerianos, Apostolos. *See* Fuca, Juan de
Vancouver, Capt. George, 35–37
Vancouver (ship), 70
Vancouver: founding, 157; as rail terminus, 157–58, 160; shipping, 158, 211; growth, 158, 159, 201, 228, 232, 237, 267; Depression, 212, 219–20; labour unrest, 204; manufacturing, 212, 227; university, 180. *See also* Granville
Vancouver Art Gallery, 263
Vancouver Island (colony): founding, 83–84; Blanshard appointed governor, 84; Douglas appointed governor, 85; legislative council appointed, 85; colonized by Puget's Sound Agricultural Company, 86–87; education system, 88; concentration of Royal Navy, 89–90; opposition to Douglas, 90–91; first legislative assembly, 91–92; impact of gold rush, 92–94, 98–99; growth of Victoria, 98–101; new government buildings, 111; Douglas retires, 112; response to union of colonies, 117–18
Vancouver Playhouse, 251

Vancouver *Province*, 243
Vancouver School of Art, 250
Vancouver Stock Exchange, 211
Vancouver *Sun*, 243
Vancouver Symphony Orchestra, 252
Vancouver Trades and Labour Council, 198, 199, 204
Vander Zalm, William, 267
Van Horne, William C., 154, 156, 157, 172
Varley, F. H., 250
Vavasour, Lieut. Mervin, 78
Verigin, Peter the Lordly, 179
Victoria, 91, 114, 118, 180, 193, 196; gold rush, 92, 98, 99–101; Confederation, 119; growth, 87–88, 111, 122, 153, 160, 173, 201–2, 228, 267; labour unrest, 204; smallpox epidemic, 130–31. *See also* Fort Victoria
Victoria College (University of Victoria), 248
Victoria Gazette (*The Anglo-American*), 105–6
Victoria Philharmonic Society, 101
Victoria Pioneer Rifle Corps, 100
Victoria Trades and Labour Council, 198, 204
Viewfield, 86
Vincennes (ship), 74
Virago (ship), 137

Waddington, Alfred, 99, 115, 133, 171
Wakashan language group, 4
Wakefield, Edward Gibbon, 86
Walhachin, 191
Walkem, George Anthony, 118, 145, 147, 148, 155
Wallace, Clarence, 239
Walsh, J. M., 215
Warre, Henry James, 78, 171
Watson, Sheila, 251
Webb, Phyllis, 251
Webber, John, 29, 128–29, 170
Weir, Dr. George, 216
Wells, 218
West Coast Allied Tribes, 260
West Coast Seamen's Union, 228
Westcoast Transmission, 230
Western Federation of Miners, 161, 176, 185
West Kootenay Power Company, 226

White, Dr., 76
White Paper on Indian Policy, 260–61
White Rock, 65, 233
Whitton, Abel, 106
Whitton, Henry Buckingham, 176
Whymper, Edward, 171
Whymper, Frederick, 133, 171
Wickanninish, Chief, 33, 59
Wicks, Lyle, 240
Wild Horse Creek, 117
Wilkes, Charles, 74
Willamette Valley, 76
William and Ann (ship), 70
Williams, Guy, 258, 259
Williams, Parker, 177
Williams Creek, 102, 103, 109
Williston, 105–6
Wilson, Charles, 90, 92
Wilson, Ethel, 251
Winch, Harold, 219, 225
winter dances, 18–20, 22, 137, 140
Wise, Jack, 250

women's suffrage, 185, 195, 196, 197, 200
Woodcock, George, 252
Woodsworth, James Shaver, 177, 214, 223
Woodward's department store, 202
Work, Jane, 210
Work, John, 60, 79, 210
Workers' Compensation (Workmen's Compensation), 177, 196
Workers' Unity League, 217
Workingmen's party, 176
Wrangell, Baron, 72
Wyeth, Nathaniel, 75–76
Wyman, Anna, 252

xy Company, 42

Yale, James Murray, 68, 80
Yale, 104, 120, 153, 154
Yates, James, 90, 91
York Factory, 67
Young, Dr. Henry Esson, 180
Yukon Telegraph, 152